SELLING THROUGH INDEPENDENT REPS

Selling Through Independent Reps

Third Edition

Harold J. Novick

AMACOM
American Management Association
New York · Atlanta · Boston · Chicago · Kansas City · San Francisco · Washington, D.C.
Brussels · Mexico City · Tokyo · Toronto

This publication is designed to provide accurate and authoritative information in regard to the subject matter covered. It is sold with the
understanding that the publisher is not engaged in rendering legal,
accounting, or other professional service. If legal advice or other expert
assistance is required, the services of a competent professional person
should be sought.

Library of Congress Cataloging-in-Publication Data

Novick, Harold J.
      Selling through independent reps / Harold J. Novick. — 3rd ed.
         p.   cm.
      Includes bibliographical references and index.
      ISBN 0-8144-0522-3
      1. Selling.   2. Sales management—United States.   3. Marketing
channels—United States.   4. Commercial agents—United States.
I. Title
HF5438.25.N68   2000
658.8/102—dc21
                                                                99-57938
                                                                     CIP

Printing number

10   9   8   7   6   5   4   3   2

To the well-conceived rep/manufacturer relationship, for it offers unique competitive advantage in the marketplace dynamics of the new millennium.

Contents

Acknowledgments   xi

Introduction   xiii

1   Independent Sales Organizations: An Overview   1
        Getting Acquainted   1
        Two Categories of ISOs   2
        Three Levels of Sales Structure   3
        Direct Sales Force   3
        Independent Sales Organizations: An Overview   5
        A Few Examples of Sales Channels   8
        Key Differences in Sales Organizations   12

2   A Systems Approach for Increased Market
        Penetration   17
        The Six-Step Process   17
        Theory Applied: The Product/Market Matrix   22
        The Next Step   25

3   The Ideal Sales Force for the New Millennium   27
        Characteristics Needed in the New Millennium
            Sales Force—Do They Suggest Direct Sales or
            Independent Reps?   28
        Another View of Alternative Channels   34
        Using Reps   34
        Using a Direct Sales Force   35
        Using Combined Rep/Direct Structures   36
        Key Questions to Consider   37
        Putting It All Together   39
        The Question of Conversion   42
        Channel Conflict   46
        The Next Step   48

4   Fisher Controls International, Inc.: A Large
        Company Using Reps   49
        Background   50
        Individual Interviews   51

	Lessons From Fisher	55
	The Next Step	60
5	The Truth About Independent Sales Reps	62
	Myths About Reps	63
	The Real Reasons for Poor Rep Performance	69
	Some True Statements About Reps	70
	What A Good Rep Can Give You	77
	Other Aspects of Reps	81
	The Next Step	83
6	Profile of the Ideal Rep	84
	How Much Is the Right Rep Worth?	85
	A Search Anomaly	88
	A Model	88
	Other Important Characteristics	93
	From the Ideal to the Pragmatic	101
	The Next Step	103
7	How to Find and Hire the Best	105
	A Search Methodology	106
	Management Commitment	107
	Planning the Search Program	107
	Assigning Responsibilities	108
	Searching for Candidates	108
	The Screening Chronology	117
	Selecting the Best: Personal Interviews	129
	Making the Selection	131
	If You Have Parallel Reps	133
	The Next Step	134
8	Building Good Working Relationships	135
	Getting the New Rep Started	136
	Working Together for Long-Term Success	139
	What Your Reps Expect From You	141
	What You Should Expect From Reps	147
	What You Should *Not* Expect From Reps	153
	The Next Step	155
9	The Importance of Total Support	156
	The Organizational Climate	157
	The Selling Team	157
	Commitment at the Top	158
	The Role of the Marketing Department	163
	Good Management and Motivation	171
	The Next Step	175
10	Evaluating and Controlling Performance	176
	Standards for Evaluating Performance	177
	Pinpointing Reasons for Success	181
	Evaluating the New Representative	181
	The Faltering Relationship	183
	The Marginal Representative	186
	The Next Step	187

11	Feedback and Control: The Rep Council and Rep Audit	188
	The Rep Council	190
	Independent Auditing	195
	Reviewing the Six Steps	207
12	Commissions and Contracts	208
	Commissions	208
	Contracts	213
13	Legal Issues and Trends, *by Gerald Salmen*	220
	Commission Protection Acts	220
	Trends in Commission Protection Acts	223
	Written Contracts	223
	Tortious Interference	228
	Litigation and Alternatives	229
	Conclusion	231
14	Selling Through Distributors and Agents Overseas, *by Gunnar Beeth*	232
	Independents or Subsidiaries?	232
	Some Initial Stumbling Blocks	234
	Market Sizes	234
	Choosing a Location for a European Subsidiary	240
	The GSM Telecom Revolution	243
	The Euro and European Monetary Union (EMU)	244
	Outsourcing	244
	Limitations in Selling Abilities of European Distributors and Agents	244
	Choosing the Right Distributor or Agent	245
	Keeping Overseas Business	248
Appendix A	Guidelines for Negotiating an Agreement Between Sales Representatives and Manufacturers, Electronics Representatives Association	251
Appendix B	Manufacturers' or Suppliers' Sales Agency Specimen Agreement Provisions, Manufacturers' Agents National Association	259
Appendix C	Sales Representative Agreement, Industrial Perforators Association	273
Appendix D	Sales Agreement, Sparks Belting Co.	289
	Resource Guide	295
	Index	335
	About the Author and Contributors	343

Acknowledgments

A number of individuals provided critical input for the third edition. Our chapter on Fisher Controls was developed with the assistance of Joe Urbanek, vice president of Fisher-Rosemount, and Ed Merwald, vice president of Fisher Controls. Thanks also to three of their reps, namely John Weekley of Proconex, Mike Aldredge of Puffer-Sweiven, and Larry Reams of Cornerstone Controls.

Gunnar Beeth of International Marketing Consultants, Brussels, Belgium, brings us up to date on the major changes in the European market. Jerry Salmen brings his view of major issues and trends in the legal picture that affect rep/manufacturer relationships.

Additional thanks go to Marilyn Stephens, executive vice president of the Manufacturers' Representatives Educational Research Foundation (MRERF), Joe Miller, president of the Manufacturers' Agents National Association (MANA), and Ray Hall, CEO of the Electronic Representatives Association (ERA) for the exhibits they provided.

Robert Glegg, CEO of Glegg Water Conditioning, has once again provided his company as an example of outstanding success with a multi-channel rep sales force. A special note of appreciation is extended to Bob Benham, my mentor, with whom I have been associated since 1964, first as a client for rep recruitment when I was in corporate life, then as my closest associate since starting my consulting practice in 1981.

Thanks again to Kathy Ehrhardt, who has now provided the word processing for our third straight edition—and to my wife, Doris, and to Lynn, Scott, Carl, Julie, Kevin, Kristin, and the most recent of the newest generation, Joey, I owe thanks for everything.

Introduction

Megatrends in the Marketplace

The third edition of *Selling Through Independent Reps* comes at the dawn of the new millennium. While the year 2000 excites the imagination of many to all sorts of unusual meanings, from a business perspective it simply marks an appropriate point in time to conduct a critical analysis of where we are, where we want to go, what obstacles face us, and how we are going to get there. Our third edition will, therefore, begin with those megatrends in the marketplace that need to be carefully considered in evaluating our current sales channels and planning the sales force for the new millennium.

Evolving trends in customer/supplier relationships clearly suggest that the need for using independent sales representatives, either as a company's primary or secondary channel, has grown substantially in recent years. Whether you are an entrepreneurial business or have sales volumes exceeding a billion dollars, the inherent advantages of using an independent rep sales force, either totally or for discrete targets, can give the great majority of business organizations competitive advantage in the marketplace. This edition will evolve the rationale for this statement and upgrade the process by which companies can make sure that their channel not only satisfies today's needs but provides the inherent strength to help achieve future objectives.

Megatrends

For the purpose of this text, the term *megatrends* will be used to define major trends in the marketplace that must be carefully considered when evaluating and upgrading sales channels in order to achieve both short- and long-term sales objectives. Several have been evolving over the past thirty to forty years. Others are still in their infancy and may not continue to grow, but are important enough to be mentioned. Following are key market trends that must be carefully analyzed:

Product Quality

This is a continuation of the commitment of American industry to consistently improve product quality. It has been a major influence in manufacturing decision-making for over thirty years. This megatrend emerged from that period in American manufacturing's history when planned product obsolescence was a primary strategy, one that abdicated a world leadership role to the Japanese and European manufacturers. American industry then rebounded with a strong quality commitment and has since achieved world-class competitiveness in manufacturing. Quality targets are continuing to be upgraded with ISO 9000 quality standards. Rejection rates of parts per billion are emerging and the literal definition of "zero defects" is on the horizon. This trend has resulted in manufacturers sharply reducing the number of their suppliers, frequently partnering with a single, sole source provider on a team basis in order to provide maximum value to the end user.

Xerox is just one example. In the late 1980s, it adopted a total quality program that promptly resulted in reducing its supplier list from 5,000 to 350. This was further reduced to 250 in the early 1990s. Over this period, Xerox achieved its objectives in becoming a world-class leader.

JIT Deliveries

Just-in-time delivery requirements in order to reduce customer inventories has also been a trend for many years. This trend is now being extended much further with a partnering process whereby the supplier not only supplies JIT parts but actually performs assembly functions within customer facilities. JIT has had a profound impact on supplier strategies to gain competitive advantage.

Predatory Purchasing

The trend toward high quality created a much higher emphasis on value contribution of a supplier to a customer. For a period of time, price was almost a secondary buying motive. This dramatically changed when the automotive industry developed a strategy of predatory purchasing whereby the term *partnering* with a supplier was perverted to mean that the supplier had to reduce its prices by specified amounts, not only this year, but in subsequent years. Comfortable partnering relationships peaked in the early 1990s.

Since then, predatory purchasing policies by many buyers have severely strained those relationships, so much so that an increasing number of suppliers have concluded that a customer who exercises predatory purchasing policies may no longer be viewed as an acceptable customer. A number of manufacturers have even re-targeted their market priorities on a strategic basis, eliminating those industries where predatory purchasing has proved to be an unprofitable practice for suppliers. Existing sales channels can become at least partially obsolete with such changes in market priorities.

Eliminating the Independent Sales Representative

While not a "megatrend" in terms of the number of cases, the visibility of this issue deserves discussion in the third edition. This subheading defines situations where the customer views an independent sales representative as an unwanted and unnecessary cost he is asked to assume in sales transactions with a supplier. The customer then tells the supplier that it should eliminate the independent rep and reduce its price by an amount equal to the commission rate that is "saved." The Wal-Mart case has been the most visible. This has evolved over several years. However, independent sales reps were never totally eliminated in sales transactions with Wal-Mart. Since then, Wal-Mart has again allowed more independent reps in its relationships with suppliers in order to avoid possible lengthy litigation from various organizations.

Still, suppliers are periodically pressured by buyers to eliminate the rep. This, in turn, has periodically resulted in manufacturers terminating reps and, in certain scenarios, reps litigating the termination. For example, here's a paragraph from a letter we received from Roger Brown, an OEM rep in Elburn, Illinois, dated November 21, 1998:

> One must wonder if the role of the sales representative is becoming an anachronism. I have lost three long time principals the past five years because of demands for price reductions and demands by the customer that they be served direct. Two terminations resulted in expensive litigation—against GE and against Richo Plastic Company. The third, an insert molder recently said in a letter ". . . the business climate is much different than it was in the past. With the on-going pressure for reduced prices, coupled with the more educated customer who resists the sales representative concept, it is next to impossible for the manufacturer to exist and remain healthy and profitable. The sales function is best serviced direct."

There is an obvious anomaly in customer demands to eliminate the rep. To provide sensitive service to the customer and create competitive advantage for the manufacturer, strong and competent sales coverage is needed. This can be obtained by either independent representatives or direct sales personnel. Costs of either channel for larger companies are comparable in many cases. For the smaller company, the cost of direct selling is prohibitive. Yet, the obviousness of a commission rate has prompted customers to suggest that this cost is not necessary and the sales channel should be eliminated, thus reducing supplier costs, which then should be passed on to the customer in the form of reduced prices.

The legal problems customers may bring on themselves and their suppliers by such demands are reviewed in Chapter 13. The anomaly is that customers are not telling manufacturers that they should eliminate their direct sales channel and reduce prices equal to the savings on all costs directly attributable to the direct channel. The bottom line is that the need for quality independent reps has never been greater.

Increased Concentration of Purchasing Power

Acquisitions, mergers, pooled purchasing practices, and long-term contracts have resulted in a significant concentration of purchasing power. Reductions in the number of suppliers started in the 1980s. This reduction continues today in many industries but with dual objectives, namely selecting the best performing vendors and offering them the incentive to lower their prices for high-volume commitments. This continues to result in fewer customers being available to manufacturers. However, it frequently has not reduced the number of customer locations that have an influence on purchasing decisions. Sales channel designs must, therefore, take these complexities into consideration.

Sharp Reductions of Customer Staffs

Somewhat hidden behind the employment surge throughout the 1990s that reduced unemployment to historic lows are the sharp head count reductions in many large organizations. Entire levels of mid-management have been replaced in order to obtain flatter organizational structures. In addition, many functional departments have been eliminated in favor of outsourcing. Every functional department in organizational life has been impacted by this trend. Manufacturing, engineering, financial functions, and computer services are now frequently outsourced. This has meant a much greater reliability by customers on their suppliers to perform many functions normally performed internally. In the process, a whole new set of competence standards is demanded of sales forces.

Global Competition for High Unit Volume Products

Despite the collapsing market opportunities in developing nations throughout the world in 1998, global competition is here to stay, particularly for high-volume, relatively standardized products. Even for more customized products, global marketing is the norm. Generally, these global competitors are the larger sized corporations that are able to constantly drive their manufacturing cost down as a result of the high volume handled. However, many small companies are now becoming global companies for niche opportunities. Integrated worldwide selling efforts are becoming the norm.

Competition Becomes More Adept at Segmenting Markets

As the great majority of manufacturers and service providers cannot be world-class competitors for large market opportunities, the most profitable alternative is to select segments of markets whereby the smaller company can provide some differentiation and, therefore, gain competitive advantage. Once again, sales channel members must upgrade their competence to best serve these niches.

Increased Computerization

Use of the computer continues its geometric expansion in our high-tech society. This trend will continue and, for many products, will result in sales being purely by e-commerce. While the computer will continue to occupy increasing amounts of our time, the astute manufacturer will recognize that there is normally a concurrent aversion to the computer. Here's where suppliers can gain competitive advantage by assuring a compassionate touch in the selling process. This will be particularly true for non-commodity-type products, systems, and services, where the need for highly competent sales personnel will be greater than ever.

Voice Messaging Systems

Originally conceived to reduce the inefficiencies of human handling of incoming calls and to provide lower communication costs, voice messaging systems have insidiously evolved into screening devices whereby customer sales personnel shield themselves from sales call intrusions. This creates considerable difficulty for sales personnel to gain access to deciders and influencers of purchasing decisions. Only the well-connected salesperson will continue to have ready access.

Each of these megatrends and perhaps others unique to your industry must be carefully considered from a specific manufacturer's point of view to determine characteristics now needed in its sales channel to gain competitive advantage. Chapter 3 takes these megatrends and converts them into a set of key characteristics desired in the new millennium sales force. Those characteristics are then compared to alternative channels.

At our public seminars[1] throughout the 1990s, attendees representing a wide diversity of manufacturers and system suppliers have increasingly pointed to independent sales representatives, rather than direct sales forces, as the closest possible fit with their needs to gain competitive advantage. Chapter 3 provides their reasoning for this conclusion.

A Systems Approach

Despite the dramatic changes in customer/supplier relationships as the millennium concludes, one of the reliable constants has been the six-step process presented in both the first and second editions for the design, development, and maintenance of highly productive sales channels. This process continues to be quite enduring and is the same one followed in the third edition.

The fundamental objective of this approach is to provide manufacturers and service providers—large and small—with a methodology to obtain intensive sales coverage of *all* targeted markets. The goal is to use highly skilled, highly motivated sales personnel who specialize in these target markets and to achieve coverage within a rational cost framework. Our systems approach allows one to take a fairly complicated task, break it down into simple elements, and provide a continuous planning and implementation process that produces results, namely increased sales and profitability. The process as described here is built primarily around one class of independent sales organization (ISO)—the manufacturer's sales representative (rep). Supplementary commentary is also offered on other types of ISOs.

It's important to point out here in the beginning that, although this book is about independent sales organizations, ISOs are not the answer for every situation; there are pluses and minuses to alternative channels. Using our six-step approach, you would first define objectives for your company and design strategies for attaining them (*Step 1*) and then determine which of several sales channels best fits those strategies (*Step 2*).

If, after completing the first two steps, you conclude that an independent sales force is the way to go, the balance of the book will help you understand how to design, develop, support, monitor, and constantly improve the channel. The four additional steps that will help you do this are as follows:

Step 3   Define the profile of the ideal rep that best matches your short- and long-term needs.

[1]Sponsored by Sales and Marketing Management Magazine, the University of Wisconsin, and the Manufacturers' Agents National Association (MANA).

Step 4   Conduct an intensive search in order to find the best available rep for each channel in each trading area.

Step 5   Develop a total support system to ensure channel commitment.

Step 6   Audit the entire system constantly, making whatever adjustments are required for changing conditions.

You'll find a complete definition of each step in Chapter 2. Step 1 is then fully developed in Chapter 2 with Steps 2 through 6 further developed in Chapters 3 through 11. The remaining chapters contain additional important information.

In this book you will learn what sales reps are all about: how they work, how they differ from direct salespeople, and what motivates them to even stronger performance. You will also learn:

- How you can design a sales channel that will give you intensive coverage of all your targeted markets
- How you can add significant profits from secondary markets
- How independent reps can make a success out of your market segmentation strategy
- How you can get more than a fair share of a rep's time
- Why many manufacturers have been dissatisfied with reps and how you can avoid these problems
- How you can assess the compatibility of your sales force with your short- and long-term needs and then promptly correct weaknesses
- How you can audit your capability to effectively support your sales force

Structure of the Book

This book shows manufacturers how to use independent sales organizations (ISOs) to develop a powerful sales channel that gives them enormous flexibility. There are several classes of ISOs: manufacturers' representatives, distributors, brokers, wholesalers, VARs, systems integrators, dealers, and others. Each holds a slightly different place in the overall scheme that moves products from manufacturer or service provider to customer (more on this in Chapter 1), but in most of the important ways they have many characteristics in common. In order to develop the explanation of a total systems approach fully, I elected to focus on just one class: the independent manufacturer's representative, or "rep." Because reps are most commonly used to sell into industrial markets, the discussions throughout a large portion of this book have an industrial orientation. However, the concepts are equally applicable to consumer markets.

One other point: This book primarily focuses on domestic marketing. Using independent sales organizations in foreign countries introduces many new complexities in terms of what is required in both the sales organization and in contract conditions dictated by the laws of each country. However, many of the concepts presented here can be used as a prelude to better understanding the job that needs to be done for successful international marketing. Chapter 14 then focuses on those characteristics unique to the international use of independent sales organizations. It is written by Gunnar Beeth, a consultant with extensive experience in international sales. Gunnar has completely updated this chapter for the third edition and gives particular attention to the European Union (EU), which was officially initiated via the use of the Euro monetary system in January 1999.

For foreign countries interested in exporting into U.S. markets, this book offers many insights into the design, development, and maintenance of the sales channels that can best serve their needs.

Other Changes

Chapter 4 examines Fisher Controls International as a major example of a large company that has been extremely successful using reps. The third edition completely updates Fisher's evolution with reps. Chapter 13 on Legal Issues and Trends introduces our guest attorney, Jerry Salmen of Wood and Lamping, a Cincinnati law firm. Also totally new are the appendices and a very valuable resource guide that is the most complete reference list compiled on independent reps. This is the bibliography periodically updated by the Manufacturers' Representatives Educational Research Foundation under the leadership of Dr. Marilyn Stephens. It is a highly valuable reference source for publications, rep associations, and rep firms.

In addition to the above new material, other chapters have been modified when appropriate based on input we have received from our clients, attendees of our public and in-house seminars, and interviews with many companies.

Gearing Up for Success

Selling through independents is not without problems. In fact, it is a much more complex management job than selling through a direct sales organization. Many manufacturers fail in their use of manufacturers' reps or succeed only marginally, generally because they lack an understanding of what it takes to be successful with reps or fail to implement the necessary programs to develop a powerful rep sales force. They may not understand the needs for a careful design of the overall channel. They may do a poor job of selecting the right rep or they may falter in supporting reps properly. They may fail to constantly audit the relationship. The answer to these failures is to develop a systematic approach to the selection, support, and evaluation of both the rep network and the company's own objectives and capabilities to support its sales organization effectively. These steps must be followed in a highly disciplined program with constant focus on all the details required for excellence.

Companies with a long history of direct sales will find that working with independents requires a different mind-set. A positive, highly supportive corporate culture is essential. This means the senior line executive—president, CEO, or division manager—must play an active role in any program with independents. If this top-level support is clearly demonstrated and if the sales network is properly designed, supported, and monitored, independent sales organizations can yield significant successes in the marketplace.

Whether your company is currently considering reps or has used them for many years, whether yours is an industrial-products or a consumer-oriented organization, whether you are in a multibillion-dollar corporation or an entrepreneurial venture, this book will offer key insights into how you can more profitably grow your business.

SELLING THROUGH INDEPENDENT REPS

1

Independent Sales Organizations: An Overview

In the competitive marketplace of the twenty-first century, the right sales organization can make the difference between surviving and thriving, between lackluster results and sterling profitability. Which one is right for your company?

Before you can determine that answer, you'll need to acquaint yourself with the various options.

Getting Acquainted

Speaking in very broad terms, there are two general classes of sales structure available based on the employment relationship with the manufacturer: the direct sales force and the independent sales organization (ISO). The essential distinction is this: Direct salespeople are employees of your company, hired and fired by you. They may earn a salary, a commission, or some combination of the two, but they are on your payroll, working under your direct control. Independent sales organizations, on the other hand, are businesses run by sales professionals who contract with your company (as well as with others) to sell your products to your customers. Traditionally, larger corporations have mostly used direct sales forces (with many having supplemental distribution systems) while smaller companies or small divisions of large companies have primarily used ISOs in order to meet all their sales channel needs.

The large-company tradition has been substantially altered in recent years as many large companies have come to recognize that their direct sales forces do not and cannot economically cover all targeted markets and geographic territories. A trend toward increased use of ISOs by large companies to complement their direct sales forces has been the result. In addition, larger firms that may at one time have considered converting from rep to direct are now staying with independent rep sales forces. Chapter 4 presents a more complete discussion on this subject.

Two Categories of ISOs

There are effectively two categories of ISOs, depending on whether they take title of the product. Within each category, there are a number of different descriptive terms used to indicate a subclass. However, in some cases the difference among subclasses is more a difference in industry semantics than in any actual differences in the ISO itself. The two categories are:

1. *Sell only.* This category applies primarily to the independent sales rep—commonly but imprecisely called an agent by many industries. Historically, the term "independent manufacturers' rep" was routinely used. However, in recent years there has been an explosion in the use of independent reps by service providers in the computer and telecommunications industry. Therefore, the term "independent manufacturers' rep" is no longer appropriate in describing this channel. "Independent sales representative" has become the more descriptive term.

The broker also fits into this category, performing exactly the same function as a rep for certain industries (i.e., in the area of industrial food ingredients). Members who fall into this category take a commission on their sales, with title to the product passing directly from manufacturer to purchaser.

2. *Buy/resell.* Distributors and wholesalers are the most recognized intermediaries in this category. Wholesalers typically sell to another level of intermediaries, while distributors may also sell directly to the end user as well as through additional intermediaries. Normally, this channel purchases the product from the manufacturer, inventories it, and, particularly in the case of distributors, may add to its value. Their compensation is the difference between their purchase price (plus associated expenses) and the selling price.

But the distinctions are not always clear. Distributors frequently offer extensive value-added capabilities, such as assembling your products with products of other manufacturers into a package they then offer to customers. Occasionally, however, they will act similarly to reps, that is, make sales and take commissions without taking title. And more and more manufacturers' reps have begun to complement their pure selling function with a buy/resell role, taking title to the goods and establishing the selling price themselves. Therefore, although theoretically there are sharply defined differences between reps and distributors, the marketplace has introduced so many differences that, at times, it may be difficult to categorize a given independent sales firm. This has lead to terms such as stocking representatives, nonstocking distributors, value-added resellers (VARs), systems integrators, and a host of others.

Three Levels of Sales Structure

In many industries, the overall sales channel will incorporate more than one type of ISO, often in combination with a direct sales team. It will seem less complicated if you visualize a structure composed of levels.

The first level is the sales team that takes the manufacturer's products out into the market. They may be either direct salespeople or manufacturers' reps (or brokers); some companies use a combination of both rep and direct. They may sell directly to the end user, in which case the company's sales structure has only one level. (Occasionally, manufacturers use distributors as the first channel level. However, this tends to be the exception rather than the rule.)

Or those in the first level can sell into a network of distributors—the second level. The distributors can sell to dealers or wholesalers—the third level—who in turn will sell to the ultimate customer. In some industries, the distributor might sell to contractors and original equipment manufacturers (OEMs), and they will sell the finished product to the customer. In truth, the possible combinations and variations are almost limitless.

Figure 1-1 shows these levels in relation to one another. While it is intended for illustration only, the sales channel shown here is similar to the sales channels employed by some industries. Normally, however, sales channels of industrial-products companies are simpler. Consumer-products channels, on the other hand, may be more complex.

The first step in sales channel design is to determine what channel approach provides the best access to sell and service your markets. This step begins with the customer, not the manufacturer. If you determine that local distributors are required, you then move back toward the manufacturer. Now determine how the distribution system and any customers not readily accessed by the distributors can be best supported—namely, by either a manufacturer's direct sales force or through independent reps.

Our focus now will primarily be on independent reps as an alternative or a complement to a direct sales force.

Direct Sales Force

A direct sales force is a sales organization in which all sales personnel are employees of the manufacturer. The key characteristic of this channel is

Figure 1-1   Alternative sales channels (industrial products).

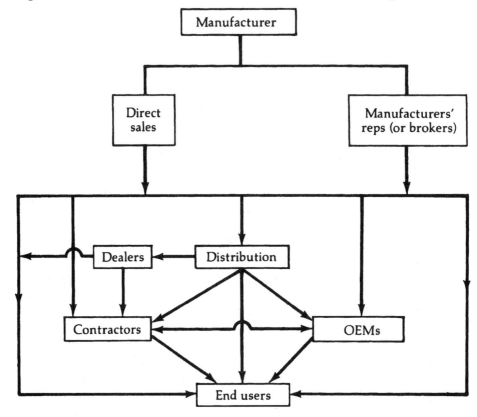

that the members dedicate their complete selling effort to their employer, who has the authority to control all their activities. They may be compensated by salary, salary plus bonus, commission, or many other variations. The selling expense is relatively fixed (except for pure commission arrangements), as most organizations do not quickly hire and fire sales personnel—even with relatively wide swings in total sales.

In most cases, a large sales volume is needed in order to afford the payroll and associated expenses of a sufficient number of salespersons to provide intensive coverage of targeted markets. A single direct sales organization is typically used for larger profit centers or organizations that have closely related products and markets. Where products and markets are highly differentiated and where the dollar volume warrants, two or more direct sales networks may be used, each handling a given set of products or markets. This is frequently the case in very large companies made up of several divisions, each with its own product line (see Figure 1-2).

A variation found in large organizations is the multidivisional direct

Figure 1-2   Autonomous divisions.

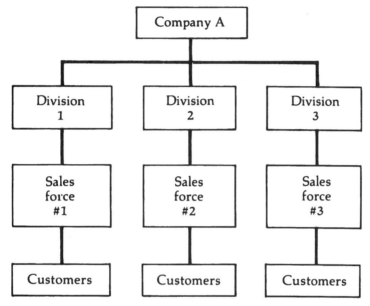

sales force (see Figure 1-3). Here, one combined corporate sales team sells the products for either a group of or all the divisions into one common market. This structure works very well, as long as all the divisions' products genuinely fit into that one common market. When one does not, the wise company will think about pulling that one out of the corporate sales force.

Note: The multidivisional sales force may also be constructed using independent reps. Again, refer to Chapter 4 where it will be noted that since the acquisition of Fisher Controls by Emerson Electric, such a multidivision structure has been established with several business units selling through a common independent rep sales force.

Independent Sales Organizations: An Overview

The terms for the various kinds of ISOs are not rigidly applied. Each industry has its own lingo, and a "wholesaler" in one industry might be called a "distributor" in another. In general, however, the functions follow the descriptions given here.

Independent Sales Representatives

Let's start with a basic definition. An independent sales representative (**rep**) is an independent business organization of one or more professional

Figure 1-3   Multidivisional sales force.

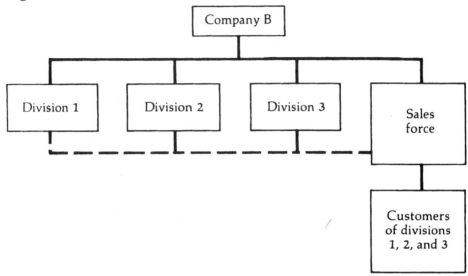

salespersons dedicated to selling in a defined territory, market, or group of customers as a career. Reps sell for more than one manufacturer under a "sales representation" contract with each and tend to specialize in selling to select customers or markets. The contract typically awards the rep an exclusive territory or market to help ensure the rep's long-term commitment. Their income is based on commissions received from the manufacturers or service providers they represent as a result of their sales for each company. They take neither title nor possession of the product, which is shipped directly to the buyer or user by each manufacturer or service provider.

Whereas most direct salespeople start out as what we might call amateurs (they are hired at entry level into a sales training program or transfer in from another department but without sales experience), most reps start out with a great deal of sales experience under their belt. In 1997, 72 percent of the owners of rep organizations surveyed had previous sales experience, and two-thirds of this total had sales management positions for manufacturers before starting their businesses. This was one of the findings in the annual rep profile developed by the Manufacturers' Agents National Association (MANA) and published in *Agency Sales*[1] magazine. In this category, one will find reps with experience as top performers in district, regional, or national sales management. Many such reps were vice-presidents of marketing. The 38 percent balance is made up of those experienced in purchasing, manufacturing, and engineering, and includes

[1]*Agency Sales,* January 1998, p. 9, Manufacturers' Agents National Association, Laguna Hills, CA.

a sprinkling of former company presidents. Typically, all were top performers with the type of self-confidence necessary to start their own businesses. This confidence and capability is also typical of the sales personnel
hired by the founders and owners of rep firms.

Reps display many of the same selling characteristics as independents
that they had as employed salespeople, except that they tend to be the
higher performers. The difference now is that they are independent, represent a number of different manufacturers, have a long-term commitment
to the territory, and receive only a commission income for their effort.

Here are some other definitions.

Sales Agents

Frequently you will hear the term *sales agent* used as a synonym for *sales
representative.* However, there is a definite legal distinction between the
two. Agents have the power to bind their principals to an agreement with
the customer. In most cases, it's a question of vocabulary used in one industry or another; even when reps are called "agents," they do not usually
function as agents in the legal sense. In this book, we use *representative* or
rep. In the total spectrum of ISOs today, it is rare that one will find conditions suggesting the use of the true agent.

Stocking Representatives

Sometimes sales reps actually purchase products for their inventory in
order to service customers better. They are normally called "stocking
reps." In this one aspect, they are functioning like distributors, but their
sales from inventory represent a very small part of their total business, so
they are not really distributors—at least not yet. As time passes in certain
industries, they may develop more and more characteristics of distributors, and you could flip a coin to decide what to call them.

Brokers

Their operation is very similar to a rep's and, in terms of their contract
relationship with a manufacturer, may be identical. They tend to be more
commodity-oriented and usually cover larger trading areas than the typical rep. For practical purposes, the differences are in name only.

Distributors and Wholesalers

These ISOs buy the product from a manufacturer, inventory it, and sell it
to their customers or to another level of resellers (i.e., dealers). Profit is the
differential between purchase and sales price less sales, administrative,

and inventory costs. At times, distributors also sell as manufacturers' reps, that is, not taking title to the goods but taking a commission on the sale. Unlike reps, distributors cannot be constrained to a given territory; once they take title to a product, law precludes restricting its sale to a given geography.

Another primary distinction of a distributor is found in the term *value-added*. The distributor, by purchasing the product and stocking it for immediate local delivery, adds value to it in the mind of the buyer. This is just one of a wide array of values a distributor can add to the product to better serve local customers. On the upper end of the value scale, systems engineering, complex product packages, and total turnkey packaging are all examples of ISOs that offer further value to their customers.

The need for distribution has gained added impetus as American industry further embraces a just-in-time (JIT) approach to purchasing. The local distributor is very well suited to perform this service. Also new is high-tech distribution, an outgrowth of customer demands for integrated system solutions.

Dealers

Dealers are similar to distributors except that they typically work in a smaller geographic area. They are frequently serviced by a distributor or a rep.

Value-Added Resellers and Systems Integrators

Newer to the sales channel jargon are these two independent sales organizations. Both represent some characteristics of distributors (stocking or nonstocking) and engineering contractors. They tend not to have as formalized a contract as distributors, and are not nearly as restricted territorial wise. Many of these firms have emerged from the application of computers to industrial and business applications. They are a second level of distribution, being reached by manufacturers through either independent reps or direct sales personnel for most companies.

A Few Examples of Sales Channels

To help you understand the structural relationships of the various types of ISOs, look at Figures 1-4, 1-5, and 1-6, which show sales configurations in three different industries. We'll be discussing these kinds of sales channels in some detail later, but for now just be aware of the various ways products flow from manufacturer to customer.

Figure 1-4 shows a system that is widely used in the electronic com-

Figure 1-4 Typical sales channel in an electronic components company.

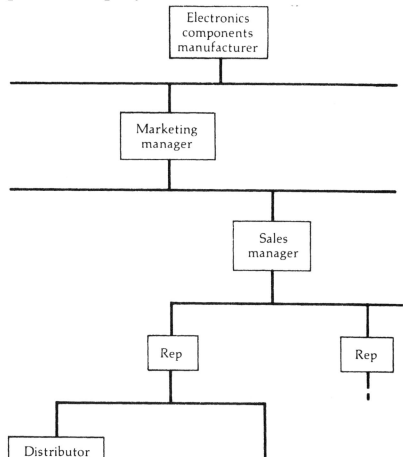

ponents industry. Regional managers, who report to a sales manager, sell through a series of reps. The reps then sell through distributors (typically recruited by the reps), who call on smaller customers in the reps' areas. The reps themselves sell to larger customers; if they happen to come across a small customer, they just turn it over to the distributors.

Figure 1-5 brings a dealer into the picture. The sales manager (either national or regional) for this manufacturer of small office equipment sells through a network of distributors, who in turn sell to local dealers, who sell to buyers.

Figure 1-5   Typical sales channel for the office products industry.

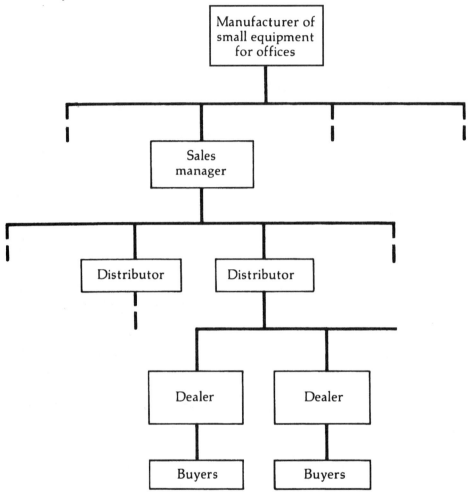

Finally, Figure 1-6 shows a combined structure, using both a network of manufacturers' reps and some direct salespeople. These hybrid channels come in many variations and are widely used in many kinds of industries. Our example happens to be a valve manufacturer. This company uses its own salespeople in its primary trading areas (meaning the geographic areas where its biggest customers are located) and a network of reps in the secondary trading areas. Both arms of the system are then split into two subcategories: sales to key customers, such as OEMs, are made directly by the salesperson, and sales to other customers, such as small end users, are made through distributors.

Figure 1-6   Combined rep/direct network in a mechanical products company.

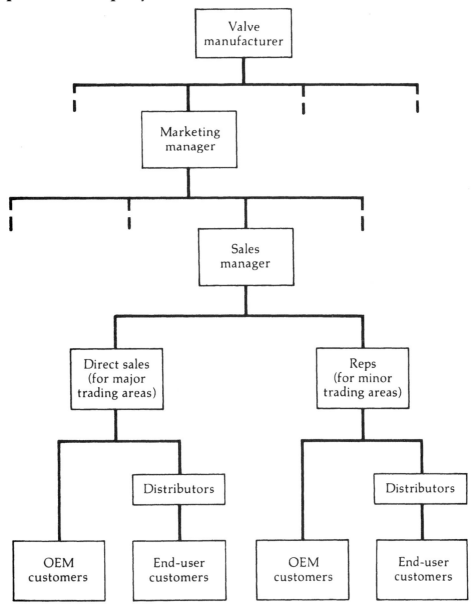

Key Differences in Sales Organizations

Independent sales organizations are, by their very nature, quite different from direct sales organizations. This means that their relationship with manufacturers will be inherently different in several significant ways. We'll be talking about many of these differences in detail throughout the book, but in this overview chapter, let's introduce four.

The Issue of Control

Because ISOs are, by definition, independent—they are not under the direct control of the organization whose products they sell—the great majority of manufacturers feel much more comfortable with a direct sales organization. This comfort index is a product of our historical management perspective involving power satisfactions (boss/subordinate relationships). Many managers say they like "having our own people," but what is often behind that statement is an inherent aversion to treating those in a sales organization as peers. All too often, this deep-seated distrust stems from senior management and is then emulated by others in the organization. This eventually develops into an anti-rep culture that is counterproductive to rep commitment and sales production for the manufacturer.

Therefore, one of the keys in successfully using ISOs is to accept and respect them as independent organizations. This means abandoning any historic boss/subordinate control practices and expectations. Independents must be treated as peer organizations that team up with your company to achieve a mutually desired objective: in-depth penetration of targeted markets in the ISO's trading area. As you will see later, this approach introduces profound differences in the way ISOs should be recruited, supported, and monitored.

Opportunities for Specialization

There is a tendency in direct selling to use each individual in the sales organization to handle all products to all markets. Many years ago, as a sales engineer for one of the divisions of what was then Westinghouse Electric, I was responsible for selling electrostatic air cleaners into residential and industrial applications, unit heaters to wholesaler markets, air handling systems in high-rise office buildings, process fans to industry, specialized fans for OEM applications, and mechanical draft fans for large boiler applications. My results were typical of similar direct sales organizations: The products that sold the easiest and that best matched my interests were the most successful ones.

Combining diverse products into diverse markets through a single sales organization is still a quite typical way to operate, but it invariably is not productive for all markets. Intensive coverage of primary markets is possible with direct personnel, but it frequently becomes cost prohibitive to obtain intensive coverage for secondary, let alone tertiary, product and market targets.

When an organization pushes a highly varied product line through diverse markets, the direct sales organization typically leaves a number of the products and markets with very poor sales coverage. In a properly designed ISO network, specialized independents with a vertical market orientation can be recruited—at least in major market areas where such rep specialization is available. A manufacturer can then "parallel" a number of independents to achieve intensive coverage of all target markets, both primary and secondary.

An Example of Successful Specialization: Glegg Water Conditioning of Guelph, Ontario, was one of the case studies used in the second edition. The firm originally used a single representative for all of its products and markets. In 1991, sales levels had reached $30 million. Glegg's single channel was primarily comprised of reps who were strong in steam generation markets.

As Glegg's market strategy expanded and focused on opportunities in ultra pure water applications for the manufacturing of semiconductor chips and pharmaceuticals, separate channels were developed for each of these two vertical markets. This paid off handsomely in the mid-1990s, particularly due to the explosive growth of chip manufacturing worldwide. Corporate sales exceeded $100 million in 1996. Essentially, the entire increase was achieved through internal growth rather than acquisition, a remarkable track record.

The semiconductor industry peaked in that year and yielded $60 million in sales for Glegg. In 1997, the expansion of plant capacity in the semiconductor industry collapsed and sales for Glegg to this industry dropped by nearly 80 percent. Yet, because it had two additional channels, one for steam generation and one for pharmaceuticals, Glegg was able to reallocate a major effort into these two other markets and minimize the decline in corporate sales to 10 percent. This is an outstanding example of the enormous benefits of strategically positioning a company in different markets that have different peaks and valleys and in constructing dedicated sales channels for each market.

As the year 2000 approaches, Glegg has strengthened its rep channels and also diversified into additional business units that are focused on other markets using a combination of new and existing channels, not only in the northern hemisphere but worldwide. The dangerous peaks and valleys of capital equipment businesses have been tempered significantly, and the future growth of the company has never looked better.

Compensation

In general, direct personnel are paid by salary or salary plus an incentive, while ISOs earn either a commission or a markup over purchase price. In other words, ISOs do not eat unless they sell. This compensation scheme has two productive results: (1) The poor performers are quickly weeded out, and (2) those who can succeed have a powerful stimulus to perform.

The point to recognize is that the total compensation for directly employed individuals is usually more limited than that for the independents. In most companies, members of the sales staff tend to be equated with members of other functional activities inside the organization as economic equals and are paid in similar hierarchical patterns as a base. Then a nominal incentive may be added in recognition of their unusual role in the company. As a result, the incentive for top sales personnel is frequently limited, and the best people tend to search out alternative opportunities—for example, promotion, transfer, company change, or change from direct sales to rep sales.

With the ISO, bureaucratization tends not to exist, and compensation potential is unlimited. Some very successful independents earn well more than a manufacturer's senior executive. Sometimes that bruises managerial egos so badly that we occasionally see one of the great paradoxes of economic life: The rep who truly excels for a manufacturer is fired and is replaced by a direct salesperson. The paradox can be explained by comparing a top-performing rep with a valued new supplier that was recruited because of a manufacturer's outsourcing program. The supplier starts with a small annual agreement, then proves its worth by shipping a high-quality product on time and backing it up with great service. The supplier then becomes a sole source for the manufacturer and is rewarded by very large annual contracts. The manufacturer does not concern itself that the supplier makes an excellent profit as a result of being this sole source supplier.

The independent rep is also the result of outsourcing. Yet, when the rep demonstrates a high level of proficiency and helps the manufacturer become increasingly successful, the same long-term relationship is frequently threatened when the manufacturer sees the commission income of the rep rivaling that of the senior executive. As commissions are purely a variable expense, the manufacturer's profits are constantly improving as a result of a rep's top performance. These high-performance reps should be viewed by the manufacturers as a major company strength and treated with tender loving care for as long as the objectives of both organizations remain common. More details on this analysis are given in Chapter 4.

Economic Independence

The degree of a rep's economic independence may also be used as a measure of describing whether or not a salesperson or sales firm is an independent rep or a direct person. In other words, an independent rep may be defined as a firm or person whose income is not dominated by one firm. On the opposite side of the coin, the direct person can be defined as one whose income is totally derived from a single company whether or not that person has an independent contractor agreement with the company. Figure 1-7, a graph of Economic Independence vs. Percent of Income Received from one company portrays the relative dependence or independence a person or firm has with its number one income contributor.

Independent reps fully understand the economic impact of a major single principal. While many reps will embrace the manufacturer who can grow rapidly and, as a result, generate an increasing share of the rep's income, other reps will become paranoid about the prospect of a single firm commanding too great a part of their income. The fear is that they will be terminated and lose too great a part of their commission income. This paranoia then becomes a self-fulfilling prophecy as any rep who limits her growth with a given manufacturer or service provider is asking to be terminated because her firm will no longer sell as aggressively as it can for that major principal. More on this complex issue later.

Figure 1-7 Economic independence vs. percent of income a rep receives from one company.

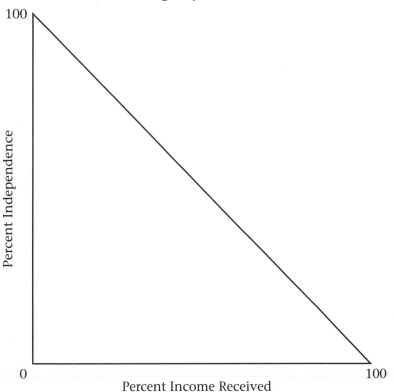

On the other hand, many reps have not been so limited by their own paranoia and have profited significantly by maintaining common objectives with their number one manufacturer. Income from that one manufacturer then will be allowed to grow as rapidly as it can. Chapter 4 presents a case on Fisher Controls where Fisher's contribution to the reps' total income ranges from 70 percent to well over 90 percent. The reps have profited significantly as they have invested in this partnership. If any of the Fisher reps had shown a reluctance to grow, they would not have remained Fisher reps very long.

2

A Systems Approach for Increased Market Penetration

Earlier I said that the objective of this book was to help manufacturers increase market share by gaining intensive sales coverage of all markets with highly skilled sales professionals—and do it cost-effectively. If you are convinced that independent reps, or some other type of ISO, are the solution for you, you might be tempted at this point to pick up the phone and hire one. Maybe someone you met at last month's trade show impressed you, or perhaps you happened to run into a rep who performed well for you at your last company.

You might be tempted, but don't do it—at least not yet. You have some work to do first.

The Six-Step Process

As a management task, selling through ISOs is more complex than selling direct. And making the choice of sales structure in the first place is complex, too. However, we can make those complex matters simpler with a systems approach that breaks larger tasks down into separate steps. For sales channel design, we use a six-step process that has been developed over time and refined with many organizations. The process is illustrated in Figure 2-1. It is structured toward reps on the assumption that using reps is the conclusion you reached after completing Step 2. However, the process is applicable to all channels.

1. *Define your objectives.* The starting point for building any sales organization is knowing specifically where you are and where you wish to go in terms of product and market objectives. You also have to develop sound

Figure 2-1   Six steps to sales channel design.

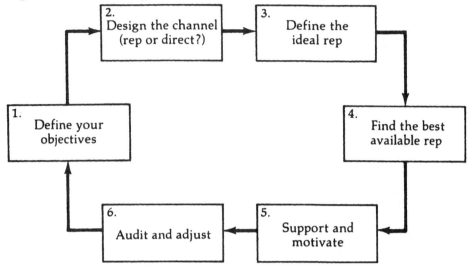

strategies to differentiate your company in the marketplace. Next, you must design the plans and programs necessary to achieve these objectives. Then, with a clear statement of where you are today and where you would like to be in the long term, you can begin to consider which sales channel will do the most effective job of getting you there.

2. *Design the channel (rep or direct?).* Now, take each targeted market segment and determine what characteristics will be required of your sales channel to serve end-user needs best; then select the channel design that best fits those needs. It may be distribution for a second level with either direct sales or reps as the first level. This choice—rep, direct, or hybrid—should take into consideration many factors, each of which will be explored later in this book. One key: Remember to consider long-term as well as short-term needs.

3. *Define the ideal rep.* Let's presume that reps are your preferred first-level channel. You now need to define the characteristics of the ideal rep for your company. This is one of the most crucial concepts in selling through an ISO, yet one of the most frequently ignored. Because you will not be able to mold and shape your reps (at least in comparison to the degree you can mold an employee), it is absolutely vital that you select those that fit closely with your objectives. And the only way to do that is to define precisely what you need. The same holds true, of course, for brokers, distributors, wholesalers, and other ISOs.

Manufacturers must be willing to invest the time to identify the characteristics a salesperson or a sales organization needs to give the best possible penetration of each product and market target. When they develop these ideal characteristics, many manufacturers discover that the best possible coverage of multiple product and market targets can be achieved only by using more than one sales channel. Frequently this may mean "paralleling" several rep organizations in a single territory, each specializing in a specific market target. The ideal rep profile is also extremely valuable in helping you select the best available rep and in understanding why some of your current reps are not performing well.

4. *Find the best available rep.* A major mistake of companies trying to succeed with reps is the failure to do the thorough search necessary to find the best available rep. A key to understanding independent reps is to recognize that what you see is what you get. Successful representatives have a very well-established modus operandi that works with a package of manufacturers they have assembled. Any new manufacturer teaming up with that rep must fit this modus operandi rather precisely if success is to be achieved. The *only* way to achieve maximum market penetration with independent reps is to hire *in the first place* those who already possess all the necessary characteristics to do the job. It is therefore imperative that the search be intensive and aggressive, with clear objectives in mind. Even a slight miss in one of the critical characteristics defined in Step 3 can result in a poor relationship and even poorer performance.

5. *Support and motivate.* Successful sales channel design results in the creation of a sales network that has not only closeness to all market targets but also the capability of converting its relationships into profitable market penetration and increasing market share over the longer term. But all that can be wasted if the manufacturer fails to provide total company-wide support for the reps. Such support includes not only the traditional tools that marketing departments provide to any sales force but a much broader foundation of support for the whole concept of using an independent professional sales organization—support that starts at the very top of the company. That kind of total support motivates reps like nothing else will. Poor support of reps' sales efforts is another critical area where manufacturers frequently fail in their relationships with reps and thereby fail to achieve their objectives.

6. *Audit and adjust.* It is very important that manufacturers develop a way of evaluating the performance of the rep network. Usually your evaluation in the early months of your relationship with a rep will be different from longer-term evaluations. Of course, you must be concerned with "numbers" performance—new orders—but you should also do a periodic comparison of the rep's characteristics with your most current definition of the "ideal rep." What was a perfectly compatible relationship yesterday may have significantly deteriorated as a result of a change in your priorities or those of your reps. Constant reappraisal is required, but not just of rep performance. It is equally important to reappraise your own company's capabilities constantly in order to support the sales organization's efforts to achieve its objectives.

Companies that use independent reps have access to two outstanding control tools: the rep council and the rep audit. These systems help senior management—not just the marketing manager—better understand the company's performance in the marketplace. Such feedback provides manufacturers a clear view of both strategic and operational issues they face and directions they should take to resolve them.

And that brings us to the end of the process—and the beginning. In any planning, by the time the ink is dry, the plan may be obsolete. This is no less true for sales channel design or even the selection of just one independent rep. Priorities change. Competitive action may demand a change in strategy. Any number of events can occur that require this system to be completely reprogrammed. This is the reason our chart shows a closed loop, with the output of the last step leading right back into the first step. As a minimum standard, the entire cycle should be repeated on an annual basis, with a watchful eye to define any event that suggests intermediate review is needed.

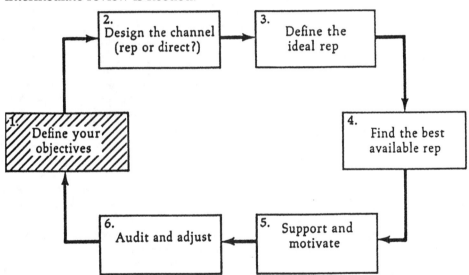

The cornerstone for developing successful sales organizations is a clear definition of a company's current and future targets, the priorities of each target, the strategies that will yield the necessary differentiation, and the subsequent plans, programs, implementation steps, and follow-up to ensure that the objectives are achieved. Surprisingly, many companies fail in building a strong sales organization because they do not pay adequate attention to this very necessary first step. (A chart focusing on Step 1 is shown above.) It is essential that an organization take the time to define its current position and the direction it wishes to pursue over the long term. With that definition in hand, a company can proceed to designing the sales channel that will best fulfill its objectives.

The tool that you need to craft your objectives is a basic business plan. It does not have to be a weighty document, but it should address certain subjects and point to a clear direction for the company. There are many excellent books available on business planning, so we'll just touch briefly on the five key tasks.

1. Situation analysis
2. Market forecasts and targeting
3. Product and market objectives
4. Strategies
5. Plans and programs

Situation Analysis

An organization needs a clear understanding of itself, the environment in which it is operating, and the factors that are likely to have a significant impact on its business over the coming years. The management staff should contribute ideas on all the trends that are affecting the company: your own historical market share and that of competitors, trends in profitability, economic issues that affect your industry, political issues, trends with major customers and major markets, technology threats, and changes among your competitors. A sales channel audit, described in detail in Step 6, is a critical part of the situation analysis and clearly defines how the system becomes a continuous process rather than a periodic event.

From the situation analysis, you should then develop a profile of the strengths and weaknesses of your own company and your competition. Out of this assessment, you can start deciding what market niches should be established and where the greatest vulnerabilities of the competition are.

Market Forecasts and Targeting

Once you have analyzed the current situation, you can develop forecasts for each key market by product. Treat the numbers with great circumspection—forecasting is at best a risky venture. Your goal is to determine the prime market opportunities that afford your company the best chance for profitable penetration. This requires both a quantification of future markets and assessments of positioning opportunities in each.

Product and Market Objectives

With the situation analysis (current) and market forecasts (future), you are ready to set preliminary product and market objectives. These should be put into a product/market matrix (more on this task later) to indicate clearly where the company has been, where it is now, and where it intends to be over the coming years. Three- to five-year targets are typical.

Strategies

Strategy development has two aspects. First is the general strategy that will guide the basic overall direction of the organization—for example, a strategy to move away from furnishing capital equipment for smokestack America and toward services for the infrastructure. The second phase involves subsets of the overall strategy. You are looking at each market segment, defining ways to differentiate your products or services to minimize competition. You will build your strategies around the concept of market segmentation.

Establishing product and market objectives is an exercise in futility unless you develop accompanying strategies that provide a reasonable chance of achieving these objectives. Be sure to take your competitors into consideration; they may be planning these very same strategies. For example, as the capital equipment markets declined, many organizations focused on the aftermarket as their opportunity to stay profitable. The result was a tremendous escalation of competition in the aftermarket and a decline in the profit opportunity.

Plans and Programs

The final step of the planning process is the development of a detailed plan with accompanying programs. The plan is the sum total of your efforts. The programs are the discrete elements that each focus on a specific objective. They provide the list of task responsibilities, budgets, and schedules. Accountability assignments are also defined to help ensure timely implementation.

Theory Applied: The Product/Market Matrix

The product/market matrix is the starting step in defining the preferred sales channel design. Figure 2-2 shows a matrix for a company with three products and three markets. If the company sells its products through a single sales organization—that is, one in which each salesperson has the responsibility for selling all products into all markets—chances are that two opportunities will not be adequately pursued. The sales organization simply will not spend the required time to do the proper job for penetrating market C or selling product 3; they have a high probability of becom-

Figure 2-2 Sample product/market matrix.

	Product #1	Product #2	Product #3	Total
Market A	40	25	0	65
Market B	15	10	5	30
Market C	2	0	3	5
Total	57	35	8	100

Typical Lost Opportunities:
- The orphan product: #3
- The orphan market: C

ing what we call "orphans," that is, opportunities that are never fully realized because of inadequate sponsorship and/or attention.

Sales personnel invariably focus on products and markets that interest them and that give them the maximum return for their effort—this is a classic shortfall of any sales organization. Many organizations have a proliferation of products—far more than three—and the list of those that receive less than adequate attention grows substantially. If an organization wishes to take advantage of the opportunities for these orphan products and markets, one excellent way is through the use of a parallel sales channel of specialists working these markets.

To be fully useful in deciding on priorities among marketing objectives, the product/market matrix needs to be expanded to include profit contribution. Figure 2-3 shows this extra dimension. In each square, the top figure is the percentage amount that each product contributes to total sales, and the bottom figure is the percentage of total profit contribution.

Product 1 in Figure 2-3 is the company's standard old-line product. It has now hit the peak of its life cycle; sales are still 57 percent of the company's totals, but the profits are only 30 percent. Product 2 is relatively new; it provides 35 percent of the company's sales but 50 percent of profits. Product 3 is newer yet; it brings only 8 percent of sales but 20

Figure 2-3   Product/market matrix: Today's performance.

	Product #1	Product #2	Product #3	Total
Market A	sales 40 / 25 profit	25 / 30	0 / 0	65 / 55
Market B	15 / 5	10 / 20	5 / 13	30 / 38
Market C	2 / 0	0 / 0	3 / 7	5 / 7
Total	57 / 30	35 / 50	8 / 20	100 / 100

percent of the company's profit. The key thing to notice about product 3, however, is that it doesn't even go into market A, which is the company's historic market, representing 55 percent of the total. Instead, its focus is on markets B and C. Usually companies like this one, with a fairly simple pattern of three products and two to three markets, have a single sales organization that is expected to cover all three markets.

But let's take a look now at the future objectives of this company, shown in Figure 2-4. We see a sharp drop in product 1, down to 15 percent of sales and only 5 percent of profitability. Product 2 grows to 62 percent of sales and 65 percent of profitability, and product 3, 23 percent of sales and 30 percent of profitability. Now, the company is really performing purely on products 2 and 3. Turning to the market profile, we find now that market B represents 52 percent of income and even market C represents 15 percent of income.

Remember, the point of comparing today's performance with future objectives is to determine whether the existing sales channel is the best design to provide intensive and highly productive sales coverage of the priority targets. In other words, will your current sales organization get you where you want to go? Let's look at what we can learn from the future objectives chart (Figure 2-4).

You will still have to maintain coverage of market A because product 2 in market A accounts for 30 percent of income. However, your major coverage has to be of market B, which is now 52 percent of income. You

Figure 2-4 Product/market matrix: Future objectives.

	Product #1	Product #2	Product #3	Total
Market A	sales 10 / 3 profit	30 / 30	0 / 0	40 / 33
Market B	5 / 2	32 / 35	13 / 15	50 / 52
Market C	0 / 0	0 / 0	10 / 15	10 / 15
Total	15 / 5	62 / 65	23 / 30	100 / 100

also need good coverage of market C, which is now up to 15 percent of income. Quite frequently this would suggest that the existing sales organization, which was primarily designed to cover market A, continue to cover that market. If it's a direct organization, you would probably reduce the head count. If it's a rep operation, you would keep them there because it's a straight variable expense.

Now you want to go after B aggressively, more so than in the past. You could set up a parallel rep network, using two reps in each geographic territory, each rep selling into a particular market on an exclusive market basis. And you could do the same with market C. Now you might have three separate rep networks, each focused on its own specialization in A, B, and C; or you could have one direct sales network and two rep networks.

The Next Step

In practice, you then have to analyze each separate trading area and determine the available mix of reps. In major trading areas, where there is a proliferation of reps who specialize in market segments, the chances are high of finding several separate specialists, each of whom is an outstanding performer in one segment. As you move to areas of lower market potential, reps specialize less because they must cover a wider diversity of markets for the same income. In these secondary trading areas you might find a single rep organization covering all three markets.

That's what the analysis is all about. First you have to find out what markets will need intensive coverage based on your future objectives. Then you have to assess if your existing organization can give that type of intensive coverage. If it cannot, you are going to need to make some changes. You'll need to begin the process of designing new sales channels—Step 2.

3

The Ideal Sales Force
for the New
Millennium

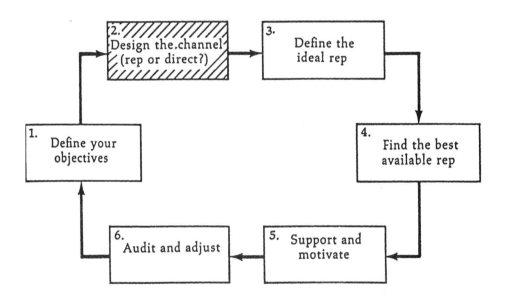

The year 2000 (Y2K) bug has emerged as a major problem facing computer programmers and users. Hundreds of millions of dollars have been spent to make up for the failure in foresight of an entire generation of programmers—not using the four-digit year designation. Still, fears exist that the new millennium will see a total collapse of many computer systems, rendering them all obsolete.

In a more subtle fashion, the new millennium will also see the obsolescence of many sales forces. This obsolescence has either slowly or rapidly evolved over the past decade based on megatrends impacting specific industries. The reasons for the obsolescence:

1. Manufacturers have given insufficient attention to the analysis of key marketplace trends in customer/supplier relationships within their targeted markets.
2. These trends have not been converted into a new set of characteristics required in a sales channel to help that manufacturer meet its short- and long-term objectives.
3. Sales channels have not been reconfigured to match the ideal characteristics as closely as possible.
4. Channel modification, where undertaken, has frequently been focused purely on macro models, i.e., national market mix objectives. What is also required is a micro view—that is, a reconfiguration of the channel in each territorial segment in order to match the market mix and local flavor of each discrete trading area.

The impact of these megatrends varies from industry to industry. Generally, though, they have culminated in the need for a new combination of characteristics a sales channel must have to help companies achieve their short- and long-term objectives. Following are a number of these characteristics followed by an assessment as to whether a direct sales force or an independent rep network best offers these critical characteristics.

Characteristics Needed in the New Millennium Sales Force—Do They Suggest Direct Sales or Independent Reps?

Following are twelve characteristics needed in a sales force to help companies achieve both short- and long-term objectives. Combinations that fit the needs of a specific industry will vary somewhat from industry to industry.

1. *System Selling*—Historically, product knowledge was king. With the sharp reductions in staff, customers now look to outsource system needs. More importantly, they are looking to suppliers to help them increase the profitability of their company. Product knowledge is, therefore, totally secondary to the capability of a supplier to offer a complete system that helps the customer increase its profitability.

Rep or Direct?—A direct salesperson excels at product knowledge—she represents only one company and allocates all of her time to that product line. The rep, on the other hand, offers a series of compatible manufacturers that together frequently comprise complete systems. Independent reps inherently have a preferred position in terms of systems understanding because of this breadth of compatible products and services.

2. *Consultative Selling With Alternative Solutions*—A salesperson with a single solution is not in a consultative selling mode compared to the salesperson with multiple solutions. Objectivity is simply not there.

Rep or Direct?—Again, the independent rep has the advantage, presuming that he has done a sound job of lining up compatible principals. By compatible, we include manufacturers who may offer functionally equivalent solutions to a customer's problem but fit somewhat different niches. As a result, their reps' offerings are multisolution, which gives them competitive advantage as they are viewed by customers as having greater objectivity.

3. *Long-Term Continuity*—In order to truly understand a customer and to develop the necessary acceptance with buyers and specifiers, a critical characteristic of the new millennium sales force will be to have sales personnel who maintain long-term continuity with customers.

Rep or Direct?—Personal growth objectives of direct sales personnel and independent reps are fundamentally different. This difference clearly puts the independent rep in a preferred position relative to gaining long-term continuity with a set of customers.

The growth objectives of top-performing direct sales personnel are to break the continuity with their existing sales assignments in order to get a better territory, move up the ladder of the sales management function, or move back into headquarters in order to get a more rounded management background. If the door is closed to these opportunities, direct salespeople frequently leave to go to a competitor or a noncompeting company to achieve their growth plans.

The independent rep, on the other hand, has personal objectives that enhance long-term continuity with customers. The rep owners buy into a territory with the sole objective of succeeding in that territory while targeting defined markets for the long term. They have no desires to grow in the corporate structure. Rather, they want to grow their own business. The key to success with these reps is just to make sure that the rep owners are good managers. As a result, they can attract and hold onto top sales personnel to maintain long-term continuity throughout the organization.

4. *Vertical Market Specialization*—To achieve the above characteristics, the channel must contain specialists in select markets. In other words, vertical market specialization in sales channels becomes necessary—at least in primary trading areas. This will require many manufacturers to reconfigure their sales channel when they have multiple market targets.

Rep or Direct?—The cost to adequately staff a direct sales force with vertical market specialists is prohibitive for all but the largest companies. The fixed costs are simply too high. Here again, selling through reps becomes preferred because of their specialization and the variable expense (i.e., commission only).

5. *Understanding Customer Needs*—Sales personnel must literally know more than customer personnel about customer issues that must be resolved and how to resolve them. The diverse responsibilities and high workload of customer personnel combined with changing responsibilities has allowed a scenario whereby supplier sales personnel can become an integral asset to a customer's organization.

Rep or Direct?—The first four characteristics, if combined in a salesperson, position that person to be of significant value to customers. As these characteristics are better attained with an independent rep network, reps offer the opportunity for in-depth understanding of customer needs.

6. *High Head Count*—There is a direct cause and effect relationship between investing in sales personnel and increasing sales. Sufficient head count is required to provide intensive coverage of all targeted markets. The penalty for not having intensive coverage is the inability to reach aggressive growth targets. Higher head count allows more time per customer account and more prospects contacted. This has a direct cause and effect relationship with sales production.

Rep or Direct?—"More feet on the street" is one of the most fundamental ways of increasing sales for a company. More precisely, we suggest that the requirement is for "more qualified feet on the street." The variable expense of independent reps combined with their vertical market specialization in major trading areas clearly gives them an edge. The only exception is where the company is very large and can afford the number of direct people needed to give the intensive coverage of all vertical markets targeted.

7. *Close Proximity to Customers*—Close physical proximity of a salesperson to an account is another significant competitive advantage. Part of the advantage is simply in the time responsiveness available to promptly respond to a customer's need. In addition, there is typically a preference for the "local person" compared to a salesperson coming in from an outside area. This is even true for metropolitan areas that are in close proximity, say, Chicago compared to Milwaukee. There is a natural preference given by southern Wisconsin buyers to a southern Wisconsin seller as compared to a Chicago-area person. Part of this is due to the sports competitiveness that is so much a part of our society. It appears to be one of the reasons why Milwaukeeans typically root for the Green Bay Packers in professional football as compared to the Chicago Bears, even though Chicago's stadium is much closer to Milwaukee than is Green Bay's. These geographic preferences can be a subtle but key deciding factor in the purchasing decisions in many areas throughout the United States.

Rep or Direct?—The higher head count and vertical market specialization offered by independent reps typically result in the much closer proximity of their sales personnel to customers than that available with a direct sales organization.

8. *Flexibility to Meet Local Needs*—Manufacturers normally develop their product and service offerings based on a macro view of market opportunities, that is, an assessment based on total U.S. opportunities. In today's market dynamics, there are many local needs that must be satisfied if a manufacturer is to make a strong penetration of that account. Sales personnel must therefore be able to flavor their offerings to meet these local needs.

Rep or Direct?—Direct personnel are at a disadvantage because of most manufacturers' macro approach to their product and service offerings. The flexibility to adapt these offerings to local needs is frequently insufficient to satisfy these unique demands. The aggressive rep, on the other hand, can take a manufacturer's shortcomings and develop the missing capability herself, and thus offer solutions tailored to local needs. This may include services not offered by the manufacturer she represents, such as local inventory, skid-mounted systems, and start-up, engineering, or maintenance services.

9. *Ability to Manage the Relationship Between Your Company and the Customers*—The sales function has dramatically changed over the past decade. The truly successful salesperson today must carefully orchestrate the relationships between the manufacturer she represents and her customers. This is a strategic as well as an operational requirement for competitive advantage. The individual must be able to influence the decisions throughout the customer's organization.

Rep or Direct?—The first eight characteristics are best matched by the independent rep firm. The bottom line is that the properly selected firm that receives sound support can offer the organizations it represents outstanding relationship management capabilities with key customers in the individual's trading area.

10. *Channel Acceptance by Customers*—Manufacturers and service providers need to develop channels that serve customers' needs and are embraced by the customers as contributors to their profitability.

Rep or Direct?—The first nine characteristics clearly suggest independent reps. However, considerable notoriety has emerged concerning a number of large customers who have at least suggested, if not demanded, that suppliers eliminate the independent rep sales channel and handle the customer on a direct basis. The Wal-Mart story was the first major example of this demand. Rite-Aid has been a more recent example. The action has been precipitated by believers in the customer organization (typically stimulated by the purchasing department) that rep commissions are an unnecessary expense that simply adds to the cost of products they have purchased. When manufacturers have taken this step, a number of cases of litigation have arisen whereby reps have sued customers for wrongful interference in their contracts with the manufacturers they represent. The legal aspects of this issue are covered in Chapter 13.

From a commercial point of view, the customer request is to delete a function of the organization that even the customers' own organizations find imperative for their success, namely maintaining an aggressive, well-connected sales organization. The customers who are suggesting to suppliers that they terminate their reps do not ask suppliers to terminate their direct sales force. This is a contradiction as the sales function is a critical element in today's business structuring. The only question facing many companies is whether or not that channel should be comprised of direct salespeople and independent reps. While there are many more problems in selling with an independent rep network than with direct sales personnel, these problems do not at all compromise the need for independent reps based on today's market scenario. It therefore becomes incumbent upon suppliers to educate customers to the fact that a sales channel is required and under what conditions independent reps are preferred over direct sales personnel.

11. *Computer Literacy*—One of the more recent megatrends has been in sales force automation. Software programs that link suppliers with customers for inventory and reordering are quite common. More recently, contact management software programs have become common to help coordinate selling efforts. The need for computer literacy in an ever-expanding software relationship between customer and supplier and between sales force members will continue to grow.

Rep or Direct?—Direct sales organizations are the clear winner relative to consistency in computer literacy combined with the use of common software programs desired by a given company. The reason is simple. Direct personnel spend 100 percent of their time on their employer's products and systems. The employer may therefore introduce hardware and software that fits his needs and gain quick compliance throughout his sales force. This is currently an almost impossible task with independent reps, who must serve many different companies with differing software needs.

12. *Economically Affordable*—Many of the above characteristics require investment by the supplier. On the surface, this investment may appear to be insurmountable. It is not insurmountable if the compensation program for the sales channel is based on a variable expense, that is, the sales channel is compensated only when it produces, not unlike subcontract manufacturing or engineering producing a part or service that is not paid for until received. From the general management point of view, variable expenses are invariably more attractive than a fixed expense. As mentioned earlier, this is one of the reasons why the vertically integrated company has become the dinosaur heading towards extinction, if not already there.

Rep or Direct?—The variable expense (i.e., pure commission payments) common to independent reps are part of the reason for their being more affordable for most companies. In fact, reps are not even paid when they produce, that is, when they receive the order. Reps are normally paid when the product is shipped or when the manufacturer is paid. Putting it all together, manufacturers sharply improve their cash flow position using reps compared to direct selling, particularly where gestation cycles between opportunity identification and shipping the order are long term. Employers must pay direct sales personnel in anticipation that they will perform. Relative to selling costs as a percent of sales, we feel the comparative ratios of direct versus rep selling are comparable for larger companies if contributed value is assessed. Smaller companies simply cannot afford a direct sales force.

The Bottom Line

The bottom line of the above megatrends and key characteristic discussions is that the great majority of manufacturers and service providers will find that independent sales representatives will much more closely meet the needs of the new millennium than direct selling will. This observation is not just the sole observation of this author. It is also the clear conclusion of attendees at our public seminar programs throughout the 1990s. During each of these seminars, we asked the class, which is typically comprised of senior sales executives up to the presidents of companies, to define megatrends they have observed in their industry. After posting these trends, they also develop a collective list of sales force characteristics they feel is required for today's and tomorrow's market environment. Discussions and consensus then follow to define whether a direct sales force or an independent rep sales channel best matches these characteristics. All of the prior comparisons are the result of the consensus of the very diverse group of executives attending these programs.

The Warts

The above is not to suggest that there are not significant disadvantages in selling through independent reps as compared to your own direct sales channel. In fact, there is quite an extensive list of issues a manufacturer or service provider faces when selling through reps, many more so than with a direct sales organization. These disadvantages are discussed in detail in Chapter 5. However, these disadvantages are of a much lower priority in deciding whether a company should use a direct or independent rep channel. The astute manufacturer will always separate those critical characteristics needed in its channel from those that are secondary, that is, more of a nuisance than a key deciding influence in the decision process.

Another View of Alternative Channels

The situation analysis, projections, and marketing strategies that you developed using the ideas in Chapter 2 and the first part of this chapter produced some important information that is key to deciding which sales channel is right for your company. In essence: Look at where you want to go and the strategies you've developed to get there, and then see what sales skills are needed to implement those strategies.

Briefly, you have three design possibilities to choose from for the first level (or only level) that will best suit your sales needs. They are:

1. *Independent reps.* Recruiting independent reps to sell to all markets. This could be either a single network if there is one main market or several networks working in parallel, covering separate markets within the same geographic territories.

2. *Direct sales organization.* Using your own salespeople to cover all your markets.

3. *A combination of rep and direct.* Adding reps to complement the efforts of your direct force by working in parallel for intensive secondary market coverage, or folded into your existing direct force to cover marginal territories, or a combination of both.

Let's look at each one, particularly in relation to your marketing programs.

Using Reps

When you have identified your primary market but do not have (or project) a sales volume high enough to support the direct sales force you would need to cover that market intensively, reps are the answer. This is the classic situation in which reps are used: a smaller manufacturer (or profit center) with a clearly defined market profile. Depending on product line and market, the line that divides "small" from "midsize" can be anywhere from $50 million to $100 million. Also, below the $50-million mark, most companies cannot afford a direct sales force if national coverage is desired. However, simply reaching "midsize" is not a reason by itself to convert from rep to direct selling. Chapter 4, for example, discusses Fisher Controls, a company that now generates nearly one billion dollars of its worldwide sales from the United States—exclusively through independent reps. Fisher is, moreover, one of the most profitable firms in its highly competitive market.

One of the main reasons for selling through reps is that it allows you to take advantage of the market specialization and in-depth contacts they have developed. If you have targeted several key markets rather than just one, you can multiply this advantage by paralleling several rep organizations, each one a specialist in one of your markets. This parallel approach allows you to focus highly specialized sales talent on each of the major opportunities you have identified. If you have developed a strategy based on market segmentation, parallel reps can make the strategy a reality. Yet, despite the many instances of organizations that have sharply increased sales at very profitable price levels, the paralleling of rep networks is still the exception rather than the rule.

> **Key to success:** Make sure the exact specialization you need actually exists in the rep firms you select. Do not parallel two reps in a territory if both sell to common markets. Eliminate potential for conflict by making the lines of demarcation between firms crystal clear. Use the reps themselves to define these lines. They know their territories better than you do and also want to make sure there is no confusion in their customers' minds.

Using a Direct Sales Force

Direct sales organizations classically are used by very large organizations, those whose sales are counted in hundreds of millions or billions of dollars. Direct sales forces are most effective at selling compatible products to one market. However, companies of this size are frequently organized into autonomous divisions (or profit centers), each with its own line of products. Each division may have its own direct sales force, responsible only for its product line (see Figure 1-2). In this case, each operates as a separate company, selling one line into one monolithic market.

However, many multidivisional organizations sell somewhat related products into common markets, and they may opt for one unified sales force. Organizationally, it is in a peer relationship with division management, rather than subordinate. To view this structure, refer again to Company B's arrangement in Figure 1-3. The important thing to notice here is that the corporate sales force sells the products of all divisions.

From the point of view of marketing strategy, there are some sound reasons for this kind of sales structure.

1. It provides a single corporate representative for each customer. From the customer's perspective, communications are simplified.

2. It facilitates a systems sale, where products and services from several divisions are combined into a single package.

3. It is a way to ensure that all geographic markets are covered. Thus it makes sense economically, particularly if one or more of the divisions cannot afford the direct staff that would be needed to cover the market fully.

It is on this third point that all too often the theory falls flat in the face of market realities. If there is one division whose target market does not match the general market profile of the others, that division is likely to get shortchanged. The sales force will simply not give it the necessary attention. In this situation, that division should be split off into a different sales channel—either its own direct force or a compatible rep organization.

> **Key to success:** Analyze market priorities of all divisions very carefully, and make sure that only those divisions and products that fit a common theme are lumped together into a single sales organization.

Using Combined Rep/Direct Structures

When an organization targets new market opportunities and develops strategies to go after them, frequently it signals the time to add supplementary sales channels to its direct team. The new markets may require different sales skills or technical knowledge. Or perhaps adding them would overburden the direct people, stretching them so thin that *every* market suffers. In this kind of situation, bringing in a rep firm to penetrate the new markets makes a great deal of sense, for the real strength of reps is their specialization. Obviously you should recruit those who specialize in that market.

Two other marketing situations call for recruiting rep firms to complement the work of the direct force. One concerns a company that has adequate coverage of its major geographic areas but finds that the minor areas cannot support a direct salesperson. Here reps can be used to handle the marginal areas while the direct people concentrate on the high-potential areas, and the company has sound total coverage.

The second is similar but involves secondary target markets rather than secondary geographic areas. If an organization with a number of secondary markets attempts to cover them all, as well as its primary market, with one direct sales organization, something is going to have to give. The laws of human nature dictate that the salespeople will develop a strong affinity for the primary market, and the others will become orphans, the very situation we saw in Chapter 2. By using reps specializing in these secondary markets, the company can realize the profit potential of *all* its targets.

Key to success: Managing a complex structure like this is somewhat more difficult but typically yields a return well in excess of the incremental investment required. Make sure you have the capability to design, develop, and support such a structure and the attentiveness to make adjustments when necessary. Keep a close eye on subtle shifts in markets so that you can shift priorities among your segmented channels. The payback will be delightful.

Key Questions to Consider

After reviewing the major types of sales channels in light of how they match up to markets and strategies, you can see how critical it is to begin the process of sales channel design with a clear definition of your own markets and the opportunities you have targeted for the future.

But what comes next? How do you make the leap from marketing plan to sales structure? Start honing in on your best channel by asking yourself the questions below (Figure 3-1, later in the chapter, provides a quick summary). Because this business of selecting the right sales channel is so very important and can seem so confusing, I will give you several different approaches to sorting out the questions.

One caution: Arriving at the right answer is something of a balancing act. It's the result of looking at every individual factor in light of all the other factors. Be on guard against making a decision on the basis of just one element.

How Large Is Your Organization?

Trying to establish a dollar level that clearly dictates whether a company should go direct or rep is no simple task. The dividing line depends on the number of units handled, the sales volume, the gross margin and profitability of the organization, the number of buyers, and the company's geographic concentration. Nevertheless, it is useful to set some general guidelines.

1. *Small organizations (either small companies or small profit centers within large organizations).* "Small" means something in the range of start-ups to $50 million. Generally, they cannot afford the fixed costs of a direct sales organization. This is the classic case in which reps are used with great effectiveness.

2. *Midsize companies.* Sales are from $50 million to $500 million. With a relatively monolithic picture—one product group going to one market—normally they would use a direct sales force. However, frequently that

volume isn't sufficient to provide for salespeople in the secondary geographic areas, so reps could provide coverage in these marginal areas while the direct people would still handle the primary trading areas.

3. *Large companies.* Sales are over $500 million. Again, if there is basically one product line going into basically one market, a direct sales organization is economically feasible (but not necessary; see Chapter 4). Situations that would call for altering this basic rule of thumb include:

- The products are highly diverse, rather than similar, and are generally sold into markets with very different characteristics. If the sales in each segment are $50 million or less, the company would be more successful using a series of parallel rep networks.

- In addition to its one primary market sector, the company has a number of secondary markets; often these can be covered more efficiently by reps. It may very well be in the company's best interests to recruit parallel rep networks to handle those secondary markets.

- The company has several divisions and uses a multidivisional sales force to sell all products, but one division does not fit well into the "mainstream" market profile. Allowing that division to set up its own rep network typically results in increased sales and profitability.

How Important Is Closeness?

The question of size goes hand in hand with another aspect that is so closely linked you really have to consider them simultaneously. Another way to put the second question is: What do you expect of your salespeople? Most manufacturers want a sales organization that is truly close to the key buyers and specifiers of their major customers around the country. They want each salesperson to develop a long-term relationship with her own set of customers. They know that long-term customer continuity builds solid contacts and earns them preferred treatment over competitors.

To develop this type of closeness to customers, salespeople must spend a lot of time with them. And that means you have to have many people in many locations around the country. In particular, areas of high potential must have adequate staffing.

The question then becomes, What size, in terms of sales dollars, does an organization have to be to afford enough direct salespeople to give this intensive coverage? And that leads us back to question 1.

On the other hand, it is possible that in your industry, personal closeness between a salesperson and a customer is not truly necessary. If a low-touch selling environment is satisfactory in your markets, then you may consider using just minimal direct people and working through telemarketing or direct mail.

Where—and What—Are Your Markets?

If your key markets are concentrated in one region of the country, you may be able to service them with just a few people; this is a situation that generally calls for using direct salespeople. For example, suppose your concern happens to be the sale of major equipment into the new-construction programs of the pulp and paper industry. Most of this activity has been in the southeastern part of the country, so locating one or two salespeople in Atlanta or Birmingham would give you close proximity to the major part of your national market. With a minimal number of direct sales personnel, you would get close coverage of the major share of your market.

It is also possible that companies with customers spread over a wide geographic territory might consider direct sales—if the customers are few. If you were selling a unique set of engineering services to existing nuclear plants, for instance, you would find a very small number of installations across the country. Therefore, you could consider using a minimal direct sales organization. The major limitation would be the long distances between customers, which typically results in less intimate contacts with the buying and specifying personnel than a local representative could generate.

Equally important (if not more so): Are your products compatible? Do the same kinds of companies buy them? If not, providing thorough coverage of many diverse markets usually calls for using reps as specialists for each target.

With direct sales organizations, smaller manufacturers are typically faced with the economic need of providing one salesperson to cover all markets in a given territory. But sales personnel working in diverse markets typically are not equally successful at all of them. In fact, it is not unusual to find a salesperson who is highly successful in one market and unsuccessful in another. If salespeople are required to serve a number of highly diverse markets, they usually invest their major effort in the markets that are most closely aligned to their interests and provide the greatest income potential. Many manufacturers find they can more profitably develop intensive sales coverage by paralleling two or more independent rep networks, each a specialist in a particular market.

Putting It All Together

Looking at the question of choosing the most effective sales channel from another angle, we can pinpoint some rather specific scenarios that suggest the use of either one format or the other. Some are purely market driven; others are the result of other factors, of corporate realities that cannot be ignored.

Six Good Reasons for Direct Selling

1. *The market size and sales volume permit intensive coverage.* If the volume of business will support the cost of sufficient staffing to provide intensive coverage, direct salespeople provide many advantages.

2. *Your primary customers are large and geographically concentrated.* When your market is concentrated geographically, or when you have just a few large customers, a minimum number of direct salespeople can give intensive coverage.

3. *Your primary customers expect it.* If your industry has historically sold direct and it's what your customers want, you really have very little choice.

4. *The boss says so.* In this case "boss" means the general manager, whether that's the president, CEO, or division manager. Some bosses simply have a very strong bias toward "having our own people." Even if the senior marketing executive comes up with an outstanding, objective argument for a sales channel based on using reps, if the boss has deep-rooted aversions to it, the chances for success are slim. The person at the top sets a tone for the entire organization, and negative attitudes toward reps will inevitably trickle down to all departments. This leads to an environment that is unmotivating for reps.

5. *You can attract and hold top performers.* A basic tenet of this book is that a key to selling success is a long-term relationship between a single salesperson and that person's set of customers. Continuity leads to closeness, and closeness leads to competitive advantage. Conversely, a break in continuity destroys that advantage.

What's behind the sales tenure issue? Two factors are driving direct salespeople to move on. The first we might call a problem of attitude. The current generation no longer seems to view selling as a profession, at least in a single company. Rather, it is seen as a stepping-stone on a career path. Today's bright, aggressive salespeople want to move to a better territory, get the boss's job, move on a fast track in-house, or go to a competitor.

The second reason for turnover appears to be the relatively limited compensation potential sales personnel face in many direct selling positions, particularly in industrial products. This is an area you *can* do something about. Frequently, the compensation schedule is developed by a wage and salary administration study that crosses all functional activities in the corporation. A sales engineer is considered roughly equivalent to a production engineer, who in turn is roughly equivalent to a cost accountant, and so on, until a common salary grade is established. Then the sales department typically is given an incentive program of commission or bonus if certain sales levels are achieved. Unfortunately, these incentives are usually capped at a relatively low percentage of the salesperson's salary. Companies willing to put aside this bureaucratic approach to wage and salary administration for the sales department, in favor of a compensation philosophy based on performance without a salary cap, have a much better chance of attracting and keeping outstanding sales personnel.

6. *You are direct now and find no compelling reason to change.* Changing your sales structure is risky, time-consuming, and expensive. There must be a truly compelling reason to change if a channel is to be redesigned. The fact that you have just brought in a new marketing manager who has "always sold through reps" is not enough.

The reasons for using reps are driven by economics. That is, you cannot afford the number and quality of highly specialized, high-achievement direct personnel you would need to meet the challenges in today's marketplace. More specifically:

Ten Good Reasons for Selling Through Reps

1. *You can't afford enough direct people to give the intensive direct coverage you need.* If your sales volume is under $50 million, you probably don't have the resources to support a sales force big enough to do the job. Your objective, remember, is a sales organization that develops closeness to customers. Because that means spending a lot of time with them, you need an adequate number of people.

2. *Your profit centers or markets are diverse and require different sales skills.* Reps are, by their very nature, specialists in certain markets. When you have a diverse market profile, you can develop a network of parallel reps geared to the specific needs of each target market. This kind of approach can be powerfully effective.

3. *Your product line is limited and competitors are outpackaging you.* The right rep will have highly compatible products he can combine with yours and many times outpackage your largest competitor.

4. *Your market is comprised of differing geographic needs.* It may be cost prohibitive to respond to the varying micro needs typically found throughout the United States. Aggressive reps will frequently develop the capability to supplement your offerings and respond to local needs.

5. *You have modest financial means.* In addition to a variable expense and a more favorable cash flow, there is a third financial advantage available with reps. It is balance sheet management, a particularly important advantage for manufacturers who are in markets requiring local services,

inventory, and value added. Fixed investments by reps improve your balance sheet.

6. *Your customers want local representation.* Customers frequently show a preference for local representatives. Unless you can afford the investment of direct salespeople in each and every key trading area in the country, reps may be the way to go. Buyers in Boston would much rather deal with sales personnel from Boston than those from New York. This is true for even short distances, such as between Milwaukee and Chicago. Local identification usually gives you a leg up.

7. *You are selling through a multidivisional corporate sales force, but your division is not a good fit with its primary focus.* Typically, these corporate sales forces have a primary market thrust that almost totally consumes the time and effort of the sales personnel. If a certain division does not fit this primary thrust, that division faces a tremendous obstacle to growth. It would be much better off negotiating a withdrawal from the corporate sales force and establishing its own sales channel. Here is where independent reps can play a very important part.

8. *You need fast entree to a new market.* Many manufacturers have stumbled when trying to use the existing sales organization to penetrate a new market. Not having contacts or familiarity with the market becomes a major roadblock, and frequently salespeople return to historical sales patterns as soon as the corporate pressure to call on the new market abates. It is typically easier and more productive to recruit a parallel network of reps who are specialists in that market.

9. *You cannot keep top-performing direct personnel.* If you're typical among manufacturers, you'll have a rather high turnover of sales personnel. This disruption of continuity minimizes your ability to maintain maximum penetration with your key customers. In contrast to the mind-set of many in a direct sales organization, a rep's whole professional life is focused on selling to a given set of customers over the long haul. Reps have higher compensation levels, a commitment to selling as a career rather than a stepping-stone, and the enticement of ownership positions in their firm. All those things create tenure with your customers, which translates into a competitive advantage for you.

10. *You're using reps now and find no compelling reason to change.* Change is tough on your organization and often on your customers as well. In practice, the change from rep selling to direct selling is even more dangerous than the other way around. I'll explain why shortly.

The Question of Conversion

The choice between reps and a direct sales channel can be a rather simple or complex decision depending on your circumstances. If you are a small company, or a start-up company without a sales organization, you typically cannot afford direct selling. Therefore, selling through independent reps becomes an obvious choice. Also, if you are very large and have hundreds of direct sales personnel, continuing to stay direct for your primary market is invariably a wise conclusion. However, companies in the middle, that is, growing out of a small size but yet to achieve truly large proportions, are faced with a difficult decision. Changing from direct to reps is tricky to manage: Changing from reps to direct can be downright disastrous.

Converting From Reps to Direct

It usually starts something like this: A controller will do some doodling, then walk into the president's office and exclaim, "Do you realize if we cancel our rep in Chicago, we can put two direct salespeople in first-class offices with full fringe benefits and a secretary and still save $75,000 a year!" The president then confronts the senior marketing executive with these "unshakable facts," and, shortly thereafter, the company takes its first step toward a direct sales force. Their number one rep, which has eight sales personnel and half of its income generated by this company, is terminated. On the battlefield of corporate strategy, this would be like winning a skirmish but losing the war.

A decision made purely on this superficial type of economics analysis can backfire. The momentum developed by your sales organization will rapidly erode, and you may lose in three ways:

1. *Lost opportunity.* The volume built in that area could have been the result of ten years or more of aggressive investment by the rep organization. When it goes, the manufacturer will lose the benefit of that long-term continuity. What are the chances that the manufacturer could replace that rep with three direct people who would have the capability for preventing a slide in that volume? There can be years of dislocation. The canceled rep would probably immediately try to sign on a competitor. If this happens, customers could very well transfer their allegiance to a competitor because of their closeness to the rep. And even if they don't, can any company withstand up to two years of significant interruption in sales performance until the conversion from rep to direct selling is fully implemented and continuity resumes?

2. *Reduced coverage.* The eight-salesperson rep generated half of its income from this manufacturer. In most cases, this means the rep gave the manufacturer four person years worth of selling effort each year. The two direct salespeople will provide only half that coverage.

3. *Lost commitment.* As soon as a manufacturer changes to direct selling from rep selling in the first area, a shock wave goes through the entire

rep network. Everyone immediately wonders, "Who is next?" The inevitable result is that reps almost immediately stop investing additional time and effort in that manufacturer and start planning how to increase sales of others in anticipation of the day they too might be canceled. That one step in Chicago destroys the image of the company's total commitment to reps, at least in the minds of those who produce: the reps themselves.

The preferred alternative to what the company regards as excessive commissions is a renegotiated rate. This is perhaps the most ticklish of subjects between rep and manufacturer, but it is one that needs addressing under certain conditions. The key in the approach is fairness to both sides, a balance between how much commission your company can afford versus how much the market suggests on the basis of your network's performance. More on this later.

In summary, making the move purely on the economics of rep commission versus direct payroll is a high-risk action that routinely results in significant upsets in sales performance. Unless there are other compelling reasons to change, it is better to maintain the same channel. When one considers all the variables involved in such a change, the economic argument becomes very uncertain. Therefore, dollar volume by itself is not a primary reason, as you will see more fully in Chapter 4, and neither is personal preference. The fact that a new president or division manager happens to prefer selling direct is one of the poorest reasons to make a conversion.

If, after a careful review of your total situation, you decide that a switch from reps to direct sales is called for, my advice is to do it all at once, and provide a vehicle for making the transition as quickly as possible. We can find a good example in National Semiconductor. This industry giant was up to well over half a billion dollars in sales, using nothing but reps, when a strategic redirection in late 1986 dictated a change. The company notified all reps of termination in one swoop and *simultaneously* offered them the opportunity to come aboard as direct sales personnel with a highly leveraged incentive program that would maintain their income levels. (Note: National again modified its direct channel in the mid-1990s by returning to the use of reps to complement their direct sales channel.)

Converting From Direct to Reps

Making the change in this direction is easier. The key is a good communication program with your staff, fully explaining what the change is all about and how they can benefit. Obviously your reason for making such a major change is the overall good of the company. The firm's value will be increased, additional jobs will be created in the plants, and so on. The salespeople themselves can also benefit directly: New sales management positions may be created, and they may have the opportunity to move into new responsibilities, such as regional sales managers. Or you can offer them the opportunity to become reps, or perhaps to join an existing rep firm.

The partial transition to rep selling for marginal territories is the easiest step to take for an incremental addition to your sales and profit. Your company may not be large enough to staff your direct sales force for intensive coverage of all geographic markets, and sales personnel may be spread too thinly for optimum coverage. Marginal areas receive little coverage, and what coverage is provided detracts from coverage of the prime areas. It is a relatively simple step to recruit reps for the secondary areas while focusing your direct force on the most promising areas. Only good things result—the added rep coverage is a variable expense, and your direct people concentrate on the major opportunities.

Often the question of converting from direct to rep arises in turnaround situations. If the turnaround manager decides that reps are the way to go, the key is to make sure the internal structure is capable of properly supporting reps before the transition takes place. Equally important is being completely open with the reps. Explain what the problems have been, what they are today, and what steps are being taken to resolve them. A well-managed transition to reps can contribute significantly to the turnaround.

A Caution About Using Sales Volume or Commission Dollars in the Decision Process

In our text, the sales range of $50 million to $100 million has been selected as a very rough dividing line to suggest a point at which a company might effectively cover its market with a direct sales force. There are many variables that go into establishing an actual dollar figure for a given company: the number of customers, the number of calls required to complete a sale, the number and complexity of negotiations required to close the sale, the number of proposals that result in a single order, the geographic dispersion of the market, the dollar value of each order, and so on.

The key point to remember is that this range should never be a factor in your decision to go from rep selling to direct selling. It tells you only that if you are direct and are within this range, you *probably* do not have to convert 100 percent to selling through reps in order to have sound market coverage.

Sound selling requires a certain number of sales calls by a certain number of highly qualified people. This is true regardless of whether one sells with a direct sales force or through reps. The true costs involved in selling are therefore somewhat constant regardless of the sales channel—as long as the overall staffing is comparable. Thus, I believe that there is rarely a strong economic rationale for a company that is even well over the $100 million class to convert from rep selling to direct selling. For example, Fisher Controls uses reps exclusively in North America despite having sales approaching one billion dollars.

There is normally only one decision point that is very dollar oriented. This applies to the smaller company, profit center, or market that simply cannot afford a direct sales force to provide the necessary coverage. This economic scenario demands selling through reps if intensive coverage is required.

As a company moves up in sales, the decision should be based on factors other than economics. If those other factors indicate that the company should go one way or another, that company will typically be making the right choice without even considering the economics of the situation. This is not to ignore economics. It is simply to suggest, first, that the many variables involved in the treatment of economics become rather subjective, and second, that once again the cost of doing the right sales job in relation to a given customer or market is essentially the same—whether the company is using a direct sales force or reps. (Figure 3-1 provides a summary of these issues.)

Channel Conflict

In this era of channel proliferation, channel conflict typically arises unless it is carefully managed. Some suggest that channel conflict is a positive factor, not unlike competition. Although channel conflict is inherently built into certain channels (i.e., those industries where nonexclusive distribution is the norm), significant channel conflict and independent reps do not mix. Most successful reps will not tolerate flagrant channel conflict. Fortunately, conflict can be avoided for the most part, at least sufficiently to keep a well-selected and well-supported rep highly motivated.

Two ground rules can be used to ensure coverage of all markets without conflict between reps:

1. Be sure that one rep does not concentrate in the same markets as the other reps. Reps tend to be market specialists; we have been able to establish as many as five different rep firms in the same trading area for one company, each concentrating on different markets without any overlap. This was a highly successful venture for a business generating $10 million in sales that grew to $40 million within four years, aided in great part by the multiple channel approach.

2. Make sure there is no confusion in the customer's eyes as to who represents the company. The chances are very high that such confusion

Figure 3-1 Choosing the most effective channel: A summary.

Consider selling through reps if:

- Your marketing strategy is built around market segmentation with sales in any one segment at or below the $50 million to $100 million range.
- Your markets are widespread geographically.
- Your customers want local representation.
- Your strategy calls for penetrating new markets quickly.
- A variable sales expense and the improved cash flow associated with a pure "pay for results only" (i.e., commission) are important to you.
- You need intense coverage of several diverse markets, and you cannot afford the fixed costs of a large direct sales force.
- You need the type of closeness to customers that can be obtained only by having your sales personnel develop long-term continuity with your customers.
- You need the synergistic effect of a grouping of your products with those of compatible manufacturers in order to thwart the advantage of a competitor's broader product line.
- You need the broadest possible perspective of a targeted market—which is available from reps who sell a broad cross section of products into that market.

Consider staying direct if:

- Your customers want it that way.
- All your product lines are compatible with each other and are sold to common markets.
- Your market is highly concentrated geographically or has very few customers.
- Sales volume (both current and future projections) is large enough that you can afford to put a big sales force in the field. *Rule of thumb:* A range of $50 million to $100 million with a broad geographic market makes it a close call. Below that, you probably can't afford direct; above that, you possibly can—but most likely with weak coverage of secondary trading areas until you reach a sales level of somewhere in the $150 million to $250 million range.
- You can attract and hold exceptional sales personnel.

Consider a combined force of direct people and reps if:

- You have a good direct sales organization for your primary geographic areas but can't afford to put people into the marginal areas.
- Your direct sales force does not have the time to devote to secondary market segments.
- One division served by your multidivisional sales force is out of the market mainstream; pull that one out and bring in reps that specialize in that particular market.

Consider converting from one type of channel to another if (and only if):

- There is a compelling reason to change.

will not exist as long as ground rule 1 is satisfied, for it suggests the recruitment of reps that do not call on the other reps' customers.

The Next Step

The exclusive use of independent reps by large companies (those with sales in excess of $500 million) is rather infrequent and unpublicized. As a result, tradition still perceives the need to convert from independent rep to direct sales forces when an organization reaches a size at which its executives believe they can economically afford direct sales organizations. This chapter has challenged this tradition. However, without an adequate case to demonstrate the highly successful use of independent reps by a large organization, the argument in favor of reps may appear to be academic. The next chapter focuses on Fisher Controls International, Inc., a very successful, large company that has stayed exclusively with independent reps in North America despite having company-wide sales exceeding one and a quarter billion dollars, approximately three-quarters of which is generated by its reps in North America.

4

Fisher Controls International, Inc.: A Large Company Using Reps

The general philosophy in U.S. industry is that you should use independent reps when your company is "small," then convert to direct selling when you become "large." The sales range generally accepted as offering sufficient mass to convert from independent reps to direct selling is roughly from $50 million to $100 million annually for a fairly simple combination of products and markets.

Perhaps the single major stimulus for this conversion is the desire on the part of management to have better control of its sales force and eliminate "excessive rep commissions." Many feel this goal is achievable only by using a directly employed sales force. But as key advantages of independent reps are lost, lower market share, lower return on investment, and lower profitability may result. This rep-to-direct conversion tradition therefore needs reexamination in light of the need for more and more sales specialization in a sales force, the increasing need for a wider array of services (including JIT and value-added), and the increasing desirability of a variable expense. For the third edition, we again offer Fisher Controls as an example of a "large" company that continues to grow very profitably while using independent reps as its sole sales force throughout North America.

The second edition introduced Fisher Controls as an example of a large company using independent reps. At that time, Fisher was going through a transition of ownership from Monsanto Company to Emerson Electric. The acquisition occurred in 1992. Fisher's worldwide sales in the prior year were $928 million. Emerson thought highly enough of Fisher that it paid Monsanto a purchase price of $1.28 billion.

Fisher historically sold through independent reps in North America. Sales in the United States and Canada were slightly in excess of $600 million in 1991. The chapter then went on to explain why Fisher chose to stay with independent reps and how it provided Fisher with a significant competitive edge in the marketplace, an advantage that led to excellent profitability for the company.

With the sale of Fisher to Emerson, some concerns were raised about the future of independent reps. Emerson Electric has long had a reputation of being extremely cost- and profit-driven. The financial community has viewed Emerson as one of the most financially astute companies on the New York Stock Exchange. The only question in some minds is perhaps that the short-term P&L influenced Emerson's decision making more than long-term returns. This edition provides an update on Fisher six years after the second edition and updates the rationale for a large company's use of independent reps rather than direct sales personnel. A brief background on Fisher is presented followed by observations of key Fisher and Fisher-Rosemount executives and several rep owners.

Background

Fisher Controls continues to be one of the world's leading valve and process control manufacturers. They are now located within a major business segment of Emerson that is called Emerson's "Process Business." This business is headed up by an executive vice president, Mr. D. N. Farr. Reporting to Mr. Farr are several individual business units, namely Fisher Controls, Rosemount, and Intellution and two operating groups. Within each group are three to four other businesses including well-known process names such as Uniloc, Micro Motion, and Brooks. The final operating entity in the Process Business is an organization known as Fisher-Rosemount, which has its own president and is matrixed with the two major divisions, Fisher and Rosemount.

Fisher-Rosemount provides large systems capabilities for both Fisher and Rosemount and is a peer organization to the two businesses, which continue to retain their individual names. In addition, the sales organizations for both Fisher and Rosemount report to a single executive vice president of global sales within Fisher-Rosemount. Here is where matrixing occurs. For example, Joe Urbanek is senior vice president of Fisher-Rosemount sales for North America. Reporting to Joe are eight area vice presidents who have the responsibility for all of the sales channels serving the three entities within North America. Presidents of Fisher's rep firms report directly to the area VPs, as do the regional managers who have the responsibility for the direct selling efforts of Rosemount and Micro Motion.

Within Fisher, Ed Merwald is vice president of sales, worldwide, for

Fisher Valve. He has a peer who is vice president of the Regulator arm of Fisher. Both are matrixed with Urbanek in managing and motivating the rep network and, in many aspects, operate as high-power product managers. It sounds a little complicated but nevertheless has proved to be effective to date.

In terms of current sales levels, the combination of valves, regulators, and systems sales is well in excess of $1.25 billion worldwide, while North American sales are not far below the $1 billion mark.

The Bottom Line: All sales of valves, regulators, and systems, now approaching $1 billion annually in the United States and Canada, are still sold through independent reps. Emerson Electric has found that reps are a valuable contributor to the success of Fisher's hardware and systems business. Despite their being viewed as hard, tightfisted money managers, Emerson's top executives have concluded, at least to date, that Fisher's reps are one of the major assets of the organization and that direct selling is not a viable alternative. This does not mean that Emerson will not continue to evaluate the pros and cons of alternative sales channel concepts. As time changes marketplace demands, channel design must always be evaluated.

Individual Interviews

Joe Urbanek, Vice President, Fisher-Rosemount North America

Urbanek's background prior to assuming the overall responsibility of Fisher-Rosemount sales throughout North America was as an executive in Rosemount, first as vice president of marketing, then as vice president of field sales. He is now responsible for all of Fisher's, Rosemount's, and Micro Motion's sales in North America. The entire rep network of Fisher and the direct and rep organizations of Rosemount report to him. The primary changes that Joe has seen over recent years are:

1. There is a more unified emphasis on growing the business, a probable influence by Emerson.

2. The reps have developed a more global vision, as there are now so many worldwide linkages with headquarters' accounts in North America.

3. Systems capabilities within Fisher-Rosemount's rep firms have expanded substantially. All of the Fisher reps now have a local solutions integration (LSI) capability that allows them to take on entire systems using both Fisher's and Rosemount's products. On the other hand, as the projects get very large, their size may exceed the financial resources of a number of reps. These large projects will then be taken on either by one of

the larger independent reps or the in-house systems capability of Fisher-Rosemount. Existing workload along with other factors will be a determining factor as to which organization will handle the larger systems.

4. The firms have gotten larger. Several of the smaller firms have eventually merged with larger reps.

As John Weekley described for us in the second edition, Fisher's reps may be called pseudo-direct organizations in that almost all of them derive a minimum of 80 percent to 90 percent of their income from Fisher. The one primary exception is Puffer-Sweiven, which is discussed in some detail later. These heavy economic ties result in extremely close working relationships between Fisher-Rosemount, Fisher, Rosemount, and the reps.

Urbanek very emphatically described the need to maintain the current Fisher rep structure for the long term. The major reason offered is the extremely good job reps do in ensuring customer satisfaction on a local basis. The total accountability and a strong infrastructure within each rep provides immediate responsiveness to customer needs. This results in a responsiveness that is not inherent in direct sales organizations where corporate decision making is primarily based on a macro view of markets with less-than-needed sensitivity to micro needs of local markets.

Ed Merwald, Vice President, Sales, Worldwide for Fisher Controls

Ed Merwald is vice president of sales worldwide for the Valve Division with annual sales of $750 million. Its North American reps handled close to 60 percent of worldwide sales or some $450 million.

Several trends observed by Merwald over recent years:

1. Reps are getting larger both by internal growth and the fact that several smaller reps have been acquired by the larger reps.

2. Several of the representatives have structured their sales organizations along the same lines as the operating divisions within Fisher and Rosemount.

3. Technology, as should be expected, has continued at a gallop. The straightforward hardware of the Valve Division has been rapidly evolving into "smart instruments," namely, valves with microprocessors. This has changed the face of their competitors. Rather than just selling against historic valve companies, they are now also selling against systems companies, e.g., Honeywell.

4. Services of a wide range have become increasingly important rather than just being a simple repair or replace function. Objectives now are to optimize installed valve performance by continual upgrades.

Concerning rep management, the primary overview is by area vice presidents reporting to Joe Urbanek for different parts of North America. These individuals are Fisher-Rosemount employees who act as the management interface between the three Fisher divisions and each rep. However, Merwald is vitally matrixed into the relationship. Needless to say, there is an enormous amount of direct contact between each division and the reps in order to maximize market penetration.

Supplementing the area vice president's role are global account directors. This is an expansion over the previous national accounts manager program. The expansion of this role is required in today's global marketing environment.

John Weekley, President of Proconex

At the time Emerson acquired Fisher, John Weekley was Fisher's vice president of sales, North America. After the acquisition, John assumed an ad hoc role that addressed all of the consolidation issues facing Fisher and Rosemount. Upon concluding that critical transitional role, Weekley took advantage of the opportunity to purchase one of the Fisher reps, the former C. B. Ives & Company, Inc., in the Philadelphia trading area. A year later, he renamed the firm Proconex.

The change is an excellent example of the transition in ownership of a Fisher firm when the owner decides that retirement is an appropriate step. While Fisher cannot dictate to whom the rep's business should be sold, their extremely strong position in terms of percent of the rep's income (85 percent to 90 percent in the case of most Fisher reps) obviously has a major influence.

In 1994, Weekley negotiated the purchase of C. B. Ives & Company that includes a seven- to ten-year payoff. Blair Ives and his son continue with a separate arm, namely Ives Equipment Corp., which is a distributor. In order to minimize the confusion of names, Weekley took on the name of Proconex, an acronym for "*process control ex*pertise," about a year after his purchase of the firm from Blair Ives.

Annual sales of the firm are now at the $45 million level, of which about 85 percent is Fisher's. Of this amount, 65 percent is handled as a rep whereby it receives a commission and the balance is invoiced by Proconex. The only other significant change in mix is that the service side of the business has expanded. This includes engineering services such as validation (a pharmaceutical industry need), configuration engineering, and process engineering. Performance services have also significantly expanded and now include diagnostic and preventive maintenance services for control valves.

Relative to the transition of ownership, Control Associates (the Tenafly, New Jersey, rep, presented in the second edition) has also gone through a change. Bob Lindner, the former president and majority stockholder, sold out to an existing member of Control Associates, Gary Gersheimer. Needless to say, this transition was also with the blessing of Fisher-Rosemount.

Mike Aldredge, President of Puffer-Sweiven, Stafford, Texas

Mike Aldredge continues as president since the second edition and provided the information for this segment. Puffer-Sweiven, Fisher's largest rep, covers the Texas Gulf Coast and part of South America. Sales exceeded $200 million in 1998, more than double that of 1992 as reported in our second edition. Puffer-Sweiven continues to blanket the Texas Gulf Coast with seven offices. It has also expanded its offices in South America, now having three in Venezuela, one in Colombia, and one in Ecuador. However, sales in the United States still account for about 95 percent of the firm's total.

Puffer-Sweiven's sales of Fisher have grown solidly over recent years, averaging a compound growth rate of a little over 9 percent. Fisher's sales now amount to nearly 70 percent of the firm's total. While this represents less of a percentage than that of 1992, the firm's sales growth for Fisher in its territory have slightly exceeded Fisher's overall growth rate during the same period. The bottom line: Puffer-Sweiven continues to do a truly outstanding job.

The firm's total head count now numbers 375. Of this number, 57 sell Fisher products in the United States, along with other principals represented, primarily Crosby Valve and Rotork. As might be expected, these firms are relatively minor factors in terms of percent of Puffer-Sweiven's total sales. Crosby represents a little less than 5 percent and Rotork 2 percent. Still, in terms of absolute dollars, the sales represent about $10 million for Crosby.

Ownership sharing is still common in Puffer-Sweiven. There are 180 stockholders resulting from individuals purchasing Puffer-Sweiven stock. Everyone who is tenured in the firm for one year is on the company's ESOP.

The firm is rather heavily computerized, including standardized order entry software connecting it with Fisher. However, individual latitude is allowed when it comes to contact management programs. Several different software programs are used depending on the preference of individuals. The contact management software activity is not interfaced with Fisher. The primary system used was designed by EDS for Puffer-Sweiven.

While still heavily a product-oriented company, a solid percentage of sales are in systems and an increasingly diversified service package. Factory automation is being increasingly tied into the hardware offerings to satisfy the increasingly precise needs of its customers.

Cornerstone Controls (formerly Donovan Controls), Cincinnati, Ohio

When Mike Donovan, owner of Donovan Controls, decided to retire, he sold the firm to Larry Reams, owner of Cornerstone Controls, Fisher's rep in Cincinnati. Cornerstone also has a branch office in Indianapolis. While Donovan's sales had grown from $3 million to $5 million between the two editions of this book, the volume was insufficient to finance the assets needed for a Fisher-type business today. Reams defines the name of the game today as increased inventory, increased people assets, and increased information technology. With the acquisition by Cornerstone, the needed critical mass for the Louisville operation was achieved.

Cornerstone today has sales of approximately $30 million and a head count of 104. Of this, about 40 individuals are systems engineers in addition to their 14 full-time sales personnel. The firm has a strong systems integration capability as well as a mix of other pre-contract and post-contract services. About 85 percent of the firm's total volume is derived from Fisher products and services.

As a side note, Larry Reams spent some fifteen years with Fisher. This covered the period from 1965 to 1979. His last position was sales manager for Fisher. He then had the opportunity to move into Cornerstone and has been on a strong growth kick since then.

Lessons From Fisher

One of the false "truisms" that has pervaded management thinking for decades is that companies should "use reps when you're small, then go direct when you're big." In addition to gaining a much higher measure of control with a direct sales organization, a rather common feeling in American industry is that there is a point in the sales growth of a company beyond which it becomes less expensive for a company to sell with a direct sales organization than with independent reps. This has been tremendously enhanced by the breakeven chart, on the next page, that suggests this very point.

Figure 4-1 suggests that "X" is the sales volume at which the cost of direct sales and selling through independent reps are the same. Then, as the slope of the direct cost line is shallower than the slope of the rep cost line, it becomes less and less expensive to sell with a direct sales force as volume continues to increase.

While the chart may appear to be theoretically rational, it is based

Figure 4-1   Breakeven chart—Cost of direct sales vs. independent reps.

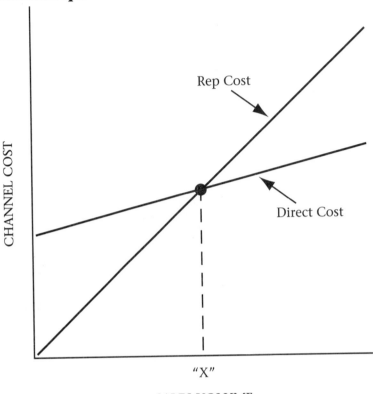

on highly questionable assumptions at best. At worst, it is based on the assumption that this is how the curve should look. Therefore, it is presented to justify a preconceived conclusion. This chart is very superficial in that it ignores some rather complex variables that affect the slope of the curves and the starting point for the direct sales curve. Here are the variables that should be considered:

Rep Cost

Cost directly attributable to a rep sales channel is defined as a variable cost. This means the cost is zero at zero volume. Cost then escalates on a straight-line basis, as it is presumed to be a constant percentage line. For example, if the chart were drawn for OEM reps, the presumption is that it is a 5 percent line. This in itself is fallacious as two major factors result in the commission not remaining a constant rate with increasing volume. These are:

Increasing Contract Size. A general characteristic of gross margin is that the rate decreases with increasing contract size. A constant pretax income is possible with this decrease as larger contracts spread fixed costs across a larger base. In other words, if a $15,000 contract at 35 percent gross margin yields 8 percent pretax, a $200,000 contract at 28 percent may also yield the same pretax. As contracts increase in size, the selling cost for a rep does not increase proportionately. The bottom line to a rep is that the commission dollars earned per unit of time invested in a sale can well be more for a larger contract on which the rep receives a lower commission rate than a small contract at a higher rate. The fact of selling is that commission rates usually decline as contracts increase in size within many industries.

The same is true where increased concentration of purchasing power results in larger and larger annual commitments with fewer and fewer suppliers. Prices and commission rates invariably are negotiated down. As a result, the commission curve does not remain a straight line. It droops as a result of lower rates at higher volumes for most companies.

Cost of Direct Selling. If we presented a sales cost analysis of a manufacturer selling exclusively through independent reps to a group of ten manufacturers and asked them the question: "How many direct personnel would you need to provide the same coverage of the existing rep network?" you could well have ten different answers. There is a major misunderstanding prevalent throughout industry about the cost of comparative coverage. Here's an example to explain the point.

At our seminars, we ask attendees the question: "If you are a $20 million company and sell exclusively through reps in the United States, what percent of their time would you expect to be spent selling your product?" The answers typically range from 10 percent to 25 percent. We then select 10 percent to minimize any bias for reps. Here are the calculations.

The manufacturer has 25 rep firms averaging a head count of 4 sales personnel per firm or 100 sales personnel. Rounding off the number of hours per year per person available for selling to 2,000, the rep network has available 200,000 hours of selling time per year for all of their principals. At 10 percent allocation to our company example, the rep network would spend 20,000 hours per year selling that company's products.

We then ask attendees the question: "How many direct sales people could your $20 million company afford?" The answers generally range from 3 or 4 up to 10. In the case of some very high gross margin consumer products, we have occasionally had the answer as high as 20. As the great majority of attendees are suppliers of industrial products and services, we have used 10 sales personnel for the example. As each would have 2,000 hours available, the direct network would also have 20,000 hours to apply selling the manufacturer's product. This becomes point "X" on the chart.

The hypothesis is that as this company exceeds $20 million in sales, it will be cheaper to sell with a direct sales force as direct selling costs do not increase at the same rate as it would with reps receiving pure commission.

One overlooked fact is that a 100-person rep sales force has much smaller trading areas per person than the 10-person direct sales force. This means that much less time is lost due to travel. It also means a much greater intensity of coverage of individual accounts as the total number of prospects in the United States would be divided by 100 rep personnel rather than ten direct personnel.

Another aspect frequently overlooked is the package of strengths inherent in a properly selected, well-supported rep sales channel. As presented in the Introduction, market dynamics facing most companies today are better served by independent reps than a direct sales force. Reps are simply better positioned in their targeted markets and can gain major competitive advantage for the companies they represent.

Then, the major light bulb goes on when we raise the question: "Do you get any advantage from the 180,000 hours the rep network spends selling other manufacturers' products?" The answer from attendees is a clear "YES!" The only caveat is that the rep network has to be properly selected. This means that the average rep firm should be calling on the same industries targeted by the manufacturer. With 100 percent match in market targets, a rep network spends 200,000 hours developing relationships in those targeted industries compared to only 20,000 hours by the direct sales organization. This is a huge advantage to the rep network.

Even presuming that the rep network is not perfectly matched and spends 50 percent of its time on markets of no interest to the manufacturer, it still spends 100,000 hours developing relationships in the targeted markets or five times that of a direct sales organization. In this latter situation, we would define the rep network as not being highly compatible with the manufacturer. This means that the manufacturer should be replacing a number of reps with those who are much more compatible with the manufacturer's market focus. It also offers the manufacturer an opportunity to quickly increase market share and profitability.

The next chart, Figure 4-2, therefore, represents the commonly published breakeven point and superimposes a second plot for both direct and rep selling costs. We have purposely drawn the curve so that the intersection point still occurs, but much further out in sales volume where the lines become almost asymptotic. It is certainly arbitrary, but no more than the historically accepted one.

The bottom line is that we believe there are no such distinct intersecting curves which clearly suggest economic benefit to the manufacturer by making this conversion. Too many larger companies have continued to use independent reps to competitive advantage. While certain aspects of sell-

Figure 4-2 Alternative breakeven chart—Direct vs. rep.

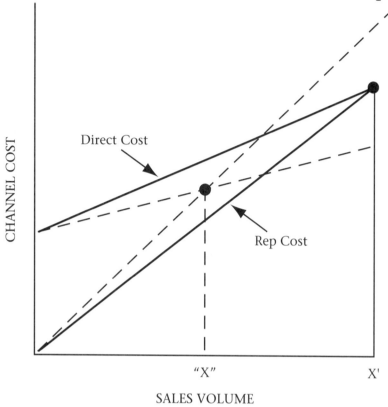

SALES VOLUME

ing through independent reps may actually be more costly than a direct sales organization, the benefits received by a well-selected, well-managed rep network have told companies like Fisher that making a conversion to direct selling is not a well-founded decision.

Control

One of the most universal reasons for a manufacturer to prefer a direct sales organization to independent sales representatives is that selling through reps means minimal control. The term control is used here to define the authority of managers to direct the allocation of time of *subordinates* to activities most desired by corporations. In this sense, the observation that you cannot control independent reps nearly as well as you can control a direct sales organization is irrefutable.

This argument is specious because control should not a managerial objective. The objective of any sales executive is to increase sales (this can be restated in many different forms) and to provide market feedback so his company can plan tomorrow's products, systems and services. "Control" is nothing more than a managerial style that is used to achieve company objectives. Yet, there is an alternative style that produces better results even with a direct sales organization than autocratic control. It is the concept of partnering, whereby the individuals closest to the work are allowed to perform the work as they see it should be performed. Literature and case studies over the years are replete with how this type of partnering has led to substantially greater results than the classic autocratic style.

The Bottom Line: The fact that you can maintain better control over a direct sales channel is no reason to terminate reps, unless the company's culture is totally autocratic. Expecting to obtain full commitment by a rep network when the manufacturer represented attempts to micro-manage everything would be a contradiction in motivation.

As a manufacturer contributes an increasingly greater percentage of a rep's income, the rep tends to develop more and more commitment to that manufacturer as well as spending more time on that manufacturer—provided the representative sees a proper long-term return without high risk, namely, she will not be terminated for doing too good a job. As the percentage of a rep's income increases, economic independence decreases. Figure 1-7 presents this relatively straightforward conclusion and should give comfort to the manufacturer who has grown in size and is concerned about whether or not a conversion to direct selling should be taken in order to improve control.

Our Fisher Controls case study is an example of each rep's strong economic dependence on Fisher. This gains a rep's attention and time. Again, as John Weekley noted: "We have a pseudo-direct sales force." Yet, Fisher has done a superb job in respecting the concept of rep independence. This, in turn, has given the Fisher rep network enormous vitality combined with responsiveness to Fisher's needs—with increasing market share and profits.

> **Key to success:** Do not fall into the traditional decision-making process of going direct just because you happen to reach a certain dollar sales level. Today's market dynamics and customer needs clearly suggest that maintaining an independent rep sales force is the preferred channel for competitive and financial advantage.

The Next Step

We've been talking about making a choice between a direct sales force and a rep network. At this point, you are probably leaning toward one structure or the other. Your marketing analysis will inevitably point you in one direction. However, there are some questions to take into account. This area, like many others in business, has its less tangible aspects, its human nature quotient. As you make your final decision, you need to be aware of these so you can factor them into the equation.

5

The Truth About Independent Sales Reps

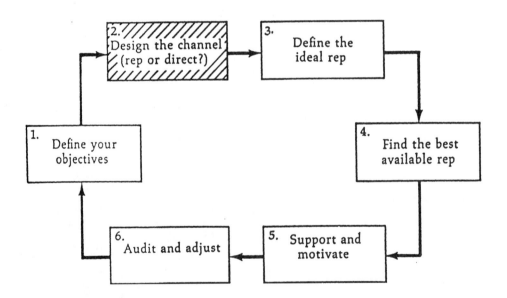

In Step 1, you analyzed your markets, both current and future, and planned the strategies you would use to achieve your objectives. Almost inevitably, at the end of that planning process, one particular sales channel presents itself as the natural and obvious choice. Because the thrust of this book is on selling through independent reps, we'll assume you're leaning toward reps. Now, to make your channel design final, you need to factor in some of the more intangible characteristics that revolve around the basic question, "Rep or direct?" Or, to reformulate the question, "What are reps really like?"

Myths About Reps

If you talk to other managers—your counterparts in other companies in your industry—sooner or later you will hear statements of dissatisfaction about reps. Often this dissatisfaction can be traced to a bad fit between manufacturer and rep, to management errors on the part of the manufacturer, or to less-than-full understanding of how to facilitate success—problems this book can help you avoid. But whatever the source, the net result is that for some people, reps have a bad reputation. Some of the complaints you will hear are simply inaccurate; others are accurate in the narrow sense but, when viewed in a total perspective, turn out not to be disadvantages after all. Let's explore some of the more common myths.

Reps Don't Sell; They Just Take Orders

This is one of the most frequent complaints. And there is no question that some manufacturers *do* find their reps are not selling for them but merely taking orders. Usually it happens because the wrong reps were selected or because the reps have become disillusioned by the manufacturer's inept management and have stopped selling. Also, objectives of either the rep or manufacturer may change and result in a dysfunctional relationship. Remember that reps do not eat unless they sell—they are not salaried. They are selling for someone. It's your job to determine why they are not selling for you and correct the problem.

When organizations are run poorly, sales suffer. Inept management results in problems in quality, timeliness, and product development. This ineptness may be relatively short term or may persevere for years, creating marginal bottom-line performance and static or declining sales.

Professional reps simply will not invest a significant amount of selling time in a poorly managed organization. Unfortunately, many reps do not cancel contracts with such a company. Instead, they let the product line hang on, make a few dollars on the occasional "over the transom" order, and live with a poor situation at arm's length. Poorly managed organizations invariably do a little better with direct salespeople because salespeople will still spend all or at least most of their time selling. Independent reps will turn their attention elsewhere.

The answer: Pick the right reps and give them plenty of support—that is, manage your business well and constantly re-audit the relationship.

Reps Are Only Interested in a Quick Dollar

Reps are often accused of having a short-term mentality that prevents them from successfully promoting products with a long selling cycle. This is a generalization, and it is untrue for many reps serving industries where products have a long gestation period between identification of the opportunity and receipt of the commission check.

In the electronics industry, many reps spend an extraordinary amount of time developing positions on new programs for the Department of Defense; literally years can pass before the first production contract is awarded. Reps are used to sell major capital equipment into the power industries, projects that may also require several years before fruition. Breaking into new industrial OEM accounts takes long-term persistence, a characteristic of many OEM reps.

Manufacturers with products or systems that have long gestation periods between inquiry and shipment can find any number of highly professional, highly qualified reps willing to commit the time required to complete the sale. If you need long-cycle selling and your reps are not providing it, that means either you haven't yet found the right reps or, if you've found them, your company's lack of support has turned them off.

Reps Don't Know the Product

Frequently you will hear it said that if you require your salespeople to have a detailed knowledge of your highly complex product, direct sales is the way to go. Reps handle many manufacturers, and they cannot be expected to learn your product as well as a direct person could. In the opinion of many highly successful marketers, a salesperson who has intimate customer acceptance and the capability of learning about a highly technical product, has a higher chance for selling successfully than vice versa. That's one plus for reps. In addition, rep specialization by market and by product or technology is commonly available, at least in the major geographic trading areas of this country. Therefore, it's not an either/or situation. Generally, you'll find that both needs—customer and product knowledge—are available in reps. The bonus with reps is that their broader product spectrum gives them a much better understanding of customer systems.

If a manufacturer feels that its reps don't know the company's products, one of two things has happened. Either the manufacturer has not picked the right rep, which means it did not search hard enough to find reps with the product knowledge or the technical background to rapidly assimilate the product; or the manufacturer failed to provide the right training programs and support material. If you pick a rep compatible with what you're all about, that rep will invest the time and effort to learn your product. It wouldn't make any sense not to; no rep wants to be ineffective in sales presentations.

Here's an example of how, with a diligent search, you can often find reps with a high level of product expertise combined with exceptional market coverage and customer acceptance. The company, Research Cottrell, manufactured highly technical air pollution control equipment for the power and heavy process industries, primarily in the area of controlling gaseous effluent from power boilers. Somewhat skeptically, it began a search for reps in the Los Angeles trading area. It found a rep organization by the name of Industrial Marketing Systems staffed by three partners:

1. A chemical engineer with more than twenty years' experience in air pollution control, including positions as product manager, marketing director for international operations, and general sales manager of a major competitor

2. A mechanical engineer who was formerly chief engineer of a major boiler company and then chief engineer in an air pollution control company

3. A chemical engineer (master's degree) who had been a product manager for a major air pollution control supplier

Together, they had more than sixty years of in-depth experience with the products this manufacturer was selling. They had intimate knowledge of both the generator of the pollutants and the equipment for removing the pollutants, an unusual combination that provided customers with a service not typically found in any other sales organization. Add to this technical base the many years of involvement with the desired industry contacts and nearly ten years as a highly successful rep in the Los Angeles area.

An exception? Yes, but the exceptions are too numerous to dismiss the possibility of locating such expertise. While manufacturers certainly cannot expect to find ideal matches of this type routinely, it can frequently be done. The key is a thorough search.

This type of match typically occurs only in the major trading areas where the size of the market opportunity allows many different rep specialists to prosper. Fortunately, these are the territories that yield most of your opportunities.

As to training, there's no denying that product training is facilitated with a direct sales organization. It's easier to pick a time and place for the training program and simply require your salespeople to be there. It's more complicated with a rep network. However, the other side of the coin is that good product training—a professional presentation of the product's capabilities and how it can be better sold against competition—is a major motivating factor for reps. It's not a question of whether reps want it—they do—it's only a question of how easy it is to get them together for it at a particular time. Good planning can overcome this.

Reps Won't Spend Enough Time on the Product

This "weakness" is the result of a number of misunderstandings. First and foremost is the fact that reps will not commit 100 percent of their sales time to a single company the way a direct salesperson will.

Selling through reps comes with a given—that is, reps will allocate their selling time among the principals they represent. Theoretically, they allocate their time objectively, namely based on the income they are receiving today balanced with income they expect to receive tomorrow from their principals. Affecting time allocation includes variables such as the relative fit a manufacturer has with the rep's objectives, commission rates, support of the rep's activities, commitment the manufacturer has in the long term to selling through reps, years of doing business with the manufacturer, personal chemistry with members of the manufacturer, and others that vary in importance from rep to rep.

The bottom line is that reps will give a fair share of time to the manufacturers that measure up well in the above variables. They will actually give more than a fair share of time to those manufacturers who excel in these variables.

A related argument is that with a direct sales organization, any goodwill that is generated with customers is totally yours. This argument does have validity. While the professional representative will do an admirable job promoting a manufacturer to a customer, the rep's own position with the customer is never forgotten. The development of goodwill is therefore shared between the rep and the manufacturer.

Many manufacturers do not get a fair share of their reps' time—a major problem, certainly, but once again it is usually the result of poor rep selection and/or poor support. This book will help you get *more* than a fair share of your rep's time.

Reps Are Not Willing to Push New Products

Established representatives evaluating new manufacturers are sometimes reluctant to take on a totally missionary effort even if the manufacturer has a nationally visible name. However, if a manufacturer with an established base business brings out a new product, reps will look forward to representing it. When a manufacturer that is well established with a rep brings out new products that are highly compatible with the rep's profile, you have the ideal situation. New product introductions of this type are one of the highest motivating factors for helping a rep and a manufacturer grow together.

Even a small manufacturer without a market position can find success with independent reps. The key is conducting an intensive search to find a rep with whom the manufacturer has a unique fit. With such a fit with a small manufacturer, even the large rep will occasionally gamble on long-term success. However, the small manufacturer will typically be better off with a well-matched smaller rep, as the potential income will be spread among fewer sales personnel.

Reps Don't Prospect

Frequently, this is true. Reps will not prospect for business from customers or industries they do not have contact with or see as a fit with their basic business. Few reps can afford to start calling on a set of new customers that represents no potential for other manufacturers they represent; the economics are not there. Even if they say with good intentions that they will try, they usually will not succeed.

However, the fact that reps will not prospect in markets that are alien to them is frequently an advantage rather than a disadvantage. The concept of specialization allows a manufacturer to recruit reps that are particularly well identified with this new market. With parallel rep networks, the manufacturer can have intensive coverage in all markets. To keep this issue in perspective, remember that direct sales organizations are subject to the same type of behavior. Although management may be able to force the salespeople into an entirely new area, if that new area does not fit the mainstream of the activities by which the salespeople are primarily compensated and evaluated, they will quickly fall back to their normal sales call patterns once the pressure is off.

The problem with a rep's failure to prospect in a particular industry it has targeted is different from the situation just described and can be a major frustration to manufacturers. The reason for this problem in an otherwise sound relationship with a rep typically has to do with that rep's lifestyle objectives. A growth-oriented rep will periodically add new sales personnel. With each addition, new prospects are solicited and new customers developed along with a deeper penetration of existing customers.

The problem occurs when a rep decides that lifestyle rather than growth is more important. This is a free choice for the rep as he is an independent businessperson. The dysfunction occurs when the manufacturer wants growth while the rep has peaked and has no desire to expend the effort necessary to accumulate new accounts. This rep does very little if any missionary work. This presents one of the more difficult situations facing a manufacturer with a well-tenured rep who has had a historically good performance. If the rep cannot be motivated to continue in a growth mode, termination frequently has to be considered. This knotty problem will be discussed in more detail in Chapter 10.

Reps Don't Have Loyalty

This fallacy can best be dispelled by looking at the fundamental objectives of rep owners versus direct personnel. The owners of rep firms are committed to developing and nurturing relationships with markets and customers they prioritize over the long term. To do this, they must attract and hold onto top manufacturers if long-term income streams are to be realized. There is simply no fundamental reason for them to be less than loyal to a manufacturer that fits their objectives well and supports them well.

The objective of the great majority of direct sales personnel is individual growth. This means getting a richer territory, getting the boss' job, or being transferred back to headquarters to round out their experience in order to further career growth. If the direct person does not see his employer providing these opportunities, that salesperson will leave to join a manufacturer who offers those opportunities.

The bottom line is that the basic objectives of reps result in their having greater loyalty to a manufacturer than does a direct salesperson.

Reps Can't Be Transferred

Some sales managers want the flexibility of transferring salespeople from one location to the other. Obviously they can't get that with reps, but this flexibility is as much a limitation as it is an advantage. Fundamentally, you want to develop continuity of your salespeople with their customers. The longer a salesperson is in contact with customers, the closer that person gets to them and the more competitive advantage can be gained. Transfers disrupt this continuity. Well-managed rep firms give you the continuity with customers that leads to strong relationship management capabilities.

Reps Are Not Willing to Perform Nonselling Activities

When managers within manufacturers say this, they're usually talking about written communications. Also, there are periodic complaints about a rep's less-than-desired commitment to helping out in trade shows or performing other nonselling functions.

Many manufacturers complain they cannot get enough paperwork from reps to satisfy internal analysis, and it is true that the rep is not a paper pusher. Think about it. If you were a rep and tried to respond to demands for call reports, special reports, lost order reports, obtained order reports, competitive analyses, market trend reports, and so on from your dozen or so principals, you would not have enough time to contact customers. You'd be too busy writing reports. There is very little correlation between this paperwork and primary selling objectives: increased profit growth and good market feedback. Customer feedback is available from reps; just don't expect it in writing. Also don't expect them to do your marketing job. They will perform the required sales job and can give you excellent market feedback so you can perform the necessary marketing job.

When it comes to trade shows, strong representatives are zealous advocates of first-class participation. They work at booths when national trade shows are in their area, or even in adjacent areas, and many really successful reps initiate local minishows for their customers. If a rep has an aversion to this type of participation, the most common reason is that the rep is really not committed to your company, so the time required for your trade show would not be a wise investment of his or her time. You don't have the right rep in this case.

There is an additional reason for not trying to impose bureaucratic reporting systems and other controls on reps. It concerns the Internal Revenue Service's (IRS) interpretation of what constitutes employer/employee relationships as opposed to independent contractor relationships. If employer qualities may be attributed to the relationship, the IRS may require withholding taxes, contributing to social security payments, and making unemployment compensation contributions on behalf of the rep. If this ruling occurs many years after the fact, it could also result in substantial tax liabilities, interest, and penalties against the manufacturer. (This issue is more fully described in Chapter 13.)

The Real Reasons for Poor Rep Performance

Those are the myths. Here are four real reasons for poor rep performance.

1. *You did not design the channel properly.* This typically occurs when a manufacturer selects a rep to handle all of its products to all markets within the rep's territory. The rep may be truly outstanding for the manufacturer's #1 market, but it has almost no coverage of the #2 market priority of the manufacturer. This not a case of poor rep selection. It is a case of poor channel design, that is, not recognizing that two separate reps were needed, one for each of the two primary targets.

2. *You did not select the right rep.* This invariably is the result of one or both of two mistakes. First is inadequate attention to profiling the ideal rep initially, a profile that clearly shows the characteristics the manufacturer needs in a top rep. All too often, this is followed up by a superficial search that simply does not yield the best available candidate in a given territory. Correcting these two limitations are subjects of Chapters 6 and 7.

3. *You did not properly support your reps.* As a result, they turned their attention to other manufacturers that better served their needs.

4. *Objectives, either yours or those of your rep, have changed*. This frequently results in a substantial lessening of the relationship's compatibility. If this deteriorating relationship is left unnoticed, market share will deteriorate in the territory.

These four causes are controllable and can be clearly defined by the Rep Audit discussed in Chapter 10. If the manufacturer does the thorough job required to design the channel properly, recruits the right rep, provides a support capability that truly makes it easy for the rep to sell, and monitors the relationship to ensure that objectives stay common, outstanding performance typically results.

Some True Statements About Reps

Reps have a number of characteristics that represent potential problems to manufacturers compared to selling direct. These concerns must be carefully understood and factored into your rep selection and evaluation process. Let's look at these situations and how you can cope successfully with several of them.

Reps Are Hard to Control

Yes, from a purely authoritarian perspective, the direct sales organization offers the manufacturer much better control. Here the relationship is between boss and subordinate. The power of authority allows a boss to tell a salesperson what to do, how, and when. All too often, the desire for tighter control has more to do with ego satisfaction than with achievement of objectives. This type of control really misses the mark. The point is not control but a greater return for the company. Control for its own sake is nothing but power, and the empty exercise of power produces nothing but ill will and low morale—whether it is with an independent rep or a direct sales force.

Control, therefore, should be defined in terms of ensuring that objectives are achieved rather than that a predetermined method for achieving them is followed. Over the long term, the best results come when all involved are dedicated to mutually developed objectives. This calls for a partnership philosophy, with the rep being allowed to decide the how-tos and the whens, rather than a boss/subordinate philosophy, with the manager dictating the rep's activities. This partnership philosophy is a positive influence on results regardless of the sales channel selected. Direct sales personnel will also be more motivated and productive when this philosophy is followed.

Some managers have a hard time viewing salespeople as peers. If they can put aside their need to be the boss and begin to view reps as partners, they will create a group of strong team players collectively looking for the best way to achieve market penetration and profit objectives. Now, we have a key question. If you can't control your reps, how can you get them to do what you want in the marketplace? Here are my answers:

- Select only reps who already have the same objectives as you do and who are currently doing precisely what you need done (see Chapters 6 and 7).

- Manage your business well and provide strong support so the reps remain highly motivated (see Chapters 8 and 9).

- Routinely audit your own company and your reps to see whether you are still marching to the beat of the same drummer. If not, make the necessary changes (see Chapters 10 and 11).

Follow these guidelines and you'll see the results. A successful, profitable relationship with your reps is an almost inevitable product of sound planning and development of the system presented in this book.

What You See Is What You Get

Many manufacturers expect more out of a rep than they should. Perhaps they tend to forget that you can mold a direct salesperson to your needs but not a successful rep.

Most manufacturers need well-established reps, so it behooves them to understand rep priorities in business development and to build on these priorities rather than try to force reps into marginal activities. Unfortunately, well-meaning reps frequently accede to a respected manufacturer's requests to spend time on activities they know are not in their best interests. In the long run—maybe even the short run—both parties will suffer. The best advice is to use reps for what they are good at and do not expect them to perform in other areas.

You Are Faced With a Second Set of Competitors

The independent representative typically has anywhere from five to fifteen additional manufacturers represented—truly an additional set of competitors because each manufacturer is vying for your rep's time. However, this situation is also an opportunity. The great majority of reps have a number of manufacturers that are not truly precise fits with the rep's capabilities and interests, and others do not properly support the rep. The astute manufacturer can gain more than a fair share of a rep's time by precise selection and support.

The Rep May Be Poorly Managed

An individual rep owner can be a truly outstanding sales performer. However, that is no assurance that she will be an equally adept manager of a rep business. Manufacturers must therefore be careful to look beyond the owner during the interviewing process with any rep. Perhaps two aspects of a rep's business are most important to analyze: (1) the quality and tenure of its most important manufacturers represented and (2) the quality and tenure of its sales personnel. If all measures rank high, one can reasonably conclude that this is a well-managed rep firm. However, all too often a rep firm represents second-rate manufacturers, has employed poorly qualified personnel, and both manufacturers represented and sales personnel have short tenures with the firm—invariably key indicators that the rep firm has survived for many years but has not been well managed. Astute manufacturers will avoid these firms.

There Is No Guarantee the Rep Firm Will Continue in Business

A 1997 survey of reps nationwide conducted by MANA[1] included the owners' plans for continuity of their firms (note that the total is more than 100 percent because of multiple answers):

No plans; agency will cease to exist upon retirement:	*37%*
Plan to sell agency to employees:	*39%*
Plan to pass agency on to heirs:	*26%*

If a number of your reps are in the first category, particularly if the owners are well into their fifties or older, you may be headed for trouble. Many reps reach a point where their primary drives are enjoying a pleasant lifestyle while maintaining some close customers, rather than growing their organization. Even if the owner plans to pass the business along to family members, this is normally good news for you only if those individuals have been active and successful in growing the business.

The moral here is to select reps who have plans for continuity and closely monitor reps who have been with you for a long time. One of the most difficult situations facing a growth-oriented manufacturer is to find that a highly productive rep has obviously plateaued and has expressed no interest in providing the continuity the business requires for future growth. This problem is addressed in Chapter 10.

[1]*Agency Sales*, January 1998, p. 9, Manufacturers' Agents National Association, Laguna Hills, California.

The Rep's Objectives May Change

One of the prime ingredients of a successful match between a rep and a manufacturer is mutuality of objectives. This means that both want to sell into a certain set of customers with certain priorities at certain decision-making levels with certain types of products. However, as time progresses, these objectives may change. If the manufacturer's objectives change, the rep may no longer fit. Of equal concern to the manufacturer is the potential changing of rep objectives.

As rep firms prosper, the owners frequently look toward additional avenues of opportunity. They may start to move into distribution with value-added programs or move more into the service area. They may start manufacturing products to fit a unique need that they have identified. More recently, rep firms have started to become national reps for foreign companies that want to penetrate the U.S. market but don't really understand how to do it.

Any of these changes may very well diminish the attention reps pay to their basic business. In some cases, for example, in service, they may actually develop a competing capability. The burden is on manufacturers to stay close to their representatives, keep abreast of any changes in rep objectives, and make changes in the relationship if objectives are becoming incompatible.

Reps That Are Compatible Today May Represent Competitive Conflict Tomorrow

Every day the financial pages are full of announcements of spinoffs, acquisitions, and various other financial marriages and divorces. These structural changes in corporations occasionally have a significantly negative impact on a manufacturer selling through reps. Suppose some of your reps have another manufacturer, highly compatible, that contributes a substantial part of their income. Then suppose that compatible manufacturer acquires a small company that is your competitor and gives your reps an ultimatum: "Drop the competition (i.e., your company) or lose our business." In this scenario, the rep is usually faced with no choice, and your company will lose.

A second competitive conflict occurs when a compatible manufacturer of importance to your rep introduces a new product that competes with one of your products. This is an uncontrollable event, and in its worst scenario may result in the rep canceling your contract if the competing manufacturer has a much stronger economic position and demands that your company be dropped.

Reps May Stop Selling for You But Not Tell You

We have already touched on the problem of reps' drastically losing interest in promoting a manufacturer's products or services. This can occur when their objectives substantially change or when they become disenchanted with a manufacturer because of poor sales support or poor customer service. Reps that have had a good performance record will be very vocal in their concerns to the manufacturer once they see problems starting. However, if the manufacturer is unable to improve this performance, reps will eventually reach a point where they essentially give up on that manufacturer.

Unfortunately, reps frequently do not tell the manufacturer that they are no longer actively selling its account. They may be thinking, "We'll put them on a back burner. Perhaps sometime in the future they'll turn around." Or perhaps, "We can still make a few dollars off them. They're not bad enough to jeopardize our position with customers. We'll just collect the easy money." Either one is bad news for the manufacturer.

This is a problem created by the manufacturer and one that must be solved by that manufacturer. The best solution is to start managing the business effectively just as soon as it is *at all* possible. The other key is to be on the lookout for symptoms of problems. The first is an absence of "noise"—that is, the rep becomes hardly noticeable. This is the time to sit down with your reps and regain their commitment before they totally cross you off.

It Is Difficult to Obtain Common Software Utilization

The explosion in sales force automation has seen the introduction of a number of excellent contact management software programs. These programs allow manufacturers to sharply improve their capabilities to track customers, prospects, new negotiations, and a host of other selling activities. Programs such as *Act, Gold Mine,* and *Maximizer* allow manufacturers to much more closely manage their selling efforts. However, this ease occurs only with direct sales organizations. Manufacturers can simply mandate to the direct sales force that: "As of next Monday, we will introduce our new contact management software program!" Then it's a relatively simple matter for introducing the training program and implementation dates. However, if your sales channel is made up of independent reps, the rep is faced with trying to reconcile the contact management needs of many different manufacturers, frequently each having its own software or manual reporting needs. As of the writing of this third edition, there is no simple solution over the near term for most manufacturers who wish to implement a contact management software program with their reps.

Reps Are Generally Weak With Written Communications

This is a characteristic of most reps. While there are notable exceptions, many reps in many industries have little time and little interest in responding to requests in writing. Reps are outstanding communicators if the proper communication medium is selected. This medium is verbal communications, either face-to-face or via telephone. Reps love to talk; they hate to write. Take advantage of their basic nature. In addition, you'll find a complementary benefit. Written communications are sterile and can frequently be misunderstood. Verbal communications allow one to probe and truly reach a meeting of minds. In addition, they provide a much closer tie with reps than cold, written communications.

You Cannot Fire Just One Member of a Rep Firm

It is most unusual to find that all members of a multisalesperson rep firm will support each manufacturer with equal enthusiasm. In fact, occasionally a member of a rep firm will do a very poor job with one manufacturer while other members of the firm excel. The first step in attacking this problem is to work with the rep member in an empathetic fashion. If this fails, discussion of the issue with the rep owners should be undertaken to see if they can come up with a solution. Still, there will be times when nothing corrects the problem. The manufacturer is then faced with two alternatives: (1) Accept poor performance from one member of the rep firm because the firm as a whole is still performing more than satisfactorily or (2) terminate the firm itself.

Very Successful Reps May Deliberately Limit Sales Volume

Successful reps face a preposterous "catch-22" situation: If they do a good job, they earn good commissions; if they do an outstanding job, they get canceled and the manufacturer goes direct. Many companies have a sort of threshold beyond which commissions are considered "too high." (They tend to lose sight of the fact that this high commission inevitably means they also have higher sales and profits.) Maybe a rep's commission is higher than a senior officer's compensation. Or maybe an accountant calculates that substituting direct salespeople for high-producing reps will "save the company money." Whatever the rationale, reps know that outstanding performance can be rewarded with termination. How can they protect themselves?

Many reps adopt an unwritten policy that they will not allow any one manufacturer to become a major part of their income. Many get very uncomfortable once a manufacturer starts to exceed the 25 to 30 percent level. In addition to the financial threat, at that point manufacturers often start demanding more of the rep. The higher their contribution is to a rep's total income, the more manufacturers feel they can "control" the rep. These demands usually lead the rep to work harder to increase the contribution from *other* manufacturers.

Is there an answer to this catch-22? Yes. As long as the manufacturer recognizes and respects the rep's independence and continues to treat the relationship as a partnership rather than increasing bureaucratic control pressures, the relationship has an excellent chance of continuing growth. On top of this, reps have to see a complete corporate commitment to the rep concept, starting with the manufacturer's senior officer. If that commitment is present, most reps will allow the percentage of that manufacturer's contribution to their income to grow disproportionately to others represented—such as experienced by Fisher Controls.

They May Not Be Responsive to Requests They Consider Superficial or Bureaucratic

Reps typically are the product of unfulfilled company personnel who resign to become reps for several reasons. The opportunity for unconstrained income, the opportunity to be their own boss and avoid bureaucracy all are key motivating factors. This leads to their reluctance, if not recalcitrance, in responding to requests from manufacturers they represent that are considered superficial or bureaucratic. If it doesn't directly contribute to the rep's success in selling, many reps will not be particularly responsive to corporate requests for reports or other actions. The positive side of this issue is that it becomes a clear indicator to manufacturers that the request is not directly sales related and perhaps it should be withdrawn. If it is information that is needed, such as considered forecasting, part if not all of the work can be done internally. The key to success in resolving this issue is to recognize that as reps are independent, the quality and timeliness of response that you can expect for any series of requests will vary significantly from rep to rep. Verbal communications can go a long way toward resolving this issue. Then, the manufacturer can reduce all of the inputs to writing at headquarters.

Working With Reps Means a More Complex Management Job

The very independence of a rep demands a change from the simplistic, autocratic style of decision making historically used in industrial America. The other manufacturers that are represented actually create a new set of competitors. These manufacturers now compete with you for a rep's time, making your job as an executive more complex.

Well-managed manufacturers that properly support their reps have an opportunity to get more than a fair share of the rep's time. Manufacturers with less astute management and without the proper organizational culture suffer in comparison. Yes, the job is more complex, but it can be broken down to readily managed small units that, effectively handled, will yield outstanding successes in the marketplace.

You Lose Key Control Elements of the Sales Management Function

Having an independent rep network relieves the manufacturer of certain elements of the sales management job: recruiting, assignments, compensation, and so on. Many define this as an advantage, but I consider it a disadvantage, for too frequently rep owners don't do a very good job at administrative tasks. Manufacturers cannot control the staffing quality— except in two ways:

- Recruit only those reps that have demonstrated the ability to attract and keep top sales personnel—talent that is well equipped to sell your products.
- Closely monitor your existing rep to be sure that turnover is not excessive. If the rate of turnover does seem high, consider getting yourself another rep.

Using Reps Deprives You of One Internal Source of Management Talent

In the ever-increasingly competitive environment facing American industry, management must develop broader perspectives of the world in which it operates if it is to succeed. One of the major failings in organizational life is the narrowness of perspective in general management. Even functional managers, such as the vice-president of engineering, of operations, or of finance, need the broad perspective that comes from direct experience in several areas. And one of these should be sales, for that is where one can best develop sensitivity to customers.

With a direct sales organization, companies can institute a program of job rotation to provide this breadth of exposure. With independent representatives, job rotation becomes considerably more difficult, although not impossible. Some manufacturers place young engineers trained in their organization with representatives, on an open-ended agreement. The engineer can make a career with the rep or, at a mutually agreeable time, return to the manufacturer.

What a Good Rep Can Give You

One point you should now be well aware of is that selling through reps is more complex than working with a direct sales organization. The question then becomes, Is it worth it? Providing your market profile is right, I believe the answer is emphatically yes. Let's look at what a well-selected rep network can offer your company.

- *More qualified feet on the street.* The leveraging available by the added principals represented combined with the opportunity to frequently use more than one rep firm in a given area, each specializing in a set of markets, gives a manufacturer many more hours of available selling time to develop relationships with its targeted markets. If the manufacturer is properly fit with each rep and supports them well, sharp advances in market share are available.

- *Ability to satisfy local needs.* As noted by Joe Urbanek in our chapter on Fisher, the entrepreneurship of a local rep results in its being much more responsive to local needs. If a specific manufacturer doesn't satisfy those needs, a rep frequently has a way to satisfy them to the benefit of the manufacturer it represents, the customer, and the rep—a truly win-win-win situation.

- *Professional salesmanship.* Rep firms are usually started by one or two individuals who have already established strong credentials as sales producers. They build on this experience to continue their professional development over the long term. With great pride, dedication, and a sense of achievement, reps have freely chosen sales as their career. You'll have outstanding professionals working for you—not looking for your job. Owners who also have excellent management capabilities will also attract and hold on to top sales personnel as employees over the long term. These are the reps you want to recruit.

- *Customer continuity.* Closeness to customers is built in part by continuity between salesperson and customer. Reps, with their much longer average tenure, give long-term continuity that generally cannot be found in most direct sales organizations. Their trading area and their customers are the focus of their existence. For them it is their life, not just some stepping-stone within a corporate hierarchy. Their interests are in the long-term well-being of their customers. Good reps know how to use these contacts for the benefit of the manufacturers they represent.

- *Commitment to selling.* Another major characteristic of reps is their extremely high drive level. Because their very life depends purely on selling, reps will give that extra effort, making calls at the end of the day and working weekends and nights. In addition, they often blend personal life and business life, developing personal friendships with customers. In many cases, personal life and business life become inseparable, reinforcing the close relationship between rep and customer.

- *Entertainment.* Reps are not constrained by typical corporate limitations in the area of entertainment. As a result, they frequently invest more in entertainment than direct organizations. Because this is directly out of their income, they also try to make sure they get maximum mileage out of each entertainment dollar.

- *The benefits of synergistic products.* Good reps handle products that are highly complementary to one another. This means they can call on the same specifiers and influencers in the same industries on the same types of applications that you need for market penetration. Ideally, the reps should have other products that are specified or purchased earlier in a customer's decision cycle. This gives you leading indicators of opportunity. Also, when reps have truly compatible product lines, frequently they can develop a larger package of products and services than your competitor, even if the competitor is larger than you. Your competitor's advantage is not just negated—*you* now have the advantage.

- *Knowledge of the customer's processes.* Independent reps, because of their more intensive coverage and their wider spectrum of products, typically develop a more comprehensive understanding of each customer. The additional products bring them into contact more frequently and in greater depth throughout the organization with the decision makers. This product breadth also gives reps a greater understanding of the system needs of their customers. The reps can then provide manufacturers with excellent feedback to plan future action.

- *Cash flow.* Improved cash flow is one of several inherent financial advantages of working with reps. With direct organizations, the investment in salary occurs before results can be expected. With independent reps and the normal commission method, you incur sales expense only for results achieved. Reps are typically paid commission either when the product is shipped or when the customer pays the invoice. For manufacturers that have a fairly long lead time in shipment, selling through reps can provide a significant improvement in cash flow.

- *A variable selling expense.* A direct sales organization is perhaps best described as a semifixed sales expense. Some might even consider it fixed, as organizations tend to maintain staff levels as business volume rises or drops (unless, of course, the change is really significant). This fixed expense means a rapidly increased selling cost as a percentage of sales in a down cycle.

The commission payment to reps results in a purely variable expense, because the commission rate stays relatively constant throughout varying sales volumes. In practice, even the rate typically declines during a down cycle. As markets contract, competitors fight to maintain sales volumes. One typical tool is price concessions, and many contracts stipulate that the rep's commission must be reduced according to some mutually agreed-upon basis.

While some might suggest that there are equal advantages and disadvantages to the variable expense, that is, an advantage with reps on the down volume and a disadvantage on the up volume, standards of performance for companies and their presidents do not value both sides of this coin equally. Protection on the down side—being able to maintain the same selling cost ratio at reduced volume—is typically much more important than reducing the sales expense ratio on an upward surge. Avoidance of loss is one of the primary criteria in judging general management performance. The variable expense helps. Once volume surges, fixed expenses become fully absorbed and the profit line benefits rapidly. The ability to drop an additional 1 or 2 percent of pretax income on the high side is not normally considered a reason to go direct.

- *Improved return on investment (ROI).* The balance sheet will be better managed and ROI increased when using independent reps, particularly as rep firms move more and more to becoming stocking reps. Instead of having these fixed assets on the manufacturer's balance sheet, they move to the rep's balance sheet.
- *Lower administrative cost.* When companies sell through reps, their personnel administration costs drop as rep owners assume this function.
- *A business advisory source.* One powerful benefit, often underused by manufacturers, is the outstanding source of business advice available from reps. In fact, one of the concerns frequently voiced about independent reps is that "they keep telling us how to run our business!" The truth is that good reps *should* be telling their manufacturers how to run their business—at least as far as the requirements for penetrating the markets in the reps' territories are concerned.

Good reps know what's required to succeed with their customers. If a manufacturer has product or service deficiencies, reps can very quickly point them out. Frequently they can suggest what should be done to penetrate a given customer or an industry in their area. If your reps are not telling you how to run your business, you do not have the right reps.

Not only do reps have the capability of providing excellent feedback based on their customer contacts, they also have another excellent frame of reference: They can compare your company's capabilities with the others they represent, giving you objective business advice that can be invaluable.

Rep feedback is usually candid and right on the mark. Reps are interested primarily in one thing: growing their income with each of the manufacturers they represent. If a manufacturer has limitations that minimize this, most reps will be quite open about discussing the issues and possible resolutions to problems. After all, they are not encumbered by your internal politics and will continue to be a vocal proponent of change even in the face of reticent corporate management. Chapter 11 presents two unique tools for obtaining this feedback in a usable form.

Other Aspects of Reps

Horizontal vs. Vertical Reps

A *horizontal rep* handles a given class of products for all industries using those products. Nonferrous castings is one example. In this case, the rep would handle different types of nonferrous castings and sell them to a wide variety of applications from aerospace to automotive to medical products and other industries.

A *vertical rep* concentrates on one or two industries selling an array of products that have at least one common denominator—for example, a rep concentrating on mechanical and electromechanical components for the aerospace industry. Within the rep's mechanical product spectrum could be aluminum and zinc die castings, injection-molded plastic parts, PC boards, harnesses, and a wide array of other products. The common denominator tying the vertical rep's products together is its focus on the aerospace industry.

Both types of representatives offer advantages to manufacturers. The horizontal rep is more of a technical expert in the particular product than the vertical rep. The vertical rep tends to develop a much more intense relationship with a particular industry. As a result, the vertical rep gets to know and understand one specific industry to much greater depth than the horizontal rep. It is because of this relationship, so important in today's market dynamics, that our preference leans toward the vertical rep. However, when both vertical and horizontal reps are available for a manufacturer, we suggest carefully looking at both before deciding.

Territorial Variations

Independent reps may have a wide variation in the territory they cover, even though a number of them may be headquartered in the same city. New England, a rather standard trading area for many industries, may have reps headquartered in any number of cities or towns stretching from Boston to Hartford. Most operate out of one office, but a number have branch offices inside the six-state trading area. All things being equal (which they obviously never are), we lean toward a rep with a branch office, because it provides a higher degree of local identification.

On the other hand, aggressive reps at times go beyond a normal trading area and open up a branch office in an adjacent trading area. Using the same example, the rep owners could be located in Boston and have expanded into upstate New York, opening a branch office in Syracuse, Rochester, or Albany. The manufacturer will therefore be faced with a choice between two separate independent reps covering these two trading areas or one rep having a branch office in the second trading area. We have generally found that two separate reps are preferred by most manufacturers. This situation gives them greater flexibility in managing performance. A rep that is not performing well can be terminated. Terminating a branch office of a larger rep is most difficult. In addition, there is a tendency toward less continuity of personnel in branch offices of these multiarea reps. Top personnel of the branch offices tend eventually to leave their employers and start their own business. After all, why should they share in the commission rate with a rep owner in an entirely different trading area if they feel they can maintain the same sales level as an independent?

The regional rep and the national rep are additional steps in extended territorial coverage. Generally, the larger the rep becomes, the more it is faced with problems in attracting and holding top sales talent. Our personal preference is to stay within normal trading areas defined by the industry and avoid the multiarea rep. This a general guideline only and refers only to industries where there are good populations of qualified reps covering the smaller territories.

The "Captive" Rep

This term describes a representative that sells for only one company. As might be expected, it is difficult to consider such an individual or individuals truly independent if their income comes from one source. The IRS may view such a relationship as an employee relationship rather than an independent contractor relationship and therefore require the employer to observe the tax laws for employees with these reps. On such matters, a tax attorney should be consulted.

The Rep-Distributor and Other Classes of ISOs

Historically, we have had entirely different definitions of a rep and a distributor. As market dynamics have changed, many industries are now finding it difficult to define an independent sales organization as a rep or a distributor because each may combine elements of the other. Fisher Controls is just one example. Although Fisher's channel is defined as a rep network, there are not only major distributor overtones throughout the channel. Their reps may perform functions of a systems integrator, value-added reseller (VAR) and other ISO classifications. We believe that this trend will continue and that for many industries, a single descriptive term will no longer be descriptive. For other industries, the historic definitions will still hold.

The Next Step

Designing the appropriate sales channel for your organization is one of the most critical decisions you will make. It's worth the investment of time and energy to do things right. That means a thorough analysis of the "numbers" issues surrounding market analysis and your business plan and also the "people" questions that revolve around some of the less tangible aspects.

There are advantages to using direct people and disadvantages; there are advantages and disadvantages to using reps. In the final analysis, if your market situation calls for using them, properly selected reps can make a powerful contribution to your company.

Many of the complaints you will hear about reps really come down to one quite simple matter: The manufacturer and the rep are not a good fit. Avoiding the problem is also simple: It is incumbent on manufacturers to do the necessary research to select the right rep. That brings us to Step 3.

6
Profile of the Ideal Rep

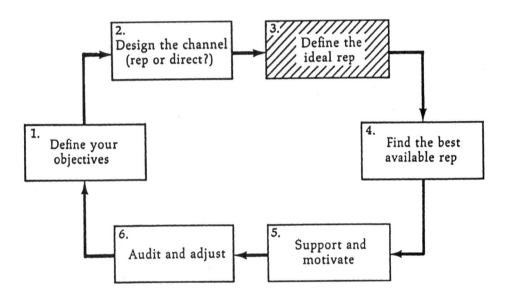

One of the primary reasons that manufacturers do not always get the results they would like from reps is simply this: They did not pick the right rep. After all the hard work you did in Steps 1 and 2 deciding whether or not to use reps, it may seem tempting to relax here and just hire the first rep firm you bump into. I've seen too many manufacturers approach rep selection with a philosophy that almost sounds like, "Any old rep will do."

Recruiting reps requires much greater care than hiring direct sales employees. There is a fundamental difference between independent reps and direct salespeople. We've talked about this difference before, but it's worth repeating here, for it is critical that it be fully understood and assimilated into your thinking.

Direct employees spend 100 percent of their time on your company and frequently can be molded to do things the way you want them done and within your priority system. That is not true for independent reps. Established, successful reps have their own way of working and their own priority system. The markets they serve and their way of approaching these markets have been worked out over a long time, and it well serves the combination of manufacturers they represent. Reps don't usually change their modus operandi as long as it produces successful results. You, as a new manufacturer, will have to fit into their system; they will not fit into yours. Once the two of you make your deal, any success will be based on what the rep *is*, not what you might hope the rep will *become*. It therefore is imperative that you carefully select only reps that already have the characteristics that your company needs. Recruiting a rep with even one key characteristic missing may substantially reduce your market share possibilities in that territory. Finding the right rep creates a high probability for a true win-win situation as both "partners" have common objectives.

It is only through an intensive, well-planned search that this one best available rep in each territory can be located. (For companies with multiple market targets, two or more reps in each area may be required, each rep concentrating on different markets.) Once found and properly supported, the return on your search investment typically exceeds other types of corporate investments and with much less risk.

How Much Is the Right Rep Worth?

Let's assume:

- You manage a company or a division with $25,000,000 sales.
- Your sales represent a 20 percent share of a $125 million U.S. market.
- Your company covers the U.S. market with 25 rep firms.
- As an "average territory," the Cincinnati trading area represents 4 percent of the U.S. potential. You should therefore have $1,000,000 sales (a 20 percent share).
- However, your Cincinnati rep has been generating only $500,000 (a 10 percent market share)—and you now realize it is because the rep's objectives do not match yours.

Question—If you terminated that rep, hired a really well-matched rep today and provided excellent support, how long would it take that rep to increase your market share to your national average of 20 percent and thereby increase your sales from $500,000 to $1,000,000?

Answer—The answers from attendees of our public seminar programs have varied significantly. The more simplistic the product, the shorter the time required. A number of consumer-products people stipulated thirty days. Suppliers of large, complex systems indicated that it might take as long as four years. The great majority of companies, however, concluded that they could raise the market share to their national average well within the second year after the recruitment of the *right* rep. Let's use two years for our example.

Calculating the Return—Table 6-1 converts the above hypothetical example into a table for calculating return. The first group of numbers (Basic Data) simply repeats the above information. The second group of numbers (percent Pretax Contribution) presents typical fixed overhead expenses, fixed selling, general and administrative expenses, and pretax income—all as a percentage of sales. If you are not a manufacturing based company, factory overhead would be zero, but the fixed SG&A would probably be higher. The sum of the three figures provides the pretax income impact of each incremental sales dollar. In other words, if your company already had absorbed all of its fixed expenses (i.e., reached breakeven), 30 cents on every incremental dollar would fall to pretax income. If you had yet to

Table 6-1   What is the value of the right rep?

Calculation Work Sheet	
Basic Data	*Example*
Market	$125,000,000
Your Company's Sales	$25,000,000
Your Market Share	20%
Trading Area to Be Examined	Cincinnati
Area Market in % of Total and $	4%—$5,000,000
Sales for This Area Should Be	$1,000,000
Actual Sales for This Area Are	$500,000
Expected Gain With the Right Rep	$500,000
Time to Reach National Market Share	2 years
% Pretax Contribution	
Fixed Overhead as % of Sales	15%
Fixed SG&A	7%
Pretax Income	8%
Pretax Contribution	30%
Actual $ and % Return	
Pretax Contribution per Dollar Sales	$.30
Incremental Sales	$500,000
Pretax Return	$150,000
Evaluated Cost of Search	$30,000
With the right rep, your return is	500%
_____% within _____years	in 2 years

reach breakeven, 30 cents of each incremental dollar would go toward decreasing your company's loss.

Let's also assume that you invested $30,000 of evaluated time and effort in conducting a highly intensive rep search program in order to help ensure that the best available candidate in the territory is identified and recruited. This means that a $30,000 investment would yield a $150,000 operating income return within the second year. The 500 percent return in the second year is vastly superior to the great majority of investments any corporation can make. We have not found any other investment that can offer such a high return to a company for so little risk—and you normally don't have to spend anywhere near $30,000 to find the right rep.

Figure 6-1 graphically portrays a typical recovery in terms of sales by replacing the underperforming rep with a very well-matched rep that is properly supported. For a two-year turnaround, the rep will be performing at somewhat under the national market share average for the first part of the second year and then perform above the market share average for the remainder of that year. The result is your national market share average for year two.

Figure 6-1   Sales recovery duration.

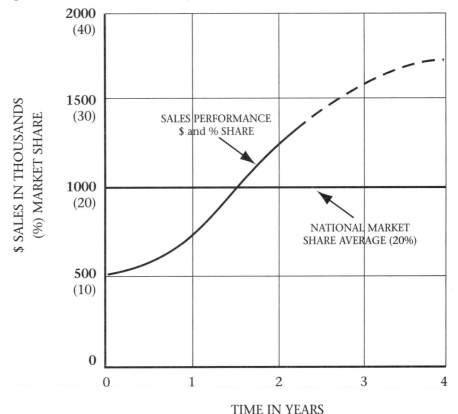

The bonus occurs because the recovery typically carries performance through the national market share *average* to a higher level. The amount of the bonus depends on your company's market share potential. This can be determined by analyzing the various market shares that your reps have. For a company having a 20 percent market share, the shares in the various trading areas throughout the United States can very well vary from 5 percent to 35 percent. Presuming the scenario in the best performing area does not contain a nonreproducible reason for its sales performance excellence, the newly recruited rep may very well reach the 35 percent market share level if properly supported. This may then result in the territory yielding $1.75 million in sales rather than just $1 million over the ensuing one to two years after reaching the 20 percent share level.

The bottom line: Leave no stone unturned to find that best available rep in all important territories.

A Search Anomaly

The anomaly that exists in a rep search is that manufacturers typically invest more time and effort in recruiting a direct salesperson than they do in recruiting an independent rep. The opposite is required. Manufacturers can recruit a highly talented direct salesperson who does not precisely match their needs with little risk because they can train that individual and direct time allocation to specific markets. Successful reps, on the other hand, will not substantially change what they are doing or how they are doing it for the great majority of new manufacturers taken on. A fit of independent rep and manufacturer must therefore be much more precise than that between direct salesperson and manufacturer.

The two critical steps in selecting the right rep are:

1. Define a model of the ideal rep by which candidates can be compared.
2. Develop and implement a highly aggressive methodology for rep search that helps ensure that the top candidates in each territory are identified and interviewed in order to select that one best available candidate.

This chapter addresses Step 1—defining a profile of the ideal rep. Chapter 7 defines how you can find and hire the best available rep.

A Model

Normally, for a given product and market combination, there is a specific class or type of representative that will best fit a manufacturer's needs.

Within that class, you want to find the *best* rep available in *each* trading area for *each* priority target. To do that, define the characteristics that are required to achieve success with your product line—in other words, a profile of your ideal rep. Surprisingly, many companies omit this most critical step.

The "ideal rep" profile will be a model you will use in your rep search. You may not be able to find the exact match, but going through the mechanics of the modeling exercise will help you select the best from the available candidates. You can use the model quantitatively, in a methodology that allows a mathematical analysis of alternative candidates, or qualitatively. Most companies choose a more qualitative approach to the evaluation process, since many of the variables in evaluating a rep are judgmental.

Characteristics discussed here might be called the foundation blocks for locating and selecting the very best rep for your needs. If any of these elements is missing in a candidate, there are significant risks that rep will not be as effective as desired. In the major trading areas throughout the country, you can usually find strong rep candidates with excellent credentials in most, if not all, of these key foundation characteristics.

All the characteristics discussed here should be considered as you develop a model of the ideal rep. Then, to determine the exact profile of the ideal rep for the product and market under consideration, it is up to you to decide the priority of the various characteristics. Where they fall in priority rank may differ somewhat with each product and market segment.

Does the Rep Firm Have Successful, Professional Sales Capability?

One of the basic reasons for going to a rep firm is that it gives you access to highly experienced and successful sales talent who have made a career out of selling in their home territory. For most, if not all, major trading areas, truly professional sales representatives can be found who fit the primary criteria most manufacturers want in a rep.

This does not mean that you should necessarily rule out a rep with less-than-solid sales experience. For example, let's consider a rep firm that was founded by the former chief engineer of a highly compatible company three years ago. In that three-year period, this chief engineer has rapidly demonstrated a flair for selling, and sales growth has been dramatic. If the chief engineer's background, other than her lack of sales experience, exactly fits the technical profile you require, then this firm could be a very strong candidate, particularly if the nature of the products required a strong technical rep. In certain cases, the technical experience might even be more important than sales experience.

Does the Firm Have In-Depth Contacts With Your Market Targets?

Long-term continuity with your key customers has been defined as one of the major advantages of working through reps. You should generally not even consider a rep that does not have these usable contacts. Even the chief-engineer-turned-rep should have in-depth market contacts developed from her engineering role over the years. These contacts should then have been sharpened during her short tenure as a rep.

The rep's current business and projected activities should match your market targets. Relative market priorities should be the same for both rep and manufacturer. Just because a rep calls on a market does not mean that rep spends the amount of time necessary to build the influential contacts required to influence the sale of your product. The key is the rep's ability to use contacts, not just to have them. Reps can demonstrate this by pointing to the results they have achieved for other manufacturers with their key customers over a fairly long period. These other manufacturers and key customer personnel can verify this capability.

Does the Rep Firm Have Compatible Products?

A compatible product may be defined as a product or service sold by the representative for another manufacturer that has the same market priorities as your product line, has its procurement influenced by the same individuals in the customer's hierarchy, is directly related to your product line in the customer's process (for example, the product would go on the same production system as yours), and ideally requires rep discussion with the customer *before* your product enters into the purchase cycle. This last characteristic usually will not be present, but when it is, it's a wonderful benefit, for it gives you an early indicator that an opportunity is emerging for your product line.

Identifying compatible products early in your search process has another benefit. One of the major ways of identifying compatible reps is to search for those that represent compatible product lines. The compatible-product definition is critical for selecting the right rep and also for evaluating the existing rep network. Unless the rep has demonstrated success in compatible products, there is a good chance that rep will not be successful with yours. What other aspects of compatibility should you look for? Here are three more, but there may be others that are applicable to your company in particular.

1. *Order gestation.* Reps with a short-term mentality generally focus their business on product lines with a short buying cycle. Generally they will not be successful with your company if the buying cycle for your

products is long. Many reps (just as many direct salespeople) do not have the emotional profile to enjoy long-gestation projects or the patience to stay with them. Unless they see a prompt commission return for their invested effort, they will not spend the time required to penetrate that opportunity.

It is definitely *not* true that *all* reps have a short-term mentality. Many reps working in many industries will happily invest what is required to close long-gestation projects as long as their return compensates fairly for their time investment.

One of the keys for success on long-term projects is that reps have been in business long enough to have a backlog of commissions that pays not only today's bills but many of those of the next one to three years. This allows them to work on a number of projects with long payoffs. Also, many of these reps will complement long-lead-time principals with a sprinkling of shorter cycle ones to smooth out their cash flow.

There is one exception to this need for an established rep to handle long-term projects. Occasionally, a new rep firm has personnel who ideally satisfy a manufacturer's needs but lacks the necessary working capital to invest the type of time and effort required to blanket a long-gestation-time project. In these cases, a manufacturer might offer an advance against future commissions to provide the rep with the working capital to invest the time required by the manufacturer. This approach can work extremely well.

2. *Contract size and commission rate.* These characteristics tend to come naturally with compatible product lines. A rep who typically sells $500 to $1,000 items at 20 to 30 percent commission will tend to have a problem handling contracts that average $500,000 to $1 million and pay $2^1/2$ to 5 percent. The problem lies both in the major differences involved in selling the two product types that differ so greatly in price and in the aversion reps have to commission rates that are much lower than those they currently receive.

3. *Cost versus value selling.* Compatibility of product also means that the appeals used in the sales process should be similar. Some reps are not value oriented in their selling approach. Their strength is essentially in selling "me too" products on the appeal of low price. These reps are a natural fit with manufacturers of commodity products or products that offer no unique benefits other than a low price.

If your company needs a rep that sells the highest priced product based on its real or perceived value to a customer, the preferred rep should have already demonstrated this capability by successfully selling products for manufacturers of products having similar needs over an extended period.

The bottom line: Compatibility of product is therefore a two-step process. First, products have to be generically compatible. Second, one must determine which manufacturers within a given product class are most compatible with your products or services. There is no more critical undertaking in rep search than this compatibility definition.

Does the Rep Firm Have the Appropriate Technical Capability?

This is not the same as technical knowledge of your specific product. Technical capability means that the rep has the ability to assimilate rapidly the technical aspects of your own or other similar product lines. That capability comes from academic and work experience, personal temperament, and the knowledge gained from representing other manufacturers in current market targets. For example, a rep with a background in chemical process design with a heavy emphasis on systems that handle corrosive and abrasive slurries could very quickly learn the basics of a slurry pump line that he has never handled before.

Specific product knowledge, while highly desirable and frequently attainable, is really not as important as closeness to the buyers and specifiers combined with a strong technical capability to assimilate a product rapidly. This is frequently not well grasped by manufacturers of highly technical products.

Does the Rep Firm Have Adequate Knowledge of Your Product?

The ideal rep will know and understand your product in the depth required to sell all targeted industries properly. This knowledge might come from prior background as a corporate employee or experience as a rep handling your type of products. The highest chance of finding such people is in the major trading areas, where there are many more specialized reps.

Even in fairly small product/market situations, such product expertise is frequently found. One small profit center of a Fortune 500 company needed reps for its analytical online process analyzers. This was a rather small, highly specialized industry, primarily serving the chemical and petrochemical industry. In the New England trading area, the organization found three separate rep firms that had exceptional degrees of product knowledge of the analyzers in question. The owner of one firm had designed and developed the same type of analyzers as an engineer and then as an officer of a research firm. As a rep she had been selling similar analytical instrumentation for sixteen years. The owner of the second firm was formerly a sales manager and marketing manager for a major competitor. His firm had been heavily involved in analytical equipment for thirteen years. The third owner, of a relatively new rep organization, had previously been product manager for a major competitor as well as product manager and marketing manager for allied equipment at another manufacturer. In addition, the search identified several other representatives with histories of ten to fifteen years of experience in similar analytical instruments. Clearly, a sound search program in major trading areas typically finds reps with excellent product knowledge as well as specific technical capabilities.

There will be many situations, however, where one will not be able to locate a qualified and interested rep who has a background in your company's specific products or services. While such knowledge is preferred, it is not a make-or-break situation in rep success. For decades, it has been clearly understood by both business executives and academics that knowledge of the customer is much more important than knowledge of the product. If one cannot find a rep who has the specific product knowledge, the objective then is to locate one who has all of the necessary compatible products and the technical ability to rapidly assimilate your product line combined with being associated with a rep firm whose objectives are compatible with your company's. This minimum required characteristic is readily available through a sound search effort.

Does the Rep Firm Handle Any Competing Lines?

Straightforward contract language usually states that representatives may not handle any competing lines. It sounds simple, but in fact a rather large degree of subjectivity is used in defining whether a product is truly competing or truly compatible. This definition is critical and therefore must be carefully assessed.

Other Important Characteristics

In addition to the "building blocks" described above, there are many other characteristics that can be considered in developing the profile of the ideal rep. The list here is not intended to be complete, but merely to stimulate thought. You should sit down and develop a complete list of characteristics you feel are important in your particular product/market situation.

Purity of the Business

Manufacturers that wish their reps to perform only one function—selling their products or services—should have reps who are not distracted by other business activities. It is not unusual to find reps growing into a number of different business spin-offs: product service, value-added functions (including assembly of components into subassemblies or finished packages), manufacturing their own products, and a number of satellite ventures that may not be at all related to selling products. For example, it is not unusual to find really successful reps in real estate and other financial ventures. All of these ventures take time away from the primary focus, at least for the owners of the rep firm—the very ones who usually are the most important to you.

On the other hand, changing market demands now require that manufacturers furnish a variety of services on a local level. Where such services do not well fit a manufacturer's capability, finding a rep who offers those services can provide significant competitive advantage.

Manufacturing can be a particular distraction, for rep firm owners can see the potential for much greater income from manufacturing than from sales commissions. This can influence the rep firm's sales personnel, as they try to help the owners build the manufacturing business. Service capability by the rep can also create some very troublesome situations. Most professional reps rank extremely high in loyalty, professionalism, integrity, and ethics, but that same high road has not always been taken in service. Although I have seen it only as a rare exception, the sale of replacement parts can be a problem. This may occur if the manufacturer's parts can be easily copied or if a major segment of the parts business can be directly purchased by a rep from suppliers to the manufacturer, then marked up and resold to customers, completely bypassing the manufacturer.

Reps receive a straight commission for selling a manufacturer's part, typically 5–20 percent, depending on the company. The manufacturer's gross margin on manufactured parts is typically very high, and even the gross margin on parts purchased for resale is frequently higher than the original-equipment gross margin. By buying parts directly from the parts supplier and reselling them to the customer, the rep can double or triple the income on the sale. Obviously, manufacturers must be vigilant in this type of situation.

Loyalty and Integrity

You wouldn't really want a rep who didn't display these two important traits, but how do you determine if they are present? A major indicator is the rep's tenure with the manufacturers it represents (particularly the top-of-the-line manufacturers) and the tenure of qualified sales personnel. If this tenure is long, you can reasonably assume that the rep does a good job of business management and has a history of loyalty, integrity, and professionalism.

If there is any question, you can always interview the rep's principals or customers. While it may be difficult to get a totally candid appraisal of reps from another manufacturer, if there is a major problem, the conversations usually reveal it.

Life Cycle and Maturity

The life cycle of the firm and the ages of its members are generally interrelated. There are all degrees of age and maturity in reps. Many manufacturers prefer to have "young tigers" selling for them. Others value the "old pros" for their long-term contacts and demonstrated ability to influence purchasing decisions.

For most manufacturers, the ideal rep organization would exhibit a balance of ages. A well-balanced four-person operation (a fairly average size) in a major trading area might have two principals in their mid-fifties who started the business ten to fifteen years ago and two younger sales personnel in their thirties or forties who have been with the firm four to eight years. Many organizations have what might be called three generations. At the top is a part-time president whose partner may have retired some years ago. There are then two or three individuals in their late forties to early fifties who have been with the firm an average of fifteen years. Finally, there are several younger salespeople, in their mid-thirties to early forties, with the shortest tenure of this younger group in the three- to four-year range.

Now let's bring in the life cycle of the rep firm itself. In the earlier phases, the owners' primary objective is to develop a cash flow to give them some breathing room. They will scramble in a number of different directions, not necessarily closely related, to assemble lines and develop the cash flow required for survival.

In this earlier period, many manufacturers are able to get commitments from reps to perform a number of activities or call on customer groups that really are not compatible with the rep's ideal profile. As reps start to mature and gain in liquidity, they can proceed in a much more planned manner and reject work that does not make sense in their overall business scheme. They will drop marginal product lines and move away from ineffective activities requested by manufacturers.

At this point, the founding members will have already made a conscious or subconscious decision about their growth aspirations. The really aggressive owners may have already added their first hired salesperson and may be thinking in terms of building a strong organization for the future, one that will continue after they retire. Other reps may find that they have no interest in increasing the size of their organizations. Their joy comes from selling, not from building an organization. Once they have become established, their income generally exceeds all their needs. Lifestyle can then become more important, and they may prefer not to disrupt it with the distractions of hiring and managing other people. We now have two different rep firms, both of which had the same start. One is geared to growth over the long term. The other is destined to peak at some point, then decline, and finally disappear.

To help you evaluate potential firms you will be interviewing later, it is important that you be able to assess where each is in its life cycle. Figure 6-2 depicts "life curves" for two rep firms. Both started in business fifteen years ago, but they have different growth objectives. On the chart, the fifteenth year is today; the solid lines represent actual performance, and the dashed lines a forecast. Rep #1 is the firm that has chosen lifestyle as its primary objective with no plans for continuity of the firm. Rep #2 is the growth-oriented firm.

Thus, as Rep #1 approaches the thirteenth year, it shows an abrupt drop in sales and then another drop a couple of years later. These instantaneous drops represent the cancellation of the rep by principals who have finally decided that they can no longer afford the stagnant environment provided by this rep. Other manufacturers will stay with the firm until it closes, sometime around the twentieth year.

Rep #2 has planned for growth and then achieved it, also providing for the firm's continuity. This type of firm is the ideal match for manufacturers interested in the same growth objectives. For the first several years after inception, the two rep firms may be identical. Both can show extreme aggressiveness, excellent sales capability, and a sharp increase in sales. After this start-up phase is completed, the aggressive rep firm adds personnel for continued growth. At the fifteen-year mark, it is still adding people and growing. The difference between the two curves is solely the result of differing priorities of the rep owners.

Figure 6-2   Rep life cycles.

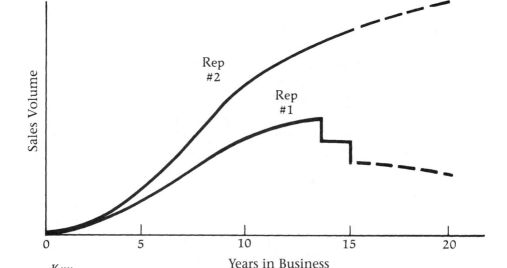

In summary, then, if you are interested in growth, your ideal rep firm will have a balance of ages, including mature owners who will retain an interest in dynamic growth.

Employee Tenure

A mistake many manufacturers make is to evaluate only the owners of the rep firm and not their employed sales personnel. Yet often the employed sales personnel are the ones primarily charged with the responsibility for selling your products.

Employee tenure is significant for two reasons. First, it tends to be a very clear indication of good management by the owners. In addition, employee tenure is the most critical ingredient for the success of any representative because most manufacturers need long-term continuity between their sales personnel and customers to obtain competitive advantage in their marketplace. Rep firms with high turnover cannot provide this continuity.

There are many well-managed reps that provide the right environment for employees to maintain tenure. There is no reason to accept a firm that has a history of two- or three-year turnover rates.

One ingredient in a rep's business management scheme that really helps the founders retain top sales talent is a provision for these top sellers to own the business partially. This should lead to a smooth transition (that is, continuity) of the business because there will be a total buy-out of the firm as each founder retires. This ownership position is a natural desire. If it is not satisfied, outstanding sales talent will frequently leave after a number of years to start their own rep firms.

Unfortunately, many rep principals refuse to allow these buy-ins despite the fact that a rep business is not asset based, and as a result, the buy-in is more a psychological reward than a real one. Nevertheless, it is important. Many of the truly top reps have buy-in provisions for employees. This situation not only allows key sales performers the psychological reward of ownership but typically leads toward a longer association, which benefits both the rep founders and the manufacturers represented.

On the other hand, it is possible for reps to develop tenure in sales personnel even if buy-in provisions do not exist. We have seen a number of outstanding reps develop long tenure in outstanding sales talent without these buy-in provisions. However, this omission is typically the only element missing from the total motivational picture. In such instances the commission sharing on each sale is usually very favorable to the salesperson. On top of that, these employees are generally offered excellent fringe benefits and profit-sharing measures combined with empathetic owner-ship.

The bottom line is that outstanding rep organizations retain their employees. Manufacturers would do well to avoid reps that have demonstrated that they cannot keep outstanding sales talent.

Manufacturer Tenure

A rep's tenure with manufacturers represented is also a key indicator of that agency's ability to produce, in every sense of the word, over the long term. This is particularly true when the rep has premier accounts, that is, the top one or two manufacturers in a number of product lines. For many industries, a top rep in business for fifteen years typically still retains one or two of its initial principals; most of its other important manufacturers fall in the four- to ten-year range.

Unless a manufacturer experiences a major shift in markets that would suggest the need for a change in reps, a high turnover of manufacturers normally indicates a poorly managed rep firm. Reps that have been in business for fifteen years and regularly keep principals only three years or so should be avoided; your company might be the next statistic.

Remember also that terminations do not take place when a poor relationship is first defined but are typically dragged out for a rather long period. Separations between reps and manufacturers at the three-year period probably indicate that there were major problems by the end of the first year.

Successorship

You may recall from Chapter 5 that fully one-third of the reps interviewed in a 1997 survey said their agency would go out of business when they retired. Most relationships between rep and manufacturer are developed with a long-term view in mind. In most cases, your ideal rep is the one who has planned for her future economic health and that of the manufacturer she represents. Obviously, the fact that two reps are in their late fifties, have been in business for fifteen years, and have yet to add an additional salesperson raises major concerns about their interest in providing a long-term, aggressive, growth-oriented firm for their principals.

To give you an extreme example, I know of one rep firm whose two founders were the only salespersons in the organization for over twenty years. In 1982 I asked them about plans to bring younger individuals into the firm, and they responded that they intended to sell for a number of years (they were then sixty-two and sixty-eight years old) and it was premature to bring others in. At that time, they represented eight significant manufacturers. Three years later, when the founders were then sixty-five and seventy-one, respectively, I learned they were starting to think of bringing somebody into the organization. They represented only five manufacturers. The surprising part is that only three of the manufacturers had terminated this organization whose growth motivation had long since dissipated.

Your Anticipated Segment of the Rep's Income

The "best rep in the area" may very well not be the best rep for you. Manufacturers that can generate only a small amount of income for a rep are typically best served by the smaller rep. This is not a hard-and-fast rule in all cases, but it has been reasonably demonstrated over the years.

It's a matter of how much attention an organization can get from a sales force. Manufacturers that generate at least 10 percent of a rep's income seem to be put into a class that gets routine attention from the reps. When the commission generation is substantially less than 10 percent, reps from a number of industries tend to treat those manufacturers as complementary lines, meaning lines that they will talk about if they have time.

There are a number of exceptions. One occurs when a rep routinely packages a number of principals together. Here, a manufacturer that contributes only a small part of the rep's income but neatly fits into the package is carried along with the rest of the sale. Another exception occurs when the products of a small manufacturer act as a key in that rep's product mix, that is, they function as a leading indicator of opportunities for other products or as a unique product that ties several others together.

The bottom line is that the smaller you are, the more exactly you have to match up to the rep's selling profile in order to receive adequate attention. In addition, you should generally look for the small rep firm where your relatively meager commissions are spread over fewer salespeople; thus, your commissions are a relatively larger percentage of each salesperson's total income.

Appropriate Support Services

The level of support services by the rep that will be necessary varies over an enormous range from industry to industry and even within industries. For some industries, a truly proficient rep may need no more than a small rented office and a good professional answering service; correspondence can be done by subcontract secretarial services. On the other end of the scale, some firms make major investments in electronic data processing, offering not just in-house computers for business control but also computer interfacing with manufacturer and customer inventories. The electronics industry particularly has seen a major expansion into high-tech services.

When you are considering the support services of your ideal rep, the key question is, Do they really make a substantive contribution to the selling function? First-class offices, for example, normally have no relationship to a rep's effectiveness, because in many industries customers are rarely brought to the rep's office. Even when they are, reps that have been highly productive for years do not have to demonstrate to customers that they can afford beautiful surroundings. Of course, there are exceptions. Occasionally, reps will do a significant amount of selling from their offices, particularly where there are major demonstrations. In this case, initial impressions may be important, and first-class quarters in readily accessible locations may become an imperative.

Appropriate Trading Areas

A necessary part of your thinking about ideal reps has to do with questions of geography. If you need reps in all the areas where your major customers are located, you must be concerned about matching up your trading areas with the rep's existing territories.

Reps that serve particular markets have their own relatively standard trading areas. It's important that you work with a map of typical trading areas in your industry. However, within each industry, there may be significant variations in trading areas of reps headquartered in the same city. If there are no maps published for your industry, you can create one by contacting manufacturers of compatible products and finding out the territories of their reps. They may even send you a copy of their map of trading areas, although they might not include the rep names. If you can define the trading areas of competitors' reps, you'll have another key input. Then each area can be fine-tuned as you interview compatible reps in each trading area.

How many trading areas do you need for national coverage? Here again there are major variations from industry to industry. Segments of the electronics industry frequently get complete national coverage with sixteen or seventeen rep organizations. General industrial products typically require anywhere from twenty-five to thirty-two separate rep organizations. The heating, ventilating, and air-conditioning industry may require fifty or more reps. Some companies require over sixty independent rep organizations, each in an exclusive trading area, for complete national coverage. Some rep organizations cover significant regions of the country, thus allowing a manufacturer to obtain national coverage with as few as three or four reps. National reps—one organization that covers the entire country—are available in certain markets.

In deciding what your own company should have in terms of trading areas, use these ground rules:

1. Know what your competitors have in terms of trading areas.
2. Determine the trading areas for manufacturers that produce compatible products.
3. Recognize that, on balance, independent organizations with the smallest territories tend to give more sustained coverage over the long term. Reps with many branch offices, covering larger territories, tend to have sales turnover problems that are not typical of the rep firms where the salespeople are also principals.

On the basis of this, you can rather quickly define the preferred trading areas for any given product and market combination.

Here's a tip for manufacturers recruiting reps for the first time: If there is an open territory adjacent to the boundaries claimed by the rep you are interviewing, always insist that the specific boundaries remain flexible until the adjoining rep is recruited.

From the Ideal to the Pragmatic

Using the characteristics discussed in this chapter as your starting point, together with your knowledge of your industry, carefully develop a list of all ingredients you feel are desirable in a manufacturers' rep. There should be anywhere from ten to twenty-five or even more characteristics contained in the profile. Once this list has been established, you are ready for the next step: developing a *pragmatic* model from the ideal.

There are two reasons for developing a more practical model from a simple list of ideal characteristics. First, the probability is close to zero that you will find a rep who not only has every characteristic listed but is clearly superior in each aspect to alternative candidates. You have to get closer to real life with the model. Second, you need to make certain that you keep your focus on those characteristics that are the best predictors of success rather than on more superficial attributes, which will only confuse the picture.

The pragmatic model can be qualitative or quantitative; even the qualitative model has to have a priority system that introduces at least a modest quantification. The choice of model depends on management philosophies and styles in decision making. The intuitive manager will lean strongly toward the qualitative assessment; the more analytical manager will lean toward the development of at least a simplified mathematical model to assist in decision making. Let's look a little at both.

The Qualitative Model

The qualitative model is nothing more than a priority ranking of all the ideal rep characteristics that you identified. I use three classes of priority:

1. An absolute must
2. Very important but not critical
3. Nice to have

The first priority is characteristics the rep *must* have to be considered a candidate. Obviously, after a thorough search of a given territory, if no single rep emerges with these top-priority classifications, a reclassification of priorities is required. At some point, one or more available candidates will have these "absolute must" characteristics. "Very important" is simply a notch behind "absolute must." It's a small but important differentiation. The third category comprises characteristics that are not truly bottom line.

How should you go about creating the three classes? Let's assume you have defined some twenty characteristics of your ideal rep. Start with the one or two that clearly emerge as "absolute musts" and one or two that are obviously "nice to have." Continue this sorting process until a predetermined percentage is reached, perhaps one third each for the two categories. When you reach the one-third point for each category, you can stop temporarily, because you have also identified the "important" class by the process of elimination.

Having made that first cut, step back and really ponder the priorities. This is best done at a consensus meeting of several people in your organization crossing functional lines, including the general manager. Each individual selected to this team should first go through the same preliminary sorting exercise. Then, as a team exercise, all should agree on primary, secondary, and tertiary characteristics.

This qualitative model then needs to be tested and adjusted to fit actual rep profiles available in different trading areas. Recognize that your model will not be applicable to all trading areas in the country; rather, it should be initially designed for the most important trading areas, where the major volume will be generated. In these major trading areas (i.e., New York, Chicago, Atlanta, Houston, Los Angeles), a much higher degree of rep specialization is available, so you have a much higher chance of finding rep candidates closest to the model. In the secondary trading areas, you might need a second model, to make sure the focus is on those few key characteristics that really make for a highly productive relationship.

The Quantitative Model

To develop a quantified model, convert the qualitative priorities into quantitative terms. For one example, you might select a scale of 1–20 as the weighting range for characteristics, giving a 1 to the least important characteristic and a 20 to the most important. You can then evaluate rep candidates against each characteristic on another number scale, say 1–10.

This simple quantitative analysis would yield scores from a low of 1 (the lowest priority characteristic and the weakest characteristic of that rep) to a maximum of 200 (the most important characteristic and the strongest rep characteristic). Then summarize ratings of all the rep candidates, and you will have a bottom-line number comparing candidates.

The major danger is too much reliance on the numbers formula. The variables involved here are, after all, somewhat subjective. The key is to arrive at a system of converting the ideal model to a pragmatic model in which you have faith.

As your organization changes along with changes in the world around you, the model will require upgrading. At a minimum, it should be reevaluated on an annual basis, more often if something happens that suggests the model may no longer be completely valid. If there are major changes in the marketplace or in your product or market priorities, you may need to select new reps, which means starting the process over again. A key point is to be as specific as you can in defining each characteristic. Without specificity, the model's potential contribution is very much weakened. For an example, let's look at the concept of compatible product lines.

A gross overgeneralization would be to say simply that your reps must have "compatible product lines." To be really useful, this characteristic must be expanded with great care because it is one of the most critical characteristics of a rep that will bring about success for your company.

First, identify generic product classes that are most compatible with your product. For example, a manufacturer of thermostats focused on the electric heating OEM market would want to select electric heating elements as a generic class. The next key step is to identify manufacturers within that generic product classification that are very similar to your company when it comes to the type of selling required for success.

Having identified these truly compatible manufacturers, you can then identify their reps. This is a major starting point for accumulating a list of possible rep candidates. However, be cautious about one item: Just because you have identified a compatible manufacturer, do not assume that the manufacturer has done the right job in rep selection. All you have achieved at this step is identification of a rep who may be a candidate.

The Next Step

You have now profiled the type of rep that will fit your short- and long-term needs. You are to be congratulated. An amazing number of companies omit this crucial step. Now you are ready to move on to Step 4, where you will identify candidates that match your profile and interview them to select the very best. You may not find reps that align with your ideal in every single respect, but you can come close—at least in the main trading areas where most of your market is located. The fact that you have undertaken the profiling process will make the search much more successful.

7

How to Find and Hire the Best

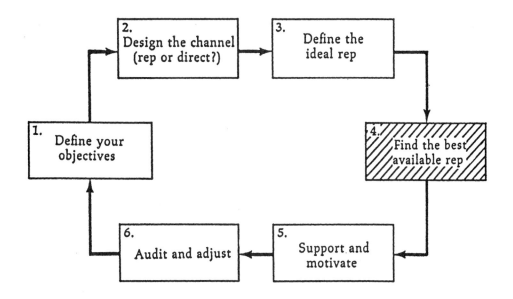

The entire process of developing a truly productive rep sales force can be summarized in eight words: Pick the right reps and support them well. This chapter will deal with picking the right rep, Step 4 of our six-step systems approach for increasing your sales and profit.

As we noted earlier, manufacturers usually devote significantly less attention to selecting reps than they would to hiring direct sales personnel, when they should do just the opposite. Remember, you can mold a direct salesperson to do things your way, but with the established, successful rep, what you get should be viewed as essentially unchangeable. Therefore, to be confident that reps will really be working those industries and accounts in the way you want, you must choose those that share your objectives going in.

It is not off base to say that most bad experiences with sales reps could have been avoided if the company had hired the right rep in the first place. Therefore it is vitally important that you do a thorough job of locating the perfect reps: Search all possible sources for candidate names, uncover all the information you can about them and how they work, and bring all your corporate wisdom to bear on the problem of selecting the ones that come closest to your ideal vision. A poorly conceived or superficially conducted search program will produce mediocrity—or worse. An intelligent, aggressive search program will yield bountiful results.

You may be tempted at this point to utter a protest about cost. Yes, it's true that a thorough search program will involve both time and dollars, but think what you get from that investment. In Chapter 6, we demonstrated that in a highly representative situation for a company that was generating only $500,000 in sales in a given territory, or a 10 percent market share when the national average was 20 percent, sales could be doubled within the second year by picking and then supporting the right rep. An evaluated investment of $30,000 in time and effort could yield a $150,000 impact on bottom line in the second year, a truly outstanding investment by any company. In most cases, the investment—even when using a search consultant for assistance—will not exceed $15,000. This includes the search fee and your time, plus associated expenses for interviewing. So, proceed in the faith that the results will more than justify the cost.

A Search Methodology

Unless you already know all the available candidates, finding the best available rep in a given territory is not a simple task. Even then, a segment of the rep population is in constant change because of breakups, mergers, and new formations, so that a clear picture of candidates in any one area becomes rapidly foggy as a function of time. You must make haste slowly in a rep search program if you intend to use performance excellence as the major criterion. The right rep will help you achieve high performance. A mediocre rep will prevent excellent performance. A poor match will drag you down.

A sound approach to a search involves six components. Briefly, they are:

1. *Commitment.* Management must be committed to giving each search the full dedication and resources needed.
2. *Planning.* The search program should be planned in detail so that all involved agree on the key steps to be followed.
3. *Responsibility.* Specific responsibilities are to be assigned.

4. *Search.* All available sources should be used to develop a list of all potentially compatible representatives for each trading area.
5. *Screening.* The candidates should be screened in stages, to narrow the list to a select few. The top candidates should be interviewed in depth to develop a sound picture of comparative strengths and weaknesses.
6. *Selection.* The best available rep should be selected.

Management Commitment

The senior executive in the profit center, whether division manager or president, should have a complete understanding of the search program and should be a participant in select segments, particularly in the high-potential trading areas. This commitment is needed to ensure that the necessary time and resource allocation is available to do a proper search.

The senior executive should be involved in selective interviews. Again, this should be primarily in the major trading areas. This serves two purposes. First, rep candidates will clearly see that your company is dedicated to reps because the profit center manager has taken the time to interview them. Second, it keeps the senior executive in close touch with the reality of the marketplace and how reps are able to contribute. Reps' comments during the interviews also represent an opportunity to hear an objective view of the marketplace, which will be valued by executives who welcome outside viewpoints to widen their perspective.

Planning the Search Program

If the search program is to be undertaken totally within your organization, those who will be involved should agree on the methodology. This methodology should also be put in writing. This will help to minimize the shortcutting of what has been demonstrated over the years to be sound search practices. It is just too easy for a regional manager or national sales manager to say, "I know these guys. They're good." The statement may be true, but frequently there will be even better candidates available.

Picking a rep from a sample of one is typically done because a manager has certain biases, usually based on a historic relationship. That introduces subjectivity. Success in picking reps comes from the ability to objectively compare strengths and weaknesses of highly compatible reps that are very interested in representing your company.

Even when search consultants are retained, elements of the search should be clearly agreed upon and the relationship of the consultant with your management personnel clearly spelled out.

Assigning Responsibilities

Clear responsibility should be assigned for each of the tasks in the program. The senior sales executive should have the ultimate responsibility for the selection. Then, depending upon the size and staffing of the organization, responsibilities can be separated into discrete tasks. For example, in larger companies, the research for candidate names can be assigned to a staff function. Others in the organization should have responsibility for submitting names to this single focal point. For example, regional managements should be constantly developing lists of contacts and feeding them to a central collection and data storage point. In a smaller company, where the senior sales executive is also the marketing manager, the regional manager, and marketing staff wrapped up into one, the responsibility becomes evident.

At times, the president is also the sales manager in a small firm. Because careful rep selection is even more important to the small firm than to the large manufacturer, the president needs to be very actively involved. If she doesn't have a near perfect fit with the best available rep, her small firm will lose a major growth opportunity. Recruiting really top reps is greatly aided by the activist president of the small company.

Searching for Candidates

There are many sources of candidate names. The key is to conduct a thorough search of these sources to identify as many compatible candidates as reasonably possible. To get a sound candidate list, manufacturers generally need a mix of sources.

The most commonly used sources for collecting rep candidate names appear here, broken down into primary and secondary classifications.[1] "Primary" means sources that yield the highest number of candidates for many companies.

Primary Sources

There are four primary sources of rep candidates that can, depending on the situation, help identify excellent candidates.

1. *Key customers and specifiers*. These are particularly valuable if the number of buyers and specifiers in a given trading area is few and very

[1]These classifications are based on assessments made by approximately 2,000 companies that attended seminars on independent reps conducted by Harold Novick over a ten-year period for continuing executive education programs at the University of Wisconsin and for other organizations.

important. In many cases telephone interviews will be sufficient. However, at times customers are reluctant to give references over the telephone; this may require face-to-face visits. In other cases, particularly at larger corporations, references of any form have become increasingly difficult. For years, human resource departments have advised their executives not to say anything negative about an employee or an organization who was associated with their company. More recently, "no comment" is being heard even when the individual firm has been a top producer. Customer references have therefore substantially declined as a major source of candidate names. Nevertheless, it's certainly worth a try.

Don't ask for names right away. Start by describing the type of capabilities (i.e., the required characteristics of your ideal rep profile) you feel a rep should have to serve your customers' needs best. Then ask if this profile contains all of the elements that customer wishes to have in a sales representative. Once they buy in to the profile, the question can then be raised, Which reps call on you now who best fit this profile? With this type of preconditioning, customers will not automatically think purely in terms of specific people they know. But they will think of people who really have the capabilities of serving the company's needs. Without this preconditioning, "hip-shot" responses too frequently include names of reps that really don't fit your needs. Only after there is an agreement on the type of rep that can best serve that company should the customer be asked for specific recommendations.

There are two concerns here. First, if a customer strongly urges a particular representative and you do not select that rep, there is a chance your business relationships with this firm can be damaged. Fortunately, this is the exception rather than the rule. A second and more minor reservation is the potential bias that can occur because of friendships between customer personnel and reps. Use of the model and alternative search techniques can normally verify whether the recommendation is sound.

When there are many customers in an area, this source is not nearly as important. Also, if you do not have a significant position in the market, there is a good chance that you may not know which potential customers to talk to.

2. *Rep directories.* A routine tool in many search campaigns is a directory of reps organized by geography or by industry. A number of excellent sources exist. The Recommended References list at the end of this book lists organizations that provide directories with rep lists. Figures 7-1 and 7-2 show typical pages from two directories, one published by the Manufacturers' Agents National Association (MANA) and one by the Electronic Representatives Association (ERA). The MANA Directory is also available on CD-ROM.

Rep directories, like other sources, have a weakness: They cannot in-

(Text continues on page 114.)

Figure 7-1   Samples from the MANA Rep Directory.

JUNTA INDUSTRIAL MARKETING
25W155 Geneva Rd., Wheaton, IL 60187-2322.
James A. Junta. (630) 260-0930, *Fax:* (630)
260-1450
Services Offered: After Sales Service, Market
Research, Technical, Promotion.
Customers: Distribution/Dealers/Mass
Marketers, Government, OEM.
Products Sold: Material handling equipment,
lifting equipment, janitorial equipment, dock /
packaging equipment, industrial supplies,
safety / ergonomic equipment, recycling
containers.
Salespeople: 2.
Territory: IL; WI; MN; Upper Peninsula MI.
Est.: 1980. *MANA:* 1989

W.F. JUST CO., INC.
5029 W. 56th St., Minneapolis, MN 55436-2425.
William Just. (612) 925-1220, *Fax:* (612) 925-
9179
Customers: End Users, OEM.
Products Sold: Perforated metal, foam / cork
tape, special circular bronze parts, springs,
wire forms, hardware, forgings, die cut parts,
shims, wire products, hinge, gaskets.
Salespeople: 1.
Territory: MN; ND; SD.
Est.: 1965. *MANA:* 1969

JIM JUSTICE & ASSOCS.
P.O. Box 14107, Palm Desert, CA 92255-4107.
Jim Justice. (760) 772-0826, *Fax:* (760) 772-
0836
Email: jyjustice@aol.com
Services Offered: Market Research,
Promotion, Warehousing.
Customers: Contractors, Distribution/Dealers/
Mass Marketers, OEM.
Products Sold: Window / door products, spiral
balances; injection molded / die cast parts;
acrylic block windows / panels; knocked down
sliding, french patio doors.
Salespeople: 3.
Territory: CA; AZ; NV; UT; CO; NM; ID; WY;
HI.
Branch Offices: Denver, CO.
Est.: 1986. *MANA:* 1987

K

KBM, INC.
P.O. Box 98, Weston, MA 02193. Karl B.
Malafey. (781) 444-9660, *Fax:* (888) 253-8367
Website: thomasregional.com/one/kbmamerica
Services Offered: After Sales Service,
Installation, Technical, Warehousing.
Customers: Contractors, Distribution/Dealers/
Mass Marketers, End Users, Government, OEM.
Products Sold: Industrial process controls for
food, dairy, electronic metal finishing, general
industry, textiles, pharmaceutical, medical
research (genetics), temperature, pressure,
flow, test equipment, wastewater.
Salespeople: 5.
Territory: MA; ME; NH; RI; CT; VT.
Branch Offices: Belmont, NH.
Est.: 1975. *MANA:* 1976

K B SPECIALTY METALS
505 Regan Dr., East Dundee, IL 60118. Kevin
Robert Bordner. (847) 844-9388
Services Offered: After Sales Service, Market
Research, Promotion.
Customers: Automotive/Truck, Contractors,
Distribution/Dealers/Mass Marketers, End
Users, OEM.
Products Sold: Steel tubing: carbon, stainless,
special alloys, steel related products.
Salespeople: 4.
Territory: IL; IA; WI; MI.
Branch Offices: Schaumburg, IL.
Est.: 1995. *MANA:* 1998

K-C ASSOCS.
P.O. Box 1185, Arlington Heights, IL 60006-
1185. Carl H. Maysack. (847) 670-0256, *Fax:*
(847) 670-0260
Email: maysack@ix.netcom.com
Customers: OEM.
Products Sold: Plastic extrusions, injection /
molding, compounded resins; aluminum / zinc
die castings; perforated / fabricated metal,
coatings.
Salespeople: 1.
Territory: IL; WI.
Est.: 1990. *MANA:* 1995

K.C.H. CO.
800 Compton Rd., Ste. 3, Cincinnati, OH 45231.
Kenneth C. Hoffman, Jr. (513) 931-1686, *Fax:*
(513) 931-1691
Email: kchco@msn.com
Services Offered: Technical, Promotion,
Warehousing.
Customers: Automotive/Truck, Distribution/
Dealers/Mass Marketers, End Users,
Government, OEM.
Products Sold: Motors, belts, bearings, cases
(aluminum / plastic), clutches, power supplies,
safety products / switches, connectors,
actuators, linear bearings / slides, motion
controller, drives / gearboxes.
Salespeople: 5.
Territory: OH; W. PA; WV; KY; IN; MI.
Branch Offices: Pittsburg, PA
Est.: 1981. *MANA:* 1986

K.C. SALES
46 W. Hudson Ave., Englewood, NJ 07631-
1719. John Henry Schreiner. (201) 567-2392,
Fax: (201) 871-2297
Services Offered: Technical.
Customers: Distribution/Dealers/Mass
Marketers, End Users, OEM.
Products Sold: Contractors / starters, printed
circuit boards, battery systems, UPS, digital /
analog panel meters, transducers, protective
relays, PLCs, transformers, telecom power
systems.
Salespeople: 1.
Territory: N. / S. NJ; E. PA; NY - Orange,
Rockland counties.
Est.: 1993. *MANA:* 1995

KGA ENGINEERING CO., INC.
1008 N. Milwaukee Ave., P.O. Box 710,
Libertyville, IL 60048. Donald L. Watson. (847)
367-5700, *Fax:* (847) 367-0675
Email: kgaeng@aol.com
Services Offered: Computer, Market Research,
Promotion.
Customers: Contractors, Distribution/Dealers/
Mass Marketers, End Users, OEM.
Products Sold: Electrical products:
enclosures, power / safety products,
transformers, power supplies, connectors,
cables, accessories.
Salespeople: 7.
Territory: IL; IA; IN; WI.
Branch Offices: Decatur, IL; Rockford, IL.
Est.: 1953. *MANA:* 1992
*For further information see ad in IL in the
Geographic Section.*

K & H SALES CO., INC.
7804 Conser, P.O. Box 4097, Overland Park,
KS 66204. Charles W. Hubbard. (913) 642-
9564
Products Sold: Machined parts; moulds (build
/ run injection); sheet metal (short run /
stamping, metalworking).
Salespeople: 1.
Territory: Kansas City, KS; Dallas, TX;
Oklahoma City, OK; Denver, CO.
Branch Offices: Plano, TX.
Est.: 1988. *MANA:* 1988

K & L AGENCY, INC.
4325 Vestview Ln., Birmingham, AL 35242-

2553. Ken H. Laurendine. (205) 969-1388, *Fax:*
(205) 969-1388
Email: klaurendin@aol.com
Customers: Automotive/Truck, Distribution/
Dealers/Mass Marketers, Government, OEM.
Products Sold: Casting, plastic molding,
gears, machining, screw machining, metal
stampings.
Salespeople: 2.
Territory: AL; TN; GA; MS.
Est.: 1985. *MANA:* 1985

KLS SALES
251 Currier Dr., Orange, CT 06477. Ken B.
Schultz. (203) 795-6210, *Fax:* (203) 799-3195
Customers: Automotive/Truck, End Users,
OEM.
Products Sold: Fine / ultra fine diameter wire:
gold / silver plated, enamel coated; wire cloth
(woven / knitted); fabricated wire cloth; wire
harnesses; wire forms.
Salespeople: 1.
Territory: CT; MA; ME; VT; RI; NH; NY; NJ; PA;
NC; SC; MD; DE.
Est.: 1976. *MANA:* 1982

K-MOORE SALES ASSOCIATES
593 Mahalo Ct., Bastrop, TX 78602. Kendall
Moore. (512) 321-4577, (800) 856-1586, *Fax:*
(512) 321-4575
Services Offered: After Sales Service, Market
Research, Promotion, Other.
Customers: Distribution/Dealers/Mass
Marketers.
Products Sold: Building material products &
services.
Salespeople: 5.
Territory: TX; LA; OK; AR.
Est.: 1989. *MANA:* 1995

K & P SALES ENGINEERS, INC.
P.O. Box 11945, Glendale, AZ 85318-1945.
William Molden. (602) 572-9098, *Fax:* (602)
572-9113
Email: kpsales@aol.com
Services Offered: After Sales Service,
Technical, Warehousing.
Customers: Distribution/Dealers/Mass
Marketers, End Users, OEM.
Products Sold: Bulk material handling,
process controls.
Salespeople: 2.
Territory: NM; AZ; W. TX.
Branch Offices: Albuquerque, NM.
Est.: 1980. *MANA:* 1993

K & P SALES ENGINEERS, INC.
777 Nile St., Golden, CO 80401. Stan A.
Tredway. (303) 279-7777, *Fax:* (303) 279-1303
Services Offered: After Sales Service,
Installation, Technical, Warehousing.
Customers: Contractors, Distribution/Dealers/
Mass Marketers, End Users, OEM.
Products Sold: Weighing systems, bulk
material handling, level controls, vibrating
feeders / screens; batch weighing loadout
systems, metal detectors, magnetic separators.
Salespeople: 3.
Territory: CO; E. WY; E. MT; W. SD; W. NE
Est.: 1980. *MANA:* 1989

K & P SALES ENGINEERS, INC.
P.O. Box 577, Sandy, UT 84091-0577. Robert
M. Keddington. (801) 571-8322, (800) 758-
8322, *Fax:* (801) 571-0297
Services Offered: After Sales Service,
Installation, Warehousing.
Customers: Contractors, End Users, OEM.
Products Sold: Scales, samplers, screens,
feeders, gates, train loadouts, conveyor safety
switches, grinding mills, classifiers, pneumatic
conveying, industrial vacuums, fans, dust
collectors, crushers.
Salespeople: 4.
Territory: UT; ID; NV; WY; MT.
Est.: 1978. *MANA:* 1980

Phone: (612) 472-1763. *Products Sold:* Lubricants - name brand / private label; tie down devices, lubrication equipment, fuel pumps / nozzles, bulk containers, automotive chemicals, automotive aftermarket products.

ASSOCIATED MANUFACTURERS' REPRESENTATIVES - Villa Park, IL. *Phone:* (630) 530-7180. *Products Sold:* Special fasteners, springs, clamps, stampings from design thru proto-type, production; fine blanking, investment castings, cable, engineered cable assembly.

CHARLES D. ATWATER ASSOCS., INC. - Crystal Lake, IL. *Phone:* (815) 356-5075. *Products Sold:* Transformer / electric motor components, plastic injection molded parts, screw machine, powdered metal, soft ferrites, stampings, rubber molded parts, bobbins.

AUTOMATION CONCEPTS INT'L., LLC. - Carmel, IN. *Phone:* (317) 848-7008. *Products Sold:* Welding automation devices, systems, micro - plasma, mico - tig, flux recovery, weldwire, gas purification, weld process development, automation conceptualizing, welding manufacturing process evaluation.

AUTOMOTIVE SALES GROUP, INC. - Troy, MI. *Phone:* (248) 729-2200. *Products Sold:* Original equipment to all automotive manufacturers / tier I suppliers in the automotive industry.

AVALANCHE, INC. - Hudson, WI. *Phone:* (715) 386-6245. *Products Sold:* Components used in the production of windows / doors.

B&B INTERNATIONAL CORP. - Omaha, NE. *Phone:* (402) 334-2482. *Products Sold:* Electrical hardware / service; global positioning satellite applications hardware / software; electro / mechanical hardware / service.

B F E COMPANY - Stillwater, MN. *Phone:* (612) 351-0215. *Products Sold:* Material handling equipment, primarily for use in automated unit load handling systems.

BFM EQUIPMENT SALES, LLC - Fall River, WI. *Phone:* (920) 484-3341. *Products Sold:* Equipment / supplies for use in the processing of food.

BJ & ASSOCS. - Palatine, IL. *Phone:* (847) 963-9575. *Products Sold:* Process dryers, thermal oxidizers, catalytic oxidizers for VOC's, fans, mixers, solvent recovery systems, non-hazardous cleaning solutions, backup propane systems, flare / flare systems.

BPSR, INC. - Crystal Lake, IL. *Phone:* (815) 459-4785. *Products Sold:* Heating elements, insulation, replacement parts for the metals industry; mold insulation for rubber, plastic mold builder, molders; laboratory furnaces, ovens.

B & P SALES, INC. - Indianapolis, IN. *Phone:* (317) 577-2477. *Products Sold:* Automatic pool cleaners, electric motors, fiber-optic pool lighting specialty chemicals, alternative pool sanitizers, spa accessories, internet access, web page design.

BSI, LTD. - Bettendorf, IA. *Phone:* (319) 332-5377. *Products Sold:* Drives, instrumentation, controls, components, OEM.

B.T.B., INC. - Palatine, IL. *Phone:* (847) 359-0452. *Products Sold:* Metal shearing, slitting tooling; alloy wear parts; tungsten carbide rolls, wearparts; grinding services; tooling storage cabinets, boxes; custom fabrication, process machinery building.

BTU CO., INC. - Prairie Village, KS. *Phone:* (913) 362-8540. *Products Sold:* Custom engineered products - utility, cogeneration, public works, petrochemical, gas transmission industries.

BADGER-AMERICAN INDUSTRIES, INC. - Mequon, WI. *Phone:* (414) 241-5050. *Products Sold:* Engineered component parts.

THE BAILEY GROUP, INC. - St. Louis, MO. *Phone:* (314) 994-7599. *Products Sold:* Industrial machines, supplies, power tools, chemicals, abrasives, cutting tools, precision measuring tools, machine tool accessories, work holding.

BAILLIE SALES & ENGINEERING, INC. - Minneapolis, MN. *Phone:* (612) 546-2960. *Products Sold:* Auto screw driving systems, special auto system machines, o-ring installation machines, leak / decay testing devices, spring detangling, coil winding, laser gauging, special design / build automatic production systems.

F.H. BARGER CO., INC. - Fairview, PA. *Phone:* (814) 474-5854. *Products Sold:* Agency specializes in selling engineered component parts: heat transfer coils, copper tubing, fabricated tubular parts, refrigeration valves / fittings to OEMs of HVAC / R equipment.

BARNETT BATES CORP. - Joliet, IL. *Phone:* (815) 726-5223. *Products Sold:* Quality industrial equipment including valves, piping specialties, process systems, walkway grating, stair treads, doors, handrail, structural components, fiberglass.

BARRY TECHNICAL SALES, INC. - Mt. Prospect, IL. *Phone:* (847) 870-9705. *Products Sold:* Electronic manufacturing test equipment, RF test equipment, instruments / controllers, automation equipment, OEM material / products, disposable medical products, electronic technical products.

BARTELS CO. - Highwood, IL. *Phone:* (847) 295-2950. *Products Sold:* Castings, forgings, welding supplies, metal components.

BASIC METAL INDUSTRIES - Wheaton, IL. *Phone:* (630) 653-7292. *Products Sold:* Forgings (all types), rolled rings, stampings, machining, castings.

S.J. BATES - Sun Valley, ID. *Phone:* (208) 622-6536. *Products Sold:* Food ingredients.

LOUIS P. BATSON CO. - Greenville, SC. *Phone:* (864) 242-5262. *Products Sold:* Textile, plastics, papermill, industrial machinery.

BELLTECH UTILITY, LLC - West Chicago, IL. *Phone:* (630) 876-8495. *Products Sold:* Sell to utilities, steel, paper, petroleum, grain processing industries that require steam for their operations.

BELMONT ENTERPRISES, INC. - Garland, TX. *Phone:* (972) 271-4484. *Products Sold:* Sell to the traditional industrial / hardware trade through distribution in our territory.

BENNETT GROUP, INC. - Overland Park, KS. *Phone:* (913) 642-2689. *Products Sold:* Craft / floral supplies.

BENSON ENGINEERING CO. - Dallas, TX. *Phone:* (214) 342-0438. *Products Sold:* Power transmission.

JAY BERWANGER, INC. - Downers Grove, IL. *Phone:* (630) 963-1800. *Products Sold:* Custom produced molded / extruded plastic; molded, extruded, die - cut, mechanical, rubber; sponge, cellular rubber; acoustical; vacuum - formed interior trim.

BETLEJEWSKI SALES, INC. - St. Louis, MO. *Phone:* (314) 843-7143. *Products Sold:* Hand tools, masonry tools, fasteners, diamond blades / bits, abrasives, HSS / carbide drill bits, pat pins / loads.

BJERKAN & CO. - Prairie Village, KS. *Phone:* (913) 362-5555. *Products Sold:* Air handling; interior air quality control; air emissions control; dust collection; sound attenuation; vacuum systems.

RON BLANK & ASSOCS., INC. - San Antonio, TX. *Phone:* (210) 494-4411. *Products Sold:* Architectural products, countertops, glass, metals, insulation, plumbing, roofing, doors, windows, coatings, chemicals, tile, drains, fencing, storefront, HVAC specialties, furnishings, electrical, mechanical, masonry, EIFS, lighting, wallboard.

G.R. BLOMMEL & ASSOCS., INC. - Menomonee Falls, WI. *Phone:* (414) 255-6060. *Products Sold:* Engineered component parts to the OEM marketplace.

THE BLOWERS CO. - Jacksonville Beach, FL. *Phone:* (904) 241-0217. *Products Sold:* Electrical / electronic, enclosures, custom metal fabrication, injection molding, vacuum forming, rim molding, custom lighting, cooling, accessories, castings, engraving, metal photo / stampings, weighing systems.

JOHN BLUM SALES CO. - Elgin, IL. *Phone:* (847) 695-7899. *Products Sold:* Powder coating; wet painting; plating; molding; metal fabrication; tube fabrication; welding; stampings; laser cutting; extrusions; plastic; rubber; die cuttings.

BORYS & ASSOCS. - Orland Park, IL. *Phone:* (708) 429-6000. *Products Sold:* Home improvement, hardware, paint / sundries; building materials; construction; warehousing.

BOSCHERT EQUIPMENT CO. - North Kansas City, MO. *Phone:* (816) 221-1510. *Products Sold:* Application / sales of heat processing equipment, insulation, controls.

BOWMAN & ASSOCS., INC. - St. Louis, MO. *Phone:* (314) 863-8318. *Products Sold:* Mechanical power transmission; laser-optic shaft alignment service.

BRAND PREFERENCE DEVELOPMENT CO. - Saint Louis, MO. *Phone:* (314) 436-0080. *Products Sold:* OEM production component hardware, custom, off the shelf hinges, latches, gaskets, foam tape, handles, bumpers, tow hooks, hitches, pintle hooks, truck, trailer, utility, boat, enclosure, cabinet hardware.

R.C. BREMER MARKETING ASSOCS., INC. - Wilmette, IL. *Phone:* (847) 256-3459. *Products Sold:* Personal protection equipment; loose equipment for the industrial / fire markets.

BRISKY ASSOCS., INC. - Orland Park, IL. *Phone:* (708) 460-5100. *Products Sold:* Mobile electrification: reels, festooning / drag chains; radio control for binary, analog data / controls, AC / DC digital drives / motors; security CCTV systems.

CHARLES BROWN INDUSTRIAL EQUIPMENT, INC. - Greendale, WI. *Phone:* (414) 325-7100. *Products Sold:* Foundry capital equipment, saud conditioning, shakeout, material handling, replacement parts, engineering services.

D.C. BROWN, INC. - Minneapolis, MN. *Phone:* (612) 896-1890. *Products Sold:* Towels, tissue, napkins, cutlery, can liners, matting, paperboard products, janitorial supplies.

W.E. BROWNSON CO. - Davenport, IA. *Phone:* (319) 388-6900. *Products Sold:* Represent various principals marketing wire forms, metal fabrications / stampings, extruded / injection molded plastics, deep draw ferrules / eyelets, powdered metal, to OEM accounts.

JOHN T. BRYANT, INC. - Lithonia, GA. *Phone:* (770) 482-7303. *Products Sold:* Medical equipment / supplies; orthopedic soft goods, oxygen monitoring equipment, laboratory equipment, wheelchairs, stretchers, medical woodenware, sterilizing equipment, alcohol testing equipment, various disposables.

BUILDING COMPONENTS SALES CO. - Kansas City, MO. *Phone:* (816) 741-6226. *Products Sold:* Architectural / industrial building products, fiberglass insulation, building fasteners, PVC panels, commercial / AG doors, windows, track, track hardware.

D.R. BULKLEY CO., INC. - Davenport, IA. *Phone:* (319) 386-0340. *Products Sold:* Corrosion resistant products: fiberglass composites, lined steel products, protective floor toppings; installation / service division.

HALPIN D. BURKE & SON - St. Louis, MO. *Phone:* (314) 968-3969. *Products Sold:* Primarily selling custom engineered components to the OEM markets; custom graphics for product identification along with man / machine interface switches.

BUSSCO, INC. - Lenexa, KS. *Phone:* (913) 236-6447. *Products Sold:* Industrial dry bulk material handling systems, equipment; food / grain processing equipment, systems; analytical equipment.

BY-DESIGN MARKETING, INC. OF MN - Prior Lake, MN. *Phone:* (612) 226-5100. *Products Sold:* Decals, pressure sensitive labels.

BYRNES SALES ASSOCS., INC. - Rockton, IL. *Phone:* (815) 624-2333. *Products Sold:* Industrial, safety equipment, welding, fire, construction.

C & A SALES LTD. - Iowa Falls, IA. *Phone:* (515) 648-5118. *Products Sold:* Powerwashers; pumps, drain jetters.

CDR INTERNATIONAL, INC. - Kingwood, TX. *Phone:* (281) 359-8288. *Products Sold:* Energy equipment: combustion air preheaters, burners, soot blowers, air cooled heat exchangers.

C.J.T. ENTERPRISES, INC. - Jackson, MI. *Phone:*

Figure 7-2   Samples from the ERA Rep Directory.

DIXIE CHAPTER

Chairman of the Board
Marc Winchester, Winchester Electronic Sales, Inc.
President
Frank Filipowicz, F & J Squared Inc.
Vice President - Huntsville
Danny Galyean, CPMR, Rep, Inc.
Vice President - Atlanta
Richard Schwintek, Matrix Marketing Inc.
Secretary/Treasurer
Rett Bean, CPMR, Cartwright & Bean, Inc.
National Delegate
Danny Galyean, CPMR, Rep, Inc.
Alternate Delegate
John Jarrard, F & J Squared Inc.

Official Dixie Chapter Mailing Address
Lori Filipowicz, Chapter Secretary
F & J Sqared Inc.
6045 Atlantic Blvd.
Norcross, GA 30071
770/368-9191
FAX: 770/368-9188

Contact Chapter for Local Directory

* Territories Covered: Alabama; Arkansas; Florida; Georgia; Louisiana; Mississippi; North Carolina; South Carolina; Tennessee; Virginia

GROUP ABBREVIATIONS

CM	Components
CE	Consumer Electronics
CP	Computer
SAVES	Sound, Audio-Visual, Electronic Security
COM	Communications
MAP	Materials, Assembly and Production
RF	RF/Microwave
IN	Instrumentation & Sensors

Company	CM	CE	CP	SAVES	COM	MAP	RF	IN
A-OK Tech Reps						● ● ●		
Adams & Associates, Inc.	● ●			● ●				
Advanced Components Mktg.	● ● ●							
Alpha Marketing	● ● ● ●							
Arthur, Harris & Assocs., Inc.	● ● ●					● ●	● ●	
BJR Manufacturing Reps. Div. of Esheault	● ● ●							
Benchmark Technical Sales, Inc.	● ● ● ●							
Blair Engineering Southeast	● ● ● ●							
CMR Associates	● ●							
Cartwright & Bean, Inc.	● ● ● ● ●				● ● ●			
D.L. Clark and Associates							●	
Communications Marketing Southeast, Inc.					● ● ● ●	● ● ●		
Complete Control, Inc.	● ●							
Current Electronics Inc.						● ● ●		
Current Solutions		●						
DHR Marketing, Inc.	● ● ● ●							
DS Electronics, Inc.	●							● ●
Effective Marketing Force	● ● ●					● ●		
Electro-Mech Sales Engineering Co.	● ● ●							
Evans Sales & Marketing, Inc.	● ●	● ●	●		● ● ●			● ●
F & J Squared Inc.	● ●							
Gebhart Associates	● ● ● ●	●						
Genesis Marketing, Inc.	● ● ● ●							
Grisco & Associates						● ● ● ●		
Group 2000 Sales, Inc.	● ● ●							

Column sub-headings:
CM: Active Components, Passive Components, Interconnect, Power Sources and Mgmt, Manufacturing Services
CE: Consumer Audio, Consumer Video, Personal Entertainment, Personal Communications, Automotive Electronics, Accessories
CP: Pers Computer & Video Games, Small Office, Home Office, LAN Products, Multi-Media and Graphics, Telecommunications
SAVES: Sound, Audio-Visual, Electronic Security
COM: Land Mobile Radio, Microwave Comm. Systems, Marine, Satellite, Cellular, Telecommunications, Avionics, Telephone Equipment, Radio Datacom, Law Enforcement, Wireless PCS
MAP: Capital Equipment, Circuit Card Assembly, Contract Manufacturing, PC Fabrication, Components and Sub-Assemblies, Discrete Devices
RF: Transmission Lines, Microwave IC, Specialized Instrumentation, Sensors
IN: Data Acquisition & Cont. Systems, Test & Measurement Instruments, Quality/Production Test/ATE

A-OK TECH REPS
355 Aspen Lake Dr. West
Newnan, GA 30263
TEL: 770/304-9068
FAX: 770/304-9142
Owners: Crusco, Louis J., Owner; Seals, Ronald, Mgr
Addl. Facilities: Appl Engrg
Territories: AL; GA; MS
Mktg. Groups: Materials, Assembly and Production (MAP)
Customer Base: 1,2,3,6,10,11,12,13,14,16,17
(for complete information see listing in Florida (formerly Sunshine) Chapter)

ADAMS & ASSOCIATES, INC.
P.O. Box 6485
Marietta, GA 30065-0485
TEL: 770/426-4667
FAX: 770/426-9640
Owners: Barnes, Robert S., VP/Sls; Teasley, David, Sls
Addl. Facilities: Computer Mail/Repts
Territories: AL; FL; GA; NC; SC; TN
Mktg. Groups: Components, Sound, Audio-Visual, Electronic Security (SAVES)
Customer Base: 1,3,4,12
(for complete information see listing in CAROLINAS CHAPTER)

ADVANCED COMPONENTS MKTG.
3054 Leeman Ferry Rd. #D
Huntsville, AL 35801
TEL: 256/881-5493
FAX: 256/883-5885
CO. E-MAIL: acm@traveller.com
Owners: Scogins, Charlie, Pres; Cody, Chuck, Sls Engr; Everett, Jeral O., Sls Engr
Addl. Facilities: Whse; Computer Mail/Repts; Appl Engrg
Territories: AL; GA; MS; TN
Mktg. Groups: Components
Employees: 5
Customer Base: 1,3,7,12
Member Since: 1988
Branch: Norcross, GA 30092
4505-K Peachtree Industrial Blvd.
Mgr: Cody, Chuck
TEL: 770/448-7025
FAX: 770/368-1163

ALPHA MARKETING
904 Bob Wallace Ave., #121
Huntsville, AL 35801
TEL: 256/533-0766
FAX: 256/534-1833
CO. E-MAIL: alphamkt@traveller.com
Owners: McCarty, Tom, Pres; Jordan, Mike, VP; Jackson, Todd, VP
Addl. Facilities: Whse; Computer Mail/Repts; Distr; Appl Engrg
Territories: AL; GA; MS; NC; SC; TN
Other Territories: FL Panhandle
Mktg. Groups: Components
Employees: 8
Customer Base: 1,3,12,17
Member Since: 1995
Branch: Murfreesboro, TN 37128
335 Creekview Dr.
Mgr: Jackson, Todd
TEL: 615/896-6102
FAX: 615/895-0933
Branch: Oak Ridge, TN 37830
19 Converse Lane
Mgr: Jordan, Mike
TEL: 423/482-4681
FAX: 423/482-1684
Branch: Gadsden, AL 35904
1304 Monte Vista Dr.
Mgr: Hott, Bill
TEL: 256/543-2928
FAX: 256/546-2691

ARTHUR, HARRIS & ASSOCS., INC.
700 Old Roswell Lake Pkwy., #330
Roswell, GA 30076
TEL: 770/640-9500
FAX: 770/640-9109
Owner: Harris, Jim
Addl. Facilities: Computer Mail/Repts; Appl Engrg
Territories: AL; GA; MS; NC; SC; TN; VA
Mktg. Groups: Components, Materials, Assembly and Production (MAP), RF/Microwave
Customer Base: 1,2,3,12,16
Branch: Huntsville, AL 35801
806 Governors Drive, #207
Mgr: Harris, Jim
TEL: 256/551-9755
FAX: 256/551-9109
(for complete information see listing in CAROLINAS CHAPTER)

BJR MANUFACTURING REPS.
DIV. OF ESNEAULT ASSOCS.
12021 S. Memorial Pkwy., #O1
Huntsville, AL 35803
TEL: 256/881-3569
FAX: 256/881-8871
Owners: Esneault, Richard N., Pres;
Esneault II, R. N., VP/Slsman; Esneault, Robert, Slsman
Addl. Facilities: Computer Mail/Repts; Appl Engrg; Svc Dept; Demo Room
Territories: AL; FL; GA; MS; TN
Other Territories: FL Panhandle
Mktg. Groups: Components
Employees: 3
Customer Base: 1,3,11,12,14
Member Since: 1977

BENCHMARK TECHNICAL SALES, INC.
3069 Amwiler Rd., Ste. 1
Atlanta, GA 30360
TEL: 770/446-1711
FAX: 770/448-2854
CO. E-MAIL: lbentley@aol.com
Owners: Bentley, Larry A., Pres; Davis, Richard S., VP
Addl. Facilities: Computer Mail/Repts; Appl Engrg; Demo Room
Territories: AL; GA; MS; NC; SC; TN; VA
Mktg. Groups: Components
Employees: 4
Customer Base: 1,3,12,14,16,17
Member Since: 1989
Branch: Huntsville, AL 35802
600 Boulevard S., #104
Mgr: Granade, Gary
TEL: 205/776-9481
FAX: 205/776-9481
Branch: Fuquay Varina, NC 27526-2607
1230 E. Academy St., #219
Mgr: Davis, Richard S.
TEL: 919/557-1985
FAX: 919/557-2287

clude all the really capable reps in a given trading area. There are too many representatives that choose not to join rep associations and therefore are not listed in the directories. No one directory can be used with that degree of confidence necessary if a manufacturer intends to be—or maintain—the number-one position. Additional sources are needed.

3. *Your existing reps.* Most representatives have excellent relationships with other reps serving the same industry and frequently can recommend people they respect. By all means use these contacts, but be a little cautious. Reps will tend to recommend others they have had a personal relationship with. As with customers, a little preconditioning will get you the most informed response.

4. *Manufacturers of compatible products.* A compatible manufacturer's list of representatives is a list of potential rep candidates for you. While manufacturers are normally reluctant to release complete lists of reps around the country, phone calls to the senior sales executive will frequently give you the name of the representative in the area being searched. The presumption here is that the compatible manufacturer has selected an outstanding rep. Obviously, you must test this presumption; other companies' objectives may not exactly match yours, or they may have made major errors in selecting their reps.

Secondary Sources

Although the following sources are generally considered secondary by most manufacturers, they may actually be prime sources in a particular industry.

1. *Competitors' reps.* There are arguments both for and against recruiting a competitor's rep. You will undoubtedly be able to locate reps that will drop a competitor because they can make more money with your product line. But do you really want a relationship founded on shaky loyalty? That rep may be willing to drop *you* the next time a better situation comes along. Fortunately, this is an exception. Reps that drop a competitor usually do so because a separation is in the offing anyway, as the result of a principal's being dissatisfied with the rep or vice versa.

Professional reps are loyal to their principals, and for this they deserve our complete respect. Here's an example. Engaged as interim president of a company in a turnaround situation, I once approached one of the best reps in the Chicago area. I knew the agency handled a smaller competitor, but I felt our product line was much broader and could generate significantly more income. The head of the rep firm acknowledged that he could see a big escalation in income with my company, but his answer had to be no. The long-term relationship with the competing manufacturer had not always been a bed of roses, but the company had treated the rep fairly and worked sincerely to resolve any problems.

On the other hand, I know of a situation involving a competitor in a very difficult financial position that had made things extremely difficult for its reps for nearly three years. In this case, reps would be justified in dropping a principal who proved inept in turning the business around within a reasonable period.

2. *Your own files.* Every manufacturer should work diligently to maintain an ongoing file of available reps. Anybody associated with a sales environment should be on the lookout for names of good representatives. These can simply be clipped out and inserted in a geographic file. Then, when an opening occurs, there will be at least a partial list of rep candidates immediately available.

3. *Rep ads.* With a few exceptions, rep ads are not a primary source of candidates. The chances that a manufacturer will be looking for a rep in a given area at the same time a highly qualified candidate is advertising from that area is very small. In many industries, representatives do not advertise at all. When the best ones decide that they need an additional principal, they go through a logical analysis to define the type of product they want and then the specific manufacturer that best fits their needs. Then they go out and make a direct contact.

4. *Your own ads.* Generally, ads placed by the manufacturer do not yield a sufficient list of highly qualified candidates to make this a recommended tool. Once again, the chances of a highly qualified rep's looking for a line at the same time the "right" manufacturer is advertising are relatively small. Furthermore, busy reps frequently don't take the time to look at manufacturers' ads.

5. *Trade shows.* In most industries, trade shows are not a major source of rep candidates for a given search. However, trade shows will give you an opportunity to meet a number of reps, and you can put their names in your file for the future. There are, nevertheless, a number of industries in which trade shows seem to be as much a matrimonial bureau between rep and manufacturer as they are a product showplace for customers. In these situations, trade shows are indeed a valuable source.

6. *Distributors.* For organizations seeking a rep that serves distributors, one of the best sources is the distributors that will be served by the selected rep. Ask these distributors which reps truly serve them best with the types of products you have to offer. This is a superb way of identifying top rep candidates that know how to sell through distributors.

7. *Sales organizations and other professional organizations.* Membership in various organizations gives you the opportunity for informal discussions with peers of compatible product manufacturers. If you ask the appropriate questions, you can get the names of potential rep candidates.

8. *The Yellow Pages.* One of the final sources of rep candidates is the business-to-business Yellow Pages. Go to the generic product class and determine from the listings who might be representing a compatible manufacturer. At times, it's hard to tell whether the telephone number is a rep or a direct office; the answer is to call and find out.

9. *Creating new rep firms.* There has been an exploding need for independent reps within computer hardware and software, telecommunications, and other high-tech industries. The need for independent reps exceeded the available number of established representatives as we entered 1999. As a result, manufacturers or service providers may be faced with the need for creating a new rep firm, doing without a rep, or finding an alternate channel for sales coverage. Personnel who may be contacted to discuss their interest in starting up a new firm and representing you are your company's employees, employees of competitors, employees of rep firms handling compatible products, or employees of firms handling competing products. In these situations, the individuals may not have sufficient working capital to launch a rep firm on their own. In these cases, we suggest providing them with the necessary cash flow to get started. This can be handled by an advance against future commissions.

10. *The Internet.* We anticipate that the Internet will become a major tool that will help companies find independent reps in the future. However, as of early 1999, use of the Internet for rep search has very limited application for most industries. There has yet to be a single search engine one may explore to locate the enormous number of independent rep firms throughout the United States. Even more fundamental, there are relatively few reps listed. We believe this scenario will rapidly change and suggest that the Internet be periodically searched as a complementary tool to other sources of candidates.

Search Consultants

Consultants who specialize in rep search are relatively few, and their services vary widely in price and quality. However, they can be a superb aid in identifying candidates in a territory. They can offer a proved methodology of search, they have developed the necessary discipline to complete a search effectively, and, as a result of continuing search programs, they have developed a cost-effective approach to the process. The key to selecting consultants is to learn as much as you can about the methodology they use and the individuals who will be conducting the search.

Make sure you understand the sources of candidates the consultant will use. Those that rely purely on historical files are missing a bet. Even if those files appear to be extensive, only rarely are they current. The most effective consultants approach a search using their most current data but also conduct the search as though such data were not available to ensure that they identify the most current members in the rep population within the targeted trading area. The best consultants use a combination of sources, tailoring the search to your industry and your specific needs. Our firm typically combines five or more sources for a given search.

Be sure you thoroughly understand the consultant's methodology and the credentials of the individual within the firm conducting the search. An aggressive search program, with telephone follow-ups of all qualified candidates, is required. A mail-only program is too passive; the best reps are very busy and frequently ignore mail solicitations, even when a good fit should be obvious.

The Screening Chronology

You have looked at all the appropriate sources for names—both primary and secondary sources—and have developed a list of all potential candidates. To select the best of the candidates, you will now follow a rather straightforward path of elimination. Your goal is to narrow the list down to those few you wish to interview in person. This refining process usually has three components.

Direct Mail

In the great majority of cases, the first round of contacts can be by mail or, in urgent cases, by fax, telephone, or e-mail. This mailing might well be extensive. It is often reasonable to use rather wide parameters in defining potential rep candidates, at least the first couple of times you do a search. The scene changes rapidly in the world of reps. A rep that was marginal yesterday can become a valuable candidate today because of a merger or the acquisition of new individuals or new principals. The rep that was an outstanding candidate yesterday may have fallen by the wayside today. Therefore, it's better to err on the high side and select a rather large number of potential candidates for the initial mailing. In our client search programs, contacting twenty-five to thirty possible candidates is common, and contacting forty or more candidates is not uncommon, at least in major trading areas.

Send a package of information on your company describing the opportunity and your potential interest in the agency. Include enough information to give the rep firm a good idea of what your company is all about, as well as the opportunity itself. Details are not needed at this point—just a reasonable description of products, sizes, and applications.

A good package includes a letter describing the company and the opportunity, a condensed product brochure, and a data sheet listing the information you'd like to have about the rep if there is interest in representation. Your goal here is to solicit responses from rep firms interested in your product. They are looking for a good fit, just as you are; they need information on the following:

1. *Your company*. Name of the company and division and a brief history of your company in the particular marketplace.

2. *Your products*. A capsule commentary accenting features and benefits. Give a range of products and prices, plus a succinct comment on competition.

3. *Markets*. A description of the market and your company's role.

4. *Area history*. How has the area been covered? Is there a rep there now? Why is the search being undertaken? What sales volume have you averaged over the recent past?

5. *Commissions*. What is the current rate, and what has been the average commission per year for the past few years? If you are converting from direct to rep selling, calculate equivalent commissions on the basis of the current commission rate. This information is necessary for reps to judge how much of their efforts will be missionary.

6. *Support*. What types of support—advertising and promotion, training programs, etc.—does your company give reps?

7. *What you want in a rep*. This will be a rather sketchy commentary. If reps are really excited by your line and know exactly what you're looking for in a rep, they may tend to color their story to fit the description of your ideal rep. Therefore, it's best to be quite general in this description—enough to have reps generally qualify themselves as a possible match for your company's needs.

8. *Action*. What specific action do you expect from the rep as a result of the package? Ask for a response within a specific period; two weeks is reasonable.

To help you assemble the materials for your mailing to your list of rep candidates, review Figures 7-3 and 7-4. Figure 7-3 shows one format for the basic letter, and Figure 7-4 is a suggested format for the data sheet designed to elicit information from the rep. Both of these represent the perspective of a search consultant, but you can adapt the approach to fit your needs.

Follow-Up

Realistically, don't expect more than a 20–25 percent response rate to your mailing. Reps tend to give prompt attention to mail if it's an inquiry or an

Figure 7-3   Sample solicitation mailing to reps.

NOVICK & ASSOCIATES, INC.   August 11, 1997
10 Shipley Court, P.O. Box 187
Pittstown, New Jersey 08867
Tel (908) 713-0808
Fax (907) 713-0909

BUCKEYE FABRICATING COMPANY
NEEDS A CHICAGO AREA REP
TO SELL ITS PRESSURE VESSELS

INTRODUCTION—Novick & Associates, Inc. are assisting Buckeye Fabricating Company (BFC) in locating a highly qualified rep to sell its pressure vessels to OEM and end user markets in the Chicago trading area. This letter introduces the opportunity to you and asks whether you are interested in discussing possible representation for it.

THE COMPANY—BFC is a privately owned builder of pressure vessels sold to a diversity of OEM and end user markets. Founded 34 years ago, it has a 20,000 sq. ft. headquarters facility in Springboro, Ohio. Dick Macaulay, President and Owner, will be the individual working closely with you to help increase sales in the Chicago area.

BFC pressure vessels are fabricated in accordance with ASME Code, Section 8, Division 1 (stamps U, UM, and R). Size and pressure capability start around six inches in diameter with pressures up to 2,000 psig. Larger sizes top off around twelve feet in diameter and up to thirty feet in length at pressures up to 50 psig. Stainless as well as carbon steel construction is available.

MARKETS—Primary OEM markets include manufacturers of environmental control or process equipment, either skid mounted or field erected, that would use pressure vessels as described above. Typical OEMs include builders of process liquid filtration, water treatment and air pollution control (scrubbing/filtering) packages. Other targets include wet end paper machinery, chemical process equipment (i.e., reactors, mixers and agitators), specialized heat exchangers, vacuum pump, and compressor packages and many other types of equipment. End user markets include organic and inorganic chemicals, plastics, paints and pigments, pulp and paper, hydrocarbon processing, food, and pharmaceutical industries.

TRADING AREA AND CURRENT REPRESENTATION—While not having representation in the Chicago area, BFC has still averaged nearly $150,000 in sales per year for the past several years in this area. This business is made up of a cross section of prominent end users (primarily pulp and paper) and OEMs.

Figure 7-3 *(continued)*

SUPPORT—The Chicago rep will receive strong, hands-on support from BFC. This includes training seminars, joint sales calls, and cost sharing of local advertising. Promotional gift items are available for your customers and a marketing video will be available in April 1998. Their brochure is enclosed.

HERE'S WHAT WE LOOK FOR IN A REP—

Market Contacts: In-depth positions with OEM and end user markets as described earlier. (Note—Do not be concerned if you do not actively cover both markets. The key is to be strong in one. A separate, complementary rep may be available to cover that market you do not cover.)

Technical Knowledge: Sales personnel should have experience in environmental and/or process industries using pressure vessels.

Other Principals: Your other product lines should be compatible with BFC's pressure vessels and automatically bring you in close contact with key buyers and specifiers of these vessels.

ACTION REQUIRED—If you're interested in discussing representation of Buckeye Fabricating Company, please mail or fax us your line card and any other material that has been published on your company. Our fax number is 908-713-0909. To give you an idea of the information that we're interested in, we have attached one of our confidential data sheets. If you have any questions, just give me a call on our toll-free number, 800-548-1173. If you choose to mail or fax the information to us, we'll immediately contact you to further discuss this excellent opportunity.

Sincerely,

Harold J. Novick

Encls.

---

order—or a commission check, although even these have been known to sit around for a while in very busy times. Responding to inquiries from prospective principals is generally not a high priority among successful reps (they often receive several each month), even though there might be an excellent possible match with the manufacturer.

What's the solution? If you haven't heard anything in two weeks, make a follow-up telephone call. It might take a number of calls to get their attention. Ask whether they received the mailing, how they rate their potential compatibility with your firm, and what interest they have in pos-

Figure 7-4 Sample data sheet for prospective reps.

Sales Representatives Confidential Data Sheet

Company _____ Date _____

Address _____ Contact _____

_____ Title _____

_____

Phone _____ Fax _____

Business Specialization—Briefly describe the primary product and market specialization of your rep business, e.g., passive components for military and commercial electronics, dry bulk material handling for the process industries.

Company History—Please give a brief outline of facts. Date founded. By whom. Current ownership. Businesses other than rep.

Background Information on Sales Personnel—Please give full name, age, education (college and degree), number of years with your company, brief chronological job history (companies, job title or function).

Principals and Product Lines—Please ATTACH YOUR LINE CARD or list the principals and product lines you currently represent. Add below any principals not listed on your card. List the year you started representing them next to each name. Who are your top three principals? What percentage of your total sales is derived from each of them?

Territory Covered

Sales and Markets Served—What are your gross sales? What are your primary markets (e.g., customer groups) and roughly what percentage of your business comes from each?

Unique Qualifications—Is there anything special about your company which would make you especially qualified to be a rep for our client?

sibly representing you. Typical answers to the first question include: "I never received it," "I think I remember seeing it but I didn't have time to really look at it," "I looked at it but I'm not too sure it really fits," "It looks like it fits, but then I forgot about it."

Don't be offended by these responses or by the fact that it took several phone calls to get their attention. It's just typical of the way well-established reps react to inquiries of this type. It reinforces the need for a highly proactive search methodology if you want to get the attention of the best reps. Once you get their attention, the search will develop more smoothly.

At this point, go directly into the complete telephone interview described in the next section. If you wish, ask reps to follow up the conversation with their line card and any other information about the firm that they feel is appropriate. You might also ask them to state why you should consider them the best candidate in the territory.

> **A caution:** The failure in most search programs occurs in this early phase of the search: defining the ideal rep, conducting the necessary research, aggressively pursuing the rep, and gaining that first telephone contact. Because a search is typically performed as an ad hoc task by line sales managers and executives, maintaining the necessary discipline and allocating the appropriate time is typically compromised by line responsibilities. Yet it is during this period that the quality of the search program is most influenced. We have found that once the manufacturer is in contact with a qualified candidate, the screening process tends to go reasonably well, and a sound selection process is followed. However, all too often the best candidates in the territory have not been reached.

Telephone Interviews

This is a critical step in reducing a mass population of candidates to the most highly qualified who deserve in-depth, personal interviewing. The purpose of the telephone interview is to develop a rather complete profile so you can determine the relative fit with your company's needs. Your questions will generally conform to the items on the data sheet, but now they are expanded. You're trying to get more of a flavor of what the rep is really all about. The reps may have some preliminary questions. Try to answer them briefly; you don't want to give away answers to questions that you might want to raise during the interview. Ask questions in the following areas:

▪ *Company history.* This expands on the background of the rep organization from the time it started. The original product and market specialization will be traced to the current situation in order to determine how the organization has developed. Key concerns are the founding owners and the way ownership has evolved to today. Also critical is discussion of additional businesses (distribution, service, etc.), if any, the rep has developed.

■ *Personnel.* This should cover brief biographical sketches of each individual who would be involved in selling your company's products. All the principals should be included whether or not they will actually be selling for you. The bio should include full name, age, educational background, a brief chronological history of experience, including the types of positions and functions held, the number of years with the rep firm, any ownership position or pending ownership position, and any unique qualifications that would be of interest to your company. After the interview, you can typically condense these bios to no more than five or six typed lines of information.

■ *Principals, product lines, and sales volume.* You want to find out *all* principals represented and their product lines. Sometimes reps don't list all the manufacturers they represent; a number of minor manufacturers might not show up on their line cards. You should be aware of *all* relationships a rep has if you want to understand where the rep's priorities are focused.

You should also know the gross sales of the company in the most recent years and the manufacturers that are the major income contributors for the rep firm, including the approximate sales of each. The top three to five principals typically account for anywhere from 50 percent to 75 percent of a rep's income. It is this group of manufacturers that really tells you what the rep's primary focus is. The others are typically small, complementary items or even nonrelated items; several may be hangers-on from past years.

Normally, reps are rather free with this information because most do not consider it confidential. But when it comes to commission income, reps tend not to discuss it. You don't really need to know this to evaluate a rep's compatibility with your needs. You do need to know the gross sales figures and the top principals; that tells you how important a financial factor you might be to the rep and where the rep's primary effort is focused.

You should also discuss how long all the major income contributors have been represented. Tenure is a major indicator of sales performance and overall relationship with principals.

■ *Territory.* You want to find out the rep's trading area. Normally, reps focus on the standard trading areas for their industry but may go beyond these areas for one or more of their principals. You should learn both the nominal trading area and the trading area for major principals. The trading area for major principals will determine the rep's primary coverage area. If only minor principals allow the rep to cover wider territories, these territories will not get intensive coverage. Keep the focus on their primary trading area and there will be less chance for disappointment in the rep's performance. It will also minimize conflicting territorial claims of reps in adjoining territories.

■ *Markets and customers served.* Here you seek both qualitative and quantitative commentary from the reps on their market and customer focuses and their selling styles. In most cases, they will give a percentage approximation of their income or sales by industry category. Rarely will this breakdown be exact, as most reps do not classify their sales in this form. However, their "gut" feel is sufficient; your main objective is to understand their relative rather than absolute priorities. An example would be:

Industry Category	Percentage of Income or Sales
Chemical/petrochemical industry	50%
Power	20
Pulp and Paper	10
Municipal	10
Miscellaneous	10
Total	100%

Reps should also explain *why* their emphasis is in those markets. This will help clarify how compatible the other manufacturers are to your needs.

Most reps also have no objection about discussing their primary customers. They may not give you details, but at least you'll know who they are and at what levels in the organization the reps spend most of their time. Try to obtain the names of a rep's top five or six customers. This is another aspect of matching up the rep's profile with your needs. If there are only a few key buyers in a territory, it may be appropriate to ask for references and telephone numbers.

The telephone interview can typically be conducted in twenty to sixty minutes, depending on the complexities of the situation. At the conclusion of the interview, you should have a relatively good feel for whether that rep is a candidate to represent you in specific markets in a given trading area. It's a good idea to prepare a written summary of this interview; your report can be used in the face-to-face interview and for future reference. Figure 7-5 gives a sample of the kind of information you should include in this write-up.

(Text continues on page 129.)

Figure 7-5   Sample written summary of a telephone interview.

NOVICK & ASSOCIATES, INC.
10 Shipley Court, P.O. Box 187
Pittstown, New Jersey 08867
Tel (908) 713-0808
Fax (908) 713-0909

August 27, 1997

CHICAGO

Buckeye Fabricating Company
Springboro, Ohio

> **PUMPS & PROCESS EQUIPMENT, INC.**
> **1234 Remington Road**
> **Schaumburg, IL 60173**
> **Tel: 847-882-8116**
> **Fax: 847-882-2319**
> **Interviewee: Jim Hudson**

I. ORGANIZATION—Pumps & Process Equipment is both a rep and a distributor specializing in liquid handling and liquid process applications in the smaller edition of the Chicago trading area (i.e., they do not go into Wisconsin). It's a five salesperson firm with two father/son combinations. Founded in 1988, sales volume now exceeds $5 million. They lease 3,300 sq. ft. of warehouse and office space in an industrial complex. Looking at the key players:

James K. (Jim) Hudson is 60 years of age with a BA in merchandising from Youngstown University. Twenty-three years of his experience was with Moyno, a pump division of Robbins and Myers, where he progressed from salesman to regional manager to national sales manager. He then joined Bran + Luebbe (metering pumps and systems) where he spent six years as Vice President of Sales and Marketing before resigning to start his rep/distributor business with Ron Bogaert.

Ron Bogaert is 54 years of age with a BA in English from DePaul. Ron's background is very similar to Jim's in that he had eighteen years as sales engineer and regional manager with Moyno, then six years with Bran + Luebbe as a regional manager before teaming up with Jim in their rep firm.

Shawn Hudson, Jim's son, is 32 years of age with a BSME from the University of Michigan and an MBA from the University of St. Louis. Shawn spent six years with U.S. Electric Motors as first a sales engineer, then product manager before joining Pumps & Process in 1991.

John Bogaert is 31 years of age, the son of Ron, and has been with the firm for five years. John has a BS in marketing from Northern Illinois. His prior experience covers five years as a sales engineer for Walter Norris, an air filter distributor.

Ed Doherty is a relative newcomer to the firm, having joined them about nine months ago. He is 33 years of age with a BS in mechanical engineering from the State University of New York. His prior background was primarily nine years as a project manager for a construction company.

Mary Ann Suhi provides full-time secretarial support.

II. PRINCIPALS—Attached are the principals and product lines currently represented. Moyno (Robbins and Myers), Bran + Luebbe and Zenith are the top producers. All have been represented for significant periods of time. While a number of the principals primarily sell straight product, they do quite a bit of systems work, particularly with Bran + Luebbe.

Relative to tanks, Jim indicated that they "dabbled" in tanks once or twice but never had much interest. However, the pressure vessel line of BFC, rather than simple tankage, turned on Jim's interest. He indicated they work with a number of reactor people where he felt there were good opportunities for pressure vessels as well as at other OEM and end user customers.

III. TRADING AREA—Northern Indiana, northern Illinois, and eastern Iowa. The exact county boundaries in each state follow the line list.

IV. MARKET FOCUS—The split between end user and OEM is approximately:

End users - 75–80 percent
OEM   - 20–25 percent

In the OEM area, they include manufacturers of water and wastewater treatment equipment, various machinery builders, and a diversity of other manufacturers who purchase pumps and other equipment associated with the firm.

In the end user area, the CPI industry is number one, accounting for about 30 percent of its total business. Food is next in importance and is primarily associated with wastewater rather than sanitary process applications. After that, there's a wide diversity of industry including pharmaceuticals, utilities, steel, and general industry.

Following is a sampling of their end user customers:

Amoco, Abbott Labs, Kraft Foods, Nabisco, Nestle, M&M Mars, Northern Indiana Public Service, Commonwealth Edison, Fluor Daniel, Raytheon Engineers, Swenson, Wheelabrator, U.S. Steel, Inland Steel, Bethlehem Steel, Rhone-Poulenc, Central Soya, Morton International, Warner-Lambert, and U.S. Gypsum.

Figure 7-5 *(continued)*

V. <u>EVALUATION</u>—Pumps & Process Equipment has some rather significant strengths for BFC to consider. This is a relatively young firm but with seasoned leadership under the two owners who are very well experienced in liquid handling. The two sons suggest continuity of the firm is well in place. In addition, both sons have sound experience. The fifth person is just a plus.

Lines are quite compatible and relatively minimal in number for a firm of this type. Jim Hudson certainly exhibits a significant degree of interest in BFC. This interest is particularly important since it's focused not on tankage but on pressure vessels. The only concern is that the firm has not successfully sold tanks or pressure vessels. We do not feel this concern is a fatal weakness.

Combined with their sound market mix, we evaluate their compatibility with BFC's needs in Chicago as <u>GOOD-EXCELLENT</u> for the end user market and still <u>GOOD</u> for the OEM market. This is a rep we would consider for both end user and OEM opportunities in the limited edition (i.e., not including Wisconsin) Chicago trading area.

Harold J. Novick

Phone (847) 882-8116   1234 Remington Road   Schaumburg, IL 60173   Fax (847) 882-2319
Web Site: http//www.twoscan.com/pumps&process/   E-Mail: pumps@interaccess.com

PUMPS

Moyno® Pumps and Parts
  Progressing Cavity Pumps
  Manufactured by Robbins & Myers Inc.

Bran + Luebbe Inc.
  Plunger and Diaphragm Metering Pumps

Price Pump Co.
  Low to Medium Flow Centrifugal Pumps

Yamada America Inc.
  Air Operated Double-Diaphragm Pumps

Zenith Pumps
  Precision Gear Pumps

Warren Pump Inc.
  Composite ANSI Centrifugal Pumps

Griswold Pump Co.
  ANSI End Suction Centrifugal Pumps

Mission-Fluid King
  End Suction Centrifugal Slurry Pumps

MIXERS/AGITATORS

Brawn Mixers Inc.
  Portable Mixers
  Top Entry Mixers

Koflo Corporation
  Static In-Line Mixers

ENGINEERED SYSTEMS

Bran + Luebbe Inc.
  Continuous and Batch Metering
  and Blending Systems

Budzar Industries, Inc.
  Industrial Liquid Cooling
  and Heating Systems

PULSATION DAMPENERS

Flowguard Ltd.
  Suction Stabilizers
  Thermal Expansion Compensators
  Pipeline Surge Absorbers
  Hydraulic Accumulators

Selecting the Best: Personal Interviews

The Interviewee List

Once you have completed all the preliminary steps, a small segment of your original list will usually emerge as uniquely qualified and interested. In secondary trading areas and in narrow product/market situations, reps coming close to the pragmatic version of the ideal rep model will be less frequent. In large trading areas and/or large industries, you usually will end up with three to six candidates with excellent credentials. Occasionally, as many as ten candidates may emerge that generally fit the pragmatic model. However, when searching for reps in specialized niches, sometimes one reasonably qualified candidate is all you can find.

How many should be interviewed? When there is a small sampling of candidates—four or fewer—it's best to interview them all. This is true even if one rep clearly emerges as the preferred candidate after the telephone interview. Occasionally, face-to-face interviews give you a completely different perception from telephone interviews. Also, personal interviewing of four candidates will give you insight into the territory from the eyes of four different rep organizations. It is valuable market intelligence.

When the candidate list is long after the telephone cut, say, in the range of ten candidates, select the best five or six for personal interviewing. Typically, when there are ten candidates that have met the minimum criteria, there will still be a rather strong difference in the qualifications among the group. It is generally rather easy to drop off the few that clearly will not meet the quality level of the top group.

Next, contact your selected candidates and establish interview dates. Occasionally, a candidate may have second thoughts at this point and decide that an interview is inappropriate. Drop down to the best candidate on your secondary list to fill this void. Hold off on advising the candidates not picked to be interviewed that they are no longer candidates. It is always possible that something may turn up during the interviews that could increase the desirability of this next group of candidates.

Conducting the Interview

The location of the interview can vary from a hotel room, with each candidate scheduled at intervals, to personal visits to the reps' offices. If the physical characteristics of the office are not critical to the rep's success, there is little need to go there. However, if your industry requires professional offices with demonstration space, samples, video demonstrations, warehousing, and so on, the rep's facility should certainly be the location for the interview. It may also give you insight that would not be possible in a hotel room.

Where a hotel arrangement is acceptable, two-hour intervals between interviews are usually satisfactory. This will allow at least four interviews in a day. The close coupling also permits a better comparison of one candidate to the others.

It is best to have two people from your organization involved in the interview session. This gives you two perspectives on what the rep has conveyed. From the rep side, the key individuals who would be involved in selling the product should be present. This means the employed sales personnel, if they will be selling your product, as well as the agency owners. In the case of reps with large staffs, the owners and perhaps one or two key sales personnel should be at this interview. If they emerge as the top candidate, a final interview can be conducted with the others at the rep's office.

This interview session should be carefully planned. After the telephone interview, you will typically have a fair amount of information already at hand. However, many areas should be probed more deeply. Before the interview day, list all the subjects that should be explored in depth, and bring this checklist to the interview.

Keep introductory conversations about your company to a minimum. You want to find out what makes the rep tick. Do this by asking opening questions about the agency's business, its principals, what turns the reps on and off, what problems they may be having, and any other question that can get them talking about their business. Do your homework first; learn as much as you can about the rep before the interview. This will give you the best chance of pinpointing the best candidate. It will also demonstrate thoroughness on your part, a plus in the rep's eyes.

Dig deeply. Make sure you fully understand how the reps see your products fitting into their sales strategy. You want to pick reps that feel you fit their overall scheme of things. They should be able to convey this to you clearly and express how they plan to make money for you both.

This is especially important if yours is a small company. You need to learn how the reps view secondary manufacturers and under what conditions they give a strong sales effort. Many reps will rather automatically say to a secondary manufacturer that they treat all manufacturers the same. Take this with a grain of salt. Reps will enthusiastically support a small principal if that manufacturer is a strong fit in the overall selling strategy. Without this fit, the small manufacturer will not receive adequate sales support.

Finally, ask about selling philosophy and style. What are their primary approaches? Do they enjoy selling at the specification level or do they sell mostly as a second source? What turns them on in the challenge of selling? What new products have they successfully brought to the marketplace for their manufacturers in the recent past? Make these questions open-ended; don't frame a question that contains an answer. You want the reps to talk about how they sell and what they do to separate their principals from competition. This will be valuable input to your final selection.

From the Rep's Side

Remember that the reps are interviewing you as much as you are interviewing them. Reps are looking for a good overall fit, just as you are. You are looking for reps that match your ideal profile; they are looking for manufacturers that match what they hope to achieve, both today and tomorrow. Not all reps are long-range planners, but most have a general conception of the directions in which they want to go and the manufacturers that would really fit their needs.

Reps use five main benchmarks to evaluate you as a potential principal:

1. The image and reputation of your company as a respected supplier to their primary market targets.
2. The reputation of your company for knowing how to work effectively with reps.
3. The total commission dollars that they can expect to earn over the short term with some estimations of what the future might hold and why.
4. The fit that your product lines have with their overall scheme of things.
5. The personal chemistry factor—how comfortable they will feel with your company as projected by the people conducting the interviews.

When you have completed your interview, the floor is open for the reps' questions. Your answers should be candid; don't attempt to sell your company. Problems should be professionally stated and the approach to solutions discussed. If there are significant problems that cannot be resolved over the near term, reps should know this. It is really unfair for them to be blindsided when they start representing you. Candor is the name of the game for both parties, not only at the initial interview but throughout the entire relationship.

Making the Selection

When all the personal interviews are completed, the interviewers should get together as soon as possible to compare notes and their evaluations of each candidate. Of particular importance at this time is the question of personal chemistry. By *personal chemistry*, we mean a strong feeling of mu-

tual respect, the sense that the other party understands you and will develop a commitment to support you. Many people would express it as:
"We speak on the same wavelength." After all is said and done, this chemistry will be a key deciding factor.

Personal chemistry between rep and manufacturer has two elements.
One is the feeling of respect for the other party's ability to produce positive
results. The second is the chemistry associated with the sheer joy of working together. Ideally, you want both. Frequently you have to choose between the two. A manufacturer totally committed to maximizing long-
term profitability will lean more toward the results-oriented rep than the
one that offers an enjoyable but possibly less productive relationship.
Which rep you select depends on the culture and standards of your company. It's not a case of absolute right or wrong but rather a decision that
best fits your company's style and the rep ownership's objectives.

Chemistry has to be evaluated face-to-face; pay special attention during the interviews to indications of positive and negative chemistry. And
don't assume you can "fix" it later. A rep with poor personal chemistry
with your people will have a negative impact on the company. Too much
time is wasted wondering, "Why won't they fire that SOB?" Frequently
it's better to eliminate that irritation and get on to a more cohesive, team-
oriented style.

As you compare and assess the interviewees, you'll be evaluating
each against the primary characteristics defined in your ideal rep profile.
Fortunately, in a surprising number of situations, a single best candidate
will be very apparent—even though you canvassed perhaps eighty representatives by mail, interviewed as many as fifty by telephone, and conducted eight to ten personal interviews.

In a number of cases, the personal interviews may result in what appears to be a tie between two or more candidates. This can be quite frus-
trating unless you develop an additional methodology for breaking ties.
This can be as simple as applying a quantitative analysis of the ideal rep
profile to the alternative candidates. The quantitative analysis will frequently give a clearer indication that one rep candidate is stronger than
the other. When even this does not give a clear answer, try expanding the
"absolute must" characteristics of the ideal rep and see what impact this
has on the evaluation of the two top candidates. If that doesn't help, try
contacting the "must" list.

Managers who have an aversion to this analytical approach can make
a more subjective superimposition, perhaps simply raising the value of
intuitive judgment. Intuitive managers tend to have a rather good track
record when using these feelings for the final selection. The bottom line is
that the final decision should be made on the basis of which rep best fits
your management style.

If there is a clear-cut consensus as to the preferred candidate and thus no need for further evaluation, we suggest their appointment as your rep be made face-to-face right then and there. (We normally suggest that the best apparent candidate be interviewed last to allow the learning curve in the interviews for a given area to peak at the most important time—with the best candidate. This also permits an appointment if the rep comes through with flying colors as the clean winner.) The personalized handshake always adds a little something extra to an agreement between a rep and a manufacturer. However, there will be times when, for any number of reasons, additional time will be required before a decision can be made. Once this has been done, the manufacturer can often obtain the rep's final agreement over the telephone. Ideally, this phone call would soon be followed up with a face-to-face meeting concerning details of the start-up period. At that time, the hearty handshake can take place.

If You Have Parallel Reps

When a company decides to parallel reps, the rep selection process has two additional steps. First, be sure to convey to the rep candidates for your most important target that you would like to select another rep in a totally unrelated market. And discuss your plans during the interview process. If your market analysis is rational, you should have little problem gaining acceptance of the paralleling process.

If there are protests by reps against this paralleling concept, they usually fall into two classes. One that may indeed be a legitimate concern is that the specialization is really not very distinct and that significant conflicts will arise between parallel reps. If it is a problem, the same protest will be raised by other reps you contact. The answer: Don't push for the specialization as originally conceived. See if an alternative for splitting up the sales can be devised that is clearly acceptable to all parties. If not, forget about the specialization and pick the one best rep available to cover both targets.

The second class of protest is the subjective argument by a rep that there should be one exclusive rep in the territory. Fortunately, few reps argue this concept as there is very little *objective* argument for it. It is quite rare that such an argument will be raised by a professional rep if the market you propose to withhold is not one either currently covered by the rep or being targeted for the future. Even if one rep does protest, you'll invariably find that just about all the other reps won't raise a concern.

Your search can now continue with the second step: Recruit the best rep in the area for the first market target; then go for the parallel rep.

The search and selection process for the primary candidate for the secondary market should proceed as the initial search did. If there is any potential for conflict between parallel reps (as indicated by the classes of protest described above), the rep signed on for the primary market and the premier candidate for the secondary target should sit down with you to define whether the conflict is real. If there does appear to be one, together you can develop alternatives for minimizing any disruption.

In the great majority of well-planned searches, there is no conflict, so a meeting is not required. Where there is potential for market overlap, this meeting will rather quickly define it. Frequently, the reps themselves can define working accommodations. These may require some adjustment later, but usually there are no stumbling blocks in implementing a parallel structure.

In the event that major stumbling blocks emerge during discussions with the two reps, the idea of paralleling at least those two reps should be reconsidered. You do not want to be continually involved in adjudicating problems of who does what to whom and when with a customer.

Even more critical is the inconvenience that this might create for the customer. The bottom line is how you can best serve a given industry and key customers in that industry. If the customer sees that two reps are calling on him when it doesn't make sense, change your system. However, sometimes two different reps can call on the same customer for the same company and not be in conflict at all. This would be where the products are sold into two different functional entities inside the customer's organization. Don't be hesitant to try it. Paralleling reps offers a major opportunity for sales growth.

The Next Step

Now that you've made your choices, what next? What happens when the deal is made, the final hand is shaken, and everybody goes home? The reps do their darnedest to sell your products, that's what, and you do your darnedest to support them in every way. That's what Step 5 is all about.

8

Building Good Working Relationships

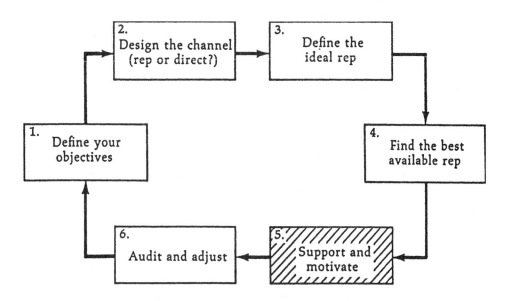

You may remember we said earlier that there are two very simple keys to success in selling through independent reps:

1. Pick the right reps.
2. Support them well.

You have picked the right reps—and they have picked you. No doubt you sealed the deal with enthusiastic handshakes all around. Now what?

Getting the New Rep Started

Too often, the initial enthusiasm quickly dissipates when manufacturers do not promptly support the new reps with the tools they need to get started and running well. Let's look at some of the important tools.

Announcements

It's usually best to let the rep define how the announcements are to be made. Frequently, the rep's customer list and the manufacturer's are merged, and the manufacturer sends announcements to this combined list indicating the appointment of the new representative. Occasionally, reps are reluctant to turn over their mailing list to a manufacturer. Usually that's because they've been burned in the past. Try to be flexible.

Material Such as Price Lists, Catalogs, and Samples

A complete package should be ready for you to put into the reps' hands so that they can hit the ground running. Obviously, you'll do an introductory training session on how to use the materials. Normally, this training will be at the reps' office, with more intensive and more formal training held later.

Historical Sales Data

Give the reps data for the past several years (five years if possible) so they can see trends of business with different customers. They can superimpose their own contacts on this past history and plan the priorities of their sales effort.

Open and Hot Negotiations

A list of all open negotiations, with specific emphasis on those that are subject to closing over the short term, should be presented to the reps and discussed with them. Together you can establish priorities and time allocation to be sure that both of you are on top of every negotiation that needs attention now.

Commission Status

A residual commission basis may be made available for the reps. This could be the destination shipment credit on certain projects or potential commissions on orders that are currently breaking. A complete detailing of the commission status should be promptly available.

Preliminary Objectives

Approach this subject carefully. In start-up situations, most reps feel that they are not in a position to set preliminary objectives until they've had an opportunity to test the waters with customer calls. Even though you gave them the historical sales levels and the open-proposal activity, these are no substitutes for the personal feel that reps develop once they actually start selling for you.

Sit down with your reps and go over historical sales data, open negotiations, recent "hit" ratios, and projected market activity in their area. From this base, you can then suggest what a purely maintenance sales activity should yield in terms of new orders. Ask the reps to comment on this background and suggest an initial objective if they feel they can establish one.

Some will answer something like this: "Hey, I can't even give you a preliminary number until we make at least one complete round with our customers. Even then, we usually find it's premature to make a forecast." This position is reasonable, and you should respect it. Forcing reps into objective-setting invariably proves counterproductive. Initial enthusiasm is dampened, and the stage is set for less-than-total commitment.

Another related key in working with reps: Don't expect all of them to fit into a neat "cookie cutter" mold in how they feed information back to you. Although you can force a uniform feedback format on direct organizations, such forcing with reps is usually counterproductive. Keep your eye on the important aspects: picking the best available rep and supporting that rep to the best of your ability. The important results—increased sales and profit—will then occur naturally.

Back to the reps' response to your request to establish an initial objective. A significant number of reps *are* willing to do so, subject to review over the coming months as they develop a learning curve on the manufacturer. Let me give you an example of how this can work. After unfolding all the historic data and comparing customer lists, I asked a new rep this question: "To give us a little indication of your feelings about how well you might be able to do with this product line, what would you guess might be a rational number for your organization to target for this first year? We're not interested in the number as a formal objective. It will just help us get a better feeling of your view about our product line as a match with your activities."

After a moment or two of silence, the rep quoted a figure that was twice the average annual sales over the previous three years. In the few moments of silence, he had reflected on the company's historic customer base; he knew that he had those customers well covered and also knew that there were many other accounts where his firm was well contacted and where the product would be an excellent fit. He then determined the amount of selling time he could see his organization offering and compared that to the amount of time the previous direct salesperson had been able to give these market segments. He cautioned, "This is just an educated guess and we wouldn't want to be held to that number." As it turned out, the rep firm exceeded his number by 20 percent in its first year.

This approach is an effective way of getting an initial number from a rep that is rationally considered. The concept of preliminary objectives is valid, for most manufacturers constantly deal in sales targets. This fulfills part of the numbers requirement of corporate life. In addition, it establishes a benchmark by which you can work with the rep to assess progress and determine mid-course corrections in forecasting. You can also use this informal number as a prelude to a formal forecast for the second year of operation—when objectives are very much in order. One other spin-off benefit is that reps who give this number typically don't forget it and tend to measure their own progress accordingly.

One caution: Reps have great confidence in their selling abilities. They are optimists. Therefore, rep forecasting should be considered in the light of their optimistic outlook on the worlds they will conquer for you. Blend history and current market appraisal with the rep's forecast before you submit a forecast for formal planning purposes.

Contracts

Key terms of the contract will have been discussed during the interviews. Reps may or may not have requested copies of your rep contract prior to agreeing to represent you. Many reps wait until after the verbal agreement is reached to address the details of a contract. At any rate, when the formal contract is drawn up, it should promptly be forwarded to the rep to be signed.

Communications Channels

Reps should receive a copy of your company's organizational chart and a clear definition of whom they should contact for what and when, and who the backups are. Advise them of the route available if they receive a negative response that they feel should be appealed. Don't back away from appeals. You must foster the attitude that appeals by the reps are one way to ensure maximum customer sensitivity. A flexible approach to appeals is a necessary safeguard for organizational health.

Joint Calls on Customers

One of the key methods in a start-up is on-the-job training (OJT). Joint calls are an important way to develop the rep's knowledge of your products and the way you do business. Joint calls are usually made with the regional manager or, if that is not possible, with the sales manager or a product manager.

Factory Visits

Factory visits, which typically include training programs and a tour of all plant facilities, are an additional key ingredient in a new rep's learning curve with a manufacturer. Let the reps decide when they should visit the plant. Most would like to spend some time with their customers before going back to the factory; that way, they develop a better idea for what questions to ask and what to look for. Others may wish to visit the plant soon after the initial handshake.

Communications

Keep the communications flowing. Routinely telephone reps during the early phases to make sure that everything is going smoothly. See to it that they are on the list of routine mailings from the factory. Make sure the rest of the reps know the new rep is on board. Likewise, the new rep should immediately receive a copy of your complete rep network, including names of firms, key personnel, telephone numbers, and territories.

Stroking

A supportive stroke at the appropriate time goes a long way. A letter from the president acknowledging the rep's first order, with congratulations and best wishes for the future, will start cementing the bond between rep and manufacturer. Others in the organization should get in the habit of expressing thanks to a rep for any particularly well-done job. These acknowledgments are more than just a routine courtesy; they are important building blocks for developing a truly committed sales force.

Working Together for Long-Term Success

These initial steps will establish a good framework for the reps' first months with you. You have selected the right reps and given them the tools they need to get off to a good start. Now you need to move beyond this start-up method into a broader mind-set. What is needed for long-term success?

To put the matter very simply, it is now up to you to provide the all-around support that motivates reps to perform at their best. You are a team. Together you will strive to build a working relationship based on reasonable expectations, genuine communication, and fair-mindedness on both sides. Each party should understand what the other needs and make every effort to provide it with professionalism and enthusiasm.

Essentially, you, the manufacturer, have two responsibilities:

1. Understand what reps expect of you—and provide it.
2. Have a clear picture of what you can expect from reps—and what you cannot.

The five general areas of concern that reps usually have in mind during their deliberations when taking on a new manufacturer are:

1. Image and reputation of the manufacturer as a respected supplier to their customers (primary targets)
2. Reputation of the manufacturer for knowing how to work effectively with reps
3. The total commission dollars—now and projected
4. The fit that the manufacturer's product lines have with the rep's scheme of things
5. The personal chemistry factor

If the selection was done wisely, the initial fit has already been judged a good one. From this point on, the rep's assessment of the new principal changes somewhat. The primary factors for the rep that now influence commitment to a manufacturer and the time spent on that company are:

1. The commission dollars per unit effort
2. Expected future commissions—that is, the ability of the manufacturer to increase the rep's income
3. The pleasure/agony factor

You, the manufacturer, have a great deal of control over these factors. This means you are in a position to motivate your reps by providing a well-managed business that satisfies their primary desires. Let's see what you can do specifically in these three areas.

Commission Dollars per Unit Effort

Reps are looking for systems, procedures, controls, and any other tools you can provide that minimize their sales costs. These range from carefully prioritized market targeting to detailed competitive analysis to professional features/benefits proposals to strong promotional and advertising programs that yield qualified leads. Essentially, it means a total marketing job, with the manufacturer putting in the rep's hands all the tools to make the rep as self-sufficient as possible. This is the most effective way of selling, for it minimizes the number of contacts a rep must make with the manufacturer in the routine conduct of business.

Expected Future Commissions

Reps develop estimates of future expectations from three ingredients: what they know of the current product and market position, your history of developing new products and new markets, and what you tell them about growth plans.

Reps are turned on by the manufacturer who is a step ahead of competition in new products, services, and systems. This gives them something new to talk about and, even more important, an edge over competition. Of course, your primary reason for pursuing these innovative concepts is your own growth in your marketplace. It's a happy side benefit that at the same time you are also providing your reps with major motivation for sales growth.

The Pleasure/Agony Factor

The agony side of the picture is the result of a manufacturer's management's not understanding reps or not training their people to work properly with them. These manufacturers frequently show a distrust for representatives and, as a result, develop antagonistic rather than mutually supportive relationships.

Established reps don't waste time with antagonism; they turn their selling energies elsewhere. New or marginal rep firms, whose highest priority is income generation, will grin and bear it—for a while. But as they move toward economic security, they start to move away from the manufacturer with an anti-rep mentality. When you select reps as your sales channel, you must not only embrace their way of doing things but train your total organization in proper rep support. If you're looking for results, this is imperative. (We will discuss the concept of total support more fully in Chapter 9.)

What Your Reps Expect From You

In addition to your positive attitude toward their primary concerns, professional reps come into the picture with certain specific expectations of what their principals should provide. Interestingly, when you provide these elements, you do more than motivate your reps; you also set up the machinery for excellence in your organization as a whole.

In an overall sense, reps expect that the manufacturers they represent will understand the *quid pro quo* in the relationship. This means there are many tradeoffs between organizations. Following are some of the typical expectations that reps have of the manufacturers they represent.

Measure Overall Rep Results, Not Activities or Individual Events

Reps achieve success by developing a selling process that fits their specific personalities, experience, objectives, and selling style. Some rely on a high number of sales calls while others rely on much fewer calls but with more pre-planning or intensity. This is an activity that should not be measured—it falls within the rep's right to manage her business the way she sees fit. Reps with different sales processes can be equally successful. The reps should be measured by their achievement of primary objectives, namely getting the orders and sound feedback, not on how they achieve it—provided that it is done in both an ethical and legal manner. The same is true concerning individual results. For example, attendees at our public seminars occasionally ask the question: "Why should we pay the rep when he did nothing to get that order?" Here is where the *quid pro quos* enter the picture. It is true that reps will occasionally receive an order through no effort on their part. However, there are many times when reps will not receive an order because the manufacturer they represented could not be competitive on price, delivery, performance, or some other measure of evaluation by the customer. The rep may have done a total selling job, including providing the manufacturer with a complete bid analysis. At times he may even be able to command a premium over the competitive price only to have the order lost because the manufacturer could not make a delivery date required by the customer. Despite a truly excellent selling job, the rep receives no commission. This is a tradeoff that the rep understands. The manufacturer needs to understand these *quid pro quo*s in the same manner.

A Marketing Job

The rep firm will do the sales job and certain aspects of sales management. Marketing, however, is your job. By "marketing," I mean the classic functions performed under marketing management: market research, market planning, advertising and promotion, product management, and so on. It's up to you to define the market focus, the overall strategy, specific target priorities, competitive analyses, the niche being filled, the features and benefits profile, and the advertising and promotional support. Reps can feed you information from the field to help in the marketing analysis, but make no mistake about it: The marketing responsibility is yours.

Responsiveness to Customers

A rep's livelihood depends on her ability to be truly responsive to customers' needs. Established representatives will not take you on if you have a track record of nonresponse. This poor response can show up in product quality, shipping schedules, poor performance, or some other key aspect of the product. Similarly, if a manufacturer currently represented develops severe problems and does not solve them, the representative at some point will try to separate the manufacturer from the customer to the point of refusing business. Above all, reps want to protect their position with the customer.

This is not to say that reps do not work effectively with manufacturers who experience problems. On the contrary, they are extremely effective in helping manufacturers through periods of unsettled conditions. The key is for manufacturers to prevent difficult conditions from becoming systemic and persisting over an extended period.

Integrity in Word and Product

A reputation of integrity ranks very high in reps' minds both when looking at new principals and when promoting existing principals. They want to have confidence that when you promise something, it will be done within the time frame expressed. And when a product is shipped, reps expect that product to perform as advertised. There are no more fundamental ingredients for building a bond between rep and manufacturer.

First Established Product Lines, Then New Products

Successful reps invariably want principals with a strong position in the marketplace. Reps have a strong aversion to doing purely missionary work for a new manufacturer unless there is a unique fit with the rep and the promise of a sound payoff in the future.

The more established reps are, the more they want established product lines. Some establish arbitrary minimum levels of commissions they can expect in the first year simply by maintaining the manufacturer's previous year's sales. I know one who expects a minimum of $35,000 per year and won't take on a manufacturer unless he can get that just by maintaining last year's level.

While some manufacturers might say this is a "giveaway," these representatives usually grow the business significantly from this starting point. These reps are at the top of their class and do an exceptional job for the right principal. Also, they will take a chance periodically on a missionary situation if it appears to be a unique fit with excellent promise.

Once a manufacturer and its business have been assimilated, then a rep looks for the introduction of new products. The growth-oriented reps see the opportunities for their own growth in new products. It also gives them something new to talk about with their customers and demonstrates to their customers that the manufacturers they represent are forward looking.

A Fair Commission Policy

Reps do not need to be enticed with unusual commission formulas. What they want is a fair commission policy for the job that is expected of them. What is fair? The industry standard for an "average" manufacturer in that industry is usually considered fair. For a new manufacturer requiring missionary effort, "fair" might well have to be a rate significantly higher than the industry average. On the other hand, where a manufacturer has been truly dominant in its industry with an outstanding track record of innovation and support, "fair" can mean a rate slightly below the average, as the rep's selling job is significantly easier and return for the invested effort is very high.

Professional Handling of All Commission Matters

One of the consistent gripes raised by representatives is the haphazard handling of their commissions. Periodic mishandling is inconvenient; routine mishandling is unacceptable. Some manufacturers, at least some financial departments, seem to view commissions as a secondary responsibility, less important than other aspects of the department's workload. This is guaranteed to sabotage sound relationships between reps and manufacturers.

Commission income is the rep's compensation for having been successful in obtaining orders. Whereas a salaried salesperson is paid in advance for expected future sales, the rep does not get paid until orders are shipped, at the earliest; half don't get paid until your invoices are paid. Commission checks should be issued promptly on the dates agreed to, just as salary checks are. Commission statements should be legible and informative. Questions should be answered promptly, accurately, and sensitively.

A Spirit of Partnership

The independent representative is just that—independent—even though mutual success is based on an interdependent relationship. The agreement between rep and manufacturer is effectively a business partnership in which two independent organizations agree to work together to achieve a common objective: maximum profitable penetration of a given trading area.

This partnership relationship should be developed in its truest sense, that is, a total give-and-take between partners dedicated to developing the best possible approaches for maximum penetration of targeted markets. Manufacturers that attempt to "boss" their reps, telling them what to do, how to do it, and when, will end up alienating them. Eventually they will receive less than a fair share of the reps' time. Boss/subordinate relationships have no place in the manufacturer/rep alliance if long-term success is your goal.

An Open Ear to Critique

Good reps know what has to be done to sell the customers in their territory. Your reps should be constantly telling you what has to be done to improve profitable penetration of the area. That does not mean you have to follow every recommendation from every rep. It does mean that you should listen to the suggestions from all your reps and then synthesize them into a list of priorities for long-term implementation. Obviously, your priority system will not satisfy all reps, but even the rep with a good suggestion will accept a turnoff if he knows you carefully considered it. Your demonstrated willingness to listen to ideas from reps is fundamental to developing a truly supportive rep network.

Action to Correct Agreed-Upon Weaknesses

Listening to criticism is one thing. Promptly implementing corrective action to eliminate weaknesses is another. All too often, manufacturers acknowledge weaknesses over and over again but fail to take the prompt steps necessary to correct them. Many of the weaknesses defined by reps can be promptly corrected, particularly when they concern procedures or policy. When you correct these weaknesses, you do more than develop an effective rep network; you ensure your survival.

Strong, Consistent Support

Reps, like most other people, look for the comfort of dependability. Manufacturers that provide strong, consistent support of their representatives with minimum upsets develop a confidence level that goes a long way toward strengthening rep commitment.

Sound Training

Professional reps look for in-depth training on products, services, competition, priority markets, and all other information they can use to improve their effectiveness in the marketplace. This not only helps them focus their activities in the areas where they can obtain maximum return but also enables them to improve their success rate in closing new business. Don't limit your training activities to the initial period with a new rep. Training should continue throughout the relationship.

Most manufacturers pay for all expenses associated with training—lodging, meals, and normal associated expenses—except for rep transportation expense to the training location.

Clear, Concise, Accurate, and Timely Communications

Weakness in communications is one of the top two criticisms that reps have of manufacturers (handling of commission matters is the other). Ironically, poor communication is also one of the major criticisms that manufacturers have about reps. Both criticisms are valid, but the solutions are somewhat different.

The expectations of many manufacturers are simply ill conceived. If you expect full written reports from reps, you are bound to be frustrated. Occasionally, you may have one or more reps that will provide rather extensive written communications. When this happens, you have one of two things: a marginal rep that needs the commission income and can be forced into doing things out of fear of alienating you, or a rep who is personally oriented to written communications and communicates well. The latter case is an exception.

To get the best from your reps, learn to accommodate your communication style to theirs. This is another major difference between direct selling and selling through reps. In a direct organization, bureaucratic conformity can be forced onto the sales network. Trying to do that with twenty-five separate independent rep organizations leads to alienation, if not rebellion. It would be much more productive to recognize these variable communication styles by the reps and accommodate your internal system to it.

This does not mean that you cannot expect sound communications from the reps on key issues. It only means you're better off using the rep's own medium for the most important communications—the telephone. Leave the paper pushing for the bureaucrats.

Consistent Procedure for Customer Contacts

Normally, most reps want all customer contacts made through them. This is not just possessiveness; it's a practical procedure for ensuring clear communication within the organization. It is very debilitating for any salesperson, whether rep or direct, to make a point to a customer and hear, "But your engineering manager [or sales manager or product manager or president] said just the opposite!"

Contacting the customer through the rep ensures that the person primarily responsible for customer relations (the rep) has an opportunity to control the sale. If reps know the customer, they are in the best position to get the answers required to any question from the manufacturer. If they do not know the customer, making the contact gives them the opportunity to develop a relationship.

Copies of All Customer Communications

Normally, a rep should receive a copy of all communications that go to a customer. This includes all routine communications, such as order acknowledgments, confirmations of order changes, shipping notices, invoices, and so on. This is good practice; it keeps the sales organization current on the status of each order. However, there are times when it may be appropriate to eliminate major segments of communications. One case would be major capital-equipment projects involving project managers. The reams of routine correspondence on major projects would choke most reps. Therefore, reps on these projects typically request they not be included on all copies but only on selected subjects, such as change requests, invoices, and new pricing. Work the system out with your reps.

Measuring Motivation

Dick Berry, professor of management at the University of Wisconsin, has studied the question of motivation thoroughly. In his book *Understanding and Motivating the Manufacturers' Agent* (1981), he presents the results of a research study on reps. Berry asked his rep respondents to evaluate the value to them of twenty motivational techniques. Their answers, grouped here into high, medium, and low, appear in Table 8-1. The statements that appear in the area of high motivational value clearly define the type of company that can really turn a rep on: the well-managed manufacturing company whose leadership maintains a long-term outlook.

What You Should Expect From Reps

The ideal relationship between rep and manufacturer is in essence a partnership, with the two organizations working as a team toward common goals. But a partnership is a two-way street; the rep expects certain things of you, and you have a right to expect certain things from the rep. If you have picked the right rep and are now providing good support, your rep

Table 8-1   Reps' evaluation of motivational techniques.

Statement	Percent of Respondents
High Degree of Motivational Value	
Image and reputation of principal in markets you serve	98
Product quality and reliability	98
Attitude of principal (esprit de corps)	96
Commission rate (fair)	95
Backup and support (specialized help in selling situations)	93
Introduction of new products	87
Product training (on specifications and applications)	84
Advertising programs directed at your customers	83
Solicitation of your recommendations for product, marketing, or advertising programs	81
Medium Degree of Motivational Value	
Financial incentives for new accounts or increased business	75
Visitations by principal at your convenience	74
Periodic sales performance reports (tabulated by account and product)	70
Volume progressive commission (increases as you attain higher sales levels)	66
Promotional offers you can extend to your customers (quantity discounts, special packaging, etc.)	63
Low Degree of Motivational Value	
Training on sales techniques	58
Recognition for outstanding performance (awards, publicity, etc.)	51
Overage splitting (normal commission plus split difference on any overage above minimum price)	48
Warnings to improve performance or lose the product line	35
Mutually established quotas (with commission based on attainment)	34
Contests (short term, with prizes awarded for sales attainment)	30

Adapted from Dick Berry, *Understanding and Motivating the Manufacturers' Agent* (New York: Van Nostrand Reinhold, 1981); used by permission.

should be providing you with the kinds of assistance and feedback described in the following sections.

On an overall basis, reps should understand the *quid pro quos* in their relationships with manufacturers. They have to appreciate that manufacturers have bureaucratic needs that include planning and forecasting. While reps dislike paperwork and bureaucracy (one of the reasons many reps leave corporate life to become entrepreneurs is to avoid these scenarios), they have to understand that their responsibility is to help the manu-facturers do an adequate job of planning and forecasting.

Other rational expectations you should have include:

In-Depth Knowledge and Influence With Key Customers

Knowledge alone is insufficient. What counts is the rep's ability to influ-ence customers to your advantage. This means being able to gain the right audience at the right time, to obtain necessary information to give you a better understanding of the customer or a specific negotiation, and to cre-ate a selling approach that will provide the best opportunity for closing the order.

Guidance on How to Sell in Their Territory

Reps should tell you how to run your business, at least when it comes to selling in their territory. Committed reps are not meek. They will push and shove manufacturers to the point of being an annoyance to some sales executives and presidents. However, this agitation is aimed at helping that manufacturer increase market share in the territory. Too frequently, mana-gerial egos take exception to having these independent organizations con-tinually press for action. It is when you hear nothing from reps that you should worry. This is a symptom of a rep that is not committed and is not selling for you.

Mutual Development and Pursuit of Objectives

By the time the rep is moving into the second year with you, there should be a fairly clear understanding of common objectives for that year. These must be developed mutually and should never be imposed unilaterally by the manufacturer. If they are, they lose all motivational value. The rep must buy into them, just as direct employees should buy into a set of objectives by which they will be measured.

Occasionally you may find maverick reps that refuse the whole con-cept of objectives. They may believe that objectives are rather meaningless, or that they do not have time to spend on setting objectives (at least sales volume objectives) for all of their principals. Fortunately, this hard-nosed stance is rare.

What should you do if a rep refuses to talk objectives? Try to remem-ber that the purpose of working through reps is not to set an objective but to achieve maximum market penetration of the area over the long term.

Attempting to force a rep into conformance with this numbers game is another extension of the boss/subordinate syndrome and the bureau-cratic need for having all numbers uniformly prepared. It is not a productive exercise with certain reps. If you find yourself in this situation, set a fair and reasonable objective and communicate that to the representative; say that it is simply a number you need for forecasting and for helping to monitor progress along with other key tools, such as successful hit ratios, gross margin generation, and so on. This approach satisfies the corporate numbers game, lets the rep know part of the evaluation methods, and yet avoids a counterproductive confrontation.

Considered, Timely Response to Your Inquiries

This does not necessarily mean *instant* response. Put yourself in the rep's shoes. Manufacturers must recognize that independent reps serve a number of masters. They will do their best to respond to requests from manufacturers, but any given request may rank well down their immediate priority list. This is a trade-off you must learn to accept.

However, you have a right to expect their considered response within a rational period. In most cases, reps will get you the answers you need within reasonable time constraints. If you cannot get this type of response, the chances are you don't have the right rep.

Handling Customer Negotiations

Depending on the nature of the products they handle, reps may be involved merely in offering guidance during the negotiation cycle or may be totally responsible for the application, sizing, pricing, negotiation, and order closing. Normally, the more you can put in the rep's hands, the more effective he will be for you. Having the power to make these negotiations enables the rep to appear more authoritative to the customer, offer prompter service, and have the maximum flexibility to operate successfully. The result is that your chances of beating out competition are increased.

A Fair Share of the Rep's Time

Theoretically, if you contribute 10 percent of a rep's income, you should expect 10 percent of her selling time. In practice, it's very difficult for reps to define the actual percentage of time they allocate to each principal. Your target should therefore be somewhat qualitative. A much better objective for you is to become the representative's preferred principal by virtue of good fit and good support.

As your position improves in a rep's evaluation, you will receive an increase in the discretionary time that the rep has available for selling. The manufacturer with the best fit and that best supports a rep will win out in the key conflict situations. As a result, the manufacturer receives more than a fair share of the rep's time. The pleasure a rep derives from the working relationship should never be overlooked, or underestimated, as a major source of getting more time spent on your company.

A Fair Share of Market in a Rational Period of Time

What is "fair" and what is "rational"? If you have an excellent current market position, the new rep should be expected to maintain that share almost from the start. If you have a poor share of market, at least compared to your average share around the country, the rep should be expected to increase market share at least to the national average. The only question is, What would be a "reasonable" time?

Generally, the first year with a new rep is a get-acquainted period. It takes time for a rep to understand new manufacturers and the problems they face in the field. While this period obviously will vary by the nature of the product handled, normally you will not see sharp increases until the second year. This improvement of an underperforming area to the national market share average in the second year is a relatively conservative assumption for many product and market combinations. That does not mean significant increases cannot be achieved within the first year. Many reps have taken an underperforming territory and made it an overperforming territory within the first year. Obviously, for companies that have very long lead times between definition of opportunity and order placement, the time period will be longer.

Once the historic average has been attained, the next objective is to increase market share above historic national averages. Market share is typically the result of yesterday's capabilities, not today's plans and programs, even though the manufacturer may have been working on them for a long time. Increasing a share of market requires making changes from past practice, even if the change is only increasing the support of more compatible representatives. Change takes time. Again, expectations should be *mutually* developed with each rep to determine logical targets and reasonable time frames.

Appropriate Promotion of Your Products

Reps will invest in promotion to varying degrees depending upon the industry and their own selling profile. Make sure you understand the norms for your industry and compare them against your reps' programs. It is not unusual for reps to have direct mail programs, telemarketing programs, seminars to acquaint customers with products and services, mini-trade shows devoted exclusively to their principals (normally on a shared-cost basis), and still participate in any number of other promotions. Which promotion is selected depends on not only the industry but the reps within that industry. You should understand that success is the result not of conformity in promotional approaches but of fitting sound promotion to each rep's style.

No Competing Lines

This requirement will be in your contract. However, the definition of just what is competing and what is not can be very subjective.

Prompt Announcement of Changes in Principals and Employees

This should also be a contract term. When reps change principals, their other manufacturers should be advised. This is not to suggest that manufacturers should have a deciding vote in any change. Rather, it is to alert each manufacturer represented that a change has occurred. Changes in principals might indicate a change in the reps' objectives or in their performance. You should investigate any noteworthy change to determine its cause and its potential impact on your relationship with the rep.

The same is true of personnel changes. If a productive employee leaves the rep firm, that could very well be an indication of the owner's inability to hold good talent. You should also be advised when new people are added; you have a right to know their background and how they will fit into the rep organization and the sale of your products. Professional reps routinely advise their principals of these changes, even without a contractual agreement.

However, be very careful to not give the impression that you are trying to interfere in the relationship between the rep owners and their employees. The rep firm is purely the owner's business. Flagrant interference in the business, such as canceling a rep and enticing one or more of that rep's employees to become direct salespeople, would leave you subject to litigation.

Professionalism

Reps should be professional at all times and in all matters. The concept of professionalism includes honesty, integrity, high standards of performance, empathy for your position, having your interest as well as the customer's interest at heart, and willingness to make commitments and live up to them.

Investment in Product Training

You will not have problems with reps being unwilling to devote time to product training, at least not with those who are a good match. The problem will primarily be in setting compatible schedules. A properly selected rep will want to understand all the nuances of your product and how it is differentiated in the marketplace. This knowledge will give the rep a leg up in making strong presentations against competition. Product training is one of the strongest motivating factors for developing committed rep networks.

Assistance in Collection Problems

Many manufacturers do not use their reps to help resolve receivable problems. They should, for reps recognize their role here. Resolving collection problems is not just a responsibility of the manufacturer. Reps also feel a responsibility to the customer to eliminate aggravations that can result from receivable problems. For reps being paid a commission when the manufacturer gets paid, their active involvement speeds up the flow of commission dollars.

A Well-Managed Business

You should expect to see a sound approach to growing current and future business. Assembly of complementary lines with a sharp focus on discrete markets, the retention of strong principals, the retention of skilled employees, and the provision of sufficient staff for continuing growth of the business are all marks of the well-managed independent rep firm.

What You Should *Not* Expect From Reps

Maintaining your half of a sound partnership also entails knowing what *not* to expect from reps.

Patience With Ineptness

Reps will work with you during problem periods, as long as they see genuine interest and effort on your part and logical, timely steps for correcting the problems. If you demonstrate an ineptitude for solving these problems within a reasonable period, reps' patience, and their support, will disappear. They will start to insulate you from their customers so as not to jeopardize the position of other manufacturers they represent.

Unethical or Illegal Conduct

Reps are professionals. Treat them that way. Don't expect more from them than you would expect of yourself—or less.

Compliance With Bureaucracy

Reps are interested in getting things done in the most expeditious way possible. Slow-moving bureaucracy is a major obstacle to highly productive professionals because it inhibits sales effectiveness. This is particularly true in relation to the paperwork of reporting systems. Manufacturers have to learn to separate form from substance in their requests to reps. You should seek profitable orders, minimal problems, and good verbal feedback—not a series of written reports. Reps have too many masters to serve to do it in writing. Do you want your reps producing paperwork or producing sales?

Instant Response

Timely response, yes; instant response, sometimes. As we've said earlier, representing multiple manufacturers means reps have to do a delicate balancing of priorities. They'll do their best to respond to your needs, but sometimes other manufacturers may be a higher priority.

Boss/Subordinate Relationships

The most productive relationship occurs when your company views the independent sales organization as an equal. Treat reps as your partners working to achieve mutually agreeable goals in their territory. Forget the authority. It may be good for your ego, but it will just backfire. If you expect success with reps, you must foster a peer relationship.

Missionary Effort

Reps assemble a number of compatible manufacturers that allow them to prioritize their selling efforts into select markets. Unless your company fits these priorities, you're not going to get maximum mileage out of a rep. If you need reps to do missionary work in industries they are not now calling on, you will get only lip service at best. However, you can count on a strong missionary effort from reps to penetrate their current customers and add new customers from their targets, as long as the reps are growth oriented.

Uneconomical Services

Do you really "need" a predetermined set of services from your reps (for example, computer or word processing services, full-time secretarial services, or fax)? What is needed in the mind of one rep may be totally superfluous in the mind of a second. All reps sell with their own style and with their own methods. To get maximum mileage out of your reps, recognize these differences and respect them. Put yourself in the rep's shoes, and look at the economics of what you're requesting. If it doesn't make sense economically, don't ask for it.

The Next Step

In this chapter you have learned the tools new reps need to get started efficiently, and you have increased your understanding of what you can reasonably expect from them. You have also learned some of the things they will expect from you. Reasonable expectations, openly communicated, lay the foundation for mutual respect. Upon this foundation, you must now create the environment in which your reps can do their best work.

9

The Importance of
Total Support

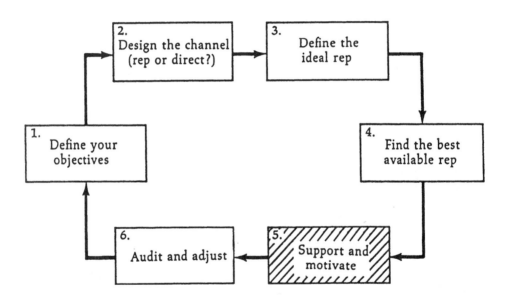

Support and motivation are two faces of the same coin. Companies that know how to create a climate in which reps find all-encompassing support will be rewarded with highly motivated sales performers. In that kind of climate, reps tend to give extra effort, to give you, in effect, *more* than your fair share of their time. And that is your goal.

Can that be done? Can you really hope to get more than your share of a rep's time? Absolutely. It's all a matter of understanding what turns a rep on and developing an organization in which those values flourish. Companies that fail to learn this will get *less* than a fair share of the representative's time. Typically, these manufacturers are the ones that have the most gripes about poor rep performance.

The Organizational Climate

Numerous studies have demonstrated conclusively that money is not the main thing that motivates people to do their best work. Reps are no exception. In fact, it is probably more true for them than for the general population. The "average" rep (let's agree for the moment there is such a thing) is already very successful financially.

So your sales pro, who is not dependent on any one manufacturer, has developed a solid net worth, maintains a strong and still-growing income, has achieved most of the personal financial goals for her family, including college education for her kids, and is still seeking new challenges.

What can you do? Simple: Focus all your efforts on doing the best management job possible. The best reps, the truly outstanding achievers, get their kicks from working on a good team, that is, with a well-run organization. The moral is clear: To get the best performance from reps, get your own house in order. Develop an organizational culture that prides itself on long-term success with decision-making excellence obtained through highly interactive team play. This type of team culture, oriented toward excellence, provides the ideal environment to excite most reps. At the same time, of course, you are also providing a highly productive climate for *all* your employees.

The Selling Team

With apologies to readers whose enthusiasms lie elsewhere, let's talk football for a moment. Figure 9-1 shows one schematic of a selling team. In this team, reps are the primary scorers. They are the ones who score the touchdowns—that is, get the orders. Yet, how many receivers or running backs score touchdowns without a strong team behind them?

Marketing is essentially the quarterback of the selling team. The marketing specialists are the ones who read the opposition and feed back to the organization the actions that should be taken to become more effective. They probe for the competitor's weak spots and provide the on-field leadership to penetrate those weaknesses. But marketing can only call the signals and provide one part of the offense. If any operational entity is weak, implementation of the "play" (such as a new-product program) typically falls well short of expected results.

The functional departments (engineering, operations, finance, R&D) are the defensive team, the offensive linemen, and the blocking backs. They are the infrastructure of the team; they allow plans to be successful. If there's a weakness in any link, the total team is less than successful.

Figure 9-1   The selling team.

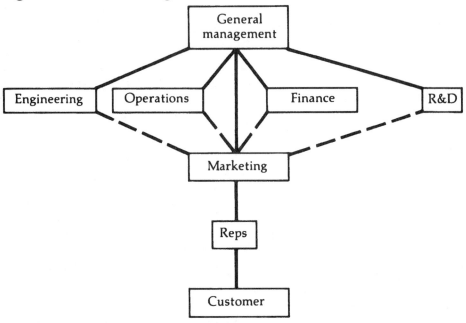

Without good information from marketing, for instance, they do not have the direction they need to be successful. Even with sound information, there can be weaknesses—for example, organizations with a history of engineering leadership frequently develop an engineering arrogance: "We know what's best for you, Mr. Customer!" As a result, customer *wants* are ignored, and the team fails.

General management is the coach, responsible for ensuring a total integration of all capabilities into a cohesive unit. Teamwork is the major ingredient in success; true teamwork can go a long way toward optimizing available talents. Obviously, the general manager is responsible for seeing that weak members are upgraded.

Commitment at the Top

Success with reps starts at the top. It is the person at the top of an organization who determines that organization's culture, and a properly supportive culture is crucial for rep sales excellence. Reps thrive in the right kind of culture and tend to lose interest when it is not present.

"Corporate culture" can be defined as the set of values commonly shared by personnel in an organization that guide decision making throughout the organization. The senior executive sets the tone for the organization's culture, for only that executive has the total responsibility and authority to ensure that the best possible decisions are made. This is achieved by developing the optimal environment for decision making and performance excellence.

The kind of culture that provides fertile ground for top performance by independent reps is one that puts a high emphasis on customer sensitivity and on strong support of the rep network. In this culture, reps are recognized as a conduit between the manufacturer and its customers; in a very real sense they are an extension of the customer.

This all adds up to one simple truth: No organization can really excel with reps unless the person at the top is wholeheartedly committed to the idea of using them. (For simplicity, let's call that person the president, although it could also be the division manager in the case of a highly autonomous division.) Any reservation the president shows about the rep network will be picked up by others in the organization. Then, no matter how hard the sales manager or marketing manager works to promote the reps, any negative attitudes of the president will be echoed by those in the engineering, operations, and financial departments in their contacts with the rep network. This negativism will eventually result in an organizational culture that diminishes, rather than strengthens, rep performance. If there is a common denominator among organizations that do not do well with reps, it is an anti-rep culture.

The solution is open, enthusiastic, and total commitment to the selected sales channel and total active involvement by the president to ensure that the organization follows suit. The president must obtain the commitment of the senior managers. They in turn have to work down through the organization so that a totally rep-sensitive group develops. In this way a manufacturer can get more than its fair share of rep time.

Training the Company to Work With Reps

If a president needs to turn around a culture that is negative toward reps, several tools are available. A number of public seminars provide sound training grounds in various aspects of working through reps. Seminars are offered by universities and other organizations around the country, including a two-day program at the University of Wisconsin in Madison, Wisconsin, and by MANA (Manufacturers' Agents National Association, Laguna Hills, CA) at various locations around the United States.

Public seminars are probably best suited to a relatively small number of individuals from a given organization. For larger numbers and for organizational training, in-house programs aimed at educating all personnel who directly and indirectly deal with reps are more cost-effective.

All these programs are purely starting points. As with most other seminars, retention is rapidly lost unless the ideas are constantly reinforced and practice becomes habit.

Proactive Presidential Style

Leaders of organizations that are built on teamwork and dedicated to excellence have learned the difference between delegation and abdication. (Those who need a review should study Figure 9-2.) This is particularly important in working with independent rep organizations. Successful reps recognize that the real leader of their principal is not the senior marketing executive but the president. They are really turned on by a president who plays a *proactive* role in ensuring the company stays both customer sensitive and rep sensitive.

That kind of president can be recognized by hands-on involvement, by the way information is gathered, and by participation in key marketing decisions.

Figure 9-2   Delegation vs. abdication.

The president of the organization said earnestly, "I've told my vice-president of marketing that my door is always open and that she should come in for help anytime she needs it. I'm always available."

That is not delegation; it is abdication of responsibility.

Here's the difference, particularly in relation to the organization's marketing department.

General Style

- Abdicators are reactive.
  Delegators are proactive.

Sources of Information

- Abdicators get filtered reports from the marketing executive.
  Delegators get reports directly from supervisors.
- Abdicators get one-perspective evaluation reports from the marketing executive.
  Delegators solicit independent audits and evaluations.
- Abdicators limit their questions to the marketing executive.
  Delegators collect all kinds of perspectives because they practice "managing by walking around" (MBWA) or "managing by telephoning around" (MBTA).
- Abdicators make a token appearance, at best, at meetings of the rep council.
  Delegators take an active participatory role in the rep council.

Key Marketing Decisions

- Abdicators turn responsibility for key decisions over to the marketing executive, who must then stand or fall on the company's market position.
  Delegators promote consensus decision making.

General Involvement in Marketing. Proactive presidents routinely engage in "ad hocracy"—periodic involvement in work groups that are addressing select issues in the company. They know this gives them a much better perception of the issues their organizations face.

Proactive presidents regularly poke around in their various departments. Managers, steeped in the president's value system that emphasizes team excellence, welcome this involvement. They know that open-ended questions from the boss help ensure they are on top of key issues in their department and on the right track toward finding solutions.

Collecting and Evaluating Information. In a classic bureaucratic reporting scheme, salespeople send reports to the regional manager, who integrates them and overlays her bias, eliminating points she considers sensitive. Regional managers then report to a sales manager, who repeats the same type of censorship, and so on up to the senior marketing executive's report to the president. By the time the president receives the report, he has little information on issues facing the organization. Proactive presidents want reports from lower levels to come directly to them, at least on a sampling basis.

Proactive presidents solicit independent evaluations (audits) of the organization's activities. They know that this kind of independent evaluation can help ensure that all issues and opportunities in the organization have been identified and that resolutions are being diligently pursued. Reactive presidents, on the other hand, will ask a key functional manager to audit a given situation in that manager's department and will rely solely on that evaluation.

Proactive presidents collect information at all levels of the organization. They believe in, and practice, "management by walking around" (MBWA). That simply means that the president periodically visits employees in lower levels of the organizational hierarchy and asks open-ended questions about their view of issues facing the company, their department, and their work responsibilities. In a culture conducive to candor, employees will quickly define for the president issues that she may not learn of otherwise.

With the rep network, there is a parallel approach. We'll call it "managing by telephoning around" (MBTA). The inherent independence of reps breeds a candor that is not normally found in direct salespeople. Although periodic telephone calls are no substitute for the various other means of maintaining a personal understanding of the marketplace, random calls to reps provide excellent *supplemental* feedback to the senior executive.

Proactive presidents welcome the feedback they get from the rep council (see Chapter 11) and themselves play an active role in the council.

Key Marketing Decisions. Presidents, particularly those who do not have a marketing background, too often abdicate their responsibilities in the area of proactive marketing involvement. When share erodes because of poor marketing decisions, then the marketing executive is replaced. The price of this type of abdication is too high. Key marketing decisions should be made by consensus, with the president an active participant.

Presidential Commitment and Success

Successful reps, as we have said, like to be associated with successful organizations. They know how to recognize them. They look for qualities like those listed here—all of which emanate directly from the commitment of the president. Over the long term, an organization tends to develop the personality of its leader.

Greater Customer Sensitivity. The successful organization gets closer to customers and moves faster in response to customer needs than its less successful competitors. The senior executive must make sure—by zealously preaching, practicing, and monitoring—that this sensitivity permeates the entire organization.

Creation of Successful Niches. Shotgun marketing is generally doomed to low profit margins. The successful organization clearly defines those segments of a broad market where differentiation can be obtained. This is a critical step in developing a strong market position and obtaining those few extra percentage points in price realization that lead toward profitable rather than marginal performance.

Rapid Innovation. Innovation characterizes all aspects of the successful business: product development, quality improvement, schedule improvements, and improvements in system procedures and controls. Everybody in a really successful organization is constantly searching for ways to improve performance.

Emphasis on Team Building. No one manager has all the answers. General managers are as fallible as any functional manager—if not more so. Usually they come up through the ranks of one functional department, gaining all their experience in one area, until suddenly they are responsible for decisions in many functional areas. Their most critical tool is a decision-making process built around consensus, bringing in the ideas and values of all key people.

Successful companies have managed to reorient managerial egos from "I" to "we." Managers in these companies take more pride in the success of the organization than in their own success. Individual pride comes from knowing that they made a contribution to the whole. It's the same pride felt by members of a winning sports team. When the president backs off from a decision because someone well down in the organization made an unsolicited comment that introduced a new perspective, he should feel proud—and so should the employee.

The Role of the Marketing Department

The marketing department, the quarterback of the selling team, provides direct support to the rep organization and defines the support needed from other departments.

In the area of marketing support, reps look for effective market planning, market niching, well-prepared application data, success stories with clear instructions on how to duplicate these successes, well-targeted advertising and promotion programs that yield qualified leads, and a continued flow of professional marketing support. We look in detail at several of these.

Structuring the Department for Maximum Effectiveness

The structure of marketing departments varies widely, based on the volume and profitability of an organization, the nature of the products sold, the senior executive's commitment to marketing, and her approach to management (short term or long term). However, structure per se has little to do with marketing success. The key is to make sure the functions are being performed rather than to agonize about the structural form of the organization.

The organizational chart of a rather typical industrial products organization with sales of $50 million to $100 million is shown in Figure 9-3. In larger organizations, there may be more functional areas; in smaller organizations, there will be fewer regional managers, down to zero, with the sales manager assuming all the major regional responsibilities. In even smaller organizations, the marketing manager will also wear the hat of the sales manager and even that of the product manager. In very small companies, say, in the $1 million to $5 million class, the marketing role might even be assumed by the president.

The actual position titles vary, as do reporting lines. What the chart shows as "marketing services" could also be "manager of advertising and promotion," with other members of the department responsible for research and planning. Customer services, the department that handles the incoming paperwork after an order is received, may be called "order service" where there is little complexity. With larger contracts, it may be called "contract administration." With multimillion-dollar projects, this

Figure 9-3   Organization of a typical marketing department.

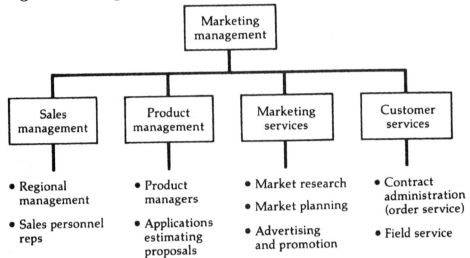

department might be called "product management" and might report directly to the senior executive.

There is no magical textbook answer to structuring the marketing department. It depends on the company, the products, the markets, the people involved, and the personal preferences of key managers. The key is to develop a series of subfunctions critically needed for effective marketing support. The structure and positions should represent a rational span of control in terms of numbers, issues faced, and the capabilities of each manager. The primary needs to be satisfied are customer sensitivity and a rational balance of expense for the basic business and the objectives to be achieved. Lines and blocks on paper only hope to suggest a rational relationship between jobs to be done. After all, it is committed people working effectively together that really achieves success.

Department/Rep Interaction. Organizations that are the most effective with reps simplify all interactive relationships with the rep network. Frequently this means each rep contacts one person at the company for any information required to close an order and a second person for all information about the order after it is entered. Ideally, though this is not necessarily practical for many companies, each rep would have a *single* contact for all routine matters.

The other end of the scale is a structure built on bureaucracy. Let's look at the product management function of an organization in the $50 million to $100 million range with a network of twenty-five separate rep firms and five product specialists or application engineers (AEs) to serve the reps' proposal needs. Schematically it would look like Figure 9-4. The

Figure 9-4   Load-leveling product management structure.

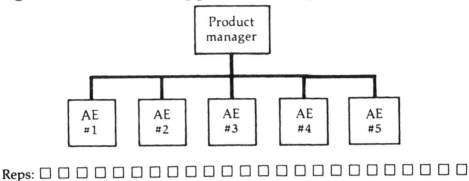

bureaucratic structure, under the guise of efficiency, would use load-leveling techniques to balance out the workload among the five application engineers. An inquiry from a rep would be sent to the product manager, who would then assign it to the application engineer with the lightest load.

On the surface, this is very efficient. In practice, it introduces major roadblocks to effective selling. The organization that is sensitive to rep needs would assign a single application engineer to a block of representatives, typically from a given region. Or reps could be grouped in common markets. Each rep then knows there is only one individual to contact in the negotiation phase, and the inquiry goes directly to a specific application engineer. This also permits the application engineers to better understand the idiosyncrasies of the reps under their responsibility and adapt to them. It breeds efficiency and team play.

Conversely, reps who don't know who is going to handle their inquiries face a number of problems. Really good reps try to maneuver around those problems by working behind the scenes to see that their inquiries go to the individual of their choice. This breeds all sorts of strains in the organization. If you can, keep it simple, with a one-on-one relationship between a rep and the person who has the answers that rep needs.

Support Activities

The scope of the support activities required for effective rep performance varies significantly depending on the nature of the product and the market. Smaller companies can do less than larger firms can in terms of quantity, but in other respects they must provide similar support activities. A number of the more important support activities you should consider for maximum rep effectiveness are presented here. Don't view this list as an order of priority; different product/market combinations call for different priorities. It is up to each manufacturer to select those that are most appropriate.

- The marketing plan
- Product manuals
- Competitive analyses
- Training
- Field visits
- Newsletters
- Activities records
- Commission status report
- An industry voice
- Advertising and promotion
- Miscellaneous support tools

The Marketing Plan. The properly selected rep should be an extension of the marketing plan, and the plan has to be clearly conveyed to the rep. The specific industry priorities should be clearly spelled out and overall company objectives should be clearly understood, along with the specific programs the company is undertaking to achieve these objectives. Reps should have a very clear picture of exactly how they fit into this plan and what is expected of them. This permits them to allocate their time to those activities that can yield the maximum return for the effort.

Some manufacturers believe the marketing plan is confidential and that reps, as independent "outsiders," should not have access to it. Some information, of course, is properly confidential and should not be disclosed to reps indiscriminately: pending acquisitions, breakthrough technology before patent disclosure, and privileged information, for example. For the most part, however, keeping the reps in the dark does little else than prevent them from helping you achieve your objectives in the marketplace. Treating reps as confidential partners is one of the cornerstones for building an outstanding team.

Product Manuals. The primary objective of the product manual is to put as much information as possible into the reps' hands to make them self-sufficient in negotiations with customers. Include background on each product, its application, sizing parameters, pricing, delivery information, and so on. Commission schedules should also be included in a separate section of the binder so that the reps have a clear understanding of what compensation will be received under what situations.

If the product is highly technical, the product manuals frequently cannot convey all the information reps need. In that case, custom applications, custom sizing, and pricing may have to come from the products department. However, product manuals are still required to help reps fully understand the product for their sales role.

Competitive Analyses. Actually, competitive analyses should be included in the product manual, but they are discussed separately because of their great significance. The analyses should clearly define the strengths and weaknesses of each significant competitor and should also give the reps a frame of reference for understanding the edge they have with your products. Little information is more critical than these analyses; they provide the rep with keen insights on how they can upset competition. It's a good idea to put these analyses in a separate section of the manual and constantly upgrade it as new information is received.

Training. Training for new products, systems, or services is really the launch vehicle for success. Take extreme care to orchestrate the introduction process properly. It is one of the great opportunities not only for motivating reps but for having a major impact in the marketplace. All the necessary preparation of application data, shipping schedules, commissions, market focus, publicity, and so forth, should be put in place for a kickoff target date. Just before the announcement, implement the training program, preferably in a series of fast-moving regional meetings so you can keep the classes to a practical size for effective interaction. Reps should walk away from this training session with a complete package.

The need for retraining is a judgment call. Talking to a number of reps will give you the best sense. Even if the need is not pronounced, retraining can be logically combined with other meetings. For example, a biennial sales meeting can provide opportunities for condensed retraining programs.

Field Visits. Product managers and regional managers should make routine field visits. The regional manager provides support for general training and specific job negotiations; the product manager gets involved for more technical presentations and more formal training programs.

If you asked reps how frequently they would like to be visited by a principal, you'd get a wide range of answers. More often than not, reps mutter something like, "I wouldn't mind seeing the regional manager once a quarter (but not more frequently than that)." Yet, some reps, even in important areas, don't see a principal for six months to a year or even longer. Such nominal contact with reps, particularly in important trading areas, is hardly conducive to getting more than a fair share of their time. Reps are only human. They will respond to the "squeaking wheel," the company that makes itself abundantly visible in a constructive sense. Even reps who feel a little put out about the number of times they see emissaries of a manufacturer agree that this does make them spend more time on that manufacturer's product. The key is to locate that fine line between what reps view as being aggressive in a positive way and what they consider being overly demanding.

Newsletters. Newsletters are an excellent way of communicating to reps routine information that can help them improve their effectiveness for you. The key is to make sure that you have sufficient information to publish a letter on a regular basis; even a quarterly letter can be effective. It is too easy to rush into the idea of doing a newsletter, only to find after three or four issues that there is little meat left to present, and the newsletter has degenerated into a social column.

Even if you don't have reason to publish a regular newsletter, make sure you have some device (such as letters or memos) for getting information to reps, including:

- *Success stories.* Reps enjoy hearing about their peers' sales successes. Frequently, this gives them an idea of how to apply the same techniques to their territory.
- *Industry trends.* Customer industries typically have changes that some reps might not be aware of. If you don't have a newsletter, announce these changes in letter form.
- *Organizational changes.* As soon as a change is made in your organization that even indirectly affects a rep, send a letter explaining the nature of the change and its impact on the rep.

Activities Records. Again, depending on the nature of the product and the number of units handled, you might publish a monthly report of open negotiations and new-orders activity for each rep. Publishing open negotiations provides a control influence; reps know that you are aware of each and every one.

Commission Status Report. One report activity that must be completely accurate and timely is the commission status report. Monthly statements should clearly identify the commission backlog, as well as how much was paid that month. All figures should be cross-referenced for ready identification.

An Industry Voice. Being associated with an industry leader is one of the major motivations of reps. To be a leader, you have to act like one. Establish your company as an industry voice by writing technical articles, presenting technical papers at trade association and technical society meetings, and taking a lead in industry activities. All these activities add to the stature of your organization and to the motivation of a rep. Send copies of each article and speech to the reps for their information.

Advertising and Promotion. Reps want strong advertising support, normally with very focused appeals. This effort includes participation in key trade shows, advertising and promotional activities in trade magazines, institutional advertising where appropriate, direct mail, telemarketing, and a variety of local promotions, usually in conjunction with a rep.

Direct mail can be an excellent complement to more conventional advertising and sales promotion activities, particularly when specific individuals must be reached with a very specific message. Assuming these individuals can be readily defined, direct mail can be used to highlight a specific opportunity or issue; a program of two to three consecutive mailings is particularly effective.

Telemarketing is becoming increasingly important in view of the ever-escalating cost of selling. At a minimum, use it as a screening device to qualify advertising and promotional leads. Unqualified leads are a waste of a rep's time. Responses to the typical "bingo" card in magazines (readers check off products they want more information on, and the magazine forwards names to the manufacturer) frequently include students, professors, competitors, and any number of other different classes of readers who offer no opportunities. If a rep receives a stack of bingo cards and finds that none of the first five or six he telephones has even the remotest connection with a customer, chances are the whole stack will be shoved aside.

Taken to the next level, telemarketing can be used effectively to help create demand for new products or services, improve market intelligence feedback, support selling activities in market segments that are not strengths of the rep network (such as aftermarketing), and engender other opportunities unique to specific industries.

Computer Hardware and Software. The 1990s have seen a major transition in communication tools by manufacturers—from fax and U.S. mail services to computer interfacing. This transition has progressed at widely divergent rates depending on the industry. The higher tech industries, as might be expected, have progressed the furthest, particularly where selling from either the manufacturer's or the rep's inventory is involved. Common software programs have been established interfacing the manufacturer's inventory with each of the reps in order to provide the fastest possible communications and the most effective use of inventory levels throughout all trading areas.

Software programs are also being used whereby reps can input customer inquiries to the manufacturer's host computer and receive a complete proposal of rather complex products and systems on almost a real-time basis. Financial information systems including commission status, new orders, past performance, etc., are also widely used.

One area of major opportunity for helping manufacturers achieve sales growth objectives is the group of software generally described as *contact management.* The primary initial program used by manufacturers and reps was *ACT.* The next entrée was *Gold Mine* and then a software program with wider capabilities, *Maximizer.* However, major problems arise when a manufacturer attempts to integrate a contact management software program with all of its reps. Each rep may have an average of ten to fifteen manufacturers under contract. Manufacturers can vary widely from rep to rep within one manufacturer's rep network. This creates major problems for a rep to select a single piece of contact management software that might be useable with all of his principals. There are simply too many software programs being used, too many reps or manufacturers not using such programs, and too many reps who still have no interest in same. These highly effective software programs can be readily used with a direct sales organization. But unless one manufacturer really dominates the income of the rep and therefore has economic leverage to assure its implementation, the use of contact management software programs throughout rep networks are still a vision of the future. The key step will be for at least one given industry to standardize a given software package for contact management. Then, it should be reasonable to expect all reps in a given sales channel to use common software.

Miscellaneous Support Tools. Fax, voice mail systems, e-mail, and similar tools to improve the communication between rep and manufacturer are being used more each year. In particular, use of an 800 number has gained favor rather rapidly. It helps minimize the reps' concern about managing their telephone expense with your company. Obviously, there is the chance that it can be abused, but the benefits usually far outweigh the occasional abuse. The need for these tools varies with the industry and the style of individual companies. The key is to pick the ones that are most cost-effective in helping your company achieve its objectives in the marketplace.

Sales Meetings

Sales meetings have a definite role in the information flow to the representatives and in building a strong relationship between rep and manufacturer. However, strong discourse is usually attainable only at smaller meetings. The larger the attendance is at a sales meeting, the more it tends to be one-way information flow—from manufacturer to rep—and the more it becomes a social affair designed to foster stronger personal relationships.

Certainly sales meetings have a place in the relationship between the manufacturer and its rep network. However, most companies don't need one every year. A biennial meeting is sufficient; save the money for higher priority activities, such as regional training sessions.

Even so, don't schedule a sales meeting simply because it's been two years since the last one. You must have valid reasons for calling the meeting. Make sure there is sufficient information to transfer to the reps to make their time investment worthwhile.

A few ground rules for a national sales meeting:

1. Prepare each meeting with great care and total professionalism.
2. Announce the meeting well in advance so the representatives can schedule their time appropriately. Six months ahead is not too soon; you may need even longer lead time to reserve the accommodations you want.
3. Consult the rep council (see Chapter 11) for agenda items.
4. Establish a very clear set of objectives.
5. Select company personnel carefully for their abilities to contribute to the objectives and to make sound presentations.
6. Rehearse presentations and make sure they are properly polished and conform to the allocated time.
7. Use off-site locations to minimize interruption.
8. Allow time for informal networking. Golf, fishing, or relaxing by the pool and discussing subjects of mutual interest is effective in building a closer bond.
9. Design a format that is hard-hitting, time-sensitive, informal, and results-oriented.
10. Clarify expense arrangement. Travel-in and travel-out costs are usually borne by the representatives, with all other normal expenses assumed by the manufacturer. Some manufacturers pick up the entire expense, but they are in the minority.
11. Summarize meeting highlights, and promptly confirm in writing any new action items committed to.

In addition to national sales meetings, regional sales meetings offer an excellent vehicle for motivation. The smaller group allows for a more dynamic interchange between manufacturer and reps. These meetings can also address regional problems, solicit feedback on issues and opportunities perceived by the representatives, and offer workshops to address these issues. They also enable the reps to get to know their neighboring reps better.

Good Management and Motivation

In the early 1980s, I made a speech in California at the Western Electronics Show and Convention (WESCON) to members of the electronics industry, presenting what I felt were ten ingredients for organizational success in the coming decade. These ingredients remain essential. In fact, all will be critical for organization success well into the 21st century. They are:

1. *Customer sensitivity.* Manufacturers must maintain a close touch with their key customer industries so that they fully know customer needs

as customers perceive them. It then remains for the manufacturers to respond to these needs promptly.

The company that is truly responsive to customers invariably receives a strong commitment from a properly selected and supported independent network. Responsiveness to customers is probably the major single attribute that reps want in companies they represent. Your reps' unique closeness to customers can help you develop this needed sensitivity—if you listen to them carefully.

2. *Product quality and service.* Every time a company sells a product to a new customer, it creates the opportunity for developing repeat business. Whether that new customer becomes a repeat customer depends on the quality of that product and the service the manufacturer provides if a problem arises. Manufacturers should also look toward additional support services the customer may need.

Product quality and service are major characteristics that can turn independent sales reps on or off to a manufacturer. They want manufacturers that produce quality products and provide quality service. If you have a problem with either one, rest assured your reps will let you know about it. If you *solve* that problem, you're way ahead of the game.

The success of TruHeat Corporation, an electric heating element manufacturer in Allegan, Michigan, points out the critical need for these two qualities. As one of the company's reps said, "Once TruHeat gets a customer, they just don't lose them!" This testifies to the enduring relationship that builds between a customer and a manufacturer when that manufacturer provides product quality and service. Then, if the manufacturer can add a number of other positive ingredients to its overall profile, true long-term success can be achieved.

3. *Innovation.* This means not only product innovation but innovation in all forms of technology, services, systems, procedures, communications—in fact, all organizational activity. Every individual in every department should constantly be searching out ways to improve everything that person touches. The status quo should be viewed as unacceptable. The risk of not having this type of creative culture is that a competitor will have it and will stampede right past you.

While reps primarily want to take on established companies, they are extremely responsive to manufacturers that can, and do, produce new products. This gives the reps additional uniqueness in the marketplace and new solutions to offer their customers. A properly motivated rep is an excellent source of ideas for improving your products, services, systems, and procedures. Her experience with other manufacturers can give you insight into many successful practices.

4. *Nichemanship.* Shotgun marketing is a luxury that should be used by extremely few manufacturers. The great majority of companies need to

focus on segments of broad markets in order to obtain some differentiation of their products and services. It is only through this differentiation that truly strong market positions can be obtained, leading a company into the number one spot and holding it there. This position is necessary to generate the price realization that will allow a manufacturer to remain profitable.

Reps are market segment specialists. They mesh beautifully with a market segmentation strategy.

5. *Sense of urgency.* "Get it done now." That was the clear cry from Peters and Waterman. It has also been a definite characteristic of truly successful companies down through the years. Put yourself in an independent salesperson's shoes and consider which company you would work hardest for: the company that tries to give you sound answers with a clear sense of urgency, responding to customer questions and yours on time, or the company that limps along without enthusiasm, frequently missing deadlines?

Some manufacturers complain that reps are too demanding. *"They think we can do everything now!"* is the cry. Yet many companies do "get it done now." They not only gain the respect of their reps; they get more than a fair share of their reps' time.

6. *Being the best.* If we do not set high standards, we will not know how far we can go. Being the best is typically measured by being first in your market, at least in the niche that you have defined for yourself. Being the best has a number of valuable spin-offs. First, the morale of an organization that really knows it is tops in its field is outstanding. This tends to develop excellence in new personnel joining the company and fosters a "can-do" attitude. It invariably leads toward enhancement of top market positions and the strongest profitability in the industry.

Obviously, the best professional independent sales organizations want to be associated with the best manufacturers. The two partners then build on each other, developing an outstanding strength in the marketplace that is intimidating to the competition.

7. *Respect for the individual.* Each individual in an organization has a contribution to make, not only in the specific job function but also in broader issues via interfunctional activities. Each individual deserves the highest respect. Those who are treated with respect tend to reach even higher and contribute even more. They also tend to treat others with respect, creating an upward spiral of effectiveness. Reps play a key role in this spiral. Their very nature—independent, highly self-motivated— demands that others work with them in an attitude of respect, and this nourishes a productive atmosphere of mutual respect throughout the organization.

8. *Highly interactive teams.* A corporate culture based on teamwork and consensus decision making promotes excellence in all aspects of the

business. This has been demonstrated many times over. Extending this concept to the rep network can only yield improved performance over both the short and the long term. Without this team relationship with reps, you probably will not get a fair share of their time.

9. *Total selling.* As you increase customer sensitivity, you should also increase the personal exposure of key members of the organization to customers. It is amazing to see the number of key managers who never have direct customer contact. There are major advantages to having managers of manufacturing, engineering, R&D, quality control, and so on get out and visit customers. They will thereby gain a greater appreciation of customer needs and a more balanced perspective for decision making.

In addition, these key managers can become a vital part of the selling effort. For example, in a major negotiation when scheduling is critical, an astute presentation by the manufacturing manager and the individual who manages the material requirements planning system can be the major single ingredient in closing the sale.

The senior executive—whether president, CEO, or division manager—also needs to play a role in this selling effort. This has a threefold purpose. First, in certain negotiations the president can be the most effective individual in the organization when helping to close a major project, penetrate a new customer, or even resolve a key issue. Second, it gives the president a fresh perspective of what the business is all about. The president who stays within the confines of the infrastructure typically develops a very stilted point of view as to the issues and opportunities facing the business. In the classic ''belly to belly'' selling role, the president's perspective is constantly invigorated. A third advantage is the strong posture that is presented to the independent sales network. Knowing the senior executive is fully behind their efforts really strengthens their commitment to the company—another factor that helps you get more than a fair share of their time.

10. *Audit and adjustment.* Your organization must continually reexamine its progress toward objectives and make the necessary adjustments as conditions warrant. The very best strategic and operational plans can be blown out of the water before the final version is typed. You must be totally open to symptoms of emerging issues and opportunities and constantly solicit critique from all areas of your organization. The independent sales network, with its uniquely objective position in the outside world, can be of tremendous advantage here. If you cultivate an action-oriented feedback system, you will be alerted, early on, to changing events, and you'll be able to change your own course of action accordingly.

Key to success: Rep motivation is not bugle blowing or drumbeating; reps are not motivated by showy splashes. They are motivated by organizations that manage their business well and understand how to work effectively with independent reps.

The Next Step

Well-chosen reps, properly supported, almost invariably give you the kind of outstanding sales performance you expect—perhaps more. That doesn't mean you can disassociate yourself from the scene. A system of accountability standards, performance criteria, and evaluation checkpoints will ensure that you are getting what you want from your reps, and that potential trouble spots are discovered early. Step 6 is evaluation.

10

Evaluating and Controlling Performance

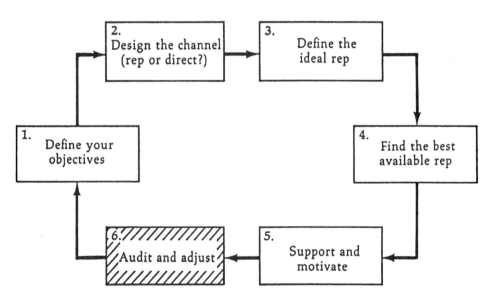

The bottom line is corporate performance over the *long term.* The measure of rep performance is the generation of profitable new orders, also over the long term. A shortfall in any one year could be triggered by any number of things, not necessarily occurring in that year. A drop in sales for one year with a rep does not necessarily mean that rep is not performing. Conversely, a rep that has increased sales in the current year compared to the previous year may really have done a poor job that, if continued, will reflect in declining sales over the long term.

You, the manufacturer, are therefore faced with the rather difficult task of evaluating whether a rep's performance is good, marginal, or submarginal. You can't safely rely just on the number and value of new orders; several other factors bear on a rep's current performance and the probability of future success. Your assessment should therefore include, among other factors:

- Orders performance
- Market share performance
- Inquiry-generation activity
- Current compatibility profile

Standards for Evaluating Performance

Orders Performance

Presuming you are assessing an existing representative with whom you have worked for some time, the trend of his orders performance relative to other reps is one of the most appropriate measures. You track new orders generated by that rep against overall company numbers (percentage of total) and possibly against a group of reps with very similar market opportunities.

The key to this evaluation is ensuring that you use a logical reference point. For example, a rep that formerly dominated a territory that is now receiving a lot of attention from competitors may be hard pressed to maintain the same share as past years. In that case, even a flat level of new orders could be considered excellent performance. On the other hand, a rep that has had a poor track record for years may, as a result of any number of factors, start to catch on with your company. This rep could show a sharp gain over previous years—higher than the national average—while applying the same effort.

Along with orders performance, you should also overlay the success ratio on closing new orders as compared to proposals. However, this calculation is appropriate only if you prepare and track the proposals or if your reps routinely submit a list of new proposals (which is not common). Therefore, percentage of success in closing rate is only for select manufacturers and industries. If you can track it, you have an excellent tool to determine how discerning the rep is in selecting sales opportunities and how strong a closer the salesperson is.

Another measure is performance compared to objectives agreed upon by the rep and the manufacturer for that period. Here again, attainment or nonattainment of objectives has to be put in the proper context: Were the targets reasonable, or were they perhaps overly optimistic? If you see any developing shortfall from objectives, promptly communicate with the rep about why and discuss whether any suitable action program by either party can help get the performance on target.

Market Share Performance

The true measure of performance is the market share that a rep or a manufacturer takes and the trend of that share over time. Unfortunately, market share cannot always be reasonably measured. For many companies, the actual value of a market in a given trading area for any given period of time is unknown. In other cases, it becomes an educated guess. Only a fortunate minority of reps sell into a market that permits a ready definition of market and therefore of share.

As with new orders, a rep's performance in market share should be tracked over time and compared to that of reps that serve a similar market profile, as well as to the company's overall average.

Inquiry Activity

A plot of new inquiries per month on a cumulative basis, combined with a plot of total open proposals on a month-by-month basis, offers another valid measure of rep performance. This is more appropriate for products with a long buying cycle and large unit value, and it presumes the rep does not do pricing. It is an excellent measure of how effective a rep has been in generating new opportunities and building an inquiry backlog. It can also be used as a basis for forecasting new orders. The forecast is based on lead time from inquiry to new-order lead and historic success percentages.

Current Compatibility Profile

When you first selected your reps, you used a model of an ideal rep, one that exactly fit with your product, your market, and your objectives. The question you should be asking yourself during this evaluation phase is, Has anything changed?

In a fast-moving, intensely competitive marketplace, many factors are continually at work modifying the profile of both the company and the rep network. From the company's side, changes may occur in market mix, competitors, technology, and customer mix, to name just a few. In addition, as time goes by, you should have developed a better understanding of the exact kind of rep that best serves your needs. During this same period, the rep's profile and interests can also change significantly. Old principals are dropped and new principals are acquired, giving a somewhat different complexion to the firm. People in the rep's organization can change. Drive levels can accelerate or diminish.

It therefore becomes imperative to audit a rep network in detail on a regular basis, at least annually, or anytime change occurs that raises questions about the rep's ability to do the job. The decision to downgrade the position in a major market is one such change. The decision to go after a significant new market, or to increase penetration of a market sharply that was previously viewed as totally secondary, are two other changes. In all such cases, reexamine your rep network to make sure each firm satisfies the requirements for success in the new game.

As you compare the rep's current profile to your changing needs, one area you should pay particular attention to is the matter of life cycle. Let's take another look at the life cycle curve of two rep firms, only this time we'll look at age of the owners rather than years the firm has been in business (Figure 10-1).

Owner A and Owner B both started their business at the age of forty and plan to retire at age seventy. At around age fifty-five, Owner B added some younger people and gave them the opportunity to eventually buy into the firm. Owner A, exercising her freedom of choice as an independent, opted for a different lifestyle, in which she had no desire to perpetuate the firm—and you can see what happened. One or more manufacturers eventually recognized that she was not going to provide continuity for her business and had peaked out in her selling effort, so they canceled. The rep's volume decreased in a straight line equal to the amount of business lost owing to the first cancellation, and then leveled out—until the second cancellation, and the third. Eventually the rep dropped out of the business.

Most growth-oriented reps start adding personnel around the time

Figure 10-1   Life cycle of two rep firms.

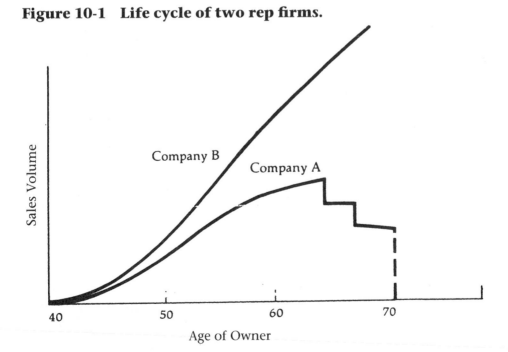

they clearly establish a sound working-capital position and have a sharp view of the direction they wish to take. Depending on the industry, this can be as short as two years to well over five years. However, if ten years passes since a firm was first established and no new people have been brought in, you would be hard pressed to consider this a growth-oriented rep firm. If you, the manufacturer, *are* growth oriented, you now have a problem. What can be done? Once you judge that there is a high probability of a rep's peaking out and there is no plan for continuity through hiring younger blood, agreements need to be worked out with the rep to provide you some protection before your market position in the area deteriorates.

Fortunately, the threat of cancellation is not the only alternative. First, push to have the rep provide for continuity by adding personnel. If this is an important trading area for you, perhaps you can provide some funding assistance. If this is not possible, try negotiating the split-off of markets, assigning segments to another rep specializing in those markets. If the rep digs in her heels against all your overtures, cancellation should be considered for all or part of the contract.

These are tough decisions if the rep has been a valuable member of your network. However, true partnership requires that both sides work together toward the same goal. If objectives are out of sync, corrections must take place.

By the way, this is not a one-way street. The same holds true for aggressive reps that find themselves with a manufacturer committed to the status quo rather than growth. Reps are faced with the same difficult decision of whether to maintain or sever long-term, friendly relationships.

Other Factors Involved in Assessing a Rep's Performance

There are a number of qualitative assessments that can be made in order to help evaluate the degree of commitment a rep has to your firm. These include assessing the quality of rep feedback, the degree of cooperative spirit displayed by the rep, and the degree to which the rep is aggressively promoting your product. Let's look briefly at each.

Quality of rep feedback covers a wide range of subjects that are not directly related to new orders. Information from the rep on customer and industry trends, suggestions that your company look at alternative opportunities, and so on are the types of feedback typically received from committed reps.

A rep with a cooperative spirit stands out in many ways. When urgent questions are raised to the rep by a manufacturer, the rep somehow finds a way of responding with a quality reply and in a timely fashion, despite the fact of having to serve several "masters." These reps are always looking at the relationship from the "we" point of view and wholeheartedly participate in any rational venture with the manufacturers they represent.

Committed reps aggressively promote their manufacturers' products in fashions that are compatible with their modus operandi. Reps may ask for a significant supply of material for direct mail programs. Others will request your participation in local equipment shows that they put on for all their manufacturers. The committed rep is always out there hustling.

All these factors, as well as a number of others, should be carefully considered in your overall evaluation of a rep's accomplishments.

Pinpointing Reasons for Success

Use your ideal rep profile to help you understand not only lack of performance but the reasons for *good* performance. Understanding the whys of good performance is extremely important. If you try to reproduce the profile of a successful rep without identifying the reasons behind that success, you may find that these "carbon copies" turn out to be failures. Here is an example that illustrates this point. It concerns distributors but applies just as well to manufacturers' reps.

A manufacturer selected one branch office of a regional distributor in a small midwestern city to sell its product line. In short order, that branch did a bang-up job, sharply escalating historic orders performance. The branch had an excellent position with four major chemical companies in the area and became the dominant supplier to those companies. The company concluded it had a winner and promptly signed on additional branch offices of that distributor in three larger cities, two with significantly greater potential. All three failed to even maintain the previous share of business. What happened?

The first branch had two unusual assets that made it atypical. First, the branch manager had an unusual affinity for the product, based on his experience. Second, competition had no local inventory in that area. The branch manager saw this as a major opportunity, promptly invested in a strong inventory position, and cleaned up in the area. Unfortunately, in the other three areas, competition had local inventory with its distributors. Also, the managers of these three operations had no particular attraction to the product. The product was almost commodity in nature, and competition was extremely tough.

By signing on these three branches, the manufacturer failed in its penetration objectives. The lesson was hard but beneficial. From that point on, the company carefully profiled the whys and wherefores of other successes and developed an ideal distributor profile to use in evaluating new candidates.

Evaluating the New Representative

Evaluating a new representative takes on a rather different flavor from evaluating a rep that has been with you for two years or more.

Let's define a new representative as one that has not been with you long enough to be able to establish a performance record, in terms of new orders compared to opportunities in the area. The exact time period will vary significantly, depending on the gestation period between opportunity identification and order closing. For a quick-turnaround business, you can evaluate new-orders performance in as little as several months. However, long-term projects, like those found in capital equipment, OEMs, or Department of Defense programs, may require several years. A similar situation occurs when a company brings on a rep to do a totally missionary job of establishing the company in a trading area. New-orders performance in these cases cannot be measured for a rather significant period.

In these longer term situations, it's critical that you devise some method of ensuring that the rep you selected is the right one. If you have to wait for three or four years to determine whether the rep is the right fit, you stand to lose three to four years of sales effort.

One of the best measures for evaluating new reps is what I call noise; we might even define it as "beautiful noise." The great majority of sales managers will quickly recognize this term. It means the sum of all the positive communications from the representative that clearly conveys the rep is out there actively and effectively promoting your products, systems, or services. "Beautiful noise" takes many forms.

"Can you do this?" It takes a while for a rep to really understand what you can and cannot do. New reps that are digging for sales will rather promptly come across situations for which they have no quick answer, so they must contact you to determine what can and cannot be done. It is a definite sign that a rep is working for you.

"Your competitor is doing this." Key in a rep's learning curve is understanding how customers perceive competitors' offerings versus your products. This question typically arises from reps that have been presenting your product or asking questions about customer usages and have come up against a competitor they do not fully know. Again, the noise shows that the rep is working for you.

"Can you send specific product information?" The noise turns beautiful when the questions evolve into the next phase: requests for more details on the product so that it can be incorporated into a customer's budget, preliminary layouts, or some other part of the customer specification and purchasing cycle. Requests might be, "I need three quick drawings of product A in this arrangement" or, "I need two or three good references for product C on these applications."

"I need a proposal!" Another phase of noise is a bona fide inquiry for a proposal. This can be a telephone or a written inquiry. The most beautiful noise, short of an actual order, is a customer inquiry that incorporates specifications that obviously came from the rep.

If a rep makes these kinds of noises, in approximately this sequence, in a reasonable time frame, you will know that rep is right on track and that new-orders performance will logically flow. If your industry has noise as a normal characteristic prior to orders and you're not getting it from your reps, you should be very concerned.

Occasionally reps take on new manufacturers only to determine rather promptly that it was a mistake—that they are not really a good fit or that the manufacturer's internal culture is a major turnoff. As the reps aggressively probe their customers, there may be some initial noise. However, when the rude awakening occurs that it is really a mismatch, frequently reps will just pull their horns in without telling the manufacturer. Your job, then, is to monitor not only the level of noise but how it develops and evolves. Reps that have stopped selling for you deserve criticism for not telling you. But the blame is just as much on you for not paying enough attention to what each rep is doing.

The Faltering Relationship

Occasionally, even though you periodically reassess the compatibility between your company and the rep firm, verifying that the objectives are still common, performance still slips. What you need then is an empathetic analysis of the situation and appropriate actions to correct any major weakness.

Let's assume you have sound documentation that a specific rep's performance has fallen well below what you expected. (This is not a case of a consistently good performer who has a shortfall because of some explainable bad breaks; this is a situation where there is some question about the long-term viability of the relationship.) How do you handle it? In one fashion or another, you will take steps in these three areas:

1. Joint assessment of issues
2. Development of action programs, if continuation is to occur
3. Reassessment and the go/no-go decision

Astute sales managers should handle routine performance assessment as a matter-of-fact part of the relationship with the rep network. Shortfalls in performance tend to become readily apparent to both sales management and reps well before the numbers turn really sour. Step in quickly and take prompt action. The sales manager (it could be the regional manager in a large organization or even the president of a very small company) should address the issue in a pragmatic, team-oriented way.

First, carefully compile the documentation outlining your specific concerns along with any ideas about why the rep is not performing. Call the rep, briefly express your concerns, and suggest a date when the two of you can get together to discuss the matter in detail. The meeting with the rep should be based on a partnership philosophy: *We* have not achieved what *we* expected to achieve; why do you think *we* have missed? Because you have a common objective—reaching a sales target—any shortfall should be considered a *mutual* shortfall. Both parties should probe all aspects of the issue to reach a clear agreement of causes.

In the discussions, probe for information empathetically. There are times when a shortfall is caused by a temporary situation, such as loss of a loved one, a divorce, a breakup in the partnership, or similar happenings that will interrupt a small business for a while. In other cases, the source may be strictly a reduced market, competition's pricing becoming increasingly aggressive at levels you choose not to match, changes in customer technology resulting in less demand for your product, or any number of other noncontrollable events. The key is to investigate all aspects of the shortfall in a completely open manner.

At the end of the first meeting, you might reach any one of several conclusions.

1. *Both sides agree to terminate.* Occasionally, rep and manufacturer will clearly see that, for any number of reasons, the relationship no longer makes sense. If so, it's best to terminate immediately, under normal contract provisions. Ask the rep to continue until you find a suitable replacement. (For more on terminations, see Chapter 12.)

2. *Both rep and manufacturer agree that the causes for the shortfall were beyond the rep's control and that the rep's performance was reasonable under the circumstances.* The objectives simply did not make sense in the light of the ensuing events. This is not uncommon. In fact, for a properly supported rep compatible with your needs, this is the *most* common shortfall situation.

If you clearly agree with this assessment, it means you understand that the shortfall is not in the rep's sales abilities but in the team's forecasting skills. Perhaps next year's objectives should be reduced, in case the problems cannot be eliminated.

3. *The rep agrees that he has just not done the job and also agrees that he will start cranking up again.* In this situation, establish clearly and precisely what the rep intends to do to improve performance. If you are expected to participate in this turnaround, this should also be clearly stated.

These agreements should be put in writing, starting with a basic statement of concern about the shortfall and the actions and time spans agreed upon. Establish a time frame for reassessment. During this interval, you should be in close contact with the rep (telephone will usually do) to make sure the rep is getting proper support and is living up to his part of the agreement.

As the demonstration period nears conclusion, set up another review point. If progress continues to fall short of expectations, schedule a second meeting and openly ask the rep if continuation is reasonable. Sometimes it just does not make sense to continue. If a rep has been unwilling to fulfill her commitment in the turnaround situation, it's typically because there was no real commitment. In that case, it is time to introduce the potential benefits to both sides of a separation.

If the rep strongly objects and wishes to continue, gain a second agreement on a commitment to achieve certain milestone events within defined periods. Confirm these checkpoints in writing, just as you did earlier. However, this time the confirmation should include the potential for cancellation if the rep fails to live up to her side of the bargain.

If the shortfall continues and you feel the rep still has not done the job and probably won't, your only recourse is termination. Your documentation along the way is necessary to set a proper stage for a professional termination "for cause," as we will see in Chapter 12.

4. *You are convinced that the rep is not doing the job, while the rep eloquently argues that he is.* You feel the compatibility of the rep is unacceptable; the rep is totally convinced that he can and will do the job, given adequate time and support. These situations can be very trying for both parties unless they can readily empathize with each other's point of view.

Relationships between less than fully compatible partners *can* prosper over the long term. It takes dedication to the partnership and a commitment by the rep to grow a segment of his business in some unfamiliar, unnatural areas. It is not unlike partners in marriage; certain couples can overcome segments of noncompatibility whereas others cannot. The solution comes from a blend of empathy and pragmatism. In the end, it all boils down to pure managerial judgment as to whether a termination is required.

As long as reps show a commitment to success, try to work with them. Remember, changing reps is very expensive at best. It may be that all the rep needs is a longer time to demonstrate successful performance. However, here too you should agree on a commitment to achieve key milestone events.

Obviously, your goal is to develop a winning operation. If both sides can make a genuine commitment that the relationship is essentially sound and requires only additional follow-through by both sides, then you should pursue the relationship with enthusiasm. Winners have been known to emerge from marginal situations. However, there may come a time when either you or the rep concludes that the relationship is no longer worthwhile. Once this point is reached, put your cards on the table and go your separate ways in a professional manner.

The Marginal Representative

Truly successful organizations invariably have very high standards of performance. They set their sights high and battle to achieve these heights. True excellence in rep performance requires an excellent match between rep and principal, strong support by the manufacturer, strong efforts by the rep in selling for the manufacturer, and periodic reviews to make sure that both organizations are on the same wavelength. If all goes well, the relationship prospers.

On the other hand, many relationships between rep and manufacturer have been marginal for years. Over the years I have found that only one-third of the reps are a really sound fit with the manufacturer, one-third are marginal, and one-third are a poor fit. Although this may not be a statistically accurate portrayal of all companies nationwide, it is a reasonably typical estimate of companies that use reps but are dissatisfied with rep performance. If you target your organization to be number one, this ratio of rep compatibilities is totally unacceptable.

In most cases, you should immediately terminate the submarginal relationship and recruit the best available rep. Test the marginal relationship carefully; can it be promptly brought back to a successful level? If not, end it. A continuing marginal relationship is a burden on the shoulders of both parties. Reps will make the most income off the manufacturers with which they have the best fit and a good working relationship. The same is true for the manufacturers. If excellence is to be achieved, the marginal relationship cannot be accepted.

This standard of excellence requires you to make very difficult decisions. The rep firm that has been associated with your company for a long period of time but is nearing the end of its life cycle without a plan for continuity represents one of the most difficult problems you have to face. Frequently, associations with manufacturers may last twenty years or more. Close, warm relationships result. Business associates become friends. Terminating that relationship is extremely difficult. However, you are charged with protecting the long-term interests of your stockholders and employees. Tough decisions must be made, and you must make them. You are not being unfair. The rep's objectives simply have not matched yours, and the handwriting has been on the wall for some time. If long-term survival is the target—let alone growth—there is no other decision.

The same holds true for the reps. Some reps grow aggressively over a ten-year period and outstrip the manufacturers they represent. They are then in the exact same position. Aggressive rep organizations interested in growth should seriously consider terminating any manufacturer that does not share in this growth orientation. If it is not a mainstream manufacturer, the need for termination is less pressing and the rep can afford to be a little indulgent toward a nonperforming principal because of the warm relationships.

It is, in truth, a two-way street. The name of the game is common objectives as a key basis for building a long-term, highly successful relationship.

The Next Step

With empathy, good judgment, and some common sense, you can shepherd your reps into a solid sales force of committed professionals. In return, you will get significant achievements in market penetration and competitive advantage. You'll also get something else: good intelligence from the marketplace.

Your reps are out in the field every day; they probably know of new developments before you do. Their antennas are out for market shifts, new-product needs, new applications, and early warning signs of competitors' plans. All these developments will eventually work their way into your company, but by the time they do, it may be too late. Because they see the signals early, reps can perform a very valuable information service, which brings us to the "audit" segment of Step 6. Don't let managerial ego keep you from taking advantage of what reps can teach you about your company.

11

Feedback and Control: The Rep Council and Rep Audit

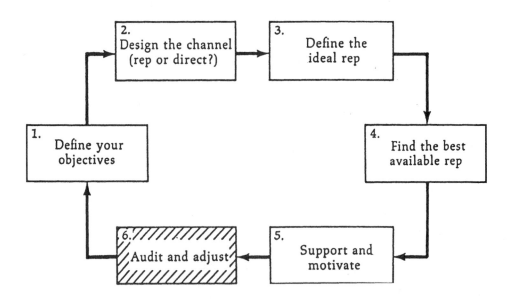

In the dynamic, fast-moving environment in which today's businesses must operate, companies face the nearly impossible burden of assessing an enormous array of factors, designing adjustments, and making them in time. Your rep network, your company, and the outside world all are in a period of rapid change, and even the best management team can get dizzy.

Some find comfort in reverting to autocratic styles, only to find that in an autocracy, issues tend to remain buried and are not discovered until major upsets occur. One remarkable aspect emerges as a common denominator among many failures: Senior executives and their management teams did not pay sufficient attention to the fundamentals of running a successful business. Breakthrough technologies, dramatic strategies, and other exceptional events lead to great successes. Failure, however, comes not from a competitor's spectacular breakthrough but from a company's neglect of the basics of good management.

An analogy to the game of golf may help here. Even the best professionals routinely go off their game. In many cases it's a simple deviation from fundamentals in grip, weight distribution, ball position, critical moves on the takeaway, or any number of other basics. Pros recognize that despite many years of highly successful competitive experience, errors can creep into their swing. As soon as trouble starts, they go back to other professionals (even their original teachers) for counsel.

Fortunately for golfers, when they forget a key fundamental, the evidence shows up promptly. First the ball flies off course (the symptom of a problem), and then they have a higher score at the end of the day (the quantified result). Unfortunately for the business community, three situations make prompt correction much more difficult. First, symptoms of a problem may not be as readily observable as the sliced golf ball. The further away senior executives are hierarchically from the grassroots operations, the greater is the risk of not knowing that something fundamental has gone awry. Issues that are just starting to fester may not be brought to the attention of the senior executive team—or, if surfaced, may be ignored.

Second, the cause/effect relationship is very immediate in a golf swing. However, in business, the time span between the cause and the negative result may be a year or more. If management waits until the overlooked fundamental problem has resulted in a negative output (a drop in market share or the creation of red ink), it may be very difficult to correct. Negative momentum is very painful and very time-consuming to turn around.

A third limitation in business management is managerial ego. Too frequently, the senior executive and other top managers in the organization feel that requesting assistance in analyzing their operations is a sign of weakness. Misplaced egos brag, "Give me the responsibility and authority, and measure me on the results. Don't muck around in my business. If I don't perform well, you can fire me." Then, after several years of mismanagement, profitability has suffocated and the executive *is* fired.

This Neanderthal approach has no place in today's highly competitive, rapidly changing environment. It ignores the higher commitment to stockholders and employees. Senior managers must use every asset at their disposal to make sure all issues are promptly surfaced and resolved and all opportunities are prioritized and profitably penetrated.

Companies with independent sales organizations have two unique tools that can provide exceptional feedback to senior management. Both tools provide an opportunity for assessing how well a management team is adhering to the fundamentals of good management practice, how well the company stacks up against competition, and what new directions must be taken to ensure long-term success. These two tools are the rep council and the rep audit. They are equally appropriate with other types of independent sales organizations (i.e., the distributor council and the distributor audit).

The Rep Council

Rep councils were initially established as advisory panels of representatives who periodically met with the senior sales or marketing executive and several members of the marketing department to discuss marketing and sales issues. The concept has been embraced by many companies, with varying degrees of success. At worst, it becomes an exercise in lip service if the manufacturer is not committed to true responsiveness to the needs of the marketplace. However, many companies reap major benefits from the panel. The representatives, if properly selected and nurtured, can give the manufacturer tremendous insights into marketplace forces, providing directions on steps needed to grow market share, penetrate new markets, improve customer relations, and raise overall profitability.

Purpose of the Council

Ideally, the purpose of the rep council should be expanded beyond that of a purely advisory body to the marketing or sales department. In a broader context, as a total business advisory council, it can make a real contribution. The rep network sees all sorts of problems and symptoms of problems in manufacturers they represent. These problems go well beyond marketing and frequently define deep-rooted, even embryonic weaknesses in engineering, manufacturing, quality control, finance, R&D, or all the subfunctions of these major departments.

Reps can measure a manufacturer's capability to be truly effective, not only against historical competition levels but also against the other manufacturers they represent. Many reps are professional businesspeople as much as they are professional salespersons, and their candid point of view can be an enormous asset to the senior executive assessing the organization's total capability.

In this expanded role, the ideal council would be a relatively small body of select reps and select *senior* management personnel, including the president. In a very candid environment, they would discuss all issues facing that company from as many points of view as possible. In addition, the panel could be a decision-making body for many issues. If the president and the senior management team participate at council meetings, resolutions to issues can frequently be reached right then and there. When others must be brought in, the council should make a commitment on the timetable for developing solutions.

Council Membership

Number of Members. The number of rep and company members on the panel should be based on whatever is needed to create a sound working body that can address and resolve issues. Meeting efficiency in general seems to suggest seven as the ideal count. In the case of the rep council, ten is perhaps the best working number—five rep personnel and five from the manufacturer. This gives a good cross section from both sides and an excellent balance for most needs.

Representation From the Company's Side. Representing the organization should be the senior executive of that profit center, whether it be a division or a corporation, and the top managers of the four departments that most affect the organization. Generally, that would be the senior marketing, engineering, manufacturing, and financial executives. If the company has a senior marketing executive, should the sales manager be a standing member of the council? Ideally, no—for two reasons:

1. One of the primary objectives of the meeting is for the senior management team to get firsthand feedback on how the organization is doing from a marketplace point of view. The sales manager routinely receives this information, so there is no reason for her to hear it again.

2. It's more efficient to have only one representative from each major function. There's little reason to have *two* people representing the marketing department. The sales manager's presence may inhibit reps' candor, particularly if the sales manager has been a stumbling block in the organization's effectiveness.

The sales manager may feel a bit put out by not being asked to participate in the council. Develop the rationale very, very carefully. Remember that the basic purpose of the rep council does not require the sales manager's attendance nearly as much as that of the senior executives in charge of the major functions reporting to the president. The council is designed to give them a better understanding of reps and a very clear picture of how the outside world views the results of their functional departments. Their representation is critical.

Selection of Reps. When it comes to selecting rep participants, there are several criteria.

1. *Longevity with the manufacturer.* Most of the reps selected should have represented the company for several years, for such reps have experienced your company over time. (This presumes you have been using reps for some time. If you are just starting with a rep network, form a rep council as soon as possible; it can provide invaluable feedback on how the company is starting up with its reps.)

Successful experience should *not* be the prime criterion. In fact, it is very appropriate to include one or two reps that have not been performing well but that have been really trying. Their problems and frustrations can be even more valuable than the input of a rep that has been highly successful and has a minimum number of burning issues to discuss.

With a council of five reps, four should be reasonably long-tenured and one a relatively recent appointment, say, six months to a year. The new person gives firsthand advice on how well you are doing in starting up with a new rep.

2. *Geographic representation.* Rep council members from different parts of the country are appropriate only if your markets are rather evenly distributed on a geographic basis. If your markets are very strongly regional, bias the panel selection toward that region. The key is to have rep councils that represent the major part of the markets you are pursuing.

3. *Commitment to your company.* Focus your selection on reps that have demonstrated a commitment to your company. This is not necessarily measured in terms of producing new orders but of aggressively trying to both sell your product and get your company to do what they feel is necessary to achieve success in the markets you have targeted. You need people who are committed. You want reps that will tell you how to run your business.

This does not mean that each panel member has to be one of the owners of the rep firm. Frequently, employed salespeople will be much better spokespersons for what is happening in their firm's territory than an owner. Owners, particularly of the larger firms, may not be as aware of the issues facing your company as one of the salespersons. If you want to include a nonowner, get the agreement of the rep firm's owners.

Commitment to the Council. Rep council members must bring a commitment to achieve the objectives of the council. This means a commitment to spend the time that is required to have an effective council. This time frame must be very carefully developed with each proposed council member before the selection is made. In my experience, reps willingly contribute their time to rep councils without compensation, knowing it helps manufacturers better understand how to be effective with reps.

Choice of Future Members. Once the first council is set up, the members themselves can elect future members. Establish ground rules about the type of member needed so that new individuals will meet your company's needs. You don't need a popularity contest.

Length of Terms. Council terms are usually for two to three years, staggered so no more than two new members are brought in at one time.

Roles of Members

Council Members and Chair. The council acts as a focal point for views of the entire rep network. Say you have a five-person council and a network of twenty-five organizations. Each of the four rep members, excluding the chair, could have the responsibility for obtaining inputs from five others so that the council speaks for the entire network. The council chair is the overall guiding hand, the leader who sees that all roles are fulfilled and acts as the funnel for primary communications between the rep council and the manufacturer outside of council meetings.

The Manufacturer. The primary function of the company is to solicit information. You want to probe the rep council members to understand their position fully about issues and opportunities facing you and to encourage suggestions for resolving them. Defensiveness has absolutely no place in the face of criticism from the rep council. When you hear the council present a marketplace issue that is endorsed by the majority of the independent reps, you can be reasonably certain that the statement reflects how your customers see your company. The problem with too many managers is their inability to see themselves as the world sees them. The rep council provides this clarity.

The Meetings

Agenda Development. Because the primary purpose of the rep council is for the reps to advise the manufacturer, they should be the ones to develop the agenda. There should be a pyramiding flow of suggestions to the council chair, who then submits the agenda to you, the manufacturer. *Every* agenda item suggested by the reps should be put on the agenda. You may introduce new items you consider appropriate for review by the council, such as possible new policies or procedures that you wish to test with the council. This is a tremendous opportunity to test changes so as not to be embarrassed by the implementation of one where a critical point of view has been overlooked.

Announcements. Suggest the meeting at least two months in advance to minimize interference with established rep schedules. Even this may require a reschedule because of a rep's prior commitments.

Conduct of the Meetings. The meeting should be results oriented. Keep the focus on subjects that are germane to the purpose of the council. The discussion should be professional at all times. Occasional emotional outbursts are rare and are quickly squelched by the other members.

Frequency of Meetings. Most rep council meetings are held annually, although occasionally more frequent meetings are required. In turnaround situations, you might hold meetings quarterly for the first year and then semiannually.

Minutes. Within several working days, your minutes of the meeting should go to the council members for an accuracy check. Approval, with any corrections, should be requested within one week. At the end of the week, telephone the representatives, review the minutes verbally, and make any changes they deem necessary—another case of the telephone being the best way of getting results. Once the minutes are frozen, they should be published to the entire rep network, along with action schedules.

Follow-Up. Particularly when action items have been indicated in the minutes, follow-up letters at the appropriate point are a good idea. Include progress on the action items and any additional appropriate information.

Duration of Meetings. One full day, from 8:00 A.M. to 5:00 P.M., is appropriate for most situations. Some companies use two half days; others allocate from two to three days, with informal activities in the afternoons and evenings to foster relationships and give ample opportunity for full discourse on all issues and opportunities. However, most reps prefer to get back to their business as soon as possible, so lean toward the one-day session.

An effective approach is to have the reps arrive on Sunday evening for dinner with the senior management team. This allows them to get to know each other a little bit more and encourages a more personal relationship between rep council and the senior management team. Many reps like the Sunday evening arrival because it means they spend only one full day away from their business.

Recreational activities are not a particularly useful supplement to the council meetings. As soon as the session is over at 5:00 P.M., the reps should be released to go back to their firms or, if they wish, to stay on for additional discussions with your company personnel in the evening or into the next day.

Expenses. All customary expenses, including all travel, should be assumed by the manufacturer because the council members are contributing a full day of free management counsel. Over the coming years, an honorarium may become standard; certainly it represents an expression of your appreciation to the reps for this informed advice.

Summary

The rep council has the potential for being an outstanding advisory body to help manufacturers locate and resolve issues. It can also define new opportunities and suggest ways that they can be realized. The key to effectiveness of the council is a proactive company president.

The proactive president does more than merely sit in on a meeting and keep a low profile. She ensures not only that each issue and opportunity will be fully explored but that all departments will start focusing on implementing actions agreed upon. The council will also help ensure that the participating management team receives a greater appreciation and understanding of the value a professional rep network can bring to the organization. This gives department managers a direct experience factor from which they can start training their own staff to become more sensitive to customer and rep needs.

Independent Auditing

Auditing and the Executive Ego

Independent auditing has yet to make its full contribution to successes in management practice, largely because of the egocentric styles that still abound in so many corporations. Egocentric managers want to do things a certain way—and without interference. The idea that someone should look over *their* shoulder and meddle in *their* business strikes them as a direct attack on their authority, autonomy, and power position. Yet profit-and-loss statements have been riddled with major upsets resulting from these same managers' failure to stay on top of their businesses. The insidious part of the problem is that even the best managers can become myopic because their involvement in a business is too intense or too protracted. Even in well-managed businesses, it is too easy to get comfortable when things seem to be going well. On top of this myopia is the problem of managers hearing, but somehow dismissing, evidence that problems exist. Yet these same managers continue to resist being "encumbered" by any form of auditing.

Common Types of Business Audits

Financial Audit. The financial audit is the most common type of business audit, and for public corporations it is a Securities and Exchange

Commission (SEC) requirement. Unfortunately, the financial audit too frequently fits the old cliché of bean counting. The audit separates the pile of beans into logical groups, weighs them, counts them, and reports them. It measures what *has* happened instead of suggesting what *will* happen because of poor decisions.

Auditing personnel generally come from a purely financial background, with strong knowledge of financial controls, systems, and procedures but without broad-based business backgrounds to help them effectively probe the decision making in manufacturing, engineering, marketing, or general management. Financial auditing, therefore, is a better means of evaluating the aftermath of a company's financial upset than of predicting that such an upset will occur.

Operations Audit. Auditors experienced in functions other than exclusively financial ones are involved in this process. Unfortunately, operations auditing is also an extension of bean counting in some respects. Operations auditors tend to be specialists in subfunctions of the manufacturing and financial process—e.g., computer systems and work scheduling—who track the systems, procedures, and controls for their narrow specialty. It is a micro approach to analysis and tends to be somewhat myopic.

Management Audit. Management auditing is an encompassing analysis. It is usually performed by a team of auditors with capability in all major functions who descend on an organization and perform a micro analysis of most departments. It is very time-consuming, very costly, and very much geared to finding the "right" systems, procedures, and controls. While mountains of suggestions can be developed from the management audit, too frequently it can miss those few core problems responsible for 90 percent of the difficulties facing the company.

Issue Audit

Issue auditing (my own term) is a rather informal system used by many general managers to help identify issues that may not come to their attention through normal communication channels. When the senior executive does it, it is sometimes called management by walking around. The primary differences between the informal issue audit and the type of issue audit I have in mind are that my approach is more systematic and is implemented by an independent auditor with the experience of a senior executive.

Issue auditing takes an entirely different approach: the macro analysis. The primary theme is that the truly major issues facing companies are known by at least a segment of the employee population. All that is needed is to get these individuals talking openly about the company, various departments in the company or profit center, their department, and their own work. It calls for interviewing a sampling of the employee population, all managers, and key interfacing positions, including those that cross functional lines, such as cost accounting, project engineering, and contract administration.

Obviously, the capabilities of the auditor are a critical ingredient. He must have very broadly based business experience (preferably at general manager levels) and a demonstrated capability for separating symptoms of issues from the core issues themselves. A nose for problems and sound intuitive judgment are also essential. The auditor must also be able to integrate all inputs into a clear picture of the issues and opportunities facing the company and have the expertise to offer resolutions for most of them.

Issue auditing is truly a predictive device. Once management makes a bad decision that could lead to significant upsets, the error—or its symptoms—quickly become apparent to people in the organization. The auditor's open-ended questioning invariably raises concerns early enough to permit corrective action.

Sales Channel Audit. The sales channel audit is a form of issue auditing that focuses on the sales organization. Normally, it has two broad objectives. The first is to assess the capabilities of the sales channel to meet a manufacturer's current and future needs. Second, with the sales channel as a sounding board through open-ended interviewing, a picture of the strategic and operational strengths the manufacturer faces in the marketplace can be readily defined and solutions offered.

Sales channel audits should be performed at least annually just as financial audits are undertaken. The reason is simple: As changes continue to proliferate, channel opportunities will also proliferate, and these opportunities can be converted into deeper penetration of each targeted market. Unless they are routinely assessed and adjustments made in design concept and/or individual members of each channel, a manufacturer will not achieve maximum performance. In addition, the audit process will help ensure that problems and opportunities observed by the sales force will be accurately defined and corrective actions taken.

Rep Audit

Rep audit is a more specific term for a sales channel audit. As the name implies, it focuses on an independent rep network. The primary difference between a rep audit and a direct sales channel audit is that, because of its inherent freedom from political pressure, the independent sales organizations can be interviewed by telephone. The political sensitivities of any deep-probing audit require that direct salespeople be interviewed face-to-face so they are more relaxed and candid.

The rep audit, in other words, uses a manufacturer's independent rep network to assess issues and opportunities facing the organization and the compatibility of the rep network design. This same approach can be used with distributors, brokers, and any other sales organization. As part of the same audit, depending on the auditor's capabilities, the sales channel compatibility with the manufacturer's short- and long-term needs can also be defined.

Objectives of a Rep Audit

The two broad objectives, therefore, are the reps' assessment of the company's capabilities and, depending on the auditor's capability, assessment of rep compatibilities with the manufacturer. In practice, these objectives should be expanded to more specific terms. In particular, the rep audit should perform the following six functions:

1. Define issues that threaten market and profit performance before market share or the profit-and-loss statement is affected. The audit can serve as a leading indicator of major upset.
2. Define new opportunities available for exploitation by the manufacturer.
3. Define the compatibility of the existing rep network design with the manufacturer's short- and long-term needs.
4. Define the compatibility of each rep organization with the company's short- and long-term needs.
5. Define the ideal representative profile for each major product/market target.
6. Provide resolutions for each identified issue.

A Critical Ingredient: The Auditor

The auditor should be selected on the basis of the objectives targeted for the audit, the experience of the senior executive, and the decision-making culture of the organization. If the objective is to make an assessment of issues and opportunities through the eyes of the rep network and if the company has a cultural style of openness and candor, any number of your organization's personnel can be selected to conduct the interviews. The key requirements are that the reps recognize candor as the organization's cultural style and that the auditor have a reasonably good perspective of the total business.

If the senior executive is fairly new and unsure about the degree of candor in his organization, if the decision-making style is or has been autocratic, or if the senior executive inherently prefers an unbiased viewpoint, an independent auditor should be selected, again with all the credentials that match the objectives. This could be a consultant or someone with a general management background from a peer organization or corporate headquarters. If all six objectives are to be attained, the auditor should combine a strong background in sales channel design, intimate knowledge of manufacturers' representatives, and a general management background. Independence is necessary to ensure total objectivity.

Other Advantages of the Rep Audit

In addition to achieving these objectives, the rep audit is quick, nondisruptive, and cost-effective. Typically, an in-depth audit among twenty-five rep organizations can be completed in eight calendar weeks or less, taking about fifteen workdays for an experienced general manager/auditor to complete. This includes a planning meeting, a comprehensive report, and a day to review the report with senior management to gain agreement on actions to be taken.

It is nondisruptive because there is minimal internal interviewing, only a kickoff meeting and a final review meeting. All the interviewing is conducted with the representatives. Finally, conducting telephone interviews is very cost-effective.

Steps in a Rep Audit

The logical evolution of the rep audit has eleven steps.

1. *Carefully define the objectives and scope.* This is primarily decided by the president (or division manager) in conjunction with the senior management team.

2. *Select the auditor.* The auditor should have the capability of successfully achieving the audit's objectives.

3. *Advise reps and company personnel.* The president should write to the reps, indicating that she needs their assistance to define current issues and opportunities facing the company and their candid suggestions on how the company can be a better principal. The president should also indicate that she clearly recognizes that the independent representatives are in an excellent position to assess the organization's capabilities relative to both competition and the other manufacturers they represent. Reps have the objectivity and independence to allow this very clear view of issues and opportunities facing the company.

The letter should announce the auditor's name and note that the auditor will be in contact with them shortly. The primary objective should be stated: to improve the manufacturer's effectiveness so that both manufacturer and reps will increase profitability.

The internal organization should also be advised because the results of the audit can very well affect any or all functions. This advice should be part of the general process of training the organization to accept auditing as a routine constructive tool to enhance decision-making excellence and not to point fingers.

4. *Contact the reps.* The auditor's initial contact with the reps is a letter of introduction, a statement of objectives, and a questionnaire the rep can use as a work sheet to prepare for the interview. Samples of this announcement letter to the reps and a typical work sheet are included here as Figures 11-1 and 11-2. They are written from a consultant's viewpoint; you may need to make minor format adjustments.

The questionnaire is to be completed by the reps but not returned in the mail. It is purely a work sheet to focus their attention on key issues and opportunities. Other specific questions can be included. However, for normal audit purposes, you are mainly interested in open-ended questions that encourage reps to talk at length about issues and opportunities facing your company.

The auditor must design the questions so that they avoid leading the rep to answers. You want to find out what is important to the rep because this is an expression of the marketplace view of your company. Once questions start to focus on specific subjects, you run the risk of prejudicing the rep's answers.

Consider having the auditor send these letters by certified mail with a signed receipt requested. It will make the letter stand out. Remember that incoming mail to a rep is so voluminous that anything that looks like a routine letter can be quickly put aside or even mistakenly thrown out.

5. *Make preliminary telephone contact.* The auditor calls the rep to establish the basis for the interview. First the auditor should ask whether the rep has thoroughly reviewed the questionnaire and has developed some thoughtful answers. Second, he should ask the rep to set a date and time for the interview, which will take anywhere from thirty minutes to two hours. The key is to make sure that the rep has given thoughtful consideration to the questions and allows the necessary time in an unpressured environment to discuss all the issues. Reps should be reminded that their critiques will be kept confidential.

6. *Conduct the interview.* The interview topics should be discussed in the order presented on the questionnaire to allow for a smooth flow. However, it is extremely important that the interviewer probe as the rep starts to define key issues. Frequently reps will discuss symptoms of problems rather than core issues. It is therefore critical that the interviewer have sufficient intuitive feeling for broad-based business problems to pick up

Figure 11-1   Sample rep audit announcement.

April 10, 200X

William W. Gotherman
Interstate Utility Sales, Inc.
P.O. Box 33338
Charlotte, NC 28233

<u>Research-Cottrell's Air Pollution Control Division</u>

Dear Bill:

Bob Hyde's recent letter introduced us to you. We have been retained by Bob to help him better plan APCD's future growth. To do this, we need your assistance as we have found that a client's rep network typically has many of the answers required to properly plan a company's future.

Our primary approach is through a system we call the REP AUDIT. This is a system by which we use the manufacturers' reps to audit the manufacturer. We have found that after interviewing our client's reps, we can put together a very clear picture of our client's strengths and weaknesses and the steps that should be taken to improve its effectiveness in the marketplace. Obviously, as its effectiveness increases, your commission opportunities will also increase. At the same time, we'll discuss with you how well a number of products and services fit with what your firm is all about.

This letter requests your assistance in helping Research-Cottrell become more effective in the marketplace. Enclosed is a confidential work sheet that addresses this question and others. We ask that you give careful consideration to each question. Use the work sheet to jot down your comments. You do not have to mail the work sheet to us. Just hold on to it until we get together on the telephone to discuss your answers. We'll contact you shortly to establish a convenient telephone interview schedule.

<u>Also, so we can properly reference your views, please send us a list of the manufacturers you represent along with their major product lines. To make it a little easier, simply send your line card to us and any other information you have available about your firm. Concise biographical profiles of your sales personnel would be appreciated. A stamped, self-addressed envelope is enclosed for your convenience—or if you prefer, fax it to us at 908-722-3724.</u>

If you prefer to return the work sheet to us, keep a copy. You will want it as a reference to help make our phone conversations as productive as possible. As our reports to APCD will represent an integration of critiques from everyone we contact, no single critique will be identified unless you specifically request it. Your suggestion for improving APCD will be entirely confidential in nature.

Let me re-emphasize the need for you to <u>complete</u> the work sheet before we discuss APCD. This pre-work will help ensure that our client receive your most considered analysis to help it be more effective and, in the process, increase your income potential with the company.

Don't hesitate to phone me at any time if you have any questions. Our toll-free number is 1-800-548-1173. I look forward to our phone conversation.

Figure 11-2   Sample rep audit work sheet.

Consultants to Industrial Management

April 10, 200X

RESEARCH-COTTRELL AIR POLLUTION CONTROL DIVISION
REPRESENTATIVE WORK SHEET

PART I—APCD'S CAPABILITIES

1. What do you feel are APCD's strengths?

2. What do you feel are APCD's weaknesses?

3. If you could change only one thing in APCD, what would you change? Why?

4. What other stumbling blocks do you encounter that inhibit your effectiveness in selling APCD's products and services?

5. Are there any new opportunities APCD should be addressing?

6. What other suggestions do you have to improve your sales for APCD?

PART II—APCD'S COMPETITION AND MARKETS

1. Who are APCD's major competitors in your area and what are the major differences between APCD and each competitor?

2. What are your most important customer markets for your total business, not just for APCD? Please give us your sales by each market (utility, cogeneration, chemical, refinery, etc.) in your area in percentage of your total sales. Your educated "guesstimate" is fine. For example:

Your Markets	% of Total
_____	_____
_____	_____
_____	_____
_____	_____
_____	_____
_____	_____
TOTAL	100%

PART III—APCD VERSUS YOUR OTHER PRINCIPALS

1. How does APCD compare with your other principals relative to:
   a. current income?
   b. future income?

      c. overall ease of working relationships?
      d. sales support?
      e. marketing support?
      f. technical support?
      g. communications in general?
      h. literature?
      i. any other comparisons?

2. Which of your current principals are your highest income producers? Where does APCD rank?

3. If there are any other subject areas you feel should be fed back to APCD to enhance your mutual income-earning potential, please raise them during our conversation.

---

every nuance in the conversation and to explore thoroughly the rep's perception of the manufacturer.

The auditor must also assemble information on the rep: principals represented, territory covered, personnel, market focus, and similar data that clearly define what the rep's business is all about. This puts answers to questions in proper context and also helps the auditor determine how compatible that rep is with the manufacturer.

Almost without exception, reps gladly and fully cooperate with these interviews. They want to help their principals improve in any way possible.

7. *Take notes and put together a spreadsheet.* The interviewer should be taking copious notes during the interview (taping tends to suppress candor). At the end of the interview, the auditor must carefully review those notes for accuracy. Then he can start putting the responses on a spreadsheet that will tabulate issues identified and resolutions suggested. This permits the accumulation of responses in a matrix form that simplifies summarization.

8. *Synthesize the responses.* Once the matrix has been completed, the key job is then to synthesize all the comments into a statement of issues and opportunities facing the organization and resolutions suggested for each. In addition, the auditor now develops the analysis of the compatibility of the overall rep network design and the compatibilities of each rep.

Nowhere in the entire audit process is the capability of the auditor so critical. Here is where all key judgments must be made. Here is where issues are defined, whereas only symptoms of those issues might have been apparent during the interview. A good auditor knows that significant issues are not merely those defined by the majority of the reps. The auditor's intuitive, experienced judgment is therefore critical to identify minority views as legitimate positions that require serious evaluation.

9. *Write and distribute the report.* At the conclusion of the synthesis, the auditor develops an issue-oriented report and distributes it to key management personnel. Each manager should have time to digest the report thoroughly and note questions or disagreements with the findings in preparation for a review meeting with the auditor.

10. *Hold a review meeting.* As soon as possible after submission of the report, a review meeting should be held with the appropriate management team. Here the auditor presents an encapsulated commentary on the highlights of the audit and the key issues and opportunities. In a work session, the management team raises any questions about the report and voices any objections about its conclusions.

Differences of opinion between the reps and the management team are not unusual. Frequently this indicates only that the manufacturer has not advised the representative of programs under way to correct problems. However, many times the differences of opinion demonstrate that management is not able to step back and take a clear, candid look at the operations from the perspective of the outside world. This is one of the most significant contributions of the audit process.

The work session should continue until consensus is reached on the issues and their resolutions. In addition, the company should commit to actions it intends to take toward resolving the issues. Schedules can frequently be established, at least for the first milestone event in issue resolution and for evaluating or attacking opportunities.

A similar consensus should be reached on evaluations of the rep network design and each individual rep. Companies often note, with some surprise, that they now understand why performances of a segment of their rep network have been marginal or submarginal. An objective view, without personal closeness to the reps, provides a clear vision of rep compatibility for the first time. Friendships and other subjective factors no longer cloud evaluations, and sound judgments can be made on upgrading the rep network to fit current and future needs.

11. *Implement the program and follow up.* The final step of the audit process is to implement the action programs and to ensure that they are diligently pursued. This requires follow-up by the president. While part of the follow-up may be delegated, the rep audit is a business control tool and should remain within the oversight of the senior executive officer as a way to help minimize the chances of unpleasant surprises in the company's market share and profitability.

Typical Results of Rep Auditing

Table 11-1 depicts the compatibilities defined by twenty-four rep audits conducted by Novick & Associates, Inc., for its clients in the period from 1989 to 1998. Products or applications of these manufacturers include:

Table 11-1 Rep/manufacturer compatibility ratings compiled from rep audits for twenty-four manufacturers.

	Compatible	Marginal	Not Compatible	Total
Number of rep firms	202	158	120	480
Percentage of total	42.1	32.9	25.0	100

- Analytical lab instruments
- Bulk solids handling equipment
- Cooling towers
- Die castings
- Dust control products
- Electrical heating elements
- Fly ash and sulfur dioxide control systems
- Food machinery
- Industrial batteries
- Instrumented monitoring systems
- Liquids/solids separation
- Medical (infection control) products
- Metering pumps
- Molded plastic components
- Pressure vessels
- Size reduction equipment
- Slurry pumps
- Storage tanks
- Uninterruptible power supplies (UPS)
- Volatile organic compound destruction systems
- Water treatment systems
- Wood veneers

The three compatibility ratings used—compatible, marginal, and not compatible—are defined as follows:

1. *Compatible.* There is a strong match of characteristics and objectives between agent and manufacturer, clearly suggesting that a highly successful long-term relationship can be maintained.

2. *Marginal.* The fit is less precise. One or more major characteristics do not line up well with the manufacturer's needs. The probabilities for sound long-term performance are not strong.

3. *Not compatible.* There are major deviations in the required match of characteristics. Chances of the relationship's being successful are very low.

The ratings themselves were strictly decisions by the manufacturers that authorized the audits. Our firm merely assisted the manufacturers in the decision process. The results are astounding: These eighteen manufacturers, all using reps for many years, concluded that only 42 percent of their reps were compatible with their short- and longer term needs.

Those reps judged as "not compatible" represented somewhat of a shock to these manufacturers in that termination in most cases should have been decided years ago. Yet, it is not the rep that is declared "not compatible" that presents the major problem to manufacturers, for that rep is simply terminated as a result of continued poor performance. The "marginal" rep is a greater problem because too many manufacturers remain indecisive about what to do with these marginal performers. The manufacturer may be ready to fire a rep for nonperformance, only to have an attractive new order be generated by that rep. This business saves the rep from termination because the manufacturer would like to believe that the rep is finally starting to produce. The scenario is then repeated and repeated.

> **Key to success:** Once you have determined that a rep has marginal credentials for your needs and produces only marginal results, terminate the rep and recruit a new one. Marginal reps that provide marginal performance reduce the manufacturer to a marginal producer.

Summary

The rep audit is invaluable for giving a company a clear perspective of itself as viewed through the outside sales force. It also helps a company to appraise candidly the capabilities of its rep network design and the compatibility of each individual rep.

The rep audit is somewhat complementary to the rep council; both are feedback mechanisms concerning company performance. The rep audit does more; it also helps appraise the capabilities of the rep network. In addition, using a qualified independent auditor eliminates the internal bias and permits the president to get a clear view of the organization's performance from individuals who are well positioned to make an objective evaluation.

Finally, the rep audit emerges as an excellent control tool for the manager of presidents, that is, the president or group executive of a multidivision corporation. It gives the senior corporate executive a unique insight into the performance of divisions reporting. It acts as an early warning device that can highlight key issues created by ineffective decision making. This advanced warning system can then be used to make sure that the divisional managers get on top of these issues and resolve them before the bottom line is affected.

Reviewing the Six Steps

The six-step systems approach presented up to this point will, if followed, invariably lead to improved market coverage and penetration. However, the manufacturer that stops with one analysis of the six-step process and expects the results to continue with equal success over the long term is headed for trouble.

Wise manufacturers—like you—will review all these steps once a year, or whenever something happens that suggests a shift in direction. It is only with dedication to solid business fundamentals and the discipline to review them constantly that true excellence in the marketplace will occur.

12

Commissions and Contracts

Commissions

The Commission Rate

In terms of commission, representatives primarily seek a fair rate. "Fairness" is a function of industry averages and of the manufacturer's position in the industry, which will determine how easy it is for the rep to develop new orders. A commission schedule should depict the rate very clearly, so that reps understand before they sell a product exactly what commission will be paid.

In cases where prices and commissions must be established on a project basis, again, commissions must be very carefully defined early in the game. If pricing and the associated commission rates need to be adjusted during the negotiation because of competing situations, the commission rate should be defined immediately. The contract should provide specifically that the rep and the manufacturer reach agreement *before* the quotation is submitted to the customer. This allows the manufacturer to know its sales cost specifically and protects the rep against an arbitrary reduction of commission after the contract is obtained.

Published Pricing and Commission

Manufacturers should put into the reps' hands as much information as possible allowing a rep to size, price, and sell equipment. This can mean publishing price lists with multiplier schedules so that, by simple multiplication, reps can quickly arrive at a selling price and their commission for a given class of customers. Sometimes (although it is not common) reps have the discretion to discount the price themselves to meet competitive situations without consulting the manufacturer. This flexibility is most appropriate in industries that have standardized equipment, low unit sales prices, minimal technical application requirements, a high degree of competition, and customer purchasing tactics that whipsaw suppliers (such as in the contracting trades).

In such cases, a schedule of price discounts and accompanying decreasing commission rates will be handy for reps. The proportion of commission reduction to price reduction varies from industry to industry. In some cases the reduction is split fifty-fifty; that is, for each one-dollar reduction on the price, the rep's commission is reduced by fifty cents. Or the share formula ranges up to a two-to-one reduction in favor of the rep; that is, for a three-dollar price cut, the rep's commission is reduced by one dollar. Manufacturers interested in developing this pricing approach should compare what compatible manufacturers, as well as competitors, in their industry are doing.

In most industries, such pricing delegation simply does not exist. The custom nature of many firms in areas such as capital equipment, defense programs, and electronic and industrial OEM businesses requires specialized pricing from the factory. In certain cases, the commission rates are a flat percentage and remain at that level even if some negotiating of price is involved. In other cases, commission rates are negotiated downward as price concessions are made to fit a competitive need.

Be very aware of industry practices on the negotiation of commission rates; in this area, as in all others, standards in your industry will suggest what you need to do if you are to attract and hold outstanding sales representatives. However, even in industries where the standard is price reduction with no change in commission rate, there have been exceptions. At times, a manufacturer reaches a point at which it can no longer reduce its price. Occasionally, a rep may drop an otherwise inflexible posture and suggest a lower commission to make sure the order is received. In industries where the commission average is relatively low, say 5 percent, this tends to be the exception rather than the rule.

Payment Timing

The manufacturer should clearly define the timing of commission payment and adhere to it closely. With some exception, most commission payments are based either on shipment or on payment by the customer of the invoice. It varies with industry and is split almost evenly; that is, about half the manufacturers pay the reps on shipment, and the other half pay when they receive payment of the invoices. This does not mean shipment of the entire contract or payment of the final invoice but each shipment and each invoice.

A small percentage of manufacturers have other payment systems. A few pay on receipt of new orders; others split the payments a number of different ways. Under certain situations when they want to give a greater incentive to the reps (for example, a small manufacturer with an unknown product trying to get established), companies might consider paying reps when the order is received, even if it is unusual in their industry. Obviously this hurts the manufacturer's cash flow a bit but may bring quicker market penetration.

The key point to remember when developing a commission payment philosophy is the element of fairness. Unfortunately, payment language sometimes runs something like this: "Commissions will be forwarded on the third Friday following the month the invoice is paid in full"—which means that the rep might not get a commission check for as many as seven weeks after the manufacturer is paid for the invoice. This manufacturer is trying to enhance cash flow at the expense of the rep. It is an unprofessional practice.

A major sore point with many reps is the handling of the stated payment policy. All too frequently, manufacturers are sloppy when it comes to issuing commission checks in line with contract terms. They make excuses like "We had a major computer run to complete" or "We were closing the year-end statement and didn't have time." Ethically and legally, this is unacceptable. Financial departments should give commission checks the same attention they give their own salary checks. Company employees are paid scrupulously on designated dates; they would never accept such excuses. Yet manufacturers' reps are expected to produce for manufacturers well *before* they get any payment. Leave no stone unturned in your efforts to make sure that commission checks are paid exactly in accordance with the payment agreements in the rep contracts.

Noncommissionable Items

The commission schedule should also indicate items that will not be subject to commission. The most common items are taxes and freight, but occasionally manufacturers list many other items as noncommissionable. Companies that go too far in this direction risk alienating their reps. They also create more paperwork for themselves.

Common examples of companies that list too many items as noncommissionable are engineering services, field services, R&D studies, and laboratory analysis. In most cases, the manufacturer has a gross margin on these activities, which can support a commission. Also, reps are frequently activists in obtaining orders for these items. Most such items really should be commissionable, a fact that can be easily established by setting commissions on a weighted average of all items covered in a customer's purchase order.

Other Forms of Compensation

Sometimes additional types of compensation are made available to representatives.

Advances Against Commission. This payment form is periodically used by manufacturers to help finance the start-up period of a new rep. Manufacturer and rep agree on the amount and payment of the advance (usually on a monthly basis) and the length of time; the agreement usually includes a maximum exposure the manufacturer is willing to assume before new orders start to build a backlog of earned commission. This helps a new rep succeed and builds a strong loyalty between rep and manufacturer.

Cash Payments. Sometimes rep organizations suggest the manufacturer pay a fixed, negotiated amount on a monthly basis as compensation for activities that don't produce a commission, such as nonselling services like market research or other special investigations. A second suggestion is that manufacturers pay reps a fixed amount—a salary, if you will—to do the missionary work of establishing a new company or a new product. Then, when the missionary work is complete, reps switch to a commission form of payment.

Most companies feel that the rep, as an independent contractor, should also assume some of the risks. Over the years, manufacturers have evolved commission structures that compensate reps not just for the order received but for other services offered. A fixed form of payment diminishes this incentive. A suggested alternative is a "bonus" commission during the missionary period: a rate higher than standard to help offset the efforts of establishing a new product.

Commission Splitting

Commission splitting is a formula manufacturers use to allocate commission among two or more reps when each rep has contributed something to the order or is expected to contribute something after the order is received. An almost infinite variety of splits can be established for various selling and service activities performed by different reps on the same customer order. Some companies have developed formulas for as many as fifteen different split arrangements. Unfortunately, even with this level of detail, the same issues still arise. Reps frequently disagree about who did how much and what is therefore deserved. In these cases the manufacturer must fairly assess the dispute and resolve it as best it can.

In recent years, a trend toward simplicity in several industries has begun, using a minimal formula with maximum participation by the reps themselves. Here's one approach:

Commission Split Formula

Location of purchase order	10%
Destination location	10%
Successful sales effort	80%
Total	100%

The first item means that the representative covering the location where the order originates will receive 10 percent (or whatever percentage is appropriate for the industry) of the commission. The rep to whose territory the product is being shipped will also receive 10 percent. This destination credit is necessary only when the rep in that territory is expected to visit the destination or be available to the customer for assistance.

The final 80 percent is compensation for successful sales effort. The reps themselves decide how it is to be split. Four separate reps may have been involved in influencing the sale: one who handled the customer's headquarters where a buying influence was contacted, a second who handled the plant location where additional influence helped in the purchase, a third who called on the architect or engineer who wrote the specifications for the product, and a fourth who called on the contractor and sold the job at a premium price over competition. Fortunately, it is rare for an order to involve four reps. Two is more common, which simplifies the problem. The majority of the time, only one rep will be involved in the sales effort.

Usually reps can promptly (if not amicably) arrive at a split they consider acceptable. At times, the company still has to adjudicate a commission split dispute. A clause should therefore be inserted in the commission split section of the contract stating that in case of any disagreement among reps, the company will investigate the claims of all parties and arrive at a final, binding split. The contract should also include a clause stating that under no circumstances shall a manufacturer be required to pay more than 100 percent of the commission due.

Changing Commission Rates

Commission rates occasionally need to be changed to accommodate new situations. The commission schedule should provide that the company has the right to change commission rates with specific advance notice.

Contracts

The Need

Surprisingly, a few manufacturers still have only verbal agreements with their rep network. This is an injustice to both. Both parties need a clear understanding of what the rep/manufacturer agreement is all about and what rights and obligations each has to the other. Of equal importance is the role the contract plays in ensuring that terminations are accomplished professionally, without rancor, and within agreements established early in the game.

The language of the contract and the subjects it contains vary enormously from industry to industry and even between companies within each industry. Contracts should be brief and simply worded. They should represent a fair quid pro quo between two business organizations. You should consult legal counsel to ensure that no key provision is omitted and that neither party assumes undue risks. However, counsel should primarily advise on, not decide, the terms. You should keep it primarily an agreement between two business organizations, utilizing business language.

If you are not using a contract now, you should develop one. First, as general background on what others are doing, try to obtain contracts used in your industry by manufacturers of compatible products. Contracts used by competitors will give you other viewpoints. In addition, you will find some help in the appendixes of this book. Contract guidelines published by two rep associations—the Electronics Representatives Association and the Manufacturers' Agents National Association—are included (Appendixes A and B). Two sample contracts (Appendixes C and D) suggest the manufacturer's point of view; one comes from the Industrial Perforators Association (guidelines offered to members of IPA), and the other is from a large company, Sparks Belting.

From these various sources, extract all items that seem appropriate to your company; then get together with your legal counsel to make a final determination on the terms and conditions that best serve your needs and are fair to the reps. If your regular counsel is not experienced in contracts and litigation between reps and manufacturers, seek out someone who is. This is a specialized field, and many precedents are rather recent.

Remember, this is a business agreement between businesspeople, not a legal treatise on how to protect yourself in every contingency. Counsel should advise *only* on the *terms* of the contract. You should take the lead in making sure the contract is fair and reasonable for both parties. However, you will need experienced legal counsel to help you develop a document that fits your needs, is fair to both parties, and does not expose you to unusual risk.

Introduction

The opening part of the contract should state the two parties, the nature of the agreement, and the effective date.

Products, Markets, and Territory

This usually follows the introduction. One very effective technique for these three subjects is a standard preprinted first page that lists each and then provides a blank space of three or four lines. With each rep agreement, details can be typed in. A company that is relatively simple in product and market and sees no rationale for establishing parallel reps can add the phrase *all products* below Products and *all markets* below Markets.

Here is a hypothetical contract for a New England rep from a manufacturer with a proliferation of products and markets. In such a case, one network may handle select products and markets, whereas an entirely separate rep network may be required elsewhere. This form permits such paralleling.

> *Products:* All liquid filtration products manufactured by XYZ Division.
> *Markets:* The chemical process markets. Specifically excluded from the contract are the power, food, pharmaceutical, and electronic industries.
> *Territory:* The entire six-state New England area, except that Fairfield County, Connecticut, is excluded. This county will be part of the metropolitan New York representative's contract.

A contract provision might be needed to cover products brought to market after the effective date of the contract. If there is any chance that new products might be introduced that would not be appropriate within the rep's contract, you should reserve the right to introduce them through alternative representatives (or other sales channels) if that's in your best interest. In our example, the market section is worded primarily to exclude those markets that will be given to another rep specializing in them. At that time, contracts of both reps in the area will be exchanged in the interest of sound communication. If any questions arise, you can arrange a meeting with both reps to resolve it.

If you are going to a rep network for the first time and don't yet know whether a parallel rep network might someday be used, cover this possibility in the contract. Essentially, the clause would state that while the current contract is based on all markets, the company reserves the right to consider alternative representatives in the future on a parallel basis to cover markets not effectively solicited by the rep currently under contract. You'll need to provide the same flexibility concerning boundaries in case you have no rep in an adjoining territory. This could save a lot of haggling and hard feelings later if the new rep in the adjoining territory provides substantially better coverage in part of the territory claimed by the first rep.

One suggestion concerning mechanics: A number of companies have put the Products, Markets, and Territory sections in an addendum. This page can then be changed without having to redo the contract.

Commissions

Keep commission language brief. Something like "commissions will be paid in accordance with the commission schedule currently in effect" is frequently sufficient. Many factors force periodic changes in the commission rate schedule. If all these were included in the contract, you would have to change the contract rather frequently. The contract should be an enduring instrument. However, aside from the rate schedule, other key aspects of commission payments *should* be included in the contract, including payment timing, backlog reporting procedure, and invoice copy distribution.

A Noncompete Clause

A standard clause should be inserted precluding the rep from signing on competing manufacturers. You may wish to require the rep to review any potential conflict with you before representing a new principal.

Duties of a Rep and of the Manufacturer

Included among the rep's duties is the requirement to service each customer in the territory, both before and after the issuance of a purchase order. The concept of service should be defined to fit the specific needs of each manufacturer. The obligations of the manufacturer are to provide copies of all purchase orders, invoices, and similar documents for the rep's use and to provide whatever specific support is suggested for the industry.

Changing Principals

Reps should be required to notify you when they either add or delete another principal. This is not intended to constrain reps from making any change they consider appropriate for their business. It is simply to keep you advised of changes that may affect the agency's commitment to you.

Changing Personnel

Similarly, reps should be responsible for promptly advising you of changes in key personnel. Occasionally only one person in the rep organization is really important to you, or maybe two or three. If these key personnel do not remain active in promoting your products, your business will suffer. Protect yourself with a clause stating that if such key personnel substantially lessen their selling efforts and are not immediately replaced with other personnel acceptable to you, the agreement may be terminated for cause.

Independent Contractor Status

This clause should clearly state that the representative is an independent contractor and cannot bind you to an agreement.

Buy/Resale

Buy/resale provisions are typically required in situations where the rep may assemble a system in which your product is a component. Where reps package several manufacturers together into a lump-sum, single-price package to more effectively fight competition, the clause may also be appropriate.

Term of Agreement

A typical historical clause, still frequently used, is that the agreement is subject to a thirty-day termination with or without cause. There are two problems here.

First, in specific situations categorized as just cause, termination with cause can be effective *immediately*. For example:

1. A breach of a material provision of the contract that remains uncorrected for a specified period after notice
2. The commencement by or against either party of voluntary or involuntary bankruptcy proceedings
3. The appointment of a receiver of the assets of either party or an assignment for the benefit of such party's creditors
4. The conviction of either party of a crime involving moral turpitude
5. Any act of omission that would induce a person similarly situated,

in the exercise of due prudence and ordinary care, to terminate the relationship forthwith

Second, the marketplace has recognized that longer termination periods may be appropriate. Carefully assess what is happening in your industry to determine a time frame that is fair and acceptable to both parties.

One possibility is a one-year term renewed on an annual basis but still subject to a thirty-day termination notice. An annual renewal gives testimony to the fact that each year both parties have reviewed the agreement and found it satisfactory. The contract then becomes a contemporary statement of agreement rather than one signed many years before, which could be significant in the case of litigation. Recent court rulings have judged that termination clauses in contracts signed many years ago may no longer be appropriate because of events that transpired over the years. As a result, settlements on terminations may be awarded to the representatives well in excess of the contract terms. These settlements may or may not be "fair," depending on the individual situations. The key is to establish mutually agreeable contracts with your reps that minimize the chances of litigation.

Terminations

A termination clause should clearly define the rights and responsibilities of both parties upon termination. Perhaps nowhere else in the rep/manufacturer relationship has there been more discussion of what is "fair."

Appendixes A–D present four contracts, two with provisions suggested by rep associations and two contracts offered by manufacturers. Examination of each will show a bias toward the rep in the Manufacturer's Agents National Association (MANA) and Electronics Representatives Association (ERA) contracts, while the bias leans toward the manufacturer in the contracts written by manufacturers. The key is to develop a contract that is fair and reasonable to both sides because the best long-term relationships are always based on mutual respect.

Suggested Commission Payments Upon Termination

Obviously, termination is a complex subject with many different points of view on what is appropriate and fair. The ideal policy is founded on industry practices and should be fair to you, to the rep being terminated, and to the new rep being signed on.

Jim Minyard, an executive committee member of the ERA, suggests a method for defining how commissions are to be divided between the terminated rep and the new rep. With some modification for the sake of graphics, I have portrayed that method in Figure 12-1. It shows one ap-

Figure 12-1   Commission transitions upon termination.

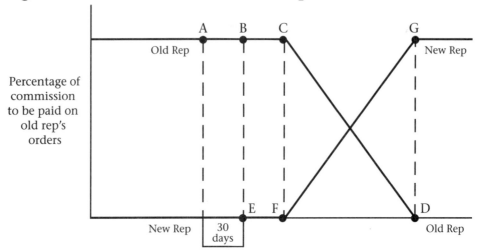

Time (in days)

proach a manufacturer can use to determine how this delicate matter might be handled.

Let's look at each point on the graph.

A: This is the date the existing rep is terminated.

B: Under the thirty-day cancellation clause, all commissions from the terminated rep's backlog at point A that are shipped up to point B will be paid in full. Any new orders received that are also shipped within the period will be paid in full. Note that at this same time, point E also occurs. This is the date the new rep is officially under contract and starts selling for your company.

C: Point C is the date after which full commission will not be paid for the backlog that existed as of B. Depending on the specific industry, more than thirty days might be allowed between points B and C. For the hypothetical situation where a manufacturer ships the product on the date the order is received, points B and C will be identical and the rep will not receive additional commissions beyond this date. However, this is the exception rather than the rule. Depending on the industry, shipments from backlog at point B can be stretched out over a number of years. The time between B and C—the added area of protection—should be developed from discussions with reps in the industry you serve (not just your own reps). You can expect a rational response; after all, reps are as interested in what they receive from backlog of new principals as they are in protection upon cancellation. In some situations backlog protection for full commission (perhaps minus destination share of commission) should be paid for up to a year or more.

At point C, commissions from backlog begin to decline, with the reduced amount going to the new rep as compensation for the service required during this period.

D: Once point D is reached, all financial obligations to the terminated rep will have been completed.

E: This is the official date that the new rep begins selling for your company. At that date, the new rep has no commission residual from previous backlog. Any commissions due to the new rep at point E would be based on that rep's closing orders as of that date.

From this point on, commissions for new orders received are credited to the new rep. Even here, there may be the need for exceptions. Suppose the old rep had worked for a long period of time, maybe years, getting a negotiation to the edge of closing, but the order does not close until after the thirty-day termination period is over and the new rep is officially selling for you. The element of fairness should come into play here. The manufacturer may ask the old rep to identify projects that are close to closing and may offer additional periods of protection beyond the normal thirty-day period. New reps accept this, for they know they will also receive similar protection.

F: In the period between points E and F, the new rep would be accumulating a backlog of commissions based on the new business booked. Once point F is reached, the new rep starts to collect a share of the commission in the backlog attained by the terminated rep.

Point F and point C occur simultaneously. The slope of the curve between F and G is the same as the declining slope between C and D, so that the total commission dollars paid to the two reps equals the actual commission dollars due on the contract.

G: At this point, all commissions will start flowing to the new rep.

You can modify this chart by superimposing whatever time periods are reasonable. Once again, consult the reps serving your industry.

13

Legal Issues and Trends

by Gerald Salmen

The marketing of products and services through manufacturers' reps must be done in accordance with applicable law. Just as importantly, the administration of the business relationship by the manufacturer must take into account the fact that reps are independent contractors, not employees. Moreover, manufacturers (and reps) are often surprised to learn that special statutes in many states have provisions that apply to the creation, performance, and termination of the rep/manufacturer relationship. This chapter provides an overview of significant legal issues and trends affecting manufacturers that market through reps.

Commission Protection Acts

Since the early 1980s, over thirty states have passed laws which apply only to reps and to those that sell through reps. These laws are generally referred to as "commission protection acts." This title, however, is somewhat misleading. These statutes also provide protection to manufacturers, and many of the laws address rep/manufacturer issues beyond commission disputes.

History of CPAs

Don't worry—this section is not the history of accounting. Rather, it's simply an explanation of the reasons for the enactment of commission protection acts (sometimes referred to as CPAs).

In the rep/manufacturer relationship, the latter holds most of the economic cards. The customer pays the manufacturer directly. Often, the manufacturer does not have to pay the commission to the rep until thirty to forty-five days after payment in full by the customer. Thus, for some period of time, the manufacturer is holding onto money that ultimately belongs to the rep.

Most of the time, this arrangement is not problematic. But upon termination or expiration of the relationship, there have been instances of some manufacturers delaying or refusing to pay commission due reps despite the rep having returned all sales literature and otherwise complying with the end-of-contract obligations.

While most manufacturers have ready access to legal counsel, reps usually do not have the financial ability to have a lawyer on a retainer. To recover wrongfully withheld earned commissions, the rep would often find that few, if any, attorneys would take such a case unless the amount involved was substantial. Accordingly, many reps simply walked away from commissions earned and due rather than getting into an expensive legal battle.

Expediting Commission Payments

While the CPAs differ in many respects from state to state, they share some common traits. First, they generally provide that commissions due at the end of the rep/manufacturer relationship must be paid within a certain amount of time. The time within which commissions must be paid after termination may often be much shorter than what is stated in the written contract between the parties or shorter than what their past practice has been. Therefore, those who administer rep contracts for a manufacturer must check any applicable CPA before making final decisions about withholding or delaying commissions after termination of a rep relationship.

If the manufacturer fails to pay commissions as required by law, most CPAs provide for a penalty payment. The rep can sue to recover not only the unpaid commissions but also for two or three times the amount due as exemplary or punitive damages. Such penalty provisions can quickly change a nominal claim into a substantial amount of money. The clear legislative intent of these provisions is to provide incentive to manufacturers to pay money to the rep entitled to it and to punish those who fail to do so.

In addition, most CPAs provide that the rep can recover attorney fees and court costs in a successful claim for unpaid commissions. This right can open the courthouse door for many reps. However, the real-world effect of this provision is to keep some commission disputes out of the legal system. Many times, the rep or an attorney on behalf of the rep will write to the manufacturer and enclose a copy of the applicable commission protection act before filing a lawsuit. Manufacturers should check with their legal counsel before withholding commission payments after termination of the contract, particularly if the rep invokes a commission protection act in asserting a claim for commission payment.

Manufacturer Protection

Many of the commission protection acts provide protection to the manufacturer from meritless lawsuits brought by a rep. If a rep brings a claim that is determined to be frivolous, the manufacturer can recover its attorney fees and court costs.

Of course, if the manufacturer complies with the contract or any applicable CPA, there are no penalty payments or attorney fees about which to be concerned.

Other Issues in the CPAs

A number of commission protection acts require agreements between reps and manufacturers to be in writing. This requirement reflects the simple fact that ink is more permanent than most human memory. Moreover, putting an understanding on paper tends to force clearer thinking as well as up-front discussion of issues that the parties are sometimes reluctant to address (e.g., house accounts or post-termination commissions).

If it turns out that the manufacturer and the rep cannot agree in writing on difficult issues or that one side is unyielding on an onerous contract term, it is much more economical (in both time and money) for the parties to face that issue prior to actual performance. The prospective business partners can then walk away from the proposed relationship before committing resources to a venture that is not meant to be.

A few commission protection acts go beyond requiring a written contract. These laws require certain specific provisions to be in the agreement, such as the identification of any house accounts and the method of accounting for charge-backs. Those interested in learning of any contract clause requirements in a particular state statute should obtain and analyze the commission protection act that applies to the actual situation in question.

It remains more common for manufacturers to prepare written contracts than for reps to do so. Typically, the manufacturer will provide that the laws of its home state govern the relationship with the rep. Most CPAs, however, state that their provisions cannot be waived, either by express waiver or by an attempt to make the laws of some other state apply. In other words, if a commission protection act in the rep's home state covers the issues in dispute, the court will, in all probability, follow that law and not follow the law selected in the contract to resolve the issue covered by the CPA. Because a manufacturer, therefore, cannot be certain that the law it selected will govern all disputes, it must become aware of and evaluate any applicable commission protection act.

Trends in Commission Protection Acts

Although the CPAs have been on the books for more than a decade, there are still relatively few published court decisions interpreting them. One state's law—Indiana—has been viewed by a federal court as providing a remedial means for reps to recover post-termination commissions if—and only if—the rep can prove the manufacturer terminated the relationship with the intent to deprive the rep of commission on actual orders fulfilled for which the principal subsequently received payment from the customer. Manufacturers can certainly make business decisions not to market through reps. Their motivation to do so may become subject to judicial scrutiny if the rep has sufficient evidence that the decision was propelled by a wrongful intent and caused actual damage.

A number of commission protection acts have been declared unconstitutional because they applied only to out-of-state manufacturers that failed to pay commissions. Legislative shielding of in-state companies from penalties that apply to out-of-state companies is rightfully seen as an unconstitutional burden on interstate commerce. After all, a failure to pay commissions due is wrongful regardless of where the principal is located.

In a number of states, legislation has either been introduced or has been passed to rectify the constitutional deficiency of the penalties applying only to out-of-state principals. Various industry and national trade associations monitor the status of commission protection acts in all the states. Interested readers can contact their associations to determine the status of a commission protection act in any particular state.

Written Contracts

It is now common for reps and manufacturers to evidence their business relationship in a written contract. As discussed above, one of the reasons is that many commission protection acts require a written agreement between a rep and its principal.

Another reason for written contracts arises from the changing marketplace. Mergers and acquisitions have eliminated manufacturers and pushed sales managers and others out of their jobs. Indeed, rep agencies are merging at an increased rate.

All this business activity naturally means that the person with whom you negotiate a rep/manufacturer relationship may not remain in the picture for a long time. Moreover, memory tends to fade with time, and money and emotions can influence the clarity with which verbal understandings are recalled.

For all these reasons, written contracts have become the norm between reps and manufacturers. It is the businesslike way to document the understanding between the parties.

Contract Clauses Must Be Clear

A detailed discussion of various contract clauses that ought to be in a written agreement is beyond the scope of this chapter. Those who want more information can review the contract discussion and specimens in this book and can obtain additional information from industry or national trade associations or from experienced counsel.

A key legal point for manufacturers (and reps) to remember when drafting a contract is *clarity*. A rule of contract law in every state is that unclear or ambiguous phrasing is construed against the person who wrote the words. The theory is that if you had a chance to write clear concepts and failed to do so, you should bear the burden of the words—not the other party, who did not phrase the agreement. Put simply, in drafting a written contract, you live by your words, and you can die by your words.

Territory: Geography or Accounts?

Traditionally, rep contracts have described territory by geography. The manufacturer wants the rep to cover a particular group of counties or states. Many reps like the prospect of business opportunities in a large territory. The vast majority of rep arrangements are still based on geography.

There is a trend, however, for some reps and principals to describe the territory by account name or market segment. In other words, the rep will call on particular identified actual or potential customers or will call only on customers in a particular market segment (e.g., governments or OEMs or utilities).

This "rifle-shot" approach is often more economical and productive for both parties because it focuses the solicitation efforts. If this approach is chosen, the parties should create a realistic account list; overinclusion, in particular, results in a territory that amounts to geography.

The parties also need to establish a system for adding or deleting accounts. One that can work well is to require the rep to give written notice of any proposed additions. The manufacturer must then respond in writing with any opposition and the reasons for it within a relatively short period of time or otherwise the proposed addition goes on the list automatically. This system permits the manufacturer to reject additions if the manufacturer has had its own pre-existing independent contacts with the potential customer.

Duties

A recurring legal issue in rep contracts is the tendency for manufacturers to list a host of detailed duties required of the rep. Sometimes, the list is a holdover from an employment contract with an employee. In other cases, the manufacturer may be reluctant or even unwilling to have minimal restraints on the day-to-day activities of a rep.

Nonetheless, it is imperative that the manufacturer realize that the rep is an independent contractor, not an employee. The legal difference is that independent contractors are not subject to the same level of detailed control as an employee.

To understand the difference, think of a typical independent contractor you may hire to paint a room in your house. The painter is *not* your employee. The painter can pick the starting and quitting times and the length of lunch. The painter determines where to start the job and how to set it up and how to clean up the job site. The painter pays taxes and hires whatever other workers are necessary.

As the homeowner hiring the painter, you are interested in the results of the work. You expect a painted room at a particular price and with a cleaned-up job site. That is how manufacturers must view reps. They must be concerned with the results of the rep's efforts and not expect to control all the details of how the rep accomplishes the goal.

The real impetus for treating reps as independent contractors rather than as employees comes from the Internal Revenue Service. The IRS regularly audits employers to determine if independent contractors should be reclassified as employees because the employer is exerting too much control over the details of the independent contractor's job performance. If so, the employer will be liable for back taxes, interest and penalties. It is therefore crucial for the parties to avoid requiring duties in the written contract which imply control over the details of the rep's work and to avoid exerting or accepting the kind of control employers have over employees.

However, the parties must still communicate for planning purposes and so that each knows the other is performing. One of the most effective ways is to include a clause in the contract that requires each party to send copies of correspondence, purchase orders, invoices, and related documents to the other party. In the business partnership between a rep and a principal, the free flow of information both ways should be a voluntary and natural process. The relationship should not be adversarial.

Notice of Termination

It is never pleasant to contemplate the end of a relationship at the beginning of it, but the fact is that every rep/manufacturer partnership will come to an end at some time. It is much better to negotiate those terms before the investment of time, money, and effort raises the stakes.

Many contracts have provided for at least thirty days' notice of termination. While that length of time is still common, it should not be considered the necessary norm. Some contracts start with that amount of notice and add increments of thirty days for each year the contract is in force up to a maximum of, say, 180 days. For example, if the contract had been in effect three years, either side would have to give the other at least ninety days' notice of termination.

Some believe, however, that if one side wants out of the partnership, it is better to cut the ties promptly and move on. For those, a thirty-day notice period will work, but thought should be given to providing for post-termination commissions to avoid litigation over what, if anything, is "fair" to pay for orders received prior to termination but fulfilled afterwards or for releases of blanket orders received after termination. Detailed discussion of this issue can be found in the following section.

A common legal mistake made by many manufacturers is to give the required days of notice of termination but to couple it with a demand to the rep to stop selling immediately. Notice means notice. It is a warning that the contract will come to an end after a certain number of days (the "effective date of termination"). But until the effective date of termination, the contract is still in effect, and both parties must continue to perform under the contract. Remember that, unless the termination is effective immediately, the date the notice of termination is given is *not* the effective date of termination.

Post-Termination Commissions

The nature of most rep/manufacturer relationships is that a great deal of work is always "in process." The rep has expended time, money, and effort to solicit orders and will not receive commission payment until weeks, months, or even years later when the customer orders; the manufacturer produces, ships, and bills; and the customer pays. What happens if the relationship ends before large blanket orders are fulfilled or before any significant commissions have resulted?

While the instinct of many is to think about what is "fair" in such a situation, the law generally says look at the contract first. Did the parties discuss post-termination commissions, and if so, what did they agree upon in their written words? Many courts say a deal is a deal and hold the parties to what they bargained for in their contract. If they failed to address the issue in writing, courts are often reluctant to find a right to post-termination commissions because they feel they are adding a term to the contract that the parties themselves did not insert.

It must be emphasized that courts do not readily embrace arguments about "fairness." The thinking is that contracts embody the agreement of the parties and that unfairness can be found in every contract from the point of view of some party.

On the other hand, manufacturers should not automatically assume post-termination commissions are never an issue if the contract is silent on that topic. A few courts have permitted some arguments for the recovery of post-termination commissions even if the contract does not directly address the issue or especially if there is no written contract. The legal theories used in the arguments include breach of a fiduciary duty, fraud, breach of an implied obligation of good faith, unjust enrichment, bad faith, bad faith denial of a contract, and others. This potpourri of possible claims explains why some attorneys argue it is the better practice to specifically address the issue of post-termination commissions in a written contract so that the focus is on the agreement of the parties and not on what might be "fair and equitable." The contract clause can permit some post-termination commissions or none at all.

Some reps try to negotiate "life of part/life of program" clauses. These provisions—often referred to as LOP/LOP clauses—state that the manufacturer shall pay commissions to the rep as long as orders come in during the life of the part or the life of the program regardless of when any termination of the rep/principal relationship occurs. LOP/LOP clauses are sought by many reps in the automotive industry and similar industries where protracted solicitation efforts may ultimately result in a part being sold through multiple model (and calendar) years.

Manufacturers who elect to consider LOP/LOP clauses can seek to have them capped after a certain number of years or to provide for reducing commissions over time or both.

From a manufacturer's point of view, a contract clause defining the limits of post-termination commissions has the benefit of establishing the extent of its liability. Without that certainty, the manufacturer may find itself subject to claims based on "fairness" that greatly exceed what it could have otherwise agreed to pay under clear contractual language limiting the right to or amount of post-termination commissions.

Moreover, some reps—particularly well-established and well-connected ones—will not enter into a rep/manufacturer relationship without adequate economic protection via post-termination commissions for pre-termination efforts. Therefore, the manufacturer who refuses to even consider some reasonable post-termination provision may be unable to attract the experienced reps who could successfully expand the manufacturer's market share. A fair post-termination provision can be a win-win clause.

Finally, manufacturers need to consider any applicable commission protection acts. As mentioned above, some CPAs, such as that of Indiana, provide a statutory claim outside the contract for post-termination commissions depending on proof of certain facts and circumstances.

Tortious Interference

"Tortious" is a fancy legalism that means "wrongful." A tortious interference is a wrongful interference with a contractual relationship. In the rep/manufacturer relationship, it can happen when a customer goes to a principal and says, in effect, break your contract with your rep; eliminate the rep; pass the savings on to us (the customer); and we will continue to do business or will do even more business with you, the manufacturer.

While the American economic system favors competition, it does not condone unfair competition or predatory actions. Unfortunately, in the face of pressure to reduce costs, a number of customers have pushed manufacturers to prematurely terminate their contracts with reps, often not aware of the legal peril in which they put themselves and their suppliers.

The legal problem arises because customers have demanded that manufacturers terminate contracts with reps regardless of the facts that the contract is not yet at an end and that usually some notice of termination must be given. The language in the customer's letter may be sugar-coated with niceties about "closer working relationships" that "add value and lower costs," but the clear point is to eliminate the rep and to do it quickly.

This demand, however, crosses the line of fair economic competition. It is not legally acceptable to require manufacturers to terminate their reps on demand—especially to demand termination prior to the normal contractual end of the relationship or without proper notice.

Nevertheless, some customers—particularly those who are big buyers ("power buyers")—believe they can impose their economic views on anyone. Reps have gone to court and to the Fair Trade Commission to seek legal protection of their contractual rights. Some years ago, Wal-Mart declared to its suppliers that it would no longer welcome reps calling on its buyers. A number of manufacturers responded by advising Wal-Mart that while their reps would not call on the buyers, the manufacturers would still honor the contracts and pay commissions to the reps. In other words, the customer was not going to dictate marketing channels to the manufacturers, and the price was not going to change. Other suppliers who did not share that view abruptly terminated contracts with their reps and found themselves mired with Wal-Mart in lawsuits.

More recently, the drugstore chain Rite-Aid has written to its suppliers and told them, effective January 1, 1999, Rite-Aid will no longer permit reps to deal with its buyers. This stance has provoked affected reps and manufacturers to evaluate the legal ramifications of Rite-Aid's edict.

Allegations of tortious interferences can be seen in a case involving the General Electric Company and the rep firm of Roger Brown & Associates, Inc. Roger Brown was a rep for one of GE's suppliers. After the sourcing relationship had been established and the supplier had agreed to locate one of its engineers at GE's facility, GE wrote to the supplier. The GE letter in no uncertain terms asked the supplier to terminate any contracts of reps who dealt with GE:

> Obviously this arrangement [the supplier engineer at GE] will make any current outside sales representatives a redundant service and unaffordable cost. In preparation for our new working arrangement, I [GE] now formally request the termination of any contracts for sales representatives that receive commission from GE Motors business. Please respond with a plan and timing to eliminate those contracts and reduce GE product costs by an appropriate amount by Monday, August 30.

The supplier subsequently told Roger Brown that it would handle GE as a direct account. Mr. Brown ultimately filed a lawsuit against GE, which was settled out of court on confidential terms.

GE's letter to its supplier suggests that it not only did not want to deal with reps but also that it wanted the manufacturer to terminate the rep contracts promptly and thereby reduce GE costs by "an appropriate amount." This kind of economic conduct puts both the customer and the manufacturer in legal jeopardy. Virtually every contract requires the manufacturer to give the rep some amount of notice of termination. Many contracts last for a specific term or can be terminated only for certain reasons. One of the functions of a contract is to set forth the requirements the parties must follow in their business actions.

A third-party customer demand that seeks to frustrate or alter the requirements the parties to the contract have agreed upon can cross the line of fair competition and become tortious interference. Manufacturers should seek legal counsel before taking actions at the insistence of customers when the actions will alter the contractual relationship with reps.

Manufacturers must be prepared to live up to the contracts they have signed regardless of economic pressure from customers. The failure to do so has resulted in some manufacturers becoming defendants in lawsuits that could have been avoided. Their actions have also impaired their ability to market products by attracting and retaining productive and successful reps.

Litigation and Alternatives

Inevitably, some rep/manufacturer disputes will result in court action. Litigation is time-consuming, emotional, and expensive for all concerned. If the case does not settle, it puts the fate of the parties in the hands of strangers on a jury who may have hidden agendas despite the best intentions to be fair and impartial. Litigation should normally be viewed as a last resort if all else fails, much like surgery is often the last option in medical care. Both are traumatic, expensive, and not always successful.

There is a trend to consider alternatives to litigation. Many contracts mandate binding arbitration instead of litigation. There are pros and cons to arbitration.

On the plus side, arbitration is usually quicker and can be less expensive than litigation. Cases may be heard within a matter of months, instead of years, and the whole process of preparation for the hearing is more streamlined. Sometimes the arbitrator can be selected from a list of those who have some experience in the issues presented, which can be in contrast to jurors who may have no such familiarity. Another advantage is that the decision of the arbitrator is final except for a very few reasons such as actual fraud.

On the negative side, arbitration does not provide for the extensive discovery rights available in civil litigation. Thus some critical facts and witnesses may never be uncovered and evaluated. A sole arbitrator may be uninterested, uninformed, or unfair, and there are no other jurors to appreciate and consider all sides of the issues. Without the right to appeal except for outrageous misconduct, the parties are stuck with a decision that may or may not be based on the facts and the law and may or may not be supported with a written explanation.

The bottom line is that arbitration is not a cure-all and should be made mandatory only after consideration of the pros and cons. In any case, the arbitration clause in the contract between the rep and the principal should provide that the prevailing party shall be awarded attorney fees, costs, and expenses.

Mediation is being ordered by more courts prior to trial. A mediation is best thought of as a formal business meeting among the parties, their counsel, and the mediator as a neutral third party. Unlike an arbitrator, the mediator cannot make a decision. The function of a mediator is to listen to each side and then to meet separately with them to explore the strengths and weaknesses of each party's position. Ultimately, the mediator tries to find any common ground that might produce a pretrial settlement.

If the mediation is successful, the parties carry out their settlement, and the case is over. If it is unsuccessful, the mediator so reports to the court, and the case is put back on the calendar for trial.

These alternative dispute resolution (ADR) mechanisms are becoming more common as the cost and delay of litigation mount. Manufacturers should consider adding an ADR provision to their contracts.

Conclusion

The law constantly evolves to meet new problems and demands. Commission protection acts will continue to proliferate, and court decisions will interpret statutory language lawmakers intend to be clear. Manufacturers must consider any applicable commission protection acts and relevant court decisions as they administer their business relationships with reps.

Written contracts will document more and more rep/manufacturer relationships. But actions must still honor words, or the contract is not worth the paper on which it is written.

Economic pressures, the Internet, and other currently unforeseen forces will challenge the best intentions, expectations, and contracts of reps and manufacturers. Thinking and acting like a business partner, together with knowledge of and adherence to the law and the contract governing the relationship, will provide the foundation manufacturers need to market their products and services successfully with reps without adverse legal consequences.

14

Selling Through Distributors and Agents Overseas

by Gunnar Beeth

Manufacturers' rep is an American term. Outside North America, and in this chapter, the term *agent* is used instead. *Agent* is here short for *commission agent,* an independent company or person who sells a product without taking title to it and gets a commission from the manufacturer for doing so. This person has no salary or retainer fee. In this book, thus far, this is the only type of independent "rep" we have discussed. When entering the overseas market, there is another breed of independent to consider: a distributor. This term refers here to an overseas company that buys—and usually imports—the goods for its own account and resells them. There is no commission, because the distributor buys the product outright from the manufacturer.

In this chapter, I'll discuss the overseas independent agents and distributors. I'll compare selling through them to selling through overseas subsidiaries, i.e., overseas sales outlets owned by the manufacturers. Establishing an overseas subsidiary is akin to setting up a direct sales organization in another country. The international business world is, of course, much more complex and includes also licensors, licensees, franchisees, overseas manufacturing subsidiaries, overseas independent manufacturing contractors, joint ventures, "piggy-backing," and other combinations. None of those will be discussed here.

Independents or Subsidiaries?

The choice of overseas independents or subsidiaries first depends on the nature of your product, but a subsidiary usually requires substantial capital investment and personnel with experience in international management. Should the political or business situation in the foreign country change, you cannot easily retrieve the capital invested in a subsidiary, so most medium- and smaller-size manufacturers do not start a sales subsidiary where any of the following situations are prevalent:

- The political, business, or legal situation is unstable
- Graft is widespread
- Currencies are, or might become, unconvertible
- There is galloping inflation
- Discrimination is intense against foreign-owned enterprise
- There are severe or unpredictable import restrictions

This means that in virtually all less-industrialized countries, most medium- and small-size American companies should sell not through subsidiaries but instead through independent local agents, or distributors. Even in most of Western Europe, most small- or medium-size American companies start selling through independents before considering subsidiaries.

Western Europe is usually the first overseas location that American companies consider for sales subsidiaries. Japan should be the second one for most products. The huge market size of Western Europe, the open and receptive attitude to imports, the legal and business stability, and many other factors contribute to considering Western Europe first.

In addition to increasing sales, there is a second reason for considering Western Europe and Japan for subsidiaries: to have your own personnel present in the three regions where nearly all new technology first appears, North America, Japan, and Western Europe. Because Japanese sales channels are more complex for Americans than European sales channels, however, many American companies continue selling through independents in Japan long after they have subsidiaries in Europe.

The advantages of independents over sales subsidiaries have been elaborated in the chapters on domestic business, but overseas the advantages of independents are augmented enormously because of the importance there of local management, incentives of local ownership, knowledge of local habits and customers, and deep understanding of local feelings. The last item is often the most important one and seriously underestimated by persons new to international business. All of these items, however, are valuable assets of independent distributors and agents. It's good to have those advantages on your side.

The manager of European operations of a medium-size company in industrial products told me that his company has one subsidiary in Europe, located in Germany; it has distributors in most other West European countries. Surprisingly, among all their distributor countries, this manufacturer has its highest sales in Austria, one of the smallest markets in Europe.

My reaction was that the company should try to duplicate in other European countries the kind of distributor selection that had provided such splendid results in Austria. The manager of European operations, however, was nervous about losing the large sales in Austria. So he mentioned that he hoped to add a subsidiary in Austria by acquiring the distributor there.

I suggested instead that he not touch the spot that works best in his area. I tried to convince him that the same Austrian employees may not achieve the same results under American ownership as under local Austrian ownership. Notwithstanding bonuses, they may lose some of the initiative and incentive they now have. They will definitely lose flexibility. In Austria, unorthodox business arrangements are particularly prevalent and impossible for an American-owned subsidiary to engage in.

So, don't change whatever is working well.

Some Initial Stumbling Blocks

To find out whether your products are competitive overseas, you might send an employee to a major international trade exhibition in the market of most interest to you. Your employee can compare prices and qualities and find out what features the customers ask for.

Before you go ahead with exporting, you probably want to investigate whether your products comply with the local safety standards and other regulations. The American National Standards Institute (ANSI) in Washington, D.C., is often helpful with information on overseas standards. The Canadian government provides similar assistance.

If your products do not comply, can they be modified easily? Most products can. Do the products have the right markings? The right packaging? Instruction manuals in the right languages? Were the translations done correctly? Whether the text has been translated by a translation bureau or a nonprofessional, it is nearly always wrong and must be corrected by a person in the country of destination before it is printed. That person has to be professionally knowledgeable in your kind of products. Advertising usually shouldn't be translated at all but created in the country of destination. It should be selected, judged, and approved by locals in the country of the buyers, never in the country of the sellers, even though they pay for it. Only the buyers know what appeals to them, and that is all that counts.

Market Sizes

Sales managers in domestic business have a habit of judging market sizes by population figures. For example, "We should sell roughly three times as much in California as in Illinois because the California population is roughly three times bigger." Such a rule based on population figures is completely invalid in international business. Instead, the GDP (gross domestic product) figures for different countries are a much better guide to rough market size comparison for most products.

A quick look at GDP statistics shows that the world has three huge markets: Western Europe, the United States, and Japan (Figure 14-1). The rest of the markets are distributed among many countries, most of which are much more difficult to penetrate than Western Europe. (The figures are based on the latest available international statistics at the time of writing, January 1999.)

Japan

Much of Japanese industry belongs to several big groupings, e.g., the Mitsui or the Mitsubishi groupings. The links within a grouping can range

Figure 14-1   Gross domestic product.

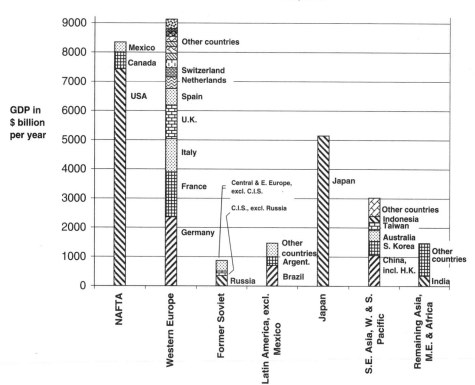

from total ownership to only loose preferences in choosing suppliers. If you are in industrial products and if most of the end users of your kind of products belong to one of the major Japanese industrial groupings, it can be fatal to have a distributor or agent belonging to its main competitor grouping. On the other hand, it can ease your sales to have a distributor or agent belonging to the same major industrial grouping as your biggest Japanese ultimate customers. There are also industrial product categories in which you may find it best to have two, three, or more Japanese distributors or agents, each one to sell principally to companies within its own industrial grouping.

For consumer goods, the Japanese distribution channels have more layers than the Western channels. Japan has twice as many retailers per million inhabitants as Western industrialized countries. Most of the retailers have little space and can neither finance nor store substantial inventories, so they are served frequently by small, secondary wholesalers, which in turn are served by primary wholesalers. Some Westerners criticize the multilayer channels, but these critics don't understand that the Japanese system works efficiently for the Japanese way of neighborhood shopping without a car. The multilayer system meets the bulk of Japanese needs better than any other system.

Many Westerners have gone to Japan and given up quickly after seeing how different Japanese distribution was, but their statements to the effect that Japan blocks imports are completely wrong for most products. Other Western businesses have made the considerable effort required to understand and penetrate the Japanese system. If their products were of good quality and suitable to Japanese needs, excellent business resulted.

Western Europe

If you sell industrial products in the United States through manufacturers' reps, it may not follow automatically that it is also best to sell in Europe through agents. One reason could be logistics: You may need stocking distributors instead of agents in Europe. That depends on the product. Another reason could be customer preferences: Their desire to speak directly to an employee of the company that manufactures the product may force you into having a subsidiary in at least one European country. The customer may feel, for example, that the employee of the manufacturer has more authority to approve immediately a design or packaging modification. A manufacturer may say that such a feeling on the part of the customer is wrong and immaterial, but if the feeling means the difference between getting orders and not getting them, it is far from immaterial, no matter how wrong it may seem to the American manufacturer.

Trends in Western Europe

Controls at most borders between countries in the European Union (EU) have been eliminated. National standards and safety regulations have been unified to a great extent and will become more similar to each other in the future. These developments benefit not only European producers but also American manufacturers selling in Europe.

1. Trucking within the new European Single Market is now so easy and inexpensive that many surface-freighted products are shipped from the United States in containers to only one, two, or at the most three stocking locations for all of the European Union. Of those companies choosing a single stocking location, many will select either Antwerp or Rotterdam, the two largest ports for goods shipped by surface.

2. The non-European manufacturers that chose to have only one stocking location for all of Europe used to put a subsidiary at that location. If no great amount of knowledge about the products is required for stocking, repackaging, and forwarding, then a specialized independent company can often perform those functions more economically. Such a forwarder usually has long-term contracts with several manufacturers of noncompeting goods. Most of these specialized forwarding and stocking firms also provide EU customs clearance.

3. In the past, American manufacturers that sold industrial equipment, which sometimes requires factory service and repair, had to provide repair and service facilities in each European country. Because of the open borders, it is now practical to have only one single repair and service facility in the EU for such equipment, at least if it is easily transportable.

4. Many electrical and other machines for industrial use, which previously needed to be manufactured in several different versions to comply with the previously conflicting standards of various European countries, can now be made in one or two models for all EU countries. For electrical consumer goods, two models will unfortunately still be required for many future years: one for the British Isles and one for the remaining countries. Safety approval and standards compliance are no longer used to protect the local manufacturers in each country, at least not to the extent that used to be the case in Western Europe.

5. Most machines now need to be approved for safety and standards in the EU country of importation only. From there they can be reshipped and sold freely across the entire EU. There remain only a few exceptions, of which automotive vehicles are the principal one.

6. French, German, and some other customers used to require instruction leaflets to be written in their own language only, a requirement that caused planning and stocking difficulties. Today, customers are in-

creasingly accepting multilingual operating instruction leaflets. For industrial goods, even multilingual packaging is becoming accepted. This means fewer forecasting, stocking, and shipping problems for American exporters.

7. The tunnel under the English Channel has sped up traffic to and from the United Kingdom. Many other new tunnels, bridges, and superhighways are being built and improved throughout Western Europe. New high-speed train lines are being built to crisscross most of Europe, except in the United Kingdom. In France, these trains now run at roughly 200 mph. The next generation of trains will be running at up to 220 mph. All of these transportation improvements are rapidly decreasing the perceived distances within Europe.

If the European Commission gets the political courage to break up the European airline oligopoly, the cost of air travel in Europe will fall drastically. Flight frequencies will multiply and convenience of routings should improve greatly. That would further improve transportation of people and goods within Europe, where some government-owned, slow-to-react airlines still prevent efficient air traffic.

8. Standardization is improving. For example, all EU countries have standardized on 400/230 V. (230 V is the single-phase voltage.) It remains 50 Hz as before.

But there are still some exceptions to standardization: For example, British and Irish electric plugs remain clumsy and different from other European electric plugs; French TV standards are different from others; some vehicle standards vary somewhat. The long-term trend, however, is toward elimination of more of the remaining differences, especially those that, from the beginning, were blatant subterfuges used to protect local manufacturers.

9. Most West European industrial customers require ISO 9000 quality registration for their industrial goods suppliers. This registration can be obtained in the United States and Canada through local organizations. Many of the companies that obtained such registration found that the exercise was worthwhile for their quality assurance alone and that the subsequent increase in exports became an additional benefit.

10. When this was written, at least Hungary, Poland, and the Czech Republic had been given limited free trade privileges with the EU. Additional countries in Central and Eastern Europe will get limited free trade arrangements with the EU, and may have gotten them by the time you read this. Poland, the Czech Republic, Hungary, Slovenia, and Estonia are first among the countries being considered for entry into the European Union, thus for entry into its common market. This is a far bigger change than just entering into a free trade area with the EU.

A free trade area (like NAFTA) requires much less integration than a common market like the European Union. Several hindrances to free trade are still retained in a free trade area. Although there are no customs duties within a free trade area, customs inspections at border crossings within a free trade area are still required in most cases. This is often to check at least the origin of merchandise so that duty can be imposed by the final country of entry on merchandise from outside the free trade area.

A common market, on the other hand, is a more complete union. It requires identical customs duties by each member toward outside countries and identical import and immigration regulations toward outsiders. Movement of goods and persons within the common market is completely free. Thus, there are no border controls between most common market members (at least the United Kingdom and Sweden still required border controls as of early 1999). American states are in a common market with each other and in a free trade area with Canada and Mexico.

11. Small- and medium-size non-European manufacturers exporting to Europe used to have a sole distributor or agent in each European country. At least in the larger European countries, there is now a trend toward having more than one distributor in each major country. For some products, the new distributors have geographic territories where each distributor can concentrate most efforts—for example, in northern, central, or southern Italy. For other products, the distributors may have different vertical markets, selling, for example, to the medical instrument market, the industrial instrument market, or the consumer instrument market throughout the country.

That trend does not in any way mean that a manufacturer should sell to anyone with an open checkbook. Nothing will destroy the efforts of your distributor faster. The foremost rule is to make your line rewarding enough for your distributor to make that company want to invest time, money, and ingenuity in promoting your business.

12. American exports of goods to Europe are rising fast. Most of these increases do not come from old giant U.S. corporations with European subsidiaries but from small manufacturers shipping to independent European distributors.

13. American exports of services to Europe are rising even faster than exports of goods. Examples include engineering design services, software, films, video, music, seminars, franchising, and (the biggest) tourism.

14. More and more American exports are being airfreighted to Europe. They are usually airfreighted directly from the United States to the country of final destination. 1991 was the first year when over half (by value) of American exports was airfreighted to Europe, and the percentage continues to rise.

15. Internet trade in both directions across the Atlantic is increasing fast. It has a huge positive trade balance for the United States. Internet

cross-Atlantic trade is used by all sorts of customers from individual consumers to giant corporations. Amazon.com was a pioneer and was quickly joined by innumerable other companies in both consumer goods and industrial products and services.

Suppliers of many services, including engineering and suppliers of products like software and books are increasingly "delivering" the purchased items via the Internet, in addition to taking orders and payments via the Internet. As an example, I have personally "printed" books in my Brussels office within minutes of providing my credit card number to U.S. sellers. I doubt that the people calculating official international trade statistics can even guess the huge and increasing amounts of such export transactions. No port or airport or customs office can collect the statistics, duties or sales taxes. And why should they? We all live in one world.

The above fifteen trends make it is easier now to export to the huge European market. The EU is also becoming an even bigger market, with its increasing number of member and affiliated countries. For many products, it is not necessary to have large investments in European subsidiaries in order to export to Europe.

For most goods, product development is progressing faster and becoming costlier. To pay for it, even small companies need larger sales volume so that the percentage of total costs spent on product development remains reasonable. To stay ahead of competitors, companies with such products need to sell in at least the three giant markets of the world.

The Largest Markets in Western Europe

Figure 14-2 superimposes a column chart onto a map of Europe to show GDP for each European country or area; this provides an overview of roughly where the markets are located and how big they are in relation to each other. A businessperson living in, say, Brussels has over half the West European market within easy driving distance and most of the remainder of the West European market within two hours' flying distance. That is how compact the large European market is geographically. Yet its total GDP is roughly the same size as the GDP of North America.

Choosing a Location for a European Subsidiary

When you choose a site for a subsidiary to work across all of Europe, you want to choose one located relatively centrally, with a good airport and within the European Monetary Union, as well as one having no border controls toward its neighbors.

How other companies have chosen their main site in Europe is not necessarily right for your products. Nevertheless, we may learn some

Figure 14-2   West European Market Sizes.

The heights of the columns are proportional to the
Gross Domestic Product of each country.

things from what many American companies have done in the past and
subsequently found out.

After World War II, the first wave of American companies poured
into the United Kingdom. Americans thought that the British, speaking
English, would pose the fewest difficulties. Their only task was to sell.
Then the Americans discovered that the culture and the attitudes in the
United Kingdom are as different from those on the European Continent
as from those in the United States. Americans discovered that it was extremely hard to run European operations from England.

The second wave of American companies poured into Europe's two
biggest markets: Germany and France. Generally, the subsidiaries sold
directly in their new home countries and through independent distribu-

tors or agents in Europe's smallest markets, as well as in the Middle East, Africa, and elsewhere.

Whether a company sold through a subsidiary, independent distributor, or agent depended on how big the European sales volume was and how much product knowledge was required for selling the goods.

For many products, there is now a growing trend toward a completely different view of what the subsidiary should do and what the independent distributors should do. For medium-size and smaller manufacturers, the new thinking is that locally owned distributors or agents are always more effective in selling than subsidiaries, even in a country where you already have a subsidiary anyway.

The independent distributors and agents will need marketing assistance, support, help, training, cajoling, and pushing from a subsidiary located not too far away and staffed by people who speak the necessary languages. In addition, these people should be able to operate within the local cultures.

The countries where one can find most multilingual and multicultural staff are Switzerland, Belgium, Holland, and Luxembourg, but since Switzerland is expensive and Luxembourg small, many of the new types of American subsidiaries have opened in Belgium or Holland. Some of the new types of subsidiaries in Belgium sell also in Belgium through independent Belgian distributors or agents. These subsidiaries do this to emphasize their undivided attention to selling through distributors and to give as much attention to distant markets as to the one outside their door. In summary, they hold that the subsidiary should not sell but should help independent distributors and agents to sell.

Of course, the above applies only to some products. For other products, such as for many of those to be incorporated in automobiles or aircraft, the cooperation between supplier and industrial customer must be so close that you do not want to have any independent between the two. Unfortunately, with time, a foreign independent nearly always becomes a filter, rarely a catalyst, between supplier and customer.

Scarcity of Multilingual and Multicultural Personnel

The trend toward selling throughout Europe has created an extremely high demand for employees who can communicate across most of Europe and motivate people in several very different European cultures.

Cultural differences remain a major communication barrier for most people. Very few people can cross the cultural barriers with gusto. When you hire staff to work across Europe, pay close attention to cross-cultural ability. Such ability is one of the main requirements in most of our executive searches. It is far more difficult to determine than knowledge of languages. Many managers are multilingual but monocultural.

The GSM Telecom Revolution

During the last half-century, the Global System for Mobile Communications (GSM) digital cell phones represented one of the few big technical advances that made its first breakthrough in Europe. Most other technical advances appeared first in the United States or Japan. As of early 1999, we expect that GSM-type cell phones will shortly change the way traveling American businesspersons work. Nevertheless, let me explain what had already happened in Europe before 1999.

Between the early 1990s and 1998, GSM telephones became predominant among businesspersons in Europe, in the Middle East, large parts of Asia except Japan, in Australia, New Zealand, and other places. The cell phones mainly used in the United States before 1998 were not of the GSM type, so they could not be used outside their country.

Elsewhere, the main reason why the GSM-type cell phones became so useful was that people traveling outside their home country could use the GSM phones in any country having GSM operators, which included nearly all the world except North America and Japan. In addition, somebody calling a businessman traveling with a GSM phone does not need to know which country he is in; dialing his single GSM number, the phone in his pocket will ring, no matter where he is. This is due to the "roaming" technology and the worldwide "roaming" agreements between nearly all the GSM operators.

At the same time, European businesspersons, especially those who travel, switched to e-mail from faxes for written communication, so they have one single e-mail address and one single (GSM) telephone number, no matter where they are. Thus, people communicating with them don't need to know where they are, whether communicating in writing or by voice.

GSM telephones are digital and laptop computers are digital, so when connecting the two with a simple wire and a small software program, you no longer need a modem to send and receive e-mail and faxes. You can do both from a car, a train, a park bench, or wherever. The cost is lower than hotel telephone rates.

Americans dealing with traveling European businesspersons have learned that it is more important to know their GSM number and e-mail address than their office phone and fax numbers.

The North American GSM traffic will be on 190 MHz, whereas the rest of the world is on 90 MHz and, increasingly, on 180 MHz. When this is being written, only Bosch makes a telephone handset spanning the main frequencies; but by the time this book is printed, we expect several manufacturers will make tri-frequency handsets. If you want to use your cell phone around the world, ask your local GSM operator which tri-frequency handset to buy for that purpose. From about 2002 or 2003, the next generation of digital cellular telephones will appear with broader bandwidth than GSM, and thus provide faster Web access together with your laptop.

The Euro and the European Monetary Union (EMU)

Variations in exchange rates have long been a bane to inter-European business, but now most of the EU countries are members of the EMU and use the Euro for trade between countries within the EMU. Those countries have fixed rates between their local currencies and the Euro. There are no more exchange costs within the EMU, just service charges for bank transfers; those we hope to get eliminated, the sooner the better. When this is being written, only four of the fifteen European Union countries haven't yet joined the EMU; but they will likely need to do so within a few years.

Within the EMU, national currencies are scheduled to continue in use for coins and bills until they are replaced by Euros in 2002. In the meantime, all written transactions, such as checks, bank transfers, credit card payments, etc., are already in Euros between the EMU countries, currently Germany, France, Spain, Portugal, Netherlands, Belgium, Luxembourg, Ireland, Finland, and Austria.

Outsourcing

There is a trend in Europe toward using independent distributors more and employed salespersons less. This is part of the overall move toward companies' concentrating on what they do best and buying from others both products and services that independent companies can provide more efficiently. It is also part of a trend away from huge, integrated companies toward smaller firms run by their owners. Services other than selling, which are increasingly bought from outside, include industrial design, management consulting, executive search, advertising, public relations, distributor search, training, repair, security, transport, and warehousing.

Limitations in Selling Abilities of European Distributors and Agents

Now that the EU is a single market, companies inexperienced in EU operations often seek a distributor or agent for all of Europe. But for over 99 percent of all products, there is no such company, although many claim to cover all of Europe. There is not even a trend toward the appearance or development of distributors or agents that really do cover all of Europe.

Furthermore, we are unlikely to see such distributors appear soon. The reason is that the selling ability of the citizens of each country is still largely limited to selling within their own country. Most American manufacturers that have tried Europe-wide selling through single independent organizations have been disappointed. There are only two exceptions: (1) companies that sell highly specialized and complex niche industrial equipment to a few end users and (2) companies that have chosen to distribute through major pan-European company groups in complementary products.

Even the many distributors or agents that call themselves regional are usually successful in their home countries only. If one agent claims to sell in the Benelux, another one claims to sell in Scandinavia, or a third one says she sells in Spain and Portugal, it is important to find out how much of these sales are actually in each country. Then consider whether you are better off with a local national agent for each country. Many German agents, for example, claim to sell well in Austria and the German-speaking part of Switzerland. I have not found a single one for whom that is true. The reason is that the cultures are very different in the three German-speaking areas.

Choosing the Right Distributor or Agent

In many countries, it is extremely costly to get rid of a distributor or agent that is not performing. So, it is important to choose the right one from the beginning. If you have done business for some time with a weak rep in Florida, you find a better one and, after thirty days, stop paying commissions to the old rep (see Chapter 12). But if you have done business for some years with an agent in one out of many overseas countries, you may owe this company commissions on new business in the country for years after terminating the company and starting with another one. The laws on this matter vary from country to country. In some countries, particularly some of those that are less industrialized, the old agent may have rights to continued commissions even if you never had any contract with the company. Local laws may consider this agent to have invested in developing the market for your products and thus to have earned the ownership of that market for your products.

Suppose that you have a contract written by your trusted North Carolina lawyer. The contract states clearly that both parties hereby agree that North Carolina law applies and that the contract can be terminated by either party upon three months' notice to the other, without any further commissions or indemnification. That contract is simply invalid in many countries, and you still may owe years of continued commissions to your fired agent. So, don't rely on just your local lawyer.

Of course, it is extremely important, also in the United States, to choose the best rep from the beginning. The difference between the sales of a good rep and an outstanding rep is not something like 20 or 30 percent but easily 200 or 300 percent or more.

To find the best distributor or agent in Country X for Product Y, do not start by going to all the potential distributors. (Here I use *distributors* to cover both distributors and agents.) Instead, go to their customers and ask them which distributors they prefer to buy from and why. Whom do they trust? Who will help them when problems arise? Who knows their products in depth? The customers know the distributors better than anyone else, so their recommendations are important.

The next step is to visit the recommended distributors and eliminate those that cannot be attracted to the new supplier and those that lack good management, adequate financing, and other important qualities.

The final choice of best distributor is the company with a key person who can and will dedicate time, effort, concern, and imagination to managing the new line successfully.

What do you do in a country where you are unhappy with the sales volume of your distributor, yet you don't want to make her business even worse by asking uncomfortable questions? Or what do you do in a country where you don't speak the language? In both cases, you can ask a consulting firm for assistance. A consultant can ask all the questions without disclosing the client's name. The consultant should know not only the language of the country but also its culture, so that he can get the customers to talk openly about the distributors.

Once you have found the outstanding distributor, no matter how enthusiastic you are about the potential relationship, your last step before starting business with the firm is to visit a local lawyer in the country of your distributor. Find out whether to draw up a contract and what it should say.

Choose Well the Person(s) to Look After Your Distributors and Agents

Suppose you seek an international sales manager for a North American company. If this person will travel from North America, he can be of the same nationality as your company. But if you seek a person to live overseas, your distributors and agents will have vastly tougher requirements on his language abilities and intercultural abilities. Your distributors may well reject the same person whom they previously accepted as a traveling visitor.

If you need a full-time person in Japan, hire a Japanese person. If you need a full-time person to travel around Europe, consider hiring one who speaks and writes English, German, and French. In addition, this person should have the rare ability to get herself accepted culturally throughout Europe. Such persons are difficult—but not impossible—to find.

Costs of Distribution

Many American companies automatically come overseas with a lot of pre-determined rules-of-thumb. What they don't realize is that these rules have been developed for their home market and are valid only there. One such rule may say, for example, that distribution may cost x percent or that a rep should receive an average of y percent commission. These may be good rules for the home market, but don't try to apply them overseas. Distribution in the United States is more efficient than in most other countries, and if you try to follow American rules, you might starve your overseas distribution channel, to the detriment of your sales volume.

Instead, observe what your best competitors are spending on distribution. If they spend $3x$ percent on distribution, maybe that is better, or maybe $2x$ percent or $4x$ percent. You really don't know until you try. A certain percentage maximizes your profit, and that percentage may vary widely from country to country. In one country, for example, Japan, the customers may demand far more attention, service, and follow-up than in another country. I never judge a distributor or agent on the commission charged but on the profit brought to the manufacturer. Japan is one of the countries with the highest distribution costs, but since you can increase the end price correspondingly, why worry?

As this is being written, exchange rates are such that most American manufacturers can get considerably higher prices for their goods in Europe than in the United States, but that situation may change. However, in countries where distribution costs are high, you can usually continue to get a high end-price for most products.

"Difficult" Distributors

All of us in international business have worked with "difficult" distributors. They make themselves unpopular by demanding shorter delivery, complaining about quality, asking the marketing department for additional advertising support, pestering the product development department for special models, and so forth. Each "difficult" foreign distributor causes the export manager more problems than five average distributors. And yet there is only one question to ask about such a "difficult" distributor: How much profit does this company bring after all the extra costs are factored in? In my experience, the "difficult" distributor often brings more profits than five average distributors. If that is the case, put up with this company and help it get whatever can increase those profits even more. Be grateful that the distributor pays attention to your line of goods!

It is the distributors I never hear from that I worry about—those that cause you no problems and rarely send you orders. Why not? Do they have the wrong person in charge of your line? Or is the right person too busy with other lines? Only by visiting these distributors proactively and going to customers with them will you find out. It is by calculating your market share for each country and area that you see where your presence is needed, not by the volume of "problems" you get from a distributor.

Training and support to distributors and agents are important in the United States, but when you are at the far end of a long supply line across an ocean, working in a different language, it is doubly important.

The distributors don't get a monthly paycheck from you; they don't have to work certain hours for you; they can start tomorrow dedicating all their time to other lines. You need to keep your line of goods present in their minds, by e-mail, mail, fax, telephone, and personal visits. If you don't make any headway with the employees of the distributing company, talk to the owners. They should be interested in earning profits on your line. If they are not, make a change.

When you have to terminate overseas distributors, here are three points to keep in mind:

1. First, get thorough advice from the most capable local lawyer you can find in the distributor's country.
2. Second, make certain that you know which better distributor you can attract. An outside consultant can help you with this—discreetly.
3. Finally, try to accomplish the change on a friendly basis with the terminated distributor. It is usually cheaper than a lawsuit dragging on for years. The distributor has a vested interest in maintaining a good reputation and not losing time in the courts—just as your company does.

Keeping Overseas Business

Some American companies have tried to go into the export market only when they have excess capacity and then abandon it when they don't. Certain American semiconductor manufacturers have even refused overseas orders or delayed export shipments once they reached full production capacity with domestic orders. When they later tried to get back into the foreign markets, they found that their former customers remembered how they had been treated. These customers blacklisted the American suppliers indefinitely. The moral is: When you are in international business, stick with it. In any case, treat your overseas customers, distributors, and agents as decently as you treat your domestic customers, and do it wholeheartedly.

Appendix A

Guidelines for Negotiating an Agreement Between Sales Representatives and Manufacturers, Electronics Representatives Association

THIS AGREEMENT made this * _____ day of _____, 19 _____.
by and between _____
a corporation incorporated under the laws of the State of _____
having its principal office at _____ ("Manufacturer"),
and _____
a corporation incorporated under the laws of the State of _____
having its principal office at _____ ("Representative"),
as follows:

* Insert date on which the agreement is signed

1.   APPOINTMENT AND ACCEPTANCE—Manufacturer appoints Representative as its exclusive representative to promote the sale of and sell its products (indicated in Provision #3 hereof); in the territory (indicated in Provision #2 hereof); and Representative accepts the appointment and agrees to sell and promote the sale of the Manufacturer's products.

2.   TERRITORY—Representative's Territory shall consist of the following:

*The territory can be designated as specific states, counties, zip codes, or a combination thereof or in any other way which clearly delineates the area. If the territory is not a specific area and is limited only to specific customers, the customers should be named. If there are any customers or "house accounts" to be excluded from the territory, they should be clearly listed by name and location along with a statement indicating that they are excluded and no commission will be paid on orders from or sales to them. ERA does not recommend any specific territory boundaries. While many "traditional territories" exist, the principal should create territories based on efficient and effective coverage.

3.   PRODUCTS—The "products" of the Manufacturer to be promoted for sale and sold by the Representative are:

*The Agreement should cover all products and services of the Manufacturer unless the Representative is to handle only specific products or services. If the Representative is not handling all the products or services, the Agreement should list the product lines, product categories or services the Rep is handling. It is preferable not to list products by model or part number as these may change from time to time. It should also indicate if new products or services developed or added by the Manufacturer are to be included.

4.   AMOUNT OF COMPENSATION—Representative's compensation for services performed hereunder shall be **___*% of the "net invoice price" of the Manufacturer's products shipped into Representative's territory. However, when engineering, execution of the order or shipment involve different territories, the Manufacturer will split the full commission among the Representatives whose territories are involved. The Manufacturer will make this determination in consultation with the Representatives involved based upon split commission applications submitted by those Representatives and advise the interested Representatives. The sum of the split commission shares shall add up to a full commission. Commissions on orders resulting from "design ins" (a design or specification indicating Manufacturer's product) procured or influenced by Representative will continue for the life of the customer's program into which the product is designed even though the commission is being split between several representatives.

Anything to the contrary notwithstanding, Representative will be compensated for orders from distributors based upon point of sale ("POS") reports received by Manufacturer from distributors. Manufacturer will pay the full commission (on the "net invoice price" to be paid by the distributor) to the Representative for the territory into which the distributor ships the products ordered by it, as indicated on the distributor's POS reports.

*This blank should be completed with the amount of the agreed commission. However, there are different arrangements that can be worked out between a Representative and a Manufacturer:

   a) The amount of commission can be a function of:

      i) The sales and marketing functions to be performed by the Representative.

      ii) Whether the Manufacturer is a new or established company.

      iii) Whether the Representative is expected to develop new markets for new or existing principals.

   b) Additional compensation could include:

      i) A fee for marketing services:

      ii) Increased commission rates based on exceeding mutually agreed upon quotas.

      iii) A monthly retainer.

   A sample Split Commission Request/Approval form is attached, and this type of form should be submitted to the Manufacturer as soon as the Representative is aware of the circumstances requiring a split commission, and the Manufacturer should be asked to approve the request within thirty (30) days after submission by the Representative.

5) COMPUTATION AND PAYMENT OF COMMISSION

a) Commissions are due and payable on or before the ___ day of the month immediately following the month in which customer is invoiced provided, however, on distributor orders commissions are due and payable on or before the ___ day of the month immediately following the month during which the Manufacturer receives a point of sale report form the distributor indicating distributor's customer and the location to which the products of the Manufacturer were shipped. However, if Manufacturer has not received a distributor Point Of Sale report reflecting the shipment of products ordered by distributor to the distributor's customers within sixty (60) days after shipment of the order to the distributor, or the Representative believes that there is an error in a Point Of Sale report received by Manufacturer, the Representative shall have the right to communicate with the distributor for the purpose of obtaining or correcting Point Of Sale information.

If the commissions are not paid when due, the amount not paid will accrue interest at ___% per annum from the date due until paid.

b) Manufacturer will send Representative copies of all invoices at the time Manufacturer invoices customer, and each invoice shall indicate the amount of commissions due Representative or the Manufacturer will send a weekly tabulation of all invoices with purchase order numbers, quantity, price and commission due.

c) At the time of payment of commissions to Representative, Manufacturer will send Representative a commission statement showing:

i) commissions due and owing Representative for that period and any prior periods, and

ii) commissions being paid (listing the invoices on which commissions are being paid).

d) "Net invoice price" shall mean the total price at which an order is invoiced to the customer including any increase or decrease in the total amount of the order (even though such increase or decrease takes place after the effective date of termination), but excluding shipping and insurance costs, sales, use and excise taxes, any allowances or discounts granted to the customer by the Manufacturer, and any tariffs, duties and export fees involved in international shipments.

e) There shall be deducted from any sums due Representative:

i) An amount equal to commissions previously paid or credited on sales of Manufacturer's products which have since been returned by the customer or on allowances credited to the customer for any reason by the Manufacturer; and;

ii) An amount equivalent to commissions previously paid or credited on sales which Manufacturer shall not have been fully paid by the customer whether by reason of the customer's bankruptcy, insolvency, or any other reason which, in Manufacturer's judgment, renders the account uncollectible. If any sums are ever realized upon such uncollectible accounts, Manufacturer will pay Representative its percentage of commission applicable at the time of the original sale upon the net proceeds of such collection.

f) "Order" shall mean any commitment to purchase Manufacturer's products which calls for shipment into Representative's territory or which is subject to a split commission in accordance with Provision #4 hereof.

* Computation and payment of Commissions—

a) The blanks should be completed with the day of the month in which commissions are to be paid and the amount of the interest to be charged on commissions due and not paid.

b) Also, commissions could be paid on or before the ___ day of the month following the month in which the order is shipped to the customer or when the Manufacturer is paid by the customer.

c) If the Representative is entitled to commissions on a Lease Agreement, the Agreement should indicate the manner in which commissions will be computed and when they are to be paid (e.g., payable in full at the time of the initial lease payment to the Manufacturer).

d) Indicate whether or not the following are to be commissionable:
(i) Engineering;
(ii) Research and development;
(iii) Non-recurring start-up costs;
(iv) Cancellation charges;
(v) Tooling;
(vi) Environmental qualification and specification;
(vii) Compliance testing;
(viii) Drawings and handbooks;
(ix) Documentation;
(x) Packaging;
(xi) Repair and reworks;
(xii) Surcharges & "add-ons" for increases in raw materials/other OEM supplies

e) The Agreement can also obligate the Manufacturer to pay attorney fees and collection costs when it is necessary for Representative to pursue the Manufacturer to recover commissions due and owing.

6.   ACCEPTANCE OF ORDERS—All orders are subject to acceptance or rejection by an authorized officer of Manufacturer at its home office and to the approval of Manufacturer's credit department. Manufacturer shall be responsible for all credit risks and collections.

If Manufacturer notifies customer of its acceptance or rejection of an order, a copy of any written notification shall be transmitted to the Representative. At least once every month Manufacturer shall supply Representative with copies of all orders received directly by Manufacturer, copies of all shipping notices, and copies of all correspondence and quotations made to customers in the territory.

7.   TERMS OF SALE—All sales shall be at prices and upon terms established by Manufacturer, and it shall have the right, in its discretion, from time to time, to establish, change, alter or amend prices and other terms and conditions of sale. Representative shall not accept orders in the Manufacturer's name or make price quotations or delivery promises without the Manufacturer's prior approval.

8.   REPRESENTATIVE'S RELATIONSHIP AND CONDUCT OF BUSINESS

a) Representative shall maintain a sales office in the territory and devote such time as may be reasonably necessary to sell and promote Manufacturer's products within the territory.

b) Representative will:

i) conduct all of its business in its own name and in such manner it may see fit,

ii) pay all expenses whatever of its office and activities, and

iii) be responsible for the acts and expenses of its employees.

c) Nothing in this Agreement shall be construed to constitute Representative as the partner, employee or agent of the Manufacturer nor shall either party have any authority to bind the other in any respect, it being intended that each shall remain an independent contractor responsible only for its own actions.

d) Representative shall not, without Manufacturer's prior written approval, alter, enlarge, or limit orders, make representations or guarantees concerning Manufacturer's products or accept the return of, or make any allowance for such products.

e) Representative shall furnish to Manufacturer's Credit Department any information which it may have from time to time relative to the credit standing of any of its customers.

f) Representative shall abide by Manufacturer's policies and communicate same to Manufacturer's customers.

g) Manufacturershall be solely responsible for the design, development, supply, production and performance of its products and the protection of its patents, trademarks and trade names. Manufacturer agrees to indemnify and hold Representative harmless from and against and to pay all losses, costs, damages or expenses whatsoever, including reasonable attorney's fees, which Representative may sustain or incur on account of infringement or alleged infringement of patents, trademarks, or trade names, or breach of warranty in any way resulting from the sale of Manufacturer's products. Manufacturer will also indemnify Representative from and hold it harmless from and against all liabilities, losses, damages, costs or expenses, including reasonable attorney's fees, which it may at any time suffer, incur, or be required to pay by reason of injury or death to any person or damage to property or both caused or allegedly caused by any products sold by Manufacturer. Manufacturer will also include Representative as an additional assured on its product liability insurance policy.

h) Manufacturer shall furnish Representative, at no expense to Representative, samples, catalogs, literature and any other material necessary for the proper promotion and sale of its products in the territory. Any literature which is not used or samples or other equipment belonging to Manufacturer shall be returned to the Manufacturer at its request.

i) If for any reason Representative, at Manufacturer's request, takes possession of Manufacturer's products, the risk of loss or damage to or destruction of such products shall be borne by Manufacturer, and Manufacturer shall indemnify and hold Representative harmless against any claims, debts, liabilities or causes of action resulting from any such loss, damage, or destruction.

j) Manufacturer will keep Representative fully informed about sales and promotional policies and programs affecting the Representative's territory.

*The Agreement can also include payment of transportation and all other expenses relating to Representative's personnel attending a sales meeting or training seminar at the request of Manufacturer.

9.   TERM OF AGREEMENT AND TERMINATION—This Agreement shall be effective on the day of _____, 19____, and shall continue in force for a ____ year period, and shall be automatically renewed for additional one (1)

year periods thereafter unless terminated by written notice from either party to the other not less than thirty (30) days prior to the end of the initial or any subsequent one year term. This Agreement may also be terminated:

a) By Manufacturer immediately upon written notice to Representative by registered or certified mail if there is a change of fifty (50%) percent or more of the present ownership or control of the Representative's business without Manufacturer's written consent.

b) By Manufacturer if Representative, without Manufacturer's written consent, offers, promotes or sells any product which is competitive with any product Representative is to offer, promote or sell for Manufacturer in accordance with the terms of this Agreement, and written notice of this breach of the Agreement is mailed to or served upon Representative, the breach is not cured within ten (10) days after receipt of such notice by Representative, and written notice of termination is mailed to or served upon Representative.

c) By Representative:

i) if Manufacturer, without Representative's written consent offers, promotes or sells any product which is competitive with any product Representative is offering or selling for any other manufacturer, and written notice of this breach of the Agreement is mailed to or served upon Manufacturer, the breach is not cured within ten (10) days after receipt of such notice by the Manufacturer, and written notice of termination is mailed to or served upon Manufacturer, or

ii) immediately upon written notice to Manufacturer by Registered or Certified mail in the event Manufacturer sells substantially all of the assets of its business or there is a change of 50% or more of its present ownership, or it is merged with another firm, corporation or business and Manufacturer is not the surviving company.

d) By either party

i) in the event of the other party's unreasonable and repeated failure to perform the terms and conditions of this Agreement, written notice of the failure is mailed to or served upon that party, the failure is not cured within thirty (30) days after receipt of such notice, and written notice of termination is mailed to or served on that party, or

ii) upon immediate written notice to the other party in the event that party has filed or has filed against it a petition in bankruptcy (which is not dismissed within thirty (30) days after it is filed) or that party makes an assignment for the benefit of creditors; or

e) By mutual written agreement.

10.   RIGHTS UPON TERMINATION

a) Upon termination of this Agreement for any reason, Representative shall be entitled to:

i) Commissions on all orders calling for shipment into Representative's territory which are dated or communicated to Manufacturer prior to the effective date of termination, regardless of when such orders are shipped, or releases and shipments on such orders take place; and

ii) Its share of split commissions on orders including those referred to in Paragraph (a) (i) of this Provision 10.

b) Commissions referred to in this Provision #10 shall be paid on or before the tenth (10th) day of the month following the month in which the Manufacturer receives payment for the orders.

c) In addition to the commissions to be paid to Representative pursuant to the other paragraphs of this provision, Manufacturer agrees to be fair and reasonable in compensating Representative at the time of or after termination, for Representative's efforts in developing customers in its territory which, because of Representative's efforts, would be likely to continue to purchase products from the Manufacturer after termination.

In addition, the following can be included:

a) In the event of termination, Manufacturer shall make its customer orders and shipping records available for inspection by the Representative, or the Representative's duly authorized agent.

b) A provision for the Representative to receive severance payments or an extended "notice of termination" period based upon the Representative's term of service.

11.   GENERAL—This Agreement contains the entire understanding of the parties, shall supersede any other oral or written agreements, and shall be binding upon and inure to the benefit of the parties' successors and assigns. It may not be modified in any way without the written consent of both parties. Representative shall not have the right to assign this Agreement in whole or in part without Manufacturer's written consent.

12.   CONSTRUCTION OF AGREEMENT—This Agreement shall be construed according to the laws of the State of _____ .

13.   DISPUTES AND ARBITRATION—The parties agree that any disputes or questions arising hereunder including the construction or application of this Agreement shall be settled by arbitration in accordance with the rules of the American Arbitration Association then in force, and that the arbitration hearings shall be held in the city in which the principal office of the party requesting arbitration (with the American Arbitration Association is located. If the parties cannot agree upon an arbitrator within ten (10) days after demand by either of them, either or both parties may request the American Arbitration Association to name a panel of five (5) arbitrators. The Manufacturer shall strike the names of two (2) on this list, the Representative shall then strike two (2) names, and the remaining name shall be the arbitrator. The decision of the arbitrator shall be final and binding upon the parties both as to law and to fact and shall not be appealable to any court in any jurisdiction. The expenses of the arbitrator shall be shared equally by the parties, unless the arbitrator determines that the expenses shall be otherwise assessed.

14.   NOTICES—All notices, demands or other communications by either party to the other shall be in writing and shall be effective upon personal delivery or if sent by mail seventy-two (72) hours after deposited in the United States mail, first class postage, prepaid, Registered or Certified, and all such notices given by mail shall be sent and addressed as follows until such time as another address is given by notice pursuant to this provision 14:

To Manufacturer: To Representative:

_____   _____
_____   _____
_____   _____

IN WITNESS WHEREOF, the parties hereto have executed this Agreement on the day and year first above written in multiple counterparts, each of which shall be considered an original.

MANUFACTURER: _____   REPRESENTATIVE: _____

By: _____   By: _____

Title: _____   Title: _____

SPLIT COMMISSION REQUEST/APPROVAL

Customer Name: _____ Date Requested: _____ Rep Making Request: _____

Part Numbers: _____

SPLITS	CUSTOMER CITY, STATE & ZIP	SPLIT	REP NAME & ACCEPTANCE	RGN. MGR. NA & APPROVAL
Design Location		___%	_____ by __ Date: __	_____ by _____ Date:
Purchase Location		___%	_____ by __ Date: __	_____ by _____ Date:
Ship To Location		___%	_____ by __ Date: __	_____ by _____ Date:
Other Location (state work done)		___%	_____ by __ Date: __	_____ by _____ Date:

Corporate Sales Approval By: _____ Date: _____
Entered Into System By: _____ Date: _____

SPECIAL COMMENTS:

PROCEDURE:
1. Request to be submitted as soon as split commission situation is realized. Include substantiation ie. sample approval etc.
2. RGN. MGR. for requesting rep territory is responsible for follow through and completion of approval process.
3. If approval is not complete in 30 days, the requested split is automatically approved.
4. After final sign-off, all signatures will receive a completed copy.

Appendix B

Manufacturers' or Suppliers' Sales Agency Specimen Agreement Provisions, Manufacturers' Agents National Association

Reprinted by permission of Manufacturers' Agents National Association, Laguna Hills, California, © 1990.

MANA®

SALES REPRESENTATIVE / PRINCIPAL AGREEMENT GUIDELINES

Guideline Information

1. General Information: The accompanying provisions are intended for use as guideline information in negotiating, preparing and evaluating agreements between manufacturers' agents and their principals (manufacturers). They are available to the members of the MANUFACTURERS' AGENTS NATIONAL ASSOCIATION ("MANA") at no charge and to other manufacturers, suppliers or sales professionals at a nominal fee. The parties should also consider any applicable laws—such as the commission protection acts in existence in over 30 states—which may affect how representative/principal agreements should be written and administered.

These guidelines are also available in Word© or WordPerfect© formats via e-mail.

The guidelines replace the following three previous documents published by MANA in 1990:
   a. *Manufacturers' or Suppliers' Sales Agency Specimen Agreement Provisions*
   b. *Sales Agency Agreement*
   c. *Sales Representative Agreement*

They are designed to provide sample information only and are furnished with the understanding that the publisher, MANA, is not engaged in rendering legal, accounting or any other professional service. One should always consult a legal professional before signing any contract. Input might also be sought from professional accounting and/or insurance advisors as circumstances warrant.

2. **Background and Rationale:** A separate document (available September 15, 1999) explains the background and rationale behind each provision and is available from MANA upon request.

3. **Status of Parties:** MANA uses the term "Representative" to describe the sales professional that is contracting to represent a manufacturer or any other form of "principal" company. "Representative" in the context of these guidelines means any individual or entity (sole proprietorship, partnership, corporation, S Corporation or LLC) contracting to promote the sale of and solicit orders for a principal.

The provisions cover *only* the case where the manufacturer or supplier of service retains title and pays the representative a commission on the sale of goods or services. If the sales professional also, or instead, operates as a dealer, jobber, distributor, design engineer, installer, franchisee, stocking agent or in any other capacity other than promoting the sale of and soliciting orders for manufacturers' products and services, then a different contract should be used with the appropriate clauses to document the alternate legal relationship.

4. **Independent Contractor:** These guidelines are designed for an independent contractor relationship. Where the parties desire an employer-employee relationship, the agreement should be tailored to so state. Irrespective of the provisions of the agreement, however, if the parties conduct themselves as if in an employer-employee relationship, the law, including the IRS, will examine the substance rather than form of the relationship and will likely impose on the parties the rights and responsibilities of an employer-employee relationship.

5. **Meaning of Words Used:** Before using the agreement guidelines, or any of its provisions, MANA urges you and your advisors to evaluate the wording carefully. The language in your agreement should be clear and relevant to your circumstances to protect your interests. Individual trade customs may give specialized meaning to a common word. Parties' actions may supply the meaning intended.

7. **Legal Consultation:** Customs, practices and interpretations applicable to certain types of issues, industries, products and marketing programs vary from state to state. Federal, state and local laws constantly change. Remember: no sample agreement can meet all possible needs, and no agreement is "bullet proof" or immune from legal interpretation. Any agreement must be tailored to your particular circumstances and to applicable law. This is why we repeatedly recommend that knowledgeable legal counsel be consulted.

Sales Representative / Principal Agreement Guidelines

This Agreement is made as of the _____ day of _____ in the year of,

by and between _____ a corporation incorporated

under _____ (Proper Manufacturer Name)

the laws of the state of _____ having its primary office at _____.
                              (State)   (Street Address)

_____ ("Manufacturer") and
                    (City, State and Zip)

_____ operating as a _____
      (Proper Representative Name)   (Proprietorship, Partnership, Corporation)

having its primary office at _____, _____.
                                        (Street Address)   (City, State and Zip)

("Representative") to be administered as follows:

1.   APPOINTMENT AND ACCEPTANCE. Manufacturer appoints Representative as its exclusive representative to promote the sale of and solicit orders for Manufacturer's products and services as defined in paragraph 3 herein, in the assigned territory as defined in paragraph 2 herein, and Representative accepts the appointment and agrees to promote the sale of and solicit orders for Manufacturer's products and services as defined by this Agreement.

2.   TERRITORY. Representative's assigned territory shall consist of the following:

(The assigned territory can be defined as specific states, counties, zip codes or a combination thereof or in any other way which clearly defines the geographical area or the particular accounts.)

3.   PRODUCTS AND SERVICES. The products and services of Manufacturer covered by this Agreement are: All the standard and custom products and services of Manufacturer as of the date of this Agreement and any new standard or custom products or services developed or added during the lifetime of this Agreement.

Representative shall not, during the duration of this Agreement, represent products or services directly competitive with Manufacturer's products or services in the assigned territory.

(The products and services of Manufacturer can also be defined by referring to a published price list, if one exists, in the case of standard products or services. If custom products or services are involved, list the product lines, categories, types or services with as much definition as required to adequately define the specific product area or service.)

4.   COMMISSION. Manufacturer shall pay Representative a commission for services performed which shall be _____% ("normal commission") of the "net invoice price" of Manufacturer's products shipped into or services provided in Representative's assigned territory on all customer orders regardless of whether the orders are transmitted to Manufacturer by Representative or received directly by Manufacturer from the customer. "Net invoice price" shall mean the total price at which an order is invoiced to the customer including any increase or decrease in the total amount of the order, but excluding shipping and insurance costs, sales, use, or excise taxes, tariffs, duties and export fees. In any case in which a price negotiation with the customer must occur to obtain an order from the customer, the percentage discount given to the customer off the published price (or normal price) will affect the percentage discount off Representative's normal commission as follows:

Percent Discount Given Customer	Effect on Representative's Normal Commission
Zero to 10%	100% of normal commission
11%	99% of normal commission
12%	98% of normal commission
Above 12%	Continue matching 1% discount off normal commission for each 1% discount given customer.

Each 1 percent discount above a 10 percent discount given to the customer will be matched and shared equally by percentage with a 1 percent discount off Representative's normal commission percentage stated above. Manufacturer shall solicit and consider Representative's input in regard to any possible customer discount in which Representative's commission will be affected before any quote or offer is made to the customer.

In the case where Manufacturer uses distributors that resell Manufacturer's product, Representative will be compensated for orders from distributors based upon point of sale (POS) reports received by Manufacturer from distributors. Manufacturer will pay full commission (on the "net invoice price" invoiced to the distributor) to Representative for the territory into which the distributor ships the products ordered by it, as indicated on the distributor's POS reports. Manufacturer will require the distributors to which they sell to provide monthly POS reports for the purposes of allocating proper commissions to Representative. (This paragraph to be deleted if Manufacturer does not sell to distributors.)

5.   COMPUTATION AND PAYMENT OF COMMISSION. Representative's commission is earned when an order is accepted by Manufacturer. "Order" shall mean any agreement to purchase Manufacturer's products or services which calls for shipment into Representative's territory or which is subject to a split commission as defined below and includes but is not limited to all follow-on orders and to all portions of any blanket order or requirements order regardless of when such portions are released or required. Commissions are due and payable on or before the 15th of the month immediately following the month in which customer is invoiced.

In those cases where Manufacturer sells to a distributor, commissions are due and payable on or before the 15th day of the month immediately following the month during which Manufacturer receives a point of sale report (POS) from the distributor indicating distributor's customer and/or the location to which the products of Manufacturer were shipped. (This paragraph to be deleted if Manufacturer does not sell to distributors.)

At the time of payment of commissions to Representative, Manufacturer will send Representative a current commission statement listing all invoices on which commissions are being paid as well as listing all commissions due and owing Representative from any prior payment periods which have not been paid.

Manufacturer shall deduct from any sums due Representative an amount equal to commissions paid or credited on sales of Manufacturer's products or services for which Manufacturer authorized the return or credit against the original invoice or for any part of an invoice if not paid within 120 days by the customer for any reason. If sums are received on any delinquent or previously classified "Uncollectible" sale, Manufacturer shall pay Representative its percentage of commission applicable at the time of the original sale upon the receipt of proceeds of such collection.

6.   SPLIT COMMISSIONS. In the event that an order or contract originates in the territory of one representative but is shipped into or provided in the territory of another representative, Manufacturer shall split the commission due using the following as a guide:

(a)   One-third of the total commission to the representative in the territory of shipment or provision of services;

(b)   One-third of the total commission to the representative in the territory in which the purchase order is issued; and

(c)   One-third of the total commission to the representative in the territory in which the product or service is designed-in or specified.

If Manufacturer does not have a representative in any one or more of the territories outlined in (a), (b), or (c) above, the total commission on any split order will be shared equally between the remaining representatives.

7.   ACCEPTANCE OF ORDERS. All orders are subject to acceptance or rejection by an authorized officer of Manufacturer at its main order entry office and to the approval of Manufacturer's credit department. Manufacturer shall advise Representative of any order rejected within 5 days of rejection. Manufacturer shall be responsible for all credit risks and collections.

8.   TERMS OF SALE. All sales shall be at prices and upon written terms established by Manufacturer, and it shall have the right, from time to time, to establish, change, alter or amend prices and other terms and conditions of sale. Representative shall not accept orders in Manufacturer's name or make price quotations or delivery promises without Manufacturer's prior approval.

9.   REPRESENTATIVE RELATIONSHIP AND CONDUCT OF BUSINESS. Representative shall promote the sale of and solicit orders for Manufacturer's products and services in the assigned territory and will conduct all its business in its own name and in such a manner as it may see fit, pay all its own expenses including all commissions, salaries, bonuses, and expenses of employees and salespersons and any and all taxes properly and lawfully associated with doing business as an independent contractor in the assigned territory.

Representative is not an employee of Manufacturer for any purpose whatsoever, but is an independent contractor with limited authority. Representative shall have sole control of the manner and means of performing under this Agreement. Manufacturer shall not have the right to require Representative to do anything which would jeopardize the relationship of independent contractor between Manufacturer and Representative. Nothing in this Agreement shall be construed to constitute Representative as a partner, employee or general agent of Manufacturer nor shall either have any authority to bind the other in any respect.

Representative shall abide by Manufacturer's terms and conditions pertaining to the sale of its products and services and shall communicate same to customers. Manufacturer shall hold Representative harmless from and shall indemnify Representative for all liability, loss, costs, expenses or damages, including court costs and reasonable attorneys' fees, howsoever caused by any products (whether or not defective), services or any act or omission of Manufacturer, including but not limited to, any injury (whether to body, property or personal or business character or reputation) sustained by any person or to property, and for infringement of any patent rights or other rights of third parties, and for any violation of municipal, state, or federal laws or regulations governing the products or services or their sale, which may result from the sale or distribution of the products by Manufacturer in which Representative was involved in the fulfillment of this Agreement. Representative shall hold Manufacturer harmless from and shall indemnify Manufacturer for all liability, loss, costs, expenses or damages, including court costs and reasonable attorneys' fees, caused by any misrepresentation made by Representative concerning Manufacturer's products or services.

Manufacturer shall include Representative in its product liability insurance coverage and list Representative as an "additional insured" in the insurance policy.

Manufacturer shall furnish Representative, at no expense to Representative, samples, catalogs, literature, demonstration equipment and any other material necessary for the proper promotion and solicitation of orders for its products and services in the assigned territory. If for any reason Representative takes possession of Manufacturer's products, reasonable use and care of the products shall be exercised by Representative while in its possession but the risk of loss or damage to the products is to be covered by Manufacturer's insurance at Manufacturer's cost. Manufacturer shall indemnify and hold Representative harmless against any claims, debts, liabilities or causes of action resulting from any loss, damage, or destruction. Any literature which is not used or samples, demonstration equipment or other items belonging to Manufacturer shall be returned by Representative to Manufacturer at its request upon reasonable notice.

If Manufacturer notifies customer of its acceptance or rejection of an order, a copy of any written notification shall be transmitted to Representative. Regarding customers in the territory and/or accounts, at least once every month, Manufacturer shall supply Representative with copies of all orders received, copies of all order acknowledgments and copies of all correspondence and Manufacturer shall send a tabulation at least every month of all invoices with purchase order numbers, quantity, price and commission due. Copies of quotations and related correspondence made by Manufacturer to customers in the assigned territory shall be faxed or mailed to Representative at the time the quotation is made. If Representative is authorized by Manufacturer to generate quotes to customers, copies of each quotation shall be faxed or mailed to Manufacturer at the time the quotation is made.

Manufacturer or Representative shall not, during the term of this Agreement or for one year after termination thereof, hire, employ, or contract with in any manner, salespersons, employees or individuals that were under contract or employed by each other's firm unless otherwise agreed to by both Manufacturer and Representative in writing.

10. TERM OF AGREEMENT AND TERMINATION. This Agreement shall be effective on the date listed on page 1 and shall continue in force without no cause termination rights for a ____-year term ("initial term"). During the initial term, neither party may terminate the Agreement without cause. This Agreement shall automatically renew for successive ____-year terms after the initial term unless it is terminated as provided below.

During the period of time from the date any notice of termination is given until the effective date of termination ("notice period"), both parties shall continue to fulfill their obligations under this Agreement. During the notice period, Manufacturer has the right to interview, evaluate, select and train a replacement representative for the assigned territory. During the notice period, Representative has the right to interview, evaluate, select and become trained by a replacement manufacturer.

This Agreement may be terminated:

(a) By Manufacturer, if Representative, without Manufacturer's written consent, promotes the sale of or solicits orders for any product or service which is competitive with any product or service of Manufacturer under the terms of this Agreement in the assigned territory.

Manufacturer shall give written notice of the alleged breach of the Agreement to Representative. If the alleged breach is not cured or otherwise resolved within 15 days after receipt of such notice by Representative, Manufacturer may give written notice of termination to Representative effective immediately.

(b) By Representative, if Manufacturer, without Representative's written consent offers, promotes or sells any product or service within the assigned territory which is competitive with any product or service Representative is promoting for sale for any other manufacturer. Representative shall give written notice of the alleged breach of the Agreement to Manufacturer. If the alleged breach is not cured or otherwise resolved within 15 days after receipt of such notice by Manufacturer, Representative may give written notice of termination to Manufacturer effective immediately.

(c) By either party:

   (i)   (But not effective during the initial term of the Agreement), for no cause upon at least 60 days' prior written notice to the other party;

   (ii) By mutual written agreement to be terminated at any time mutually agreed upon; or

   (iii) After 30 days' written notice if either party has filed or has filed against it a petition in bankruptcy (which is not dismissed within 30 days after it is filed) or after 30 days' written notice if either party has other cause.

11. RIGHTS UPON TERMINATION. Upon termination of this Agreement for any reason:

(a) Representative shall be paid commissions on all orders calling for shipment into Representative's assigned territory which are dated or communicated to Manufacturer prior to the effective date of termination, or during any added period authorized by this Agreement as set forth below regardless of when such orders are shipped or fulfilled.

(b) Representative shall be paid commissions on all orders dated or communicated to Manufacturer after the effective date of termination and during the added period described below, regardless of when such orders are shipped or fulfilled, predicated on the length of service (time this Agreement has been in effect) as follows:

Length of time Agreement has been in effect	Added period for orders transmitted after effective date of termination or reduction
Less than two years	0
Two to four years	30 days added.
Four to five years	60 days added.
Five to six years	90 days added.
Six years or more	120 days added.

(c)   Representative shall be paid commissions for the full lifetime of the customer's program or product in which Manufacturer's product, part or service is being purchased by blanket orders, by requirements orders, by monthly, annual or multi-year orders and by follow-on agreements to purchase Manufacturer's products or services that were designed in or selected by the customer during the lifetime of this Agreement.

(d)   Representative shall be paid its share of any split commissions on orders as defined in paragraph 6 of this Agreement.

(e)   Manufacturer shall continue to furnish Representative copies of orders and invoices and other documentation on all customer business in the assigned territory on which Representative has earned or is to be paid a commission under this Agreement until the date of the final commission payment to Representative.

(f)   Both parties have the right to audit (and shall retain such right after the effective date of termination of this Agreement) all documentation related to this Agreement. Such audit shall be scheduled on a date mutually agreed upon but no greater than 30 days after written request, allowing the other party or its duly appointed representative to audit documents of the other party, to be limited to documents relating to products or services sold, shipments, invoices, customer purchase orders, customer communications, customer payments, quotes and commission on sales in the assigned territory.

12.   ENTIRE AGREEMENT; MODIFICATION. This Agreement contains the entire understanding of the parties, shall supersede any other oral or written agreements, and shall be binding upon successors and assigns. It may not be modified in any way without the written consent of an officer or owner of both parties.

In the event the parties desire to decrease or reduce either the territory, accounts, products or services set forth in this Agreement, the party seeking the decrease or reduction must give at least 60 days' notice of such desire. Any such decrease or reduction shall be considered as a partial termination of this Agreement only with regard to the affected territory, accounts, products or services. Manufacturer shall pay commissions to Representative pursuant to paragraph 11 above, including but not limited to any applicable added period under paragraph 11(b) above, on sales derived from the decreased or reduced territory, accounts, products or services.

13. SURVIVABILITY OF AGREEMENT. If any provision of this Agreement is held to be invalid or unenforceable, such provision shall be considered deleted from this Agreement and shall not invalidate the remaining provisions of this Agreement.

14. CONSTRUCTION OF AGREEMENT. This Agreement shall be construed according to the laws of the State of _____.

15. WAIVER. The failure of either party to enforce, at any time or for any period of time, any provisions of this Agreement shall not be construed as a waiver of such provision or of the right of such party thereafter to enforce such provision.

16. ASSUMABILITY OF AGREEMENT. This Agreement will be binding upon any purchaser of Manufacturer's or Representative's business entity if ownership transfer or a sale of assets occurs prior to the effective date of termination of this Agreement.

17. DISPUTES AND MEDIATION. The parties agree that any disputes or questions arising hereunder, including the construction or application of this Agreement shall be submitted to mediation between Manufacturer and Representative. Any mediation settlement by the parties shall be documented in writing. If such mediation settlement modifies the language of this Agreement, the modification shall be put in writing, signed by both parties and added to this Agreement as an attachment. If mediation between the parties does not result in a mutual settlement within 180 days after submission to mediation, then each party will have the right to enforce the obligations of this Agreement in any court of law in the United States of America with all reasonable attorney fees, court costs and expenses incurred by the prevailing party in such litigation to be paid by the other party.

18. NOTICES. All notices, demands or other communications by either party to the other shall be in writing and shall be effective upon personal delivery, or if sent by mail, 72 hours after deposited in the United States mail, first class certified postage prepaid and all such notices given by mail shall be sent and addressed to the addresses set forth on page 1 until such time as another address is given by notice pursuant to this provision 18.

IN WITNESS WHEREOF, the officers or owners of both parties hereto have executed thisAgreement to be effective on the day and year listed on page one of this Agreement written in multiple counterparts, each of which shall be considered an original.

(Manufacturer)	(Representative)
(Signature)	(Signature)
(Title)	(Title)

Appendix C

Sales Representative Agreement, Industrial Perforators Association

This specimen contract was developed by Leon Wolf for the Industrial Perforators Association's members. Do not use without consulting your attorney.

THIS AGREEMENT is entered into as of the _____ day of _____
19_____ between _____
("the Industrial Perforator" or "the IP"), the address of which is _____
_____
and _____
(a corporation/partnership existing under the laws of the state of _____
/sole proprietorship) ("Representative"), the address of which is _____
_____.

The Industrial Perforator is in the business, among other things, of producing perforated materials and fabrications used by various industrial customers or offered for sale to end users or OEM manufacturers either by the IP or by its customers, and by this agreement intends to appoint the Representative as its sales representative for the solicitation of purchase orders within the territory and upon the terms and conditions hereafter set forth for the segment or segments of its services and capabilities hereafter specified; and the Representative desires to accept such appointment. In consideration of the mutual promises contained in this agreement the parties agree as follows:

1. *Definitions.* For all purposes of this agreement (a) the term "Territory" shall mean the geographic area and/or the customers and potential customers specified in the attached Schedule A; (b) the term "Products" shall mean and shall be limited to that segment or those segments of the services and capabilities provided by IP specified in the attached Schedule B, which may be amended from time to time by IP at its sole discretion

upon 30 days prior written notice to the Representative, and in this regard the various segments of the services and capabilities of IP include _____

_____

_____

_____

_____ ;

(c) the term "Net Selling Price" shall be the gross amount of any invoice rendered for Products, less any federal, state or local taxes, transportation, freight, export duty, insurance, any discounts, allowances, special packing charges, tooling, die, handling or similar charges; (d) the terms "Excluded Accounts and/or House Accounts" shall mean those customers and/or potential customers specified in the attached Schedule C.

2. *Appointment.* IP appoints the Representative as its exclusive independent authorized representative to solicit purchase orders for Products in the Territory during the term of this agreement. This appointment applies only to the Products specified in Schedule B as modified from time to time by IP. Without the express prior written consent of IP there shall be (a) no solicitation by the Representative of purchase orders other than within the Territory specified in Schedule A and (b) no solicitation of purchase orders within the territory for Product segments consisting of services and capabilities offered by IP other than those specified in Schedule B, it being understood between the parties that IP reserves the right to appoint other manufacturers' representatives to solicit purchase orders for Products beyond the Territory and to solicit purchase orders for Product segments other than those specified in Schedule B, both within and beyond the Territory.

The persons named in the attached Schedule D are key persons upon whom IP is relying to discharge the duties of the Representative under this agreement. In recognition of this reliance the Representative shall take all appropriate actions to the end that the key persons remain active in the discharge of the duties of the Representative under this agreement; and if they do not, IP may terminate this agreement as hereafter provided. IP shall, in its sole discretion, determine whether such key persons remain active as hereby required.

3. *Term.* The term of this agreement shall commence upon the date above stated and shall continue for an original term of one year, unless earlier terminated by either party. If it is not terminated by either party before the end of one year, this contract shall automatically be renewed for successive one year terms unless either party shall, not less than 60 days before the expiration of any existing term, notify the other party of its, his or her intention not to renew the agreement.

4. *Representative's Obligations.* Throughout the original and any renewal term of this agreement the Representative shall:
   (a) energetically and diligently promote the sales of Products within the Territory and protect and promote the interests and good will of IP;
   (b) solicit and receive orders for Products in accordance with proposals, quotations and prices provided by IP and promptly transmit each such order to IP;
   (c) provide each customer and potential customer in the Territory with satisfactory account servicing, including:
      (i) acting as liaison between the customer and IP before, during and after each sale, with the duty of communicating written or oral statements of problems or questions and the proposed solutions or answers thereto, related to such criteria as inquiries, testing, requests for quotations or bids, quotations, bids, proposals, orders, work in process, technical application recommendations, delivery, quality control, engineering changes, change

orders, modifications, drawings, plans, specifications, releases, requirements or pricing of any Product.

(ii) discussing payment and collection problems with customers, if necessary,

(iii) the exercise by the Representative of his, her or its best efforts to develop, support and maintain the good will of the customer toward IP, and

(iv) the performance of such other reasonable duties as may from time to time be requested of the Representative by IP such as are customarily performed by independent sales representatives and as are recognized as customary servicing practices in the sales representative business in the customer;

(d) furnish IP with sales forecasts containing estimates of the Representative's anticipated sales of Products, at such intervals and in such form as IP may prescribe;

(e) keep IP advised, at reasonable intervals, of the Representative's activities in respect of the Products, including, without limitation:

(i) procurement and training of sales personnel,

(ii) sales promotion activities available for participation by IP in the Territory,

(iii) display of Products at appropriate exhibitions;

(f) furnish IP market information concerning similar products available in the Territory;

(g) not enter into any agency or sub-representative agreement with respect to the Products without prior written consent from IP;

(h) neither advertise the Products nor engage in sales activities for the Products outside the Territory without the express prior written consent of IP;

(i) not alter any Products or documents bearing any of IP's trademarks or copyright notices without the prior written consent of IP;

(j) neither sell nor solicit or encourage the sale or purchase of any competitive item which is within the scope of the contract manufacturing services and capabilities of IP, whether or not such competitive item is within the scope of the Product segment or segments specified in Schedule B. As used herein the term "competitive" shall apply to any item or service which is similar in appearance and/or intended usage to any item or service which IP has the capability of manufacturing or providing or which may be used or availed of in place of any item or service offered by IP within the scope of its various product segments.

(k) not undertake duties similar to those described herein on behalf of any entity or person whose business or products are competitive [as that term is defined in sub-paragraph (j) hereof] with those of IP;

(l) treat as confidential and neither disclose nor make available for use or for any purpose other than for sale of Products all trade secrets of IP, including, but not limited to, its proprietary processes, materials, resources or information relating to the Products or the operations or business of IP, customer lists vendor information, sub-contractor information, pricing or discount information, sales forecasts, agreements (including this agreement), memoranda, correspondence or other information developed or procured by or on behalf of the Representative or IP, whether before, during or after the termination or expiration of this agreement; nor shall the Representative use any of such trade secrets or proprietary information for his, her or its own use, benefit or account to manufacture or sell any product without the prior written consent of IP. Such obligation of confidentiality shall not apply to information which is public or otherwise available to the public through common means; nor shall it apply to information that the Representative can demonstrate to have been lawfully in his, her or its possession prior to the date of the commencement of his, her or its services as manufacturers' representative for IP, whether pursuant to this or any prior written agreement with IP, whether written or oral;

(m) provide reasonable security measures to prevent unauthorized persons from obtaining any trade secrets or proprietary information;

(n) comply with all laws, statutes and regulations which govern the sale of Products, and with IP terms of sale of Products as communicated to the Representative from time to time in writing;

(o) attend and participate in such conventions and trade shows, whether within or outside the Territory, as may be reasonably requested by IP from time to time; and the Representative shall pay all expenses incident thereto, except that IP may, at its sole discretion, share such expenses with the Representative; and

(p) keep IP informed as to the identity, location and product line of each principal represented by him, her or it, and provide IP with copies of all brochures and other literature generated by each of such other principals describing itself and its products; and the Representative shall provide IP with such information and material within two weeks after (i) commencing representation of any new or additional principal or (ii) the addition of any new products by an existing principal. Attached hereto as Schedule E is a list setting forth the names, addresses and general product lines of each principal, other than IP, represented by the Representative as of this date.

5. *Rights and Obligations of IP.*

   (a) All promotional material shall be provided free of charge.

   (b) IP shall promptly provide the Representative with copies of all acknowledgment of purchase orders sent by it to customers in the Territory, excepting House Accounts and Excluded Accounts, as well as copies of all invoices rendered to customers in the Territory pertaining to such purchase orders upon which commissions may become due to the Representative.

   (c) IP shall provide the Representative with monthly commission statements identifying each invoice upon which IP has received payment from the customer and specifying the commission amount due and payable, and the balance not yet payable.

   (d) IP reserves the unrestricted rights to (i) refuse acceptance of any purchase order from the Territory in its sole and absolute discretion, (ii) change its prices and pricing policies from time to time and (iii) discontinue any Product segment or any portion thereof and to add other or new Product segments and/or items or services; and (iv) fulfill any purchase order through the services of subcontractors or through in-house production or both.

   (e) IP reserves the unrestricted right to sell Products to House Accounts located within the geographical boundaries of the Territory without payment of commission to the Representative, to allocate Excluded Accounts in the Territory to other representatives and to convert Excluded Accounts to House Accounts. If IP opts to cancel the House Account status of any customer in the Territory, that former House Account will be allocated to the Representative.

6. *Relationship of the Parties.* The Representative is and shall at all times be an independent contractor with no authority to bind or obligate IP in any respect. The Representative shall not be and shall not represent itself as being the general agent, employee, partner or joint venturer of or with IP. The Representative shall not perform any acts for or on behalf of IP, other than those specified in this agreement. The Representative shall fulfill all obligations under this agreement in accordance with his, her or its own methods, subject only to compliance with this agreement. IP shall not have the right to do anything which would

jeopardize the relationship of independent contractor between the parties. The Representative shall not make any representation or warranty regarding the Products, or the delivery thereof, beyond the terms of any express written warranty made by IP concerning the Products. The Representative shall bear all expenses incidental to the performance of his, her or its obligations under this agreement and shall be solely responsible for the acts, omissions, compensation and expense reimbursement of sales persons engaged by the Representative to assist in sales activities hereunder. In no event shall IP be responsible for any obligation or liability of the Representative, whether or not the obligation or liability shall have arisen in connection with the solicitation of purchase orders for the Products; provided, however, that IP shall indemnity the Representative from and against any customer claim based upon alleged breach of any express warranty given or extended by IP.

7. *Commissions.*

   (a) As the Representative's sole compensation under this agreement IP shall pay the Representative commissions as set forth in the attached Schedule F which shall be based upon the Net Selling Price upon all Products shipped or provided and invoiced to customers in the Territory; excepting however House Accounts or Excluded Accounts.

   (b) Split commissions shall be paid at the sole discretion of IP, in accordance with the following guideline:

   (i) If a commissionable purchase order placed by a customer in the Territory may, in the judgment of IP, require active participation by one or more representatives of IP assigned to other territories, IP may require such activity by such other representatives; and in that event IP shall pay one-third ($1/3$) of the commission to the representative in whose territory the order shall have originated, one-third ($1/3$) to the representative shown to have directly influenced the issuance of the order (which, in the absence of compelling evidence to the contrary, shall be presumed to be the representative who solicited the order) and the remaining one-third ($1/3$) among such other representatives in such manner as shall appear just and equitable to IP.

   (ii) In no event shall IP pay more than the full commission provided in subparagraph (a).

   (iii) Any variation of this paragraph 7 shall require the prior written consent of IP, the Representative and all participating representatives.

   (c) Commissions shall be due and payable by the 15th day of the month following the month in which IP shall have received payment thereon. If for any reason a customer returns any item to IP and/or receives a credit, IP shall deduct the commission, if any, previously paid upon the amount of such credit from any commission or other sum thereafter payable to the Representative.

   (d) Notwithstanding the foregoing, if during the course of negotiations with a customer or potential customer IP in its discretion determines that its prices must be reduced in order to maintain a competitive posture and thus make a sale, IP may propose a commission rate lower than that specified in Schedule F; and if the Representative agrees to such lower commission rate the Representative shall receive a commission upon the purchase order or orders resulting from those negotiations based upon the agreed reduced rate. If the Representative does not agree to accept a reduced commission, IP shall pay the Representative a commission based upon the rate specified in Schedule F for the initial purchase order accepted by it as the result of such negotiations (without obligating IP to accept such purchase order) but may thereafter with respect to all succeeding or follow-on purchase orders or reorders convert the customer to a House Account or to an Excluded Account and may delete such customer from the Territory, at its option.

8. *House Accounts and Excluded Accounts.* The Representative shall have neither sales nor servicing responsibilities for, nor shall the Representative be entitled to payment of commission upon sales by IP or by any other manufacturers' representative to House Accounts or to Excluded Accounts. Other than as provided in paragraph 7(d) hereof, a customer in the Territory initially procured by the Representative shall not become a House Account or an Excluded Account without the express written consent of the Representative. Any other customer or any potential customer may hereafter be included in Schedule C upon 90 days prior written notice to the Representative, and thereafter such other customer or potential customer will be deemed either a House Account to be dealt with directly by IP or an Excluded Account to be solicited and serviced by another representative.

9. *Personnel.* The Representative shall employ sufficient personnel to promote and solicit orders for the Products. Such personnel shall at all times have and maintain a level of knowledge of the technology and Products adequate to effectively promote, and obtain specification of and orders for the Products. Subject only to the foregoing, the Representative shall have the exclusive right to engage and shall be solely responsible for his, her or its own sales personnel, employees, agents and representatives, who shall be at the Representative's risk, expense and supervision and who shall not have any claim against IP for commission or other compensation or for reimbursement of expenses. If, in the sole discretion of IP, any of the Representative's personnel lack sufficient knowledge of the Products, the Representative shall, at its expense, make such personnel available to IP for training.

10. *Non-Competition.*
   (a) During the term of this agreement the Representative shall not, either directly or indirectly, sell, solicit purchase orders for, manufacture or in any way deal with any products which compete with the Products ("competitive products"); nor shall the Representative act as the sales agent, representative, employee or sub-agent for any person, firm or corporation that manufactures competing products, even though such competing products are not in the line handled by the Representative.
   (b) IP has been assued by the Representative, and therefore believes, that the Representative possesses or will develop unusual skills such as to enable the Representative to perform his, her or its duties hereunder with a high degree of expertise. The parties therefore agree that in the event of the termination of this agreement, either by the Representative for any reason or by IP for cause, IP will require a reasonable period of time to locate and train a replacement representative to the level of skill now or hereafter possessed by the Representative. Therefore the Representative agrees that if this agreement shall hereafter be terminated by the Representative for any reason or by IP for cause, the Representative will not for a period of one year after the effective date of such termination directly or indirectly display, present, solicit purchase orders for or sell competing products to any person, firm or corporation in the Territory who is or was a customer of IP within three years prior to the termination of this agreement, whether on behalf of the Representative or any other person, firm or corporation.
   (c) The parties have attempted to limit the Representative's right to compete only to the extent necessary to protect IP from unfair competition. The parties recognize, however, that reasonable people may differ in making such a determination. Consequently, the parties hereby agree that, if the scope of enforceability of the restrictive covenant is in any way disputed at any time, a court or other trier of fact may modify and enforce the covenant to the extent that it believes to be reasonable under the circumstances existing at that time.

(d) The Representative acknowledges that in the event of the termination of this agreement he, she or it will be able to earn a livelihood without violating the foregoing restrictions and that his, her or its ability to earn a livelihood without violating such restrictions is a material condition to the execution of this agreement by IP.

(e) The Representative acknowledges that compliance with this paragraph 10 is necessary to protect IP's business and good will, that IP will be irreparably harmed by the Representative's failure to comply therewith and that monetary damages are not adequate to repair such harm. Consequently the Representative agrees that if he, she or it breaches or threatens a breach of this paragraph 10, IP shall be entitled, among other cumulative remedies, to preliminary and permanent injunctive relief to prevent the continuation of such harm.

11. *Termination. A. For Cause*—This agreement may be terminated by either party for cause, by written notice to the other party, which termination shall be effective immediately upon notice being given. Cause for immediate termination shall exist upon the happening of any one or more of the following:

(a) Either party shall be in default under any material term or condition of this agreement, and shall not have cured such default to the reasonable satisfaction of the other party within 15 days after notice of default.

(b) Any act or omission by either party such as would justifiably persuade an ordinary manufacturer (as to any act or omission by the Representative) or an ordinary sales representative (as to any act or omission by IP) under the same or similar circumstances, in the exercise of reasonable prudence, to terminate this agreement.

(c) The commencement of voluntary or involuntary bankruptcy proceedings under any bankruptcy, reorganization or similar laws of any jurisdiction by or against either party or any partner of the Representative or any shareholder (if the Representative is a corporation) owning 25 percent or more of the voting stock of the Representative; or the commencement of any action, proceeding or procedure for the winding up, liquidation or dissolution of either party; or the appointment of a receiver for either party or its property.

(d) The Representative shall be merged with or into or become the subsidiary of any other company; or control of the Representative (by stock ownership or by composition of its board of directors or otherwise) shall be substantially charged; or this agreement shall be assigned by the Representative to any other person or entity without the prior written consent of IP.

(e) The inactivity, death, incapacity or incompetency of the Representative if a natural person; or, if a partnership, the death, incapacity, inactivity, incompetency or withdrawal of any partner; or, if a corporation, its *de jure* or *de facto* dissolution; or the withdrawal or inactivity of any key person in the Representative's organization, whether the Representative or any employee or sub-agent; and the failure of the Representative to replace such key person with another key person acceptable to IP within 60 days.

The exercise of the right of termination for cause shall be without prejudice to any other rights either party may have at law or in equity under this agreement or otherwise, but shall not give rise to any rights or claims for compensation, loss of profits or good will by the terminated party; provided, however, that nothing herein stated shall be construed to relieve either party from liability to the other for his, her or its breach of any express provision hereof, or acts or omission of fraud or other tortious conduct.

B. *Without Cause*—This agreement may be terminated at any time by either party, without limitation and without cause, upon the giving of 60 days prior written notice to the other party. IP and the Representative mutually stipulate that termination without cause by either party shall not be deemed an act of bad faith; and, in the event of such termination, neither party will claim from the other any damages flowing from the termination without cause, other than for the breach of any express provision of this agreement.

12. *Rights and Obligations upon Termination.* The following shall govern the rights, duties and obligations of the parties upon expiration or termination of this agreement, however occasioned:

(a) After the effective date of termination, the Representative shall discontinue to use in any manner any name, trademark, trade name, slogan, label, title or insignia now or hereafter owned, adopted or used by IP; and refrain from using in any manner any firm name or style or any product name, trademark, trade name, slogan, label, title, insignia or anything else which so nearly resembles any of the same owned, adopted or used by IP as to create confusion or uncertainty or the appearance that the Representative is an authorized representative of IP in the sale of the Products; and, if requested by IP, the Representative shall notify customers/purchasers and others that it has ceased to be IP's Representative.

(b) Immediately after the effective date of termination, the Representative shall return any property of IP then in the Representative's possession, including all manuals, books, catalogs, reference works, bulletins, mailing lists, pamphlets, kits, signs or other material of any kind previously supplied to the Representative by IP, including all copies or reproductions thereof, and all samples of the Products.

(c) IP shall pay commission upon invoices rendered by it pursuant to purchase orders received by IP prior to the effective date of termination without regard to the date upon which such purchase order shall be accepted and without reference to the date of shipment of Products or the rendering of invoices to the customer thereon. No obligation or liability on the part of IP shall exist for the payment of commissions to the Representative on sales of Products under purchase orders received by IP after the effective date of termination, regardless of any solicitation efforts by the Representative prior thereto, unless otherwise expressly provided in this agreement or agreed in a separate writing signed by the parties.

13. *Property Rights.* The Representative will promptly and fully inform and disclose to IP all inventions, designs, and improvements which he, she or it has or may hereafter have during the term of this agreement which pertain to the Products, to the line of products generally sold by IP or potential products compatible therewith, or which pertain to any experimental work carried on by IP, or by any customer, whether conceived by the Representative alone or with others. All such inventions, designs and improvements shall be the exclusive property of IP. The Representative shall assist IP in obtaining worldwide patents on all such inventions, designs and improvements deemed patentable by IP and shall execute all documents and do all things necessary at the request and expense of IP, to obtain letters patent, vest IP with full and exclusive title thereto, and protect the same against infringement by others. This paragraph 13 shall survive the termination of this agreement.

14. *Assignment.* This agreement, which shall be binding upon and inure to the benefit of the parties and their respective heirs, successors and assigns, may not be assigned by the Representative without the express prior written consent of IP, except, however, that if the Representative hereafter incorporates his or her business, this contract may be assigned to such corporation if the Representative owns and controls 70 percent or more of the voting stock thereof.

15. *Notices.* All notices required hereunder shall be in writing and shall be deemed given when either hand-delivered or mailed by certified or registered U.S. Mail, postage prepaid, addressed to the Representative or to IP at their respective addresses as set forth in this agreement or at such other addresses as may from time to time be given by either party to the other by notice as herein provided.

16. *Trade Secrets.* In addition to the confidentiality commitment of the Representative as set forth in paragraph 4(1) of this agreement, which shall be equally binding upon the Representative's successors and assigns and each of its employees, sub-representatives and/or sub-agents, the Representative shall cause each employee, sub-agent or sub-representative to sign and deliver to IP the confidentiality agreement, a copy of which is attached hereto as Schedule G.

17. *Miscellaneous.*

    (a) This agreement and all issues related to it, whether sounding in contract or in tort, shall be governed by, construed under and enforced in accordance with the laws of the state of _____.

    (b) This agreement and the accompanying schedules constitute the sole and entire agreement between the parties and supersedes all other agreements, whether written or oral, relating to the subject matter hereof. There are no covenants, assurances or representations, either express or implied, other than those expressly stated herein. No modification, rescission or waiver of this agreement, or any provision hereof, shall be binding upon IP unless evidenced by an instrument in writing, duly signed by an authorized officer or employee of IP and by the Representative.

    (c) The failure of either party to insist in any one or more instance upon performance of any of the provisions of this agreement or to take advantage of any of its rights hereunder shall not be construed as a waiver of any such provisions or the relinquishment of any such rights, and the same shall continue and remain in full force and effect. No single or partial exercise by either party of any right or remedy shall preclude other or further exercise thereof or the exercise of any other right or remedy.

    (d) Any provision (or portion thereof) of this agreement prohibited by applicable law or by court decree shall be ineffective to the extent of such prohibition, without in any way invalidating or affecting the remaining portions of such provisions or other provisions of this agreement.

IN WITNESS WHEREOF, the parties have executed this agreement upon the day and year first above written.

Industrial Perforator

By _____
Name: _____
Title: _____

(Name of Representative)

By _____
Name: _____
Name of Authorized Signatory
Title: _____

SCHEDULE A

Territory

The geographic area of the Territory referred to in Paragraph 1 and elsewhere throughout the Agreement dated _____, 19____ between

_____

("the Industrial Perforator" or "the IP") and _____

_____

_____, of which this Schedule A is an integral part, consists of:

(a) The following geographic area:

(b) The following designated customers and potential customers, at the customer facilities located in the specified states:

Authorized Signatures:

_____   _____

Date   IP

_____   _____

Date   Representative

SCHEDULE B

Products

The Products referred to in Paragraph 1 and elsewhere throughout the Agreement dated _____, 19_____ between _____

_____

("the Industrial Perforator" or "the IP") and _____

_____

of which this Schedule B is an integral part, shall consist of the following Product segments within the scope of the contract manufacturing services and capabilities offered by IP:

Authorized Signatures:

Date	IP

Date	Representative

SCHEDULE C

House Accounts and Excluded Accounts

The House Accounts and Excluded Accounts referred to in Paragraph 1 and elsewhere throughout the Agreement dated _____, 19_____

between _____
_____

("the Industrial Perforator" or "the IP") and _____
_____

of which this Schedule C is an integral part are as follows:

House Accounts:

Excluded Accounts:

Authorized Signatures:

_____   _____
Date   IP

_____   _____
Date   Representative

SCHEDULE D

Key Persons

The key persons referred to in Paragraph 2 of the Agreement dated _____, 19_____ between _____

_____

("the Industrial Perforator" or "the IP") and _____

_____

of which this Schedule D is an integral part, are as follows:

Authorized Signatures:

_____   _____

Date   IP

_____   _____

Date   Representative

SCHEDULE E

Principals

The principals referred to in Paragraph 4(p) of the Agreement dated _____, 19_____ between, _____

_____

("the Industrial Perforator" or "the IP") and _____

_____

of which this Schedule E is an integral part, are as follows:

Authorized Signatures:

_____   _____
Date   IP

_____   _____
Date   Representative

5) PURCHASE ORDERS:

Whenever possible, orders shall be taken on the buyer's Purchase Order form and signed and forwarded on to the COMPANY. When buyer's form is not used, all orders must be complete as to description, shipping instructions, buyer's full legal business name and address, purchase order number, etc. All Purchase Orders should be made out to the COMPANY and are subject to acceptance at its sole discretion by the COMPANY. The REPRESENTATIVE is held responsible for loss on all orders taken by him resulting from incorrect verbal instructions by the buyer.

The REPRESENTATIVE shall solicit all orders in the name of the COMPANY, in accordance with the COMPANY'S regular terms, credit requirements and prices. The REPRESENTATIVE shall have no authority to solicit orders in any other manner.

6) COMPENSATION:

Full payment for all services rendered by the REPRESENTATIVE is in the form of commissions paid by the COMPANY on shipments made by the COMPANY of the products covered hereby during the effective period of this Agreement.

Orders are not considered as final until the invoice is paid; however, the commission is credited to the REPRESENTATIVE at the time of invoicing and is paid on the 15th of the month for all shipments during the previous month. Commissions are not paid on freight or drayage charges or on Labor Charges.

Where losses are incurred, goods are returned or accounts are not settled, the COMPANY reserves the right to debit back all or part of the REPRESENTATIVE'S commission to cover the loss.

The effective Commission Schedule is included with the COMPANY'S Price Book.

7) SPLIT COMMISSIONS:

It is recognized that under special circumstances, shipments may be made outside the designated territory for customers located within the designated territory and that the servicing of these accounts may become, in part, the responsibility to the representative in another territory.

Similarly, shipments may be made within the designated territory for customers located outside the designated territory so that the REPRESENTATIVE may become responsible, in part, for the servicing of such accounts.

In such cases, the COMPANY may compensate each of the overlapping representatives by a portion of the commission. The exercise of the right being reserved to the COMPANY to split commissions in this fashion shall be at the COMPANY's sole discretion, although it shall try to be fair and equitable to both representatives.

However, when an order is issued, received from and shipped to the same territory, but the billing is handled in another territory, the commission will NOT BE SPLIT but the full commission will go to the REPRESENTATIVE assigned the territory where the order originated and the goods were shipped. Unusual cases will be handled at the sole discretion of the COMPANY.

Commissions on orders from Original Equipment Manufacturers (OEM accounts) where shipment is made directly to their customer outside the REPRESENTATIVE'S territory will NOT BE SPLIT. The full commission will be paid to the REPRESENTATIVE servicing the OEM account. There may be times when specification credit will be given some other representative, and then commissions will be split.

8) EXCEPTIONS TO THIS AGREEMENT:

The COMPANY reserves the right, in order to secure proper distribution, to enter into any contracts with large National concerns on highly competitive terms. When this is necessary, the commission may be small, and will not be split.

The exclusive protection given by this Agreement applies to all present items in the COMPANY'S product line, with the exception of SOLID URETHANE, RUBBER and NEOPRENE PARTS. On these specialty items, the COMPANY reserves the right to market them on a "protected account" basis. This means that if the REPRESENTATIVE develops an inquiry and is responsible for an order for any of these items, that account would be a "protected account" and would belong to that REPRESENTATIVE during the course of this Agreement. Full effective commissions would be paid to the REPRESENTATIVE on these "protected accounts" for the above mentioned items.

If at any time in the future, the COMPANY should decide to manufacture an item that does not fit properly into the general selling plan, the COMPANY reserves the right to market the item as it sees fit, with the possibility that no protection or commission will be given to the REPRESENTATIVE.

9) ALLOWANCES:

It is agreed that no allowances will be made to the REPRESENTATIVE for expenses of any kind, even though incurred in connection with the REPRESENTATIVE'S services under this Agreement. Drawing Accounts or advances against unearned commissions will not be paid.

The REPRESENTATIVE must pay for all telephone calls and telegrams to the COMPANY. Collect calls or wires will be accepted and may be charged to the REPRESENTATIVE. The COMPANY will pay for all telephone calls and telegrams to the REPRESENTATIVE.

10) PRICES:

All prices, discounts and terms governing the sale of products hereunder shall be established by the COMPANY, from time to time, and shall be under its exclusive control and/or subject to change by the COMPANY at any time without notice and without creating any liability on the part of the COMPANY to the REPRESENTATIVE or any account of the REPRESENTATIVE.

11) ADVERTISING MATERIALS AND SUPPLIES:

All advertising and sales aids shall be and remain the property of the COMPANY and the REPRESEN-TATIVE agrees to indemnify the COMPANY against loss or damage for any reason whatsoever.

Upon termination of this Agreement, such supplies (including all old or used files of correspondence, original letters received by the REPRESENTATIVE from customers, and copies of letters sent by the REPRESENTATIVE relating to the business of the COMPANY) shall be returned on demand.

For all supplies not returned, the final commission payment may be withheld until the REPRESENTA-TIVE has made a satisfactory accounting by return or payment of all COMPANY property.

12) INSURANCE:

It is agreed that the REPRESENTATIVE will carry automobile liability insurance for injuries to property in the minimum amount of Ten Thousand Dollars ($10,000), and for injuries to persons in the minimum amount of One Hundred Thousand Dollars ($100,000) per person and Three Hundred Thousand Dollars ($300,000) per accident.

It is further agreed that the REPRESENTATIVE will deliver to the COMPANY a copy of the certificate of such policy and will indemnify the COMPANY against any claim for injuries or damages caused by the REPRESENTATIVE while traveling in his automobile in the course of his services for the COMPANY. This provision shall survive the termination of this Agreement.

13) TERMINATION OF AGREEMENT:

This Agreement may be cancelled by the COMPANY or the REPRESENTATIVE with or without cause, upon thirty (30) days written notice by either party to the other. This written notice must be in the form of a registered letter and said notice begins officially from the date of registration of the letter. Violation of any part of this Agreement can provide immediate termination without the usual thirty (30) days notice.

The COMPANY shall pay the REPRESENTATIVE the full applicable commission on shipments made after this Agreement is terminated provided the order was received and accepted by the COMPANY prior to the termination of this Agreement and the COMPANY has the right to make immediate shipment upon fabrication completion.

Commission would also be paid in full on any "Blanket order" or "Hold for release order" on any shipments made against these orders within ninety (90) days of contract termination.

The COMPANY shall have no other obligation to pay the REPRESENTATIVE compensation on shipments of products after this Agreement is terminated, whether or not the sales were solicited prior to the termination of such Agreement.

The COMPANY'S franchise cannot be sold by the REPRESENTATIVE to another person or organization. The REPRESENTATIVE is not permitted to appoint a sub-agent for any part of his territory without the written permission of the COMPANY. This does not apply to a junior salesman, associates or assistants, who work under the close supervision of the REPRESENTATIVE, and whose compensation and, if required payroll taxes thereon and workman's compensation insurance, the REPRESENTATIVE is responsible as part of his expenses.

When the REPRESENTATIVE reaches age 65, the COMPANY will review all Sales Agreements. Should the REPRESENTATIVE wish to continue representing the Company beyond age 65, he should so indicate in writing at that time. Consideration will be given on an individual case by case basis with such things as health, current sales development relative to past years, etc. being key factors in the COMPANY'S decision. Any extension of this Agreement will then be reviewed periodically by the COMPANY.

14) EFFECT ON OTHER AGREEMENTS:

This Agreement cancels and supercedes all prior Agreements and understandings between the parties. No modifications or amendments of this Agreement shall be effective unless made in writing and signed by both parties.

This Agreement shall commence on the _____ day of _____, 19_____, and shall remain in full force and effect until terminated by either party.

IN TESTIMONY WHEREOF, BOTH PARTIES HAVE EXECUTED
THIS AGREEMENT AND HAVE EXECUTED IT IN DUPLICATE

SPARKS BELTING COMPANY
a division of
JSJ BELTING CORPORATION

REPRESENTATIVE

BY_____

BY_____

_____

Resource Guide

The following listing is a late 1998 compilation of a wide range of information sources concerning manufacturers' representatives. This is the most exhaustive database of information on representatives assembled. It is the work of Dr. Marilyn Stephens, Executive Vice President of the Manufacturers' Representatives Educational Research Foundation (MRERF). Copies of the information are avaiable from MRERF. If you have any questions, contact Dr. Stevens at—MRERF, P.O. Box 247, Geneva, IL 60134. Tel: (630) 208-1466; Fax: (630) 208-1475; e-mail: info@MRERF.org.

Manufacturers' Representatives Educational Research Foundation Bibliography
Table of Contents

Introduction   295
Industry-Specific Sources of Information   296
Manufacturers' Representative Assocations   297
Newsletters Pertaining to Representatives   304
Magazines Pertaining to Representatives   305
Visual Media   305
Case Studies About Manufacturers' Representatives   306
Books   307
Articles in Research/Articles From Academia   313
Unpublished Studies and Papers   315
Articles From Trade Journals and Newspapers   316
Directories of Manufacturers' Representatives   330
Legal   332

Introduction

The Following listing pulls together a wide range of information sources on manufacturers' representatives. An exhaustive search of available database files was completed to locate all printed material relative to Representatives. Some additional information resources are also identified: trade associations, other foundations, newsletters/papers, and material produced by consultants.

The Manufactures' Representatives Educational Research Foundation has copies of ONLY the information produced with MRERF funding. (Most items are protected by a copyright.) Check in your local public, college, or university library for the materials or contact the publisher and/or author. If you have any questions, contact Dr. Marilyn Stephens, Executive Vice President, MRERF, P.O. Box 247, Geneva, IL 60134. Telephone: (630) 208-1466; Fax (630) 208-1475.

Industry-Specific Sources of Information

Business Information Sources, Daniells, Lorna, M., Berkley, CA: University of California, rev. ed., 1993. (Includes Lists of publications for specific industries. 725 pages.)

Canadian National Register of Manufacturers' Agents & Distributors, published by the Manufacturers' Agents' Association of North America, 15 Toronto Street, Suite 200, Toronto, Ontario, Canada M5C 2R1.

Directory of Directories, Marlow, C.A. & R.C. Thomas (eds), Detroit, MI: Gale Research Company, 15th ed., 1997. (This is 16 directories in one with a separate section devoted to "Specific Industries and Lines of Business." A two volume set with 10,000 entries and 1,800 pages. Cost: $185. Call Toll-free [800] 223-GALE.)

Directory of Manufacturers' Agents, published by the Manufacturers' Agents National Association, 23016 Mill Creek Road, Laguna Hills, CA 92654. Tel: (714) 859-4040.

Encyclopedia of Associations, Vol. 1: National Organizations of the U.S., Part 1 (Sections 1-6), Burek, Deborah M. (ed), Detroit, MI: Gale Research Company, 1198. (A set of 4 volumes. A guide to more than 30,000 national and international organizations, including trade, business and commercial. Cost: $220/set. Call toll-free [800] 223-GALE.)

Encyclopedia of Business Information Sources, Woy, James (ed), Detroit, MI: Gale Research Company, 6th ed., 1986. (A guide to specific business topics. Cites both live and print information sources. 878 pages. Cost: $210. Call toll-free [800] 223-GALE.)

Manufacturers' Agents Guide, 1982 ed., compiled by MacRae's Blue Book, Inc., 817 Broadway, New York, NY 10003. Tel: (202) 673-4700. (List of manufacturers who sell through representatives.)

National Directory of Manufacturers' Representatives, Holtje, Herbert F., McGraw-Hill, Inc., 1221 Avenue of the Americas, New York, NY 10020. Tel: (212) 997-1221.

Verified Directory of Manufacturers' Representatives, compiled by Manufacturers' Agent Publishing Company, 554 Fifth Avenue, New York, NY 10022. (List of manufacturers who sell through representatives.)

Manufacturers' Representative Associations

Product/Market-Specific Associations

Note: Where the industry served is not obvious we have added an indication of products sold.

+ Denotes participation in the Council of Manufacturers Representatives Association (CMRA).
*Indicates that association is a member of The Manufacturers Representatives Educational Research Foundation (MRERF).

+*Agricultural & Industrial Manufacturers Representatives Association, Frank Bistrom, Executive Director, 5818 Reeds Rd., Mission, KS 66202-2740. Tel: (913) 262-0317, Fax: (913) 262-0174. Agricultural, industrial, power, lawn, and garden equipment industries.

Aircraft Electronics Association, Monte Mitchell, Executive Director, P.O. Box 1981, Independence, MO 64055. Tel: (816) 373-6565.

+*American Beauty Association, Paul Dykstra, Executive Director, 401 N. Michigan Ave., Chicago, IL 60611. Tel: (312) 245-1595. Beauty supplies.

American Hardware Manufacturers Association, Wm. P. Farrell, President/CEO; Martin O'Rourke, Manager-Membership, 801 Plaza Drive, Schaumburg, IL 60173. Tel: (708) 605-1025. An organization that includes representatives in the industry.

+*American Lighting Association, Eric Jacobsen, V.P. Membership/Development Services, World Trade Center, P.O. Box 420288, Dallas, TX 75342-0288, shipping address: 2050 Stemmons Freeway, Dallas, TX 75207. Tel: (214) 698-9898, Toll free (800) 605-4448. Lighting equipment, and products.

American Society of Refrigeration & Air Conditioning Engineers, Dan Jeffrey, President, c/o Honeywell, Inc., 217 International Circle, Hunt Valley, MD 21030. Tel: (410) 785-4202. There is a rep division of this association.

American Sports-Fishing Association, Mike Hayden, President, 1033 N. Fairfax St., Ste. 200, Alexandria, VA 22314 Tel: (703) 519-9691.

Armed Forces Marketing Council Manufacturers Representatives, Rip Rowan, Executive Director, 1750 New York Ave. N.W., Ste. 340, Washington, DC 20006. Tel: (202) 783-8228. Manufacturers' representative specializing in the military resale market, supplying military exchanges commissary stores, military club outlets, and veteran's canteens in the United States and overseas.

+*Association of Industry Manufacturers Representatives**, Eileen Robiso, Executive Director, 222 Merchandise Mart Plaza, #1360, Chicago, IL 60654. Tel: (312) 464-0092, FAX: (312) 464-0091. Plumbing, heating, cooling, and piping industry.

+*Association of Service and Marketing Companies, ASMC** (formerly NFBA), Robert Schwarze, President (staff) Karen Ribler, Senior V.P., 2100 Reston Parkway, Ste. 400, Reston, VA 22091-1208. Tel: (703) 758-7790.

Association of Visual Merchandise Representatives, Tom Raguse, 307 Cove Creek, LN, Houston, TX 77042-1023. Tel: (713) 782-5533, FAX: (713) 785-1114. Sales representative from manufacturers of visual merchandise.

Auto Parts Association—Rep Group, Bob White, Chairman, c/o Bob White Associates, 3 Cypress Lane, Berwyn, PA 19312. Tel: (301) 654-6664

Automotive Booster Clubs International, see ASIA.

Automotive Parts & Accessories Association, Alfred L. Gaspar, President, 4600 E-W Highway, #300, Bethesda, MD 20814-3415. Tel: (301) 654-6664. Umbrella organization of manufacturers, reps, and distributors.

+*Automotive Service Industry Association (Mfg. Rep Division)**, Gene Gardner , Alice Moore, Rep Liaison, 25 Northwest Point, Ste. 425, Elk Grove Village, IL 60007-1035. Tel: (847) 228-1310. "Add on" products not originally purchased with vehicle.

+*Broker Management Council**, William Bess, Executive Director, P.O. Box 150229, Arlington, TX 76015, shipping address: 7208 Forestburg Drive, Arlington, TX 76017. Tel: (817) 561-7272. Food products.

BIFMA—International (Business & Institutional Furniture Manufacturers Association) (Rep members), Russell R. Coyner, Executive Director, 2680 Horizon Drive S.E., Ste. A1, Grand Rapids, MI 49546-7500 Tel: (616) 285-3963. Office Furniture.

Bureau of Wholesale Sales Representatives, Mike Wolyn, Executive Director, 1801 Peachtree Road N.E., Suite 200, Atlanta, GA 30309. Tel: (800) 877-1808. Representatives in the apparel industry with additional complimentary items. (Example: westernwear, boots and tack gear; children's wear may be accompanied by infant's furniture lines, etc.)

+*Canadian Electrical Manufacturers Representatives Association**, Rick McCarten, Executive Director, Electro-Federation, 10 Carlson Ct. Ste. 210, Toronto, Ontario, Canada M9W 6L2. Tel: (416) 674-7410. Cable, wire, etc.

*Canadian Institute of Plumbing & Heating**, Edward R. Hardison, President/GM, 295 The West Mall, Ste. 330, Toronto, Ontario, Canada M9C 4Z4. Tel: (416) 695-0447.

Central States Hardware Association, Inc., Eleanore Salemi, P.O. Box 5309, Woodridge, IL 60532 Tel: (630) 420-0267. An organization that includes representatives in the industry.

*Communication Marketing Association, Joe O'Connell, c/o Scientific Dimensions, Inc., P.O. Box 26778 Albuquerque, NM 87125, Tel: (505) 345-8674.

Construction Industry Sales, John Hancock, Secretary/Manager, 202 N.E. Huron Street, Ste. 206, Ann Arbor, MI 48104. Tel: (313) 769-8169.

Costume Jewelry Salesman's Association, Michael Gail, President, 303 Fifth Ave., New York, NY 10016 Tel: (212) 532-7595.

Door & Hardware Institute, Jerry Heppes, 14170 Newbrook Dr., Chantilly, VA 22021 Tel: (703) 222-7010

Eastern Ski Reps Association, Linda Irvin, Executive Director, HC1 Box 7, White Haven, PA 18661. Tel: (717) 443-7180.

Electrical Equipment Representatives Association, John S. McDermott, Executive Director, 368 W. 39th St., Kansas City, MO 64111, mailing address: P.O. Box 419264, K.C., MO 64141. Tel: (816) 753-0210, FAX: (816) 753-1954.

+ **Electrical Generating Systems Association**, David Kellough, Executive Director, 1650 South Dixie Hwy, 5th floor, Boca Raton, FL 33432. Tel: (561) 750-5575. Standby gas and diesel systems.

+ ***Electronics Representatives Association**, Ray Hall, Exec. Vice President/CEO, 444 N. Michigan Ave., Ste. 1960, Chicago, IL 60611. Tel: (312) 527-3050. Electronics included in a wide range of products and industries.

+ ***The Foodservice Group, Inc.** Kenneth W. Reynolds, Executive Director, P.O. Box 76533, Atlanta, GA 30358. Shipping address: 4149 Lakeshore Way, Marietta, GA 30067. Tel: (770) 977-1476. Concentration on food delivery products.

+ ***Health Industry Representatives Association**, Karen Hone, Executive Director, 6535 South Dayton St., Ste. 3000, Englewood, CO 80111. Tel: (303) 799-0650, or (800) 777-4472. Health care equipment.

Heavy Duty Representatives Association, Cara Giebner, Executive Director, 4015 Marks Road, Ste. 2B, Medina, OH 44256. Tel: (216) 725-7160.

Hobby Industry Association, Hope Crawley, 319 E. 54th St., P.O. Box 348, Elmwood Park, NJ 07407. Tel: (201) 794-1133.

Illinois Manufacturers' Association, Karen Klemens, P.O. Box 2147, Springfield, IL 62705.

+ **Incentive Manufacturers Representatives Association**, Karen Renk, Executive Director, 1805 N. Mill St., Ste. A., Naperville, IL 60563. Tel: (630) 369-3466, FAX: (630) 369-3773.

Independent Professional Representatives Organization, Tex Morton,

Executive Director, P.O. Box 4146, Deerfield Beach, FL 33442. Tel: (800) 420-4268. Serving the audio/video, custom home installation, home theater and car audio industries.

Industrial Manufacturer's Representative Association, (contact) Peggy Quinn, 21010 Center Ridge Rd., Ste. G-4 Rocky River, OH 44116 Tel: (216) 356-5898.

+ **Infant's Furniture Representatives Association**, Jerry Jones, President, c/o Prange-Jones, 4501 N. High St., Ste. B Columbus, OH 43214. Tel: (800) 969-1985, Fax: (614) 261-7979. People in this industry may also handle other items related to infants.

+ *****International Association of Plastics Distributors**, Deborah Hamlin, Executive Director, 4707 College Blvd., Ste. 105, Leawood, KS 66211. Tel: (913) 345-1005. Reps sell: raw materials for reinforced plastics as well as pipe, fittings, valves, sheeting, rods, tubes, etc.

+ **International Home Furnishings Representatives Association**, Robert Hall, P.O. Box 670, High Point, NC 27261. Tel: (910) 889-3920. Local affiliated organization of approximately 3200 home furnishings representatives.

+ *****International Housewares Representatives Association**, William Weiner, Executive Director, 400 East Randolph Street, Ste. 500-6, Chicago, IL 60601. Tel: (312) 240-0822 , Fax: (312) 240-1005.

International Manufacturers Representatives Association, Mert Dale, P.O. Box 702678, Tulsa, OK 74170. Tel: (918) 743-5443, FAX: (918) 743-5443. Automotive accessories.

International Sanitary Supply Association, Bill Buescher, Director of Marketing, 7373 N. Lincoln Avenue, Lincolnwood, IL 60646. Tel: (847) 982-0800 or (800) 225-4772. There is a rep section in this association.

+ *****Manufacturers' Agents / Food Service Industry**, Larry Fleischman, Executive Director, Smith, Bucklin & Associates, Inc., 401 N. Michigan Ave., Chicago, IL 60611-4267. Tel: (312) 644-6610 x3311. Foodservice equipment, furnishings, and supplies.

+ *****Manufacturers' Representatives Educational Research Foundation (MRERF)**, Marilyn Stephens, P.O. Box 247, 339 Stevens St., Unit K, Geneva, IL 60134. Tel: (800) 346-7373, Fax: (630) 208-1475.

Air-conditioning and Refrigeration Wholesales Association-Membership Directory, Air-conditioning and Refrigeration Wholesalers Association, 1650 Dixie Hwy, Boca Raton, FL 33432-7462. Tel: (561) 338-3495, Fax: (561) 338- 3496, E-mail: mail@arw.org. Manufacturers' representatives included.

Gift and Decorative Accessories Center Association—Directory (New England), Gift and Decorative Accessories Center Association, 59 Middlesex Tpke., Bedford, MA 01730. Tel: (617) 275-2775, Fax: (617) 275-7479. Manufacturers' representatives included.

+ *****Manufacturers Representatives of America, Inc.**, William Bess , Executive Director, mailing address: P.O. Box 150229 Arlington, TX 76015, 7208 Forestburg Dr. Arlington, TX 76001. Tel: (817) 561-7272, FAX: (817) 561-7275. Paper, plastics, sanitary, and janitorial supply products.

Mechanical Equipment Manufacturers Representatives (MEMRA), William Schaare, Engineering Center, 1200 68th St., Baltimore, MD. Tel: (410) 866-6800, Fax: (410) 866-1048. Manufacturers representatives united to seek better ways to serve the industry and to help members improve the efficiency of their business operations.

NAM Reps, Jack Gaughan, Sec.-Treas., 116 Sandpiper Circle, Corte Madera, CA 94925-1082. Tel: (415) 927-3240. Camera industry reps.

***National Association-Division Seven Representatives**, William Weiner, Executive Director, 400 E. Randolph Street, Ste. 500-6, Chicago, IL 60611-4267. Tel: (312) 240-1004. Roofing materials and related products.

+ ***NAGMR—Consumer Products Brokers**, Jack Springer, Executive Director, Smith, Bucklin & Associates, Inc., 401 N. Michigan Ave. #2400, Chicago, IL 60611-4267. Tel: (312) 321-6806, FAX: (312) 245-1081. Health & beauty aids as well as general merchandise sold to food and drug stores.

National Association Independent Publishers Representatives, Ralph Woodward, Secretary, 111 E. 14th St., Ste. 157, New York City, NY 10003. Tel: (508) 877-5328, Fax: (508) 788-0208. Representatives selling books.

National Association of Lighting Representatives, Paul Saunders, Executive Director, P.O. Box 214, Sea Girt, NJ 08750. Tel: (908) 974-1900.

National Association of Manufacturers, Managing Director, 1331 Pennsylvania Ave., #1500 N., Washington, DC 20004.

National Association of Publishers Representatives, Florence Pressman, 150 Lynnway, Apt. 506, Lynn, MA 01902-3457. Independent publishers' representatives selling advertising space for more than one publisher of consumer, industrial, direct response, and trade publication.

National Candy Brokers Association, Edward Bjornson, 151 Salem St., North Andover, MA 01845.

+ ***National Electrical Manufacturers Representatives Association** (NEMRA), Henry P. Bergson, President, 200 Business Park Dr., Ste. 301, Armonk, NY 10504. Tel: (914) 273-6780, FAX: (914) 273-6785, E-mail: NEMRAHQ@NEMRA.org.

National Groundwater Association, David Schmitt, 6375 Riverside Dr., Dublin, OH, 43017. Tel: (800) 551-7379, Fax: (614) 761-1711.

National Housewares Manufacturers Association, 6400 Shafer Ct., #650, Des Plaines, IL 60018. Tel: (847) 292-4200.

National Marine Representatives Association, David McCloskey, Executive Director, 2742 Old Natchez Trace Trail, P.O. Box 969, Camden,

TN 38320. Tel: (901) 584-0203, Fax: (901) 584-0420. Components for manufacturing of boats and after-market accessories.

National Ornament & Electric Lights Christmas Association, Phyllis Southard, Executive Secretary, 2 Greentree Center, Ste. 225, Marlton, NJ 08053. Tel: (609) 231-8500.

National Shoe Traveler's Association, Manny Santos, Chm., 313 Adams St., #101, P.O. Box 456, Abington, MA 02531. Tel: (800) 200-6782, Fax: (617) 871-8033.

National Screw Machine Products Association, Scott Giesler, 6700 W. Snowville Rd., Brecksville, OH 44141.

National Sporting Goods Association—Buying Guide, National Sporting Goods Association (NSGA), 1699 Wall St., Mount Prospect, IL 60056-5780. Tel: (708) 439-4000, Fax: (708) 439-4000, E-mail: nsga16992 @aol. com. Manufacturers' representatives included.

National Tooling & Machining Association, Thomas H. Garcia, 9300 Livingston Rd., Fort Washington, MD 20744. Tel: (301) 248-6200.

+*NorthAmerican Industrial Representatives Association**, William Weiner, Executive Director, 400 East Randolph Street, Ste. 500-6, Chicago, IL 60601-2740. Tel: (312) 240-0820, Fax: (312) 240-1005. Industrial and construction products such as welding, specialty, and machine tools.

+**NorthAmerican Ingredients Marketing Specialists**, Kenneth W. Reynolds, Executive Director, P.O. Box 76422, Atlanta, GA 30358, shipping address: 4149 Lakeshore Way, Marietta, GA 30067. Tel: (770) 977-1476. Food ingredients sold to manufacturers of food products.

O.A.S.I.S., JoAnn Duff, 1130 E. Missouri, Ste. 750, Phoenix, AZ 85014-2717.

+*Office Products Representatives Alliance** (OPRA), Theresa McCafferty, Alliance Coordinator, 301 N. Fairfax St., Alexandria, VA 22314. Tel: (703) 549-9070 or (800) 542-6672. Office products, furniture and supplies, school supplies, information processing supplies, creative industries, art/engineering/drafting supplies, and equipment. OPRA is an alliance of the Business Products Industry Association (BPIA).

+*Power Transmission Representatives Association**, Barbara Boden, Executive Director, 330 South Wells St., Ste. 1422, Chicago, IL 60606. Tel: (312) 360-0389. Power transmission and motion control equipment.

Professional Picture Framers Association, Rex P. Boynton, Exec. Dir., 4305 Sarellen Rd., Richmond, VA 23231-4311. Tel: U.S. (800) 832-7732. Canada (800) 833-7732. Association consists of manufacturers, distributors, representatives, and publishers. Members work in the art and framing industry.

*Professional Reps Organization**, Bill Moore, Pres., 218 West Genesee St., Auburn, NY. Tel: (315) 255-2879. Sell items in the gift industry, home decor as well as nursery/garden centers.

Professional Sales Association, Don Michael (current association president), Tel: (818) 917-3456. Housewares, hardware, home improvement, lawn, and garden products. Some automotive products sold to automotive chains.

+*Safety Equipment Manufacturers' Agents Association, George Hayward, P.O. Box 30310, Cincinnati, OH 45230, Ship to: 7537 State Rd., Cincinnati, OH 45255. Tel: (513) 624-3535, Fax: (513) 231-1456. Products, supplies, and equipment. Associated with safety in all industries.

Sales Associates of the Chemical Industry, Patrick Vazquez, President, c/o A.L. Laboratories, 1 Executive Dr., Fort Lee, NJ 07024. Tel: (201) 947-7774.

Screen Printing & Graphic Imaging Association-International, John Crawsord, 10015 Main St., Fairfax, VA 22031. Tel: (703) 385-1335.

Simpson Sales Company, Inc., Dudley Simpson, 1000 Hurricane Shoals Rd. N.E. #400, Lawrenceville, GA 30243-4826.

Specialty Advertising Manufacturing Representatives Association, Leonard Blackburn, 23 Ledgebrook Dr., Norwalk, CT 06854. Tel: (203) 855-8478.

Specialty Advertising of Industrial Agents, Executive Director, 115 Garrison Ct., Langhorne, PA 19047.

*Specialty Equipment Market Association, Ellen McKoy, P.O. Box 4910, Diamond Bar, CA 91765, shipping address, 1575 Valley Vista Drive. Tel: (909) 396-0289. Automotive aftermarket products.

+Sporting Goods Agents Association, Lois E. Halinton, Executive Director, P.O. Box 998, Morton Grove, IL 60053. Tel: (847) 296-3670.

Sporting Goods Manufacturers Association, Howard J. Bruns, 200 Castlewood Drive, North Palm Beach, FL 33408.

Stationery Representatives Associations, M.S. Kellner, Managing Director, 230 Park Ave., New York, NY 10169. Tel: (212) 687-2484.

+Tackle/Shooting Sports Association, Joe Kuti, 1033 N. Fairfax St., Ste. 200 Alexandria, VA 22314. Tel: (703) 519-9691.

Textile Salesman's Association, Karen Stone, 295 Fifth Ave., Ste. 621, New York, NY 10016-7201. Tel: (212) 685-0530.

Tooling & Manufacturing Association, Bruce Baker, 1177 S. Dee Rd., Park Ridge, IL 60068.

United Sales Agents, Mark Legue, c/o ETS, Atlanta Gift Mart, 230 Spring St., Ste. #1705, Atlanta, GA 30303. Tel: (404) 681-4706, FAX: (714) 240-7001. Representatives in the gift industry.

Wire Association International, Inc. (The), Phyllis O. Conon, P.O. Box H, Guilford, CT 06437. Tel: (203) 453-2777.

Non-Industry Specific Associations

Manufacturers' Agents Association of North America, Gordon Rogers, 15 Toronto St., Ste. 200, Toronto, Ontario, Canada M5C 2R1. Tel: (416) 324-9016.

Manufacturers Agents of Cincinnati, Kathy Walter, Executive Secretary, P.O. Box 53535, Cincinnati, OH 45253. Tel: (513) 385-8091. Industrial/ OEM types of products. Cincinnati-based representatives who cover the entire midwest.

*****Manufacturers Agents National Association**, Lionel Diaz, President/ CEO, P.O. Box 3467, 23016 Mill Creek Road, Laguna Hills, CA 92654. Tel: (714) 859-4040.

Society of Manufacturers Representatives, Inc., Carol Scheid, Managing Director, 42072 Queen Anne, Northville, MI 48167. Tel: (810) 344-4748. Representatives deal mostly with automotive materials and they only cover the state of Michigan.

United Association of Manufacturers Representatives, Executive Director, Karen Mazzola, P.O. Box 986, Dana Point, CA 92629. Tel: (714) 240- 4966.

+*****Wisconsin Association of Manufacturers Agents, Inc.**, Carole Bluem, Executive Director, 1504 N. 68th St., Milwaukee, WI 53213. Tel: (414) 778-0640. Representatives sell primarily machine tools, castings, and mechanical types of products although other industries/products are also sold.

Newsletters Pertaining to Representatives

Better Rep Management. Publisher: R.W. Parsons, Talk Publications, Inc., 373 South Redwood Avenue, San Jose, CA 95128. Tel: (408) 246-4582. (Written for manufacturers who work with independent representatives.)

Contact. Publisher: Henry Lavin, Lavin Associates, 12 Promontory Drive, Cheshire, CT 06410. Tel: (203) 272-9121.

Rep Letter. Publisher: Manufacturers' Agents National Association, 23016 Mill Creek Road, Laguna Hills, CA 92654. Tel: (714) 859-4040. (A monthly publication for manufacturers who sell through manufacturers' representatives.)

Hardlines Rep Report. Published through joint efforts of *Do It Yourself Retailing Magazine*, 5822 West 74th Street, Indianapolis, IN 46278, and the American Hardware Manufacturers Association, 801 Plaza Drive, Schaumburg, IL 60194. Tel: (317) 290-0338.

Rep. Talk. Publisher: Jack Berman, Berman Institute of Agreeable Selling, 15720 Ventura Boulevard, #31, Encino, CA 91436. Tel: (818) 905-5388. (Monthly publication for representatives.)

Sales Rep's Advisor. Editor: Laurence A. Alexander. Published by Alexander Research & Communications, Inc., 215 Park Avenue South, New York, NY 10003. Tel: (212) 206-7979. (A bi-monthly publication

gic issues in operating a small service business; how to manage people, systems and structures to achieve growth and leverage. An additional issue is that of being a professional and building a professional firm.") Available from: Library, Knowledge Edge, Inc., 2479 East Bayshore Road, Suite 700, Palo Alto, CA 94303. A video tape of the 1982 Electronic Representatives Association conference includes this study being taught. The video is available from: ERA, 20 East Huron Street, Chicago, IL 60611. Tel: (312) 649-1333.

What Factors are Conducive to a Long-Term Relationship between Representatives and Manufacturers? 1991. (This study was conducted as part of a dissertation project by Dr. S.P. Dant for the Institute for the Study of business Markets at Pennsylvania State University.) Information is available from: Dr. S.P. Dant, St. Louis, MO (in 1992).

Books

Agent in the Arab World (The), Shilling, N.A. 1977.

America's Newest Profession: *a Study of the Manufacturers Representative and Other Commission Businesses*, Runglin, Walt. Late 1970's or early 1980's publication. University Publishers.

An Analysis of Non-Coercive Power and Probability of Compliance in a Manufacturers' Agents Channel of Distribution: The Development of Measures and a Causal Model. Hunt, Kenneth Allen. 1984. Available from University Microfilms International, P.O. Box 1346, Ann Arbor, MI 48106. (A dissertation study to determine if non-coercive power used by a manufacturer positively affects the manufacturers' agent's probability of complying with the wishes of the manufacturer. Analysis results were unable to determine a relationship between reward power and probability of compliance.)

An Empirical Analysis of Power in Channels of Distributions: A Systems Perspective. Keith, Janet E. 1985. Arizona State University, Tempe, AZ 85287-4106.

An Evaluation of Business Practices of Manufacturers' Agents Marketing Industrial Goods. Cairns, Donald F. 1972. Available from University Microfilms International, P.O. Box 1346, Ann Arbor, MI 41806. Tel: (313) 761-4700. (Dissertation research to gather evidence regarding specific marketing practices of manufacturers' agents as evaluated by industrial customers.)

An Examination of Manufacturers' Representatives' Performance. Patton, Charles, Ph.D. 1989. Dissertation 432 pages. Available from University Microfilms International, P.O. Box 1346, Ann Arbor, MI 48106. (A study to investigate the determinants of manufacturers' representative performance with a manufacturer's product line, i.e., territorial market share from the perspective of the manufacturer.)

Company Sales Force or Independent Representatives? Shapiro, Benson (Chapter 26) *Sales Program Management: Formulation and Implementation.* McGraw-Hill, 1221 Avenue of the Americas, New York, NY 10020.

Contracting the Selling Function: Microform: The Sales Person as Outside Agent or Employee. Anderson, Erin M. 1982.

Dartnell Sales Manager's Handbook (The). Riso, Ovid. 1977. Dartnell Corporation, 4660 Ravenswood Avenue, Chicago, IL 60640.

Effects of Switching Costs on the Termination of Distribution Channel Relationships: Working Paper. Weiss, Allen M. 1991.

FNBA Legal Manual. Maloney & Burch, 1100 Connecticut Avenue, N.W., Ste. 1900, Washington, DC 20036-4101. Tel: (202) 293-1414. (Manual is addressed to independent representatives, food brokers, and others who are involved in the food distribution and marketing industry.)

Handbook for Selling with Manufacturers' Representatives. Reinhart, Thomas C. and Donald R. Coleman. Book review by Sales & Marketing Management, Oct. 1983, page 99.

Handbook of Modern Marketing. Buell, Victor P. 1977. McGraw-Hill, 1221 Avenue of the Americas, New York, NY 10020.

How to Become a Manufacturer's Representative. Frye, Jack. 1980. Available from the author: 4148 Newland Drive East, West Bloomfield, MI 48033.

How to Become a Successful Manufacturer's Representative. Leffler, Marvin. 1952. Prentice Hall, Englewood Cliffs, NJ 07632.

How to Build Sales with Manufacturers' Agencies. Gibbons, James. Prentice Hall, Englewood Cliffs, NJ 07632.

How to Get Started as a Manufacturers' Representative. Kruse, William H. 1980. AMACOM, 135 West 50th Street, New York, NY 10020. Tel: (212) 586-8100.

How to Hire and Motivate Manufacturers' Representatives. Kruse, William H. 1976. AMACOM. See previous entry.

How to Get—and Keep!—Good Product Lines. Lavin, Henry. 2nd ed., 1988. Lavin Associates, Cheshire, CT 06410. Tel: (203) 272-9121. (How to build a rep business through professional image promotion.)

How to Get—and Keep!—Good Industrial Customers through Effective Direct Mail. Lavin, Henry. 1980. Lavin Associates. (See previous entries. A guidebook for small manufacturers, distributors, and independent representatives.)

How to Get—and Keep!—Good Industrial Representatives. Lavin, Henry. 2nd ed., 1985. Lavin Associates. (See previous entries. A guidebook for manufacturers' representatives, distributors, and small manufacturers.)

How to Get—and Keep!—A Profitable Rep Agency by Effective Marketing. Lavin, Henry. 1991. Lavin Associates. (See previous entries. A marketing guidebook for manufacturers' representatives, distributors, and small manufacturers.)

How to Hire and Motivate Manufacturers' Representatives. Kruse, William H. AMACOM. See previous entry.

How to Get and Hold Key Accounts: The Complete Guide for the Manufacturer's Rep. Clark, L.H. 1975.

How to Increase Your Sales Volume as a Manufacturer's Agent. Leffler, Marvin. 1958. Prentice Hall, Englewood Cliffs, NJ 07632.

How to Make Big Money as an Independent Sales Agent. Bobrow, Edwin E. Parker Publishing Co., Inc. (division of Prentice Hall), Englewood Cliffs, NJ 07632.

How to Sell Your Way into Your Own Business with Little or No Capital. Bobrow, Edwin E. 1977. Sales Builders (a division of Sales & Marketing Management). Bill Publications, 633 Third Avenue, New York, NY 10017.

How to Sell Your Product Through (not to) Wholesalers. Friday, William. 1980.

How to Sell Effectively through Manufacturers' Agents and Distributors. Hitchcock, Earl B. Available from Independent Marketing Counselors, Inc., P.O. Box 296, Midland Park, NJ 07432. Tel: (201) 445-6522.

How to Start and Build a Successful Manufacturers' Agency, Gibbons, James. 1988. Prentice Hall, Englewood Cliffs, NJ 07632.

Independent Marketing-Selling. Lebell, Frank. 1980. Herman Publishing, Inc. 45 Newbury St., Boston, MA 02116. Tel: (617) 536-5810.

Industrial Marketing Channels: Channel Participants. Hutt, Michael D. & Thomas W. Speh 2nd ed., 1983. Chapter from *Industrial Marketing Management*. Dryden Press, Chicago, IL.

Is the Independent Sales Agent for You? Bobrow, Edwin E. 1988. Available from Small Business Administration (Management Aid No. 200), Washington, DC, or local SBA offices.

Making $70,000-plus a Year as a Self-Employed Manufacturer's Representative. Silliphant, Leigh. Rev. ed. 1988. Ten Speed Press, Berkeley, CA.

Managing and Motivating Your Agents and Distributors: Profitable Sales Part-nerships: A Guide to Managing and Motivating Agents, Distributors, Importers, and anyone else who sells your product! Iyer, Vinoo. 1994. London Financial Times, Irwin Professional Publishers, Burr Ridge, IL.

Manufacturers' Agent. Anderson, Erin. Taken from Business research: Marketing. 3rd ed., 1986. Research Publishing, 2113 "S" Street, N.W., Washington, DC 20008-4011.

Manufacturers' Guide—Dealing with Agents (The). Manufacturers' Agents' Association of North America, 15 Toronto Street, Ste. 200, Toronto, Ontario, Canada M5C 2R1.

Manufacturers' Representative (The). Lebell, Frank. 1981. Hills Bay Press, P.O. Box 5521, San Mateo, CA 94402.

Marketer's Complete Guide to the 1980's and Marketing through the Outside Sales Force (The). Special reports by: Sales & Marketing Management. Available from Builders Division, Sales & Marketing Management, 633 Third Street, New York, NY 10164-0563.

Marketing Channels: A Management View. Rosenbloom, Bert. 3rd ed. New York: Dryden Press, 1986. (Includes case study, Hassler & Howard, Inc., that deals with effective management of a representative agency. An advanced text for upper division undergraduate and graduate students.)

Marketing Handbook Second Edition. Rines, Michael. 1981. Gower Publishing Company, Ltd., Gower House, Croft Road, Aldershot, Hampshire GU11 3HR, England.

Marketing Handbook, Vol. 1: Marketing Practices, and Vol. 11: Marketing Management. Bobrow, Edwin E. and Mark David Bobrow. 1985. Dow Jones-Irwin, Homewood, IL 60430.

Marketing Manager's Handbook. Britt and Guess. 1983. Dartnell Corporation, 4660 Ravenswood Avenue, Chicago, IL 60640-4595.

Marketing through Independent Sales Agencies. Gibbons, James. Chapter 34, Marketing Handbook, Vol. 1, Marketing Practices. Bobrow, Edwin E. and Mark David Bobrow (eds). Dow Jones-Irwin, Homewood, IL.

Marketing through Manufacturers Agents. Bobrow, Edwin E. 1976. New York: Sales builders (a division of Sales & Marketing Management). Bill Publications, 633 Third Avenue, New York, NY 10017.

Multiple-Line Selling: Developing Synergistic Selling Skills. Berman, Jack. The Research & Review Service of America, Inc., P.O. Box 1727, Indianapolis, IN.

New Manufacturer's Agent-Guide Book (The). Manufacturers' Agents' Association of North America, 15 Toronto Street, Ste. 200, Toronto, Ontario, Canada M5C 2R1.

Operations Manual for Manufacturers' Representative Firms. Hill, Tess and Marilyn Stephens. (eds.) 1989. Available from MRERF, P.O. Box 247, Geneva, IL 60134. Tel: (630) 208-1466. (A how-to book on every aspect of representative firm operations; from start-up through expansion and reorganization stages and finally the sell out. Cost: $150.)

Professional Sales Representation. Lebell, Frank. 1975. Hills Bay Press, P.O. Box 5221, San Mateo, CA 94402.

Profiling Differences Between Manufacturers' Representatives and Direct Company Salespeople: An Exploratory Study. Taylor, Ronald K. 1988. Ph.D. dissertation. 194 pages. Available from University Microfilms International, P.O. Box 1346, Ann Arbor, MI 41806. (The purpose of the study was to identify and examine specific attributes of representatives and direct salespeople and make comparisons between the two groups. The results seem to indicate the personal and selling dimensions are not significantly different statistically.)

Rep-Factory Relationship (The). (Guidelines for Improving the Marketing Partnership and Bottom-line Performance.) 1992. Developed by American Hardware Manufacturers Association, 801 Plaza Drive, Schaumburg, IL 60194. Tel: (847) 605-1025. (A source book for manufacturers and independent agents of the hardware industry. AHMA member cost: $75; nonmember cost: $125.)

Representative Selection and Maintenance Guide (A). Parsons, R.W. 2nd ed., 1985. Available from Talk Publications Inc., P.O. Box 26277, San Jose, CA 95128. Tel: (408) 246-4582. ("All about the . . . location of . . . selection of . . . appointment of . . . training of . . . on-going review of and, yes . . . the firing of . . . manufacturers' reps.")

Sales Manager's Handbook. Bobrow, Edwin E. and Larry Wizenberg. 1983. Dow Jones-Irwin, Homewood, IL 60430.

Sales Rep Strategies for Dealing with Principals Successfully: Negotiations, Contracts, Working Relationships and Termination's. Sack, Steven Mitchell. 1991. Sales Rep's Advisor, 215 Park Avenue South, Ste. 1301, New York, NY 10003. Tel: (212) 228-0426. (Cost: $79.95)

Salesperson's Legal Guide (The). Sack, Steven Mitchell and Howard J. Steinberg. 1981. Prentice-Hall, Inc., Englewood Cliffs, NJ 07632.

Salesperson as Outside Agent or Employee: A Transaction Cost Analysis. Anderson, Erin. 1984.

Sales Representatives' Business and Tax Handbook. Daskal, Melvin H. 1995. Irwin Professional Publishers, New York.

Selling through Independent Manufacturers' Representatives. Coleman, Don. 1983. Taken from: Sales Manager's Handbook. Bobrow, Edwin E. & Larry Wisenberg (eds.) Dow Jones-Irwin, Homewood, IL.

Selling through Independent Reps. Novick, Harold J. 1988. Revised 1992. AMACOM, 135 West 50th Street, New York, NY 10020. Tel: (212) 586-8100.

Selling through Independent Reps: Getting Them to Work for you. Special reports from: Sales & Marketing Management. Written 1981 or later. Available from Builder Divisions, Sales & Marketing Management, 633 Third Street, New York, NY 10164-0563. (A monograph exploring the benefits and problems that may arise while working with representatives.)

Staff Recommendations. 1975. Research Institute of America, Inc., 589 Fifth Avenue, New York, NY 10017. (When, where, and how to use manufacturers' representatives. A monograph. Approximate cost: $10.)

Study to Identify a Competency Pattern for the Manufacturer's Salesperson (A). Jacobs, Brian Colin. 1978. Available through University Microfilm International, P.O. Box 1346, Ann Arbor, MI 48106. (The Study purpose was to develop lists of tasks and competencies to be used in the development of competency-based curricula for training salespersons, the evaluation of representative salesperson, and the development of a salesperson certification program.)

Study to Identify the Roles, Tasks, and Competencies of Manufacturers' Representatives in the Electronics Industry with Implications for Sales Training. Stephens, Marilyn. 1988. Available through University Microfilms International, P.O. Box 1346, Ann Arbor, MI 48106. Also available through interlibrary loan microfiche. (Dissertation research that surveyed both veteran and novice representative salespersons. Specific roles, tasks, and competencies were identified that are necessary from the practice of the profession of manufacturers' representative. A matrix was developed to show a relationship of task to role. A schematic of the most frequently used competencies was designed for the purpose of adult continuing education for representatives.)

Synergistic Selling Course. Berman, Jack. 1984. Berman Institute of Agreeable Selling, 15720 Ventura Blvd., Ste. 311, Encino, CA 91436. Tel: (818) 905-5388.

Thriving with Reps. Frank, Jerry S. and Jack McNutt. 1992. Available from MRERF, P.O. Box 247, Geneva, IL 60134. Tel: (630) 208-1466. (Guidelines and documents for maximizing the sales results and profits of manufacturing organizations through the use of manufacturers' representatives. Cost: $289.)

Twenty Minute Marketing Plan (The). Haskell, John S. 1987. Available from Electronic Representatives Association, 20 East Huron Street, Chicago, IL 60611. Tel: (312) 649-1333.

Understanding and Motivating the Manufacturers' Agent. Berry, Dick. 1981. CBI Publishing Company, 51 Sleeper Street, Boston, MA 02210. Available from Van Norstrand Reinhold Company, Inc., 7625 Empire Drive, Florence, KY 41042. Currently out of print.

When and How to Use Manufacturers' Representatives. Lavin, Henry. 2nd ed., 1986. Chapter 75 of: *Handbook of Modern Marketing*. McGraw-Hill, 1221 Avenue of the Americas, New York, NY 10020.

Articles in Research/Articles From Academia

"An Analysis of the Food Broker—Food Manufacturer Marketing Channel Interface." Teas, Roy K. 1975. Dissertation 234 pages. (Study of how the flow of goods, services, information, etc. is facilitated between producers and consumers.) Order No. 76-3137 from University Microfilms International, P.O. Box 1346, Ann Arbor, MI 48106.

"An Analysis of Food Brokers Versus Grocery Manufacturers' Sales Forces." Alan, Terry F. 1984. Dissertation 259 pages. (Study of how food manufacturers make the choices between selling through brokers or their own direct sales forces.) Order No. DA8608514 from University Microfilms International, P.O. Box 1346, Ann Arbor, MI 48106.

"Converting from Independent to Employee Salesforces: The Role of Perceived Switching Costs." Weiss, Allen M. and Erin Anderson. Journal of Marketing Research. Feb. 1992. Pages 101–115. (Study of perceptions of costs vs. benefits in changing sales methods.)

"Determinants of Opportunistic Behavior in Marketing Channels." Anderson, Erin. (Study of cheating by representative and direct salespeople.) Available as Working Paper 85-109, Dept. of Marketing, The Wharton School, University of Pennsylvania, Philadelphia, PA 19104.

"Distribution of Industrial Products Introduced to a Foreign Markets: Integrated Versus Independent Channels." Anderson, Erin and Ann T. Coughlan. Available as working paper 85-039, Dept. of Marketing, The Wharton School. (See above address.)

"The Effects of Alternate Types of Influence Strategies Under Different Channel Dependence Structures." Keith, Janet E., Donald W. Jackson, and Lawrence A. Crosby. Journal of Marketing. July 1990. Pages 30–41.

"The Effect of Relational Characteristics of the Duration of Manufacturers Agent Relationship." Dant, Sharish. 1992. Available from University Microfilms International, P.O. Box 1346, Ann Arbor, MI 48106.

"Efficiency and Conformity: An Empirical Test of Bowman's Hypothesis." Anderson, Erin. (Impact of direct salesperson/representative salesperson on the bottom line.) Available as Working Paper 85-08, Reginald Jones Center for Management Policy, Strategy and Organization, The Wharton School, University of Pennsylvania, Philadelphia, PA 19104.

"An Empirical Analysis of Power Relations in Channels of Distribution: A Systems Perspective." Keith, Janet E. 1985. Dissertation 261 pages. (Study of food broker—food manufacturer relationships.) Order No. DA8522939 from University of Microfilms International, P.O. Box 1346, Ann Arbor, MI 48106.

"An Empirical Analysis of the Product Addition Decision Process in the Food Broker Using Cyert-March Theory or Organization Decision Making." Lacho, Kenneth J. 1969. Dissertation 486 pages. (Study of how food broker firms search for, evaluate, and choose product lines to add to their sales portfolios.) Order No. 70-10, 976 from University Microfilms International, P.O. Box 1346, Ann Arbor, MI 48106.

"The Food Broker as a Marketing Institution." Johnson, Frank. 1962. Dissertation 461 pages. (Analysis of food broker operations, their economic role in distribution and their operating efficiency.) Order No. 63-2942 from University Microfilms International, P.O. Box 1346, Ann Arbor, MI 48106.

"Global Marketing Challenges and Opportunities for Manufacturers' Representatives." Stephens, Marilyn, Rodney Carlson, J. Donald Weinrauch. Marketing Intelligence & Planning. Volume 14, Number 5, 1996. Pages 25–30.

"Implications of Transaction Cost Analysis for Management of Distribution Channels." Anderson, Erin. 1985. Taken from: Proceedings: A strategic Approach to Business Marketing, Spekman, Robert E., Ed., Chicago: American Marketing Association.

"Leading Manufacturers' Representative Voice Their Perception and Recommendations for the Future: A Challenge Marketing Educators." Mann, O. Karl, Marilyn Stephens, and J. Donald Weinrauch. March 1993. Published in conference proceedings: National Conference in Sales Management, Orlando, FL. Contact MRERF, P.O. Box 247, Geneva, IL 60134. Tel: (630) 208-1466.

"Make or Buy Decisions: A Framework for Analyzing Vertical Integration Decisions in Marketing." Anderson, Erin and Barton A. Weitz. 1986. Sloan Management Review.

"Power and Conflict in the Food Broker—Wholesaler Distribution Channel." Author and publication date unknown. Dissertation 290 pages. (Examination of the concepts of power and conflict as they affect food brokers and wholesalers.) Order No. 7921261 from University Microfilms International, P.O. Box 1346, Ann Arbor, MI 48106.

"Resource Allocation Behaviors by Channel Members: Economic and Non-Economic Determinants." Anderson, Erin et al. Available as Working Paper 84-023, Dept. of Marketing, The Wharton School, University of Pennsylvania, Philadelphia, PA 19104. Also published in *Journal of Marketing Research*, Feb. 1987.

"The Salespersons Outside Agent or Employee: A Transaction-Cost Analysis." Anderson, Erin. Marketing Science. Summer 1985. Pages 234–254. (Field study of representative-direct trade-offs made by component manufacturers.)

"The Selection of Agents and Distributors: A Descriptive Model." Moore, Richard A. Quarterly Review of Marketing (UK). Autumn 1987. Pages 12–16. (Selection criteria for choosing representatives and distributors for UK exporters. Based on 1979 study of agents and distributors in the Middle East.)

"Unraveling the Perceived Roles and Tasks of Manufacturers' Representatives: An Exploratory Study." Weinrauch, Donald, Karl Mann, and Marilyn Stephens. Professional Sales and Sales Management Practices: Leading Toward the 21st Century. April 1992. Proceedings published by Pi Sigma Epsilon. Pages 31–36.

Unpublished Studies and Papers

"An Overview and Analysis of Sales Force Size Estimation Techniques." Steinberg, Stanley M. March 1993. Contact: Dr. Stanley M. Steinberg, 3026 Overland Ave., Baltimore, MD 21214. Tel: (410) 254-3520.

"Operations Ratio Survey." Smith, Barry. 1986. (This ORS was conducted within the membership of the electronics Representatives Association.) Contact: Dr. Barry Smith, Associate Professor of Finance, New Mexico State University, Las Cruces, NM 88001.

"Organizational Culture Strength and Value Congruity as Determinants of Sales Organizational Outcomes." Barnes, John Walter. 1992. Arizona State University.

"PR for Professional Representatives." Lavin, Henry. Available from Lavin Associates, 12 Promontory Drive, Cheshire, CT 06410. Tel: (203) 272-9121.

"Professional Selling in 1990." Shannon, William N., III. Prepared for the Manufacturing Agents for Food Service Industry. 1985. (Research on professional selling in 1990 as viewed by manufacturers, users, distributors, and consultants. A similar study was completed for the National Electrical Manufacturers Representatives Association in 1986.) Contact: Professor William N. Shannon, III, Dept. of Business Administration, Saint Mary's/ Notre Dame, P.O. Box 69, Madeleva Hall, Notre Dame, IN 46614.

"Report to Respondents of Manufacturers' Agent Survey." John, George. Spring 1986. (A study undertaken to learn how manufacturers' reps and principals can work together more effectively.) Contact: Professor George John, Marketing Dept., University of Minnesota, 271 19th Avenue South, Minneapolis, MN 55455. Tel: (612) 624-6841.

"A Study to Identify the Sales Training Needs of the Bourns Manufacturers' Representatives." Jones, Curtis C. February 1987. (A study undertaken to determine the various training needs and most appropriate methods for both novice and veteran sales representatives in the sales network utilized by Bourns, Inc., and electronics industry manufacturer.) Contact: Dennis Lause, Vice President Field Sales, Electronic Components Sales, Bourns, Inc., 1200 Columbia Avenue, Riverside, CA 92507. Tel: (714) 781-5112.

"Survey of Electronic Representatives." Haskell, John S. 1985. (A survey of manufacturers' representatives in the electronic industry in the areas of principal/representative relations and firm management.) Contact: John S. Haskell, Professional Marketing Consultants, 1700 Mandeville Canyon Road, Los Angeles, CA 90049. Tel: (213) 476-3355.

"Using Lotus 1-2-3 as a Decision Support in Selecting Manufacturers Agents or Company Sales People." Steinberg, Stanley M. November 1992. Contact: Dr. Stanley M. Steinberg, 3026 Overland Ave., Baltimore, MD 21214. Tel: (410) 254-3520.

Articles From Trade Journals and Newspapers

(Arranged alphabetically by name of source publication and in order of publication date.)

Advertising Age
  "Sales Reps, Brokers Tae on Wal-Mart." Dec. 23, 1991. Page 28.
  "Wal-Mart Draws Fire: Reps, Brokers Protest Being Shut Out by New Policy (of Dealing Only with Manufacturers)." Lawrence, Jennifer. Jan. 13, 1992. Pages 3+.

Advertising Management Journal
  "Improving the Productivity of Your Manufacturers' Representative." Kruse, William H. Spring 1985. Pages 32–36. The same article is in: Ad-

vanced Management Journal. Spring 1985. Pages 32–37. (Techniques used by sales manager to help representatives become more effective.)

After Market Business
"Will Power Buyers Change Face of Competition?" (Editorial) Stambaugh-Cannon, Sandi. July 1, 1992. Page 48.

Air Conditioning Heating & Refrigeration News
"Manufacturers' Rep Gets Ahead by Keeping Track." Kowalski, Greg. Sept. 14, 1987.

American Import/Export Bulletin
"Foreign Reps: Your Door to the Overseas Market." North American Publishing Co., 401 North Broad Street, Philadelphia, PA 19108. Dec. 1980. Page 52.

American Salesman
"Market Penetration and Longevity." Jan. 1991. Pages 23–25. (Advantages of using manufacturers' agents.)
"Sales Are Up, Profits Are Up, and Owners Are Bullish on the Future." Feb. 1991. Pages 10–11.
"Manufacturers Encourage Their Independent Sales Agencies to Expand." April 1991. Pages 7–9.
"Qualified Sales Leads." May 1991. Pages 14–15.
"Business Law for Manufacturers and Agents." Feb. 1992. Pages 19–22.

Arkansas Democrat Gazette (Little Rock)
"Wal-Mart Target of Complaint Filed with FTC by Agents' Group." Jan. 18, 1992. Page D1.

Atlanta Constitution
"Slamming the Door—Wal-Mart Plans to Bypass Reps from Factories." Burritt, Chris. Nov. 23, 1991. Page C1.

Automotive News
"Stretch to Fit: A Detroit Manufacturers Rep Keeps Opening Doors for a Dutch Sunroof Manufacturer." Fleming, Al. Nov. 25, 1991. Page 101.
"The New Globetrotters: Manufacturers Reps Evolve to Meet the Challenges of the 1990's." (Special Report) Fleming, Al. Nov. 25, 1991. Pages 1i–13i.
"The New Globetrotters: Today's Manufacturers Rep Is a Combination Problem-Solver and Product-Seller." (Special Report) Fleming, Al. Nov. 25, 1991. Pages 61–62.

Baltimore Sun
"Wal-Mart Moves to Cut Out Manufacturers' Middlemen." Clark, Kim. Dec. 4, 1991. Page 7D.

Beverage Industry

"Manufacturers' Rep: Expert Middlemen Keeping Lines Rolling." Staff. Reprint available from Beverage Industry, 747 Third Avenue, New York, NY 10017.

Beverage World

"Manufacturers-agents: Directories." Databank Issue 1991–'92.

"Manufacturers' Representatives: Manufacturers' Representative Beverage-related products, systems, and services.)" Databank Issue 1995–'96.

Broadcasting & Cable

"Canadian Rep Looks for U.S. Clients." Moshavi, Sharon. March 1993.

"New World's Rep Firm With a Difference." Foisie, Geoffrey. May 23, 1994.

"Infinity Considers In-House Sales Team." By, DP. Aug. 8, 1994.

"Liberty Sports sets up In-House Rep." Brown, Rich. Nov. 21, 1994.

"Sentry Becomes Katz's Sixth Rep. Firm." By, D.P. Dec. 4, 1995.

Business America

"Overseas Trade Shows." Schafer, Joachim et al. July 18, 1988. Pages 2–9. (A good place to sign up foreign reps, distributors, and agents.)

Business Marketing

"Are Reps Right for You?" Washburn, Stewart A. June 1983. Pages 86 + .

"Keeping Manufacturers' Reps Motivated." Weaver, Donna. Nov. 1985. Pages 128 + .

"Budget-Wise Ways to Sell Your Firm to Reps." Baird, Brent J. Dec. 1985. Pages 66–68.

"You Can Lead a Rep to Prospects." Bertrand, Kate. April 1987. Page 56. (Telephone lead qualification.)

"They Don't Get No Respect." Bertrand, Kate. June 1987. Pages 38 + . (Sales managers need to keep independent representatives informed.)

"The Care and Feeding of Manufacturers' Reps." DuBois, Lois C. and Roger H. Grace. Dec. 1987. Pages 52–54. (Importance of communication between manufacturers and representatives.)

"Reps Beat the Slow-Growth Catch-22." Novick, Harold. Dec. 1987. Pages 52, 65–69.

"Tips on Rep Councils." Aug. 1988. Page 34. (Meetings in which manufacturers communicate expectations and concerns.)

"Yes, There Is a Perfect Rep." Novick, Harold. Feb. 1989. Pages 73–76. (Defining the profile of the ideal rep to fit specific needs and selecting reps who most closely match the profile.)

"The New Wave of Sales Automation: Today's Computer Use by Sales Force Goes Well Beyond the Mundane." Yovovich, B.G. June 1991. Pages 12–15.

"Xerox Pits Workers vs. Agents." Apr. 1994. Pages 1 + . (Xerox offers qualified sales personnel incentives to become independent sales agents.)

Business Outlook

"How You Can Build a Sales Rep Organization." Emry, John D. March 24, 1986. Page 8. (A look at the potential advantages of using the rep sales pattern from the perspective of firms who can't afford to underwrite an in-house sales department who desire a program emphasizing personal selling.)

Business Quarterly (Canada)

"Using Independent Sales Representatives to Penetrate the U.S. Market." Novick, Harold. Winter 1989. Pages 80–83. (Guidelines for Canadian manufacturers on the use of independent reps as a preferred channel to cover U.S. markets.)

Chicago Tribune

"Manufacturers Are Sold on Top Sales Representatives." Kleiman, Carol. Section 8. Nov. 22, 1987. (An outline for a potential career as a representative.)

Columbus C.E.O.

"Do You Need an Independent Rep? OK, Maybe Your Bottom Line Does." Nixon-Knight, Lynnell. Oct. 1993. Pages 36–37.
The Secrets to Finding Great Sales Reps and How They Can Work for You." Nixon-Knight, Lynnell Nov. 1993. Pages 34–36.

Communications

"Here Come the Carriers." Purcell, Dick. Jan. 1988. Pages 42–49. (A discussion of problems in the cellular telephone industry involving cellular agents and dealers.)
"The Future of Independent Manufacturers' Reps." Reubenstein, Stan. April 1991. Pages 95–97.

Computerworld

"Sales Reps' Data Targets Prospects." Betts, Mitch. June 23, 1986. Pages 27 and 33. (Competitive benefits derived through building a database of information gathered by representatives.)

The Counselor

"NOT the Envelope, PLEASE!" Hendrickson, Alyson R. Oct. 1991. Pages 107–116. (Specialty Advertising Association International review of the tax implications of independent contractors vs. sales employees in representative and distributor firms.)

Dallas Morning News

"Wal-Mart Move Angers Vendor Reps." Baldwin, Pat. Dec. 3, 1991. Page 1D.

"Wal-Mart CEO Defends Vendor Policy." Baldwin, Pat. Dec. 5, 1991. Page 1D.
"Sales Reps Form Group to Fight Wal-Mart." Baldwin, Pat. Dec. 14, 1991.
"Manufacturers' Reps Step Up Fight Against Wal-Mart Policy." Baldwin, Pat. Jan. 20, 1992.

Discount Store News
"Vendor Rep Move Stirs Debate." (Special Section: The World of Wal-Mart) June 15, 1992. Page 135.
"Congressmen Vent Concern over Wal-Mart Rep Policy." June 15, 1992. Page 5.

Dun & Bradstreet Reports
"What makes a Top-Notch Sales Rep? Who Knows Better Than a Buyer?" Goodman, Gerson. Dun & Bradstreet Reports. Mar.-Apr. 1985. Pages 34+. (A discussion of salesperson's skills.)
"Manufacturers Reps Are Ideal Sales Force for Small Business." July-Aug. 1986. Pages 54–56.

Editor & Publisher
"Scripps Howard Newspapers Switch Sales Rep Firms." Radolf, Andres. Jan. 11, 1986. Page 8.

Electronic Business
"Fair Exchange: How to Use Representatives Wisely." Mathews, C. Oct. 1983. Pages 22+.
"Manufacturing Reps Redefine Their Role." Kerr, John. Oct. 1987. Pages 32+.

Electronic Buyers' News
"Manufacturers' Reps Blend Engineering and Sales Skills." Magee, Harriett. July 12, 1990. Pages 50–52.

Electronic News
"ERA: Left out of Sales Rep Bill Hearings." June 23, 1980. Page 76.
"IBM Compromises on the Use of Sales Agents." Day, R. Dec. 30, 1985. Pages 1+.

Electronics Distribution Today
"Reps Relationships Change." Staff ETD. June 1987. Pages 22–23. (Material drawn from a panel presentation at the Electronics Representatives Association conference, April 1987, and an interview with two representatives who have each maintained a high volume of sales for 30+ years.)
"Some of the Most Common Mistakes Reps Make in Dealing with their Principals" and "Some of the Most Common Mistakes Principals Make in Working with their Reps." Frank, Jerry S. June 1987. Page 23. (A suc-

cinct list of mistakes on the part of both manufacturers and representatives.)

"TMC*: Shifting Back to the Basics." Staff EDT. June 1987. Pages 26–27. (An interview with a manufacturers' representative who has responded to the demands within the electronics industry by remaining flexible in his marketing strategies for twenty-five years.)

"Reps Need More Selling Back." Lavin, Henry. July 1987. Page 33. (Reps' survival depends on marketing expertise.)

"Reps Beat the Slow-Growth Catch-22." Novick, Harold J. Dec. 1987. Cover Story. (Independent reps can penetrate new markets efficiently. Here's how one manufacturer puts them to work.)

European Journal of Marketing

"Relationship States in an International Marketing Channel." Moore, Richard A. May 1991. Pages 47–59.

Folio: The Magazine of Magazine Management. "When, Why and How to Hire an Ad Rep." July 1, 1993. Page 104.

Footwear News Magazine

"Markdown Money." Heiderstadt, Donna. Jan. 1987. Pages 35–39.

"Profit Props: How Vendors Can Help." Rossi, William A. Feb. 1987. Pages 42–44.

Forbes

"Revolt of the Reps." Lappen. A.A. (136:51). Sept. 16, 1985.

"Who'll Sell What to Whom?" Staff. Mar. 23, 1987. Page 10. (Sales representatives versus retailers.)

"How Smart Agents Will Change Selling." Negroponte, Nicholas. Aug. 1995.

Fortune

"Manufacturers-agents: Customer-relations. Sales-force-management. Selling." May 1992. Pages 99–100.

Frozen Food Digest

"Manufacturers and Brokers Agree on Regional Marketing; Differ on What It's Worth." July 1988. Page 99.

Grocery Marketing

"Will Brokers Find Life After Wal-Mart?" Mathews, Ryan. Oct. 24, 1991. Pages 10+.

Health Facts

"Drug Company: Reps Misinform Doctors." June 1995.

High-Tech Marketing

"Keeping a Rep Network Strong." Carey, Carol. Oct. 1986. Pages 70–71.

Home Office Computing

"Becoming a Manufacturers' Agent." Edwards, Paul, Sarah Edwards. Sept. 1994.

"Grow Without Pains." Smith, Wesley. March 1995.

"Prove Your Independence." Carey, Patricia. July 1995.

Housewares

"Plizban Brings Rep Company into 1990." Gittlitz, Ian. Aug. 21, 1987. Pages 3–6 (Case study of a rep firm.)

"Reps at a Crossroads: Lawsuits, Retail Consolidation Blurring Future Relationships." Feb. 21, 1989. Pages 1–2.

Inc.

"Going for Brokers." May 1986. Page 167.

"A Good Sales Rep Is Hard to Find." Nov. 1986. Page 129.

"Strategy: Reps of Sales Force?" Dec. 1991. Page 154. (Start-up companies.)

"The CEO as Sales Rep (Schneider Educational Products)." May 1991. Page 142.

"The CEO as Sales Rep." Allen, S. May 1992.

"Looking for Reps in All the Right Places." Greco, Susan. July 1992. Page 117.

"A 'Finishing School' for Sales Reps." Greco, Susan. Oct. 1992.

"Bonuses Offer Breaking New Ground." Greco, Susan. Mar. 1993.

"Even the CFO Sells." Greco, Susan. May 1993.

"Recruiting the Newly Retired." Greco, Susan. Aug. 1993.

"The Double-Duty Sales Script." Hise, Phaedra. Sept. 1993.

"The Faxable International Sales-Rep. Application." Gibbons, Vera. Nov. 1993.

"Making Owners of Sales Reps." Greco, Susan. Mar. 1994.

"Sales-training Hit List." Greco, Susan. Nov. 1994.

"Managing People." Fenn, Donna. Jan. 1996.

Incentive

"Independent Sales Reps: Keeping Them Happy." Gates, Michael. July 1988. Pages 28–30 and 71. (How one manufacturer used an incentive program to help representatives maintain loyalty and motivation.)

Independent Business

"Are Reps Right for You?" Horowitz, Alan S. Sept.-Oct. 1991. Pages 20–24.

Industrial Distribution

Copies of the articles are available from University Microfilms, Ann Arbor, MI 48106.

"Now or Never." Staff. Dec. 1984. Page 25.

"Target the Buyer!" Gibbons, Jim. Aug. 1984. Page 53.

"Synergism: $1+1=3$." Bistrom, Frank. Oct. 1984. Page 117.

"Partners in Marketing." Diaz, Lionel. Jan. 1985. Page 69.

"How Good are Factory Reps?" Sharer, R.W. Mar. 1985. Pages 54–55.

"A Matter of Trust." Fields, Gene. Mar. 1985. Page 69.

"Reps Meet Distributors: An Interactive Dialog." May 1985. Page 113–115.

"Joint Calls: A Delicate Balance." Berkwitt, George. May 1985. Pages 125–126.

"The Agent as a Businessman." Gibbons, Jim. May 1985. Page 111.

"The Agent as a Trainer." McDonald, William. July 1985. Page 65.

"Working the Field." Gibbons, Jim. Oct. 1985. Page 81.

"Alternates to International Sales." O'Donnell, John. Feb. 1996. Pages S13–15. (Utilizing export trading companies, international manufacturers reps, etc.)

"When Customers Talk, Agents Listen." Gibbons, Jim. Mar. 1986. Page 90.

"The Manufacturer's Agent's Lament." Staff. May 1987. Pages 125–126.

"Finally, Reps Get Some Respect." Zurier, Steve. June 1991. Pages 27–29.

"Retail Giant Clouds Reps' Horizon (Wal-Mart Conducting Business Only with Suppliers Who Sell Through Factory Salespeople)." May 1991. Pages 10–11.

"One Step Back, Two Steps Forward." June 1994. Pages 35–36.

Industrial Marketing. Novick, Harold J.

"The Case for Reps vs. Direct Selling. Can Reps Do It Better?" March 1982. Page 90. (Pros and cons of selling through reps or company-employed salesperson and when to use each.)

"The Issue Audit: How to Diagnose Hidden Marketing Problems." Nov. 1982. Page 54. (An auditing system to help resolve and understand strategic and operational issues faced by rep firms.)

Industrial Marketing Management

"Building a More Successful Rep Organization." Aug. 1986. Pages 207–213.

"Ten Key Activities of Industrial Salespeople." Moncrief, William C. Nov. 1986. Pages 309+.

"Switching from Reps to Direct Salespeople." Powers, Thomas L. Aug. 1987. Pages 169–172.

"Products and Markets Served by Distributors and Agents." Jackson, Donald, M. Feb. 1989. Pages 27–33.

"Identifying Independent Reps." Nov. 1992. Pages 319–321.

"An Integrated Approach to the Development of Channel Strategy." Oct. 1994. Pages 315–322.

Industry Week

"Target Your Sales Channels, Too." Novick, Harold. March 6, 1989. Pages 11–12. (Attaining outstanding market penetration by selecting reps specializing in each market niche.)

Insider (A research and business publication of the National Electrical Manufacturers Representatives Association.)

"Technology and the Information Age: Implications for the Rep of the '90s." 1991.

Institutional Distribution

"Three-Hat Strategy." Salkin, Stephanie Weisman. Mar. 1985. Page 24. (Sales rep's roles.)

"Scooping Out New Accounts: Which Are Worth Pursuing?" Black, Clarence et al. Sept. 1, 1991. Page 36. (Sales clinic.)

"Taking the First Step: Opening the Sale." Blumenthal, Don. Sept. 1, 1991. Page 36. (Sales thinking.)

International Executive

"Penetrating Canada's Industrial Markets." Novick, Harold. July-Aug. 1989. Pages 14–17. (Providing cost-effective coverage to the four major Canadian trading regions.)

Jewelers Circular Keystone

"Sales as a Two-Way Street." Thompson, Michael. Oct. 1989. Pages 232–233.

Journal of Applied Management

"Working with Reps: Ten Ways to Insure Success." Koch, Peter F. May/June 1980. (Choosing a rep, establishing two-way working policies, training and finally, if necessary, rep replacement.)

Journal of Applied Psychology

"Conscientiousness and Performance of Sales Representatives: Test of the Mediating Effect of . . ." Barrick, Murray, Michael Mount. Oct. 1993.

Journal of Marketing Research

"Cost-Benefit-Analysis. Manufacturers-Agents. Vertical-Integrity. Marketing-Channels. Sales-Management: Costs." Feb. 1992.

Journal of Commerce and Commercial

"Exporter Calls Local Reps Vital." Robinson, Duncan. Nov. 9, 1990. Page 1A.

Technological Advances Not Always Welcomed by Retail Middleman." Seideman, Tony. Dec. 16, 1991. Page 3B.

Journal of Marketing

"The Role of Dependence Balancing in Safeguarding Transaction-Specific Assets in Conventional Channels." Heide, Jan. and George John. Jan. 1988. Pages 20–35.

Journal of Marketing Research

"Converting from Independent to Employee Salesforces: The Role Perceived Switching Costs." Weiss, Allen M. and Erin Anderson. Feb. 1992. Pages 101–115.

Journal of Personal Selling and Sales Management

"A Comparison of the Impact of Organizational Climate on the Job Satisfaction of Manufacturers' Agents and Company Salespeople: An Exploratory Study." Mahajan, J. et al. May 1984. Pages 1–10.

"Manufacturers' Representatives: The March to Professionalism." Taylor, Ronald K. Winter 1990. Pages 53–55.

Journal of Small Business Management

"Manufacturers' Representatives for Small Firms." Collins, Robert H. Jan. 1978. Pages 13–18.

Lavin, Henry

Dr. Lavin has written 50+ articles for 20+ magazines and many books. For a complete listing, contact Lavin Associates, 12 Promontory Drive, Cheshire, CT 06410. Tel: (203) 272-9121.

"This Little Rep Went to Market . . ." The Agent and Representative. Vol. 24. 1972.

"21 Reasons Why Independent Reps Make Sales Sense." Marketing Times. July/Aug. 1984.

"Choosing a Sales Team: Reps vs. In-House Personnel."

"10 Ways to a Profitable Affair for a Rep and His Manufacturer." The previous two articles are from Air Conditioning, Heating & Refrigeration News. Feb. 1986.

"Survival of Rep Keyed to Marketing Expertise." The Cheshire Herald. May 28, 1987. (The article stresses the importance of a professional image for representative firms.)

Los Angeles Times

"Road Gets Tough for Salesmen." LaGanga, Maria L. Jan. 1, 1991.

Marketing News

"Reps Must Assume Different Roles for Selling New Products." Kelly, P.J. Sept. 27, 1985. Pages 17–18.

"Sales Reps Win with Product Knowledge." May 8, 1987. Page 1.

"Food Brokers Seek Compensation for Expanding Role in Marketing Plans." July 4, 1988. Page 7.

"U.S. Reps Should Learn to Sell Japanese Style." Oct. 29, 1990. Page 6.

"The Right Questions Are the Most Profitable You Can Ask." Lambers, K.D. Mar. 18, 1991, Page 17.

"Successful New Products Are Products of Process." Bobrow, Edwin. April 15, 1991.

"Total Resource Selling Involves Entire Company." Bobrow, Edwin. Sept. 30, 1991. Page 10.

Minnesota Ventures

"Legislature Amends Rules (Again) for Minnesota Sales Representatives." Thomson, Joseph. Nov.-Dec. 1991. Pages 68–69.

Modern Machine Shop
   "Keeping in Contact with Your Reps." Casper, Bert. Aug. 1987. Page 102.
   "Support and Recognize Your Reps." Casper, Bert. Sept. 1987. Page 98.
   "Why Small Companies Should Sell through Manufacturers' Reps." Casper, Bert. Nov. 1990. Page 110.
   "Recruitment Process Techniques (Selecting Machine Shop Sales Representatives)." Casper, Bert. Dec. 1990. Page 102.

Nation's Business
   "How to Hire a Sales Rep." Harvey, Jeanne. May 1994. Page 60.

National Petroleum News
   "Marketing Skills for the '90s." May 1993. Page 60. (Marketing representatives on strike.)
   "The Best Equipment Sales Reps Sell Integrity and Trust." Aug. 1993. Page 12.

New Scientist
   "Why Sales Reps. Pose a Hard Problem." Sangalli, Arturo. Dec. 12, 1992.

New York Times
   "Twinkies Fans Cope." Staff. Nov. 14, 1987. Pages 16 & 56. (Hostess Twinkies sales representatives on strike.)
   "Apparel Industry Tunes in to Low-Profile Money Men." Strom, Stephanie. Dec. 16, 1991. Page D3.

Occupational Brief 417.
   "Manufacturers' Representatives." G.O.E. 08.02.01; 4th ed. D.O.T. 279. Chronicle Guidance Publications, Inc., P.O. Box 1190, Moravia, NY 13118. Nov. 1988; revised edition due in early 1993. (Career potential as a manufacturers' representative.)

Personal Selling Power
   "How to Open New Markets Overseas." Bobrow, Edwin. April 1992.
   "Your Sales Plan Begins with Your Life Plan." Bobrow, Edwin. Sept. 1992.

Philadelphia Inquirer
   "Wal-Mart Sells Anger as It Moves to Cut Out Third Party Sales Brokers." Clancy, Mike. Dec. 6, 1991.

Pittsburgh Business Times
   "Bad Connection: Cellular One Rows with Its Independent Agents." Oct. 20, 1991. Page 1.

Playthings
   "Taking a Closer Look at Manufacturers' Reps." Clark, Louis H. May 31, 1991. Pages 4–6.

Product Marketing
"Regional Sales Agents Help Cut Rising Staff Costs for Big Firms." Charleson Publishing Co., 124 East 40th Street, New York, NY 10016.

Progressive Grocer
"Brokers: Up the Creek?" Dec. 1992. Page 60–63.

"The Broker's Role (implementing category management; supermarkets)." Sept. 1993. Page 26.

"The Broker's Role (efficient consumer response; grocery trade)." Jan. 1994. Pages 33–35.

Profit-Building Strategies for Business Owners
"A Low-Investment Way to Break into Exporting." Staff. May 1988. Pages 8–11. (The importance of association membership for representatives in the publishing industry.)

Psychological Reports
"Building Exchange Relationships: Perceptions of Sales Representatives' Performance." Hawes, Jon, Thomas Baker. April 1993. Volume 72.

Publishers Weekly
"Rocky Issue: Reps on the Road." Mutter, John, Nicole Keller. Nov. 20, 1995.

"Harper Collins Names Sales Rep of the Year." Tripp, David. Jan. 22, 1996.

Purchasing
"Are Your Supplier Reps Proactive, Knowledgeable?" June 2, 1994. Pages 43 +.

"Best Sales Reps Have Ideas and a Desire to Succeed (1995 Top Sales Competition.)" Morgan, James. Nov. 9, 1995. Pages 45–46.

Purchasing World
"Electronics Reps Adopt Professional Standards to Serve Customers Better." Hall, Ray. June 1988. Pages 50–51. (Representatives who make a Commitment to Performance should provide buyers with effective sales calls, a thorough and practical knowledge, proper product application, and an understanding of the buyers' needs.)

RV Business
"Enterprises & Associates." Oct. 7, 1991. Page 42. (Newly established representative firm.)

"The Succession Issue." Longsdorf, Jr. Robert. Dec. 2, 1991. Pages 48–51. (Transfer of ownership in recreational vehicle manufacturer-dealer agreements.)

Sales and Marketing Executive Report
"The Plateaued Sales Rep: Report of Survey Findings." Staff. Prepared by Porter & Henry Co. Inc., 370 Lexington Avenue, New York, NY 10017.

Published by the Dartness Corporation, Christen P. Heide, ed. Feb. 19, 1986.

Sales and Marketing Management

"Make Sure You're Ready for Reps." Jan. 13, 1986. Page 17.

"Manufacturer's Representatives' Commissions." Feb. 16, 1987. Page 59.

"Wal-Mart's War on Reps." Bragg, Arthur. Mar. 1987. Pages 41 +.

"What's This? Send Reps to Driving School." Kelley, Bill. Oct. 1987. Pages 74–76.

"Teaming Up for the Attention of Independent Reps." Urbanski, Al. Nov. 1987. Page 110.

"What to Do When You're Tenth out of the Bag." Everett, Martin. Jan. 1989. Pages 34–39.

"The Question of Reps." Bobrow, Edwin. June 1991. Pages 32–36.

"Reps and Recognition: Understanding What Motivates." Bobrow, Edwin. Sept. 1991. Pages 82–86.

"Should Salespeople be Certified?" Sept. 1992. Page 37.

"Selecting the Right Rep Firm." Marshall, Michael, Frank Siegler. Jan. 1993. Pages 46–49.

"Please, Don't Shoot! Better Managers can Motivate Without Putting a Gun to Their Reps' Heads." Apr. 1994. Page 41.

"Rising to the Top." Apr. 1994. Page 83. (These innovative incentive programs reward salespeople for acting strategically and strengthening customer relations.)

"Simulating Sales Success." Apr. 1994. Page 33. (Computer-based training program for showing sales reps how to plan long-term sales strategies.)

"Reports from the Field." Aug. 1994. Page 31.

"Right on Target." Dec. 1994. Page 59. (Salesperson compensation linked to customer satisfaction.)

"Best Selling Practices-Revealed." Jan. 1995. Page 27.

"Agents of Change: Facing New Demands, Independent Reps are Forced to Alter the Way They Service Manufacturers or Lose Business." Feb. 1995. Page 71.

"Highly Classified: Hiring Top Salespeople May be a Manager's Most Important Responsibility. Here's How to Pick Winners." Mar. 1995. Page 75.

"Is it Worth Keeping Older Salespeople? Of Course, but Management Must Help Them Adapt to a Changing Marketplace." April 1995. Page 147.

"Should Your Salespeople be Certified?" Apr. 1995. Page 138.

"Best Supporting Role: (Independent Sales Reps)." Silberman, Sally. Dec. 1995.

Small Business Administration

"Is the Independent Sales Agent for You?" Management Aid No. 200. Washington, DC, or your local SBA office.

Small Business Report

"The Use of Sales Reps: Alternative to Direct Sales Force." Dec. 1986. Pages 72–78.

"More Feet on the Street." Apr. 1993. Pages 20–24. (Hiring independent sales reps.)

SMB Special Report. "Manufacturer—Agency Partnerships." Bobrow, Edwin. Aug. 30, 1992. Issue #1287, Section II. Bureau of Business Practices, Prentice Hall, Waterford, CT 06386.

Sporting Goods Business

"New Decade, New Reps." Sheridan, Joe. Feb. 1990. Page 152.

Success

"How to Use Sales Reps: Tips on Exploiting Your Advantage as an Entrepreneur." Harrell, Wilson L. May 1992. Page 9.

Supermarket Business Magazine

"Brokers, Manufacturer Reps: Making an FTC 'CASE' against Wal-Mart, Other 'Power Buyer' Retailers." May 1992. Page 12.

Supervision

"Business Law for Manufacturers and Agents." April 1992. Pages 23–24.

"Trust: The Key to Success for Manufacturers and Their Agents." May 1993. Pages 8–9.

TCI

"Reps for Vari-Lite's Architectural Series." By, DJ. April 1994.

Telephone Engineering & Management

"Choosing a Sales Force—Employees or Reps?" Dec. 15, 1985. Page 106.

Textile World

"Textile World '94–'95 Buyer's Guide." July 1994. Pages 17–175.

Training & Development Journal

"A Cure for Sales Trauma." Nov. 1985. Pages 56–58. (Training sales reps to handle obstreperous territories.)

Wall Street Journal

"A Few Big Retailers Rebuff Middlemen." Blumenthal, Karen. Midwest edition. Oct. 21, 1986. Page 6. (Two large retailers currently discourage their buyers from making purchases through manufactures' representatives. Interviews with the involved retailers and representatives.)

"Wal-Mart Set to Eliminate Reps, Brokers." Blumenthal, Karen. Dec. 2, 1991. Page A3.

"Wal-Mart Says Policy on Suppliers Aims Only to Ensure Stock." Dec. 5, 1991.

"Independent Sales Reps Are Squeezed by the Recession." Selz, Michael. Dec. 26, 1991. Enterprise Section.

"Florida Journal—Economic Focus: Health Alliances Succeed, But Sales Agents Grumble." Johnson, Robert. Nov. 16, 1994. Sec. F. Page 1.

"Enterprise: Small Businesses Get Big Bills as IRA Targets Free-Lancers." Selz, Michael, Stephanie Mehta. Aug. 24, 1995. Sec. B. Page 1.

"Enterprise: IRA Drafts Guidelines for Determining If Workers are Independent Contractors." Mar. 6, 1996. Sec. B. Page 2.

"Enterprise: Senate Bill Would Clarify Definition of Contractor." Mar. 14, 1996. Sec. B. Page 7.

"Britannica Ends Sales of Encyclopedias in-Home." Apr. 25, 1996, Sec. S. Page 4.

Working Woman

"Turning Art into a Business." Staff. Dec. 1986. Page 35. (Case study plus a related article on how to hire and use a sales representative.)

Women's Wear Daily

"Riding a Positive Wave: Sales Firms Strive to Create Excitement Now." McFarland, Kathy. Jan. 16, 1989. Page B44. (Women's apparel sales representatives.)

"New York Sales Reps: Gaining an Edge." Friedman, Arthur. Jan. 15, 1991. Pages 6–7.

"Bank of New York Takes For Sales Sign off Factor Unit." Rutberg, Sidney. Oct. 15, 1991. Page 17.

"Wal-Mart to Lock Out Sales Reps." Williamson, Rusty. Dec. 4, 1991.

"Staying Fresh." Dec. 9, 1991. Pages 8–9. (New York apparel representatives.)

Directories of Manufacturers' Representatives

Publications That Contain Directories

Accent—**Source book (jewelry and watches)**, The Lakin Group, 100 Wells Ave., Newton, MA 02159-9103, Tel: (617) 964-5100, Free: (800) 869-7469, Fax: (617) 964-2752.

Air Conditioning, Heating & Refrigeration News, 1992 Directory Issue. Jan. 6, 1992.

Alternative Energy Retailer—Hearth Products Industrial Buyer's Guide Issue, Zackin Publications, Inc., 70 Edwin Ave., P.O. Box 2180, Waterbury, CT 06722, Tel: (203) 755-0158, Free: (800) 325-6745, Fax: (203) 755-3480.

American Paint & Coatings Journal, Raw Material Distributors and Manufacturers' Agents Directory. Selling the Paint Manufacturing Industry. Five Volumes. Dec. 30, 1991.

American Salon Green Book (Barbers, Cosmetologists), Advanstar Communications, 7500 Old Oak Blvd., Cleveland, OH 44130-3369, Tel: (216) 243-8100, Free: (800) 225-4569.

Asian Industrial Reporter—Directory of Distributor Issue, Keller International Publishing Corp., 150 Great Neck Rd., Great Neck, NY 11021, Tel: (516) 829-9210.

Automotive Marketing, 1989 Retail Aftermarket Guide. Spring 1989.

Beverage World, Manufacturers' Representatives. 1991–92 Data bank issue.

Boating Industry, Marine Manufacturers' Rep Directory. Dec. 30, 1991.

Building, Design & Construction, Directory Section II: Manufacturers' Representatives. Six Volumes. Nov. 15, 1991.

Chicago Market—Buyer's Guide to Chicago Giftware Association Lines Issues (IL), Bolger Publications, Inc., 3301 Como Ave. S.E., Minneapolis, MN 55414, Tel: (612) 645-6311, Free: (800) 999-6311, Fax: (612) 642-2900.

Dallas Market Center—Permanent Directory (Texas), Dallas Market Center Co., 2100 Stemmons Fwy., MS. 135, Dallas, TX 75207, Tel: (214) 655-6100, Free: (800) 325-6587, Fax: (214) 749-5458, E-mail: dmc@the center.com.

Fleet Owner, Heavy Duty Representatives Association Fleet Service Directory. July 1989.

Gift and Apparel Directory (Florida), Miami International Merchandise Mart, 777 N.W. 72nd. Ave., Miami, FL 33126, Tel: (305) 261-2900. Free: (800) 323-7770, Fax: (305) 261-3659.

Groom and Board—Buyer's Guide Issue (Pet Industry), H.H. Backer Associates, Inc., 20 E, Jackson Blvd., Chicago, IL 60604 , Tel: (312) 663-4040, Fax: (312) 663-5676, E-mail: petage@aol.com.

Hardware Age Home Improvement Market , Who Makes It Buyer's Guide Issue, Chilton Co., One Chilton Way, Wayne, PA 19089, Tel: (610) 964-4283, Fax: (610) 964-4284.

Hospitality Management—Buyer's Guide Issue, Delmont Communications, Inc., 1700 Livingston Ave., St. Paul, MN 55118-5908, Tel: (612) 457-2289, Fax: (612) 457-7787.

Pet Age—Sourcebook Issue, H.H. Backer Asssociates, Inc., 20 E. Jackson Blvd., Chicago, IL 60604, Tel: (312) 663-4040, Fax: (312) 663-5676.

Playthings. Directory of Manufacturers' Representatives in Toy Sales. May 31, 1991.

Printed Circuit Fabrication—Supplier Directory Issue, Miller Freeman Publications, Inc., 2000 Powers Ferry Center, Ste. 450, Marietta, GA 30067, Tel: (404) 952-1303, Fax: (404) 952-6461.

Regional Industrial Buying Guide Series, Thomas Regional Directory Co. Inc., Subsidiary, Thomas Publishing Co., Inc. 5 Penn Plaza, New York, NY 10001, Tel: (212) 629-2147, Free: (888) 734-4662, Fax: (212) 629-1582, E-mail: info@trdnet.com.

Sources of Supply/Buyer's Guide (Paper Industry), Wm. O. Dannausen Corp., P.O. Box 795, Park Ridge, IL 60068, Tel: (847) 823-3145, Fax: (847) 696-3445.

RV Business, Manufacturers' Representatives Directory (U.S.A. and Canada). Jan. 1992.

The Northwest Electronics Buying Guide (Idaho, Oregon, Washington), Cobro Publishing Inc., 11 143rd. St. S.E., Lynnwood, WA 98037, Tel: (206) 742-6111, Free: (800) 755-6111, Fax: (206) 742-0144, E-mail: cobrobc@aol.com.

Western Floors—Buyers Guide and Directory Issue, Specialist Publications, Inc., 22801 Ventura Blvd., Ste. 115, Woodland Hills, CA 91364, (818) 224-8035, Free: (800) 835-4398, Fax: (818) 224-8042.

NOTE: Most associations of manufacturers' representatives (as listed elsewhere in this bibliography) publish directories of their members. Some of these publications are significantly detailed in their information listings, and they often contain considerable supplemental information, including sample contracts, various guidelines and code of ethics, association, and industry data, etc. Contact individual associations for further details and sample copies.

Individual Directories

Directory of Wholesale Representatives for Craft Professionals, Northwest Trading Co., 13451 Essex Ct., Eden Prairie, MN 55347, Tel: (612) 937-5275.

Manufacturers' Agents and Representatives Directory, American Business Directory, Inc., American Business Information, Inc., 5711 S. 86th Circle, Omaha, NE 68127, Tel: (402) 593-4600, Free: (800) 555-6124, Fax: (402) 331-5481.

Michigan Distributors Directory, Pick Publications, Inc., 24293 Telegraph Rd. Ste. 140, Southfield, MI 48034, Tel: (810) 827-7111, Free: (800) 247-1558, Fax: (313) 827-7119.

Legal

United States Congress. House Committee on Interstate and Foreign Commerce. Subcommittee on Consumer Protection and Finance. Sales Representatives Protection Act: hearing before the Subcommittee on Interstate and Foreign Commerce, House of Representatives, Ninety . . . 1980.

United States Congress. House Committee on Energy and Commerce. Subcommittee on commerce, Transportation, and Tourism. Sales Representatives Protection Act of 1981: hearing before the Subcommittee on Commerce, Transportation and Tourism of the Committee on Energy . . . 1981.

United States Congress. House Committee on Energy and Commerce. Subcommittee on commerce, Transportation, and Tourism. Sales Representatives Contractual Relations Act: hearing before the Subcommittee on Commerce, Transportation, and Tourism of the Committee on Energy . . . 1983.

Index

abdication, vs. delegation, 160, 160*f*
ACT software program, 169
advertising
  as source of rep candidates, 115
  as support activity for reps, 168–169
agents, international, *see* international
  agents/distributors
age, of rep firm owners, 179
agreement, *see* sales representative
  agreement
Aldredge, Mike, 54
alternative dispute resolution (ADR),
  of rep/manufacturer disputes,
  230
American National Standards Institute (ANSI), 234
arbitration, of rep/manufacturer disputes, 230
auditing
  independent, 195
  issue, 196–197
  rep, *see* rep audits
  sales channel, 197
  types of, 195–196

Berry, Dick, on motivation, 147, 148*t*
brokers, definition of, 7
Brown, Roger on role of sales reps, *xiii*
bureaucracy, as obstacle to productivity, 76, 154
business failures, as a result of mismanagement, 188–189
business planning
  key tasks of, 21–22
  see also objectives

business spin-offs, as distractions,
  93–94

candidate search, *see* recruitment
channel acceptance, by customers, 31
channel conflict, 46, 48
chemistry, personal, as factor in selecting reps, 132
collections, assistance with, 153
combined ISO/direct sales structure,
  advantages of using, 36–37, 47*f*
commission protection acts
  history of, 220–221
  and need for written contracts, 222,
    223–224
  provisions of, 221–222
  trends in, 223
commissions
  advances against, 211
  change in rates, 212
  decline of with increased contract
    size, 57
  and effect of pricing practices,
    208–209
  fairness of rates, 144, 208
  and noncommissionable items, 210
  payable upon termination, 217–219,
    218*f*
  payment policies for, 209–210
  as percentage of reps' income, 99
  post-termination, 226–227
  professional handling of, 144
  protection of, *see* commission pro-
    tection acts

commissions (*continued*)
  specified in sales rep agreement,
    215
  splitting of, 211–212, 257*f*
  status report, 168
  threshold problem of, 75–76
  as variable expense, 79–80
  see also compensation
communication
  with customers, 147
  effective style of, 146, 147
  with new reps, 139
  problem with written, 75
compatibility
  profile monitoring, 178–179
  ratings in rep audits, 205–206, 205*t*
compensation
  cash payments as, 211
  commissions as, *see* commissions
  of new millennium sales force, 32
  of reps vs. direct sales staff, 14, 55–
    59, 56*f*, 59*f*
competitive analysis, 166–167
competitors' reps, as source of rep
  candidates, 114–115
computer literacy, need for in new
  millennium sales force, 32
computer software, *see* software
consultants, specializing in recruitment, 116–117
consultative selling, as characteristic
  of new millennium sales force, 29
continuity
  as characteristic of new millennium
    sales force, 29
  need for in rep firm, 180
contract, *see* sales representative
  agreement
control, as issue in choosing sales
  structure, 59–60
Control Associates, 54
conversion of sales channels
  from direct selling to reps, 44–45,
    47*f*
  from reps to direct selling, 44, 47*f*
  sales volume effect on, 45–46
Cornerstone Controls, as rep of Fisher
  Controls, 55

corporate culture, 158–159
criticism, openness to, 145
Crosby Valve, 54
customers
  ability to influence, 149
  consistent approach to, 146–147
  needs served by sales force, 30–31
  negotiations with, 150
  responsiveness to, 143
  sensitivity to, 162, 171
  as sources of rep candidates,
    108–109

dealers, definition of, 8
delegation, vs. abdication, 160, 160*f*
direct mail
  for recruitment, 117–118, 119–120*f*,
    121*f*
  as support activity for reps, 169
directories, as sources for rep candidates, 109, 110*f*, 112*f*, 114
direct sales force
  advantages of using, 35–36, 40–41,
    47*f*
  for autonomous divisions, 4, 5*f*
  characteristics of, 3, 28–33
  conversion to reps of, 44–45, 47*f*
  cost breakeven of, 55–59, 56*f*, 59*f*
  multidivisional, 5, 6*f*
  uses of, 1
distributors
  definition of, 3, 7–8
  international, *see* international
    agents/distributors
  reps as, 82
  as source of rep candidates, 115

e-commerce
  as megatrend, *xv*
Electronic Representatives Association (ERA)
  directory, 109, 112–113*f*
  sample sales rep agreement,
    252–257
Emerson Electric, 49–50
European Monetary Union (EMU),
  244

European Union (EU), *see* Europe, Western
Europe, Eastern, trade with European Union, 238
Europe, Western
  exporting to, 239
  ISO 9000 registration in, 238
  largest markets in, 240, 241*f*
  locating a subsidiary in, 240–242
  selling in, 236–238
  standardization in, 238
Euro, use of in Western Europe, 244
expectations
  of manufacturers, 141–147
  of reps, 147–153

fairness, of commission rates, 208
fair share
  of market, 151
  of time spent by reps, 66, 150–151
Farr, D.N., 50
field visits, by management, 167
financial audit, 195–196
Fisher Controls International, Inc.
  changes in international marketing of, 52–53
  changes in rep structure of, 51–52
  corporate background of, 50–51
  reps' economic dependence on, 55, 60
  sales structure of, 51–55
Fisher-Rosemount, 50–51
flexibility, as characteristic of new millennium sales force, 31

General Electric, and termination of rep contracts, 228–229
geography, *see* territories; trading areas
Glegg Water Conditioning, 13
global competition
  as megatrend, *xiv–xv*
Global System for Mobile Communications (GSM), 243–244
Gold Mine software program, 169

head count
  high, as characteristic of new millennium sales force, 30
  reduction of, *xiv*

ideal sales rep
  characteristics of, 93–101
  key steps in selection of, 88
  models of, 89–93, 102–103
  value of, 85–86, 86*t*
independent contractor status
  IRS determination of, 225
  specified in sales rep agreement, 216
independent sales organization (ISO)
  "buy-sell" category, 2
  categories of, 2–3
  conversion to direct selling of, 44, 47*f*
  financial advantages of, 79–80
  as partnership, 144–145
  sales advantages of, 78–79
  "sell only" category, 2
  terminology, 5–8
  top management commitment to, 158–159
  see also independent sales representatives
independent sales representatives
  advantages of using, 34–35, 41–42, 47*f*
  "captive," 82
  characteristics of in new millennium, 28–33
  common myths about, 63–69
  communication problems of, 75, 76
  compensation as incentive for, 14
  competitive conflict of, 73
  contractual duties of, 225
  control over, 70–71
  conversion to direct sales force of, 44, 47*f*
  cost breakeven of, 55–59, 56*f*, 59*f*
  definition of, 5–6
  and differences from direct sales force, 12–15
  as distributors, 82
  economic independence of, 14–15, 15*f*
  elimination of, *xiii*
  fair share of time spent by, 66, 150–151

independent sales representatives
(*continued*)
  horizontal, 81
  ideal profile of, *see* ideal sales rep
  independence of, 12
  initial objectives for, 137–138
  international, *see* international
    agents/distributors
  marginal, 186–187
  parallel, 133–134
  performance evaluation of, *see* per-
    formance
  previous experience of, 6
  problems in managing, 70–77
  recruitment of, *see* recruitment
  shared expectations with, 139–140
  as source of rep candidates, 114
  specialization of, 12–13
  support materials for, 136
  vertical, 81
  see also independent sales organiza-
    tion; rep firms
individuals, respect for, 173
Industrial Perforators Association,
  sample sales rep agreement,
  273–288
innovation
  as key to success, 172
  need for, 162
inquiries, as measure of performance,
  178
integrity
  of manufacturers, 143
  of reps, 94
international agents/distributors
  problems with, 247–248
  selection of, 245–247
  termination of, 248
  vs. subsidiaries, 233
international markets
  cultural barriers in, 242
  distribution costs for, 247
  Japan, 235–236, 235f
  size of, 234–235
  suitability of products for, 234
  use of GSM-type phones in,
    243–244
  Western Europe, 236–242, 241f

international sales manager, selection
  of, 246–247
Internet, the
  cross-Atlantic trade, 239–240
  as source of rep candidates, 116
interviews
  benchmarks used by reps in, 131
  candidate selection for, 129
  conducting of, 129–131
  in rep audits, 200, 203
  telephone, 122–124, 125–127f
issue auditing, 196–197
Ives, Blair, 53

Japan, selling in, 235–236

life cycle
  of rep firms, 179–180, 179f
  of reps, 95–96, 96f
life of part / life of program clauses,
  227
Lindner, Bob, 54
litigation
  of rep/manufacturer disputes,
    229–230
  see also commission protection acts
loyalty, of reps, 67–68

management audit, 196
manufacturers
  expectations, 141–147
  integrity of, 143
  protection of against claims, 222
  as source of rep candidates, 114
Manufacturers' Agents National Association (MANA)
  directory, 109, 110–111f
  findings on sales experience, 6
  sample sales rep agreement,
    260–271
  seminars offered by, 159
market forecasting, as business planning task, 21
marketing
  niche, 162, 172–173
  in support of reps, 140–141, 142
marketing department
  interaction with reps, 164–165

load-leveling practice of, 164–165, 165*f*
structure of, 163–164, 164*f*
support activities of, 165–170
marketing plan, 166
market objectives, setting of, 21–22
markets
  segmentation of, *xv*
  specified in sales rep agreement, 214–215
Maximizer software program, 169
mediation, of rep/manufacturer disputes, 230
megatrends, *xi–xv*
Merwald, Ed, on international sales trends, 52–53
missionary activity, by reps, 66–67, 154
Monsanto Company, 49
motivation
  techniques, *see* motivational techniques
  through a supportive relationship, 141
  through future products, 141
  through total marketing, 140–141
motivational techniques, reps' evaluation of, 147, 148*t*

newsletters, as support activity for reps, 167–168
niche marketing, 162, 172–173
noncommissionable items, 210
noncompete clause, 215

objectives
  achievement of, 20–22, 142
  common pursuit of, 149
  market, 21–22
  product, 21–22
on-the-job-training, 138–139
operations audit, 196
order gestation, 90–91
organizational success, key ingredients of, 171–174

parallel reps, recruitment of, 133–134
partnering relationships, *xii*

performance
  evaluation of, *see* performance evaluation
  marginal, 186
  market share, 178
  orders, 177
  problems, *see* performance shortfall
  successful, 181
performance evaluation, 177–181
  of new reps, 181–182
  qualitative, 180–181
  standards for, 177–180
performance shortfall, 69–70
  assessment of, 183–184
  corrective action for, 184
plant visits, 139
predatory purchasing, *xii–xiii*
president
  commitment of, 162–163
  involvement of in marketing, 161, 162
  as proactive leader, 160–162, 160*f*
  role of on rep council, 195
  soliciting of feedback by, 161
pricing practices, effect of on commissions, 208–209
Proconex, 53
product knowledge, 64–65
product lines
  fair share of time spent on, 66
  selling new vs. established, 66–67, 143–144
product manuals, 166
product/market matrix
  and orphan market, 23
  and sample sales pattern, 22–23, 23*f*
  and sample sales/profit pattern, 23–24, 24*f*, 25*f*
  as step in sales channel design, 22–25
product objectives, setting of, 21–22
product quality, 172
  as megatrend, *xii*
products, specified in sales rep agreement, 214–215
product training, 152–153
professionalism, of reps, 152, 153

program development, as business planning task, 22
promotion by reps, appropriateness of, 151–152
prospecting, 67
Puffer-Sweiven, as rep of Fisher Controls, 54
Pumps & Process Equipment, Inc., 128

Reams, Larry, 55
recruitment
    candidate evaluation process, 131
    chemistry as factor in, 132
    consultants specializing in, 116–117
    executive involvement in, 107
    follow-up process, 118, 120, 122
    initial mailing for, 117–118, 119–120*f*, 121*f*
    of parallel reps, 133–134
    responsibility for, 108
    screening process, 117–118, 120, 122–124
    search methodology for, 106–107
    telephone interviews used in, 122–124, 125–127*f*
    use of primary sources in, 108–114
    use of secondary sources in, 114–116
rep audits
    advantages of, 198, 199
    auditor selection for, 198–199
    compatibility ratings, 205–206, 205*t*
    as control tool, 20
    definition of, 197–198
    interviews in, 200, 203
    objectives of, 198
    results of, 204–206
    sample announcement of, 201*f*
    sample work sheet for, 202–203*f*
    steps in, 199–200
rep council
    chair, 193
    as control tool, 20
    meeting agenda, 193–194
    meeting duration, 194
    membership in, 191

members' roles in, 193
    president's role in, 195
    purpose of, 190–191
    selection criteria, 192
    terms of, 193
rep directories, 109, 110*f*, 112*f*, 114
rep firms
    age of members of, 95–96
    characteristics of, 101–103
    compatibility of, 90–92, 103
    employee tenure of, 97–98
    ideal characteristics of, 89–93
    life cycle of, 95–96, 96*f*
    and product compatibility, 90–92, 103
    product knowledge of, 92–93
    purity of business of, 93–94
    as source of rep candidates, 116
    successorship issues in, 98–99
    support services provided by, 99–100
    technical ability of, 92
    and tenure with manufacturer, 98
    see also independent sales representatives
Rite-Aid, termination of rep contracts, 228
Roger Brown & Associates, termination of contract with GE, 228–229
Rotork, 54

sales agents, definition of, 7
sales channel audit, 197
sales channel design
    company size effect on, 37–38
    customer proximity effect on, 38–39
    market diversity effect on, 39
    six-step process for, 17–19, 18*f*, *xvi–xvii*
sales channels
    conflict of, 46, 48
    design of, *see* sales channel design
    for electronic components company, 9, 9*f*
    for mechanical products company, 10, 11*f*
    for office equipment company, 9, 10*f*

top management commitment to, 158–159

sales forces
   characteristics of in new millennium, 28–33
   potential obsolescence of, 27–28

sales meetings
   guidelines for, 171
   as support activity for reps, 170–171

sales recovery period, for new reps, 87–88, 87f

sales representative agreement, 138
   and commission protection, *see* commission protection acts
   need for, 213
   noncompete clause, 215
   provisions of, 214–217
   sample documents, 252–293
   termination clause of, 217
   term of, 216

sales structure
   classes of, 1
   levels of, 3, 4f

search, *see* recruitment

selling team, 3
   reps as part of, 157–158, 158f

selling, total, 174

seminars, on working with reps, 159

short-term orientation, of sales reps, 63–64, 91

situation analysis, as business planning task, 21

six-step process, for sales channel design, 17–19, 18f, xvi–xvii

software, contact management programs, 169–170

Sparks Belting Company, sample sales rep agreement, 290–293

stocking representatives, definition of, 7

strategy development, as business planning task, 22

subsidiaries, international, vs. agents, 233

suppliers
   reduction of, *xiv*

system selling, as characteristic of new millennium sales force, 28

systems integrators, definition of, 8

team building, 162
team culture, 157
teams, interactive, 173–174
telemarketing, used to qualify leads, 169
telephone communication
   with GSM-type cell phones, 243–244
   recruitment interviews, 122–124, 125–127f

tenure
   with manufacturers, 98
   in rep firms, 97–98

termination
   commissions due after, 226–227
   commissions payable upon, 217–219, 218f
   of international distributors, 248
   legal notice of, 225–226
   for performance shortfall, 185
   specified in sales rep agreement, 219

territories
   by account, 224–25
   by geography, 224
   specified in sales rep agreement, 214–215
   variations in, 81–82
   see also trading areas

tortuous interference, 228–229
total selling, 174
trading areas, size of, 100–101
training
   availability of, 145–146
   as support activity for reps, 167

turnover, *see* tenure

Urbanek, Joe, on Fisher Control's rep structure, 51–52

urgency, as characteristic of top companies, 173

value-added resellers, definition of, 8
value selling, 91
vertical market specialization, as characteristic of new millennium sales force, 29

voice messaging systems
  as megatrend, *xv*

Wal-Mart, termination of rep contracts, 228
Weekley, John, 52
  on purchase of Proconex, 53

Western Electronics Show and Convention, 171
wholesalers, 3
  definition of, 7–8
wrongful interference, 228–229

Xerox
  total quality program of, *xii*

About the Author and Contributors

Harold J. Novick is president of Novick & Associates, Inc., a general management and industrial marketing consulting firm located in Pittstown, New Jersey. The firm specializes in helping companies increase sales and profits by using independent reps and distributors. Among its larger clients are Alfa Laval, Babcock & Wilcox, Becton Dickinson, Bethlehem Steel, Continental Can, Deutsche Babcock, Dupont, Hewlett Packard, Mitsubishi, and Unisys. His practice is associated with International Marketing Consultants (IMACONSULT) of Brussels, Belgium. Previously, Mr. Novick served as president of the Permutit Company and of Garry Manufacturing Company, and he was a group executive at Research-Cottrell. He has also held senior sales and marketing positions at Joy Manufacturing Company and Westinghouse. His articles have appeared in *Industry Week, Business Marketing, Management Review, The International Executive, Agency Sales,* and Canada's *Business Quarterly.* Holding a BSME and an MBA, he is program leader of the highly acclaimed seminar on using independent reps offered by the University of Wisconsin and is the keynote speaker for a similar seminar offered by Manufacturers' Agents National Association (MANA).

Gerald G. Salmen is the founder of the Law Offices of Gerald G. Salmen in Cincinnati, Ohio. He has provided legal counsel to manufacturers working with manufacturers' representatives for over twenty years. He is a graduate of the University of Cincinnati College of Law. Mr. Salmen has structured and evaluated numerous contractual relationships between manufacturers and their reps, distributors, dealers, and other marketing channels. He is also a trial attorney and has participated in contractual and product liability cases throughout the United States. Mr. Salmen has written articles and spoken to industry groups and trade associations involved in the manufacture and distribution of products. He is also general counsel to a number of trade associations and industry groups.

Gunnar Beeth is the head of IMACONSULT, S.A., a management consulting firm in Brussels, Belgium. Since 1973, he has been conducting distributor search and executive search throughout all of Western Europe. Prior to becoming a consultant, Gunnar Beeth was in charge of distributor selection, training, and motivation in twenty-three countries for the Atlas Copco Group. Then, as director of international operations of Ransburg Corp., Indianapolis, now part of ITW, Beeth helped convert Ransburg from a domestic to a multinational company. Beeth received a master's degree in engineering from Sweden and an MBA from the University of Chicago. He works closely with Novick & Associates in international searches for reps, distributors, and agents.